AF361428

On Verbal Art

On Verbal Art

Ripples in a Timeless World: Essays in Honour of
Ruqaiya Hasan

Edited by Rebekah Wegener, Stella Neumann, and
Antje Oesterle

SHEFFIELD UK   BRISTOL CT

Published by Equinox Publishing Ltd.

UK: Office 415, The Workstation, 15 Paternoster Row, Sheffield, South Yorkshire,
        S1 2BX
USA: ISD, 70 Enterprise Drive, Bristol, CT 06010

www.equinoxpub.com

First published 2018

British Library Cataloguing-in-Publication Data

A catalogue record for this book is available from the British Library.

ISBN-13 978 1 78179 447 0   (hardback)
         978 1 78179 448 7   (paperback)
         978 1 78179 647 4   (ePDF)

Library of Congress Cataloging-in-Publication Data
Names: Wegener, Rebekah, editor. | Neumann, Stella, 1968- editor. | Oesterle,
    Antje, editor. | Hasan, Ruqaiya honoree.
Title: On verbal art : essays in honour of Ruqaiya Hasan / edited by Rebekah
    Wegener, Stella Neumann and Antje Oesterle.
Description: Sheffield, UK ; Bristol, CT : Equinox Publishing Ltd, 2018. |
    Includes bibliographical references and index.
Identifiers: LCCN 2017023835 (print) | LCCN 2017044090 (ebook) | ISBN
    9781781796474 (ePDF) | ISBN 9781781794470 (hardcover) | ISBN 9781781794487
    (softcover)
Subjects: LCSH: Philology, Modern.
Classification: LCC PB41 (ebook) | LCC PB41 .O43 2018 (print) | DDC 410--dc23
LC record available at https://lccn.loc.gov/2017023835

Typeset by ISB Typesetting, Sheffield, www.sheffieldtypesetting.com
Printed and bound in Great Britain by Lightning Source UK Ltd., Milton Keynes and
Lightning Source Inc., La Vergne, TN

Contents

Introduction: Ripples in a timeless world
Rebekah Wegener, Stella Neumann and Antje Oesterle — 1

1   Language, linguistics and verbal art: The contribution of Ruqaiya
    Hasan to the study of literature
    Annabelle Lukin — 6

2   On being a literature teacher: A language based perspective
    David Butt — 26

3   Software-assisted systemic socio-semantic stylistics – Appraising
    *tru** in J. M. Coetzee's *Foe*
    Donna R. Miller and Antonella Luporini — 53

4   The analysis of a sonnet
    Kathryn Tuckwell — 80

5   Foregrounding and defamiliarization in Peter Carey's
    'Conversations with Unicorns'
    Martin Tilney — 109

6   Simone de Beauvoir's construal of language and literature in
    Mémoires d'une jeune fille rangée (1958): A Hasanian perspective
    Alice Caffarel-Cayron — 132

7   Jane Austen's shapely sentence and the differentiation of dialogue
    from narrative: Towards a clause complex of her own
    Fang Li — 166

8   Appraisal and master identities in contemporary Spanish crime
    fiction: The case of *Los mares del Sur* and its translations into English
    and German
    Anna Espunya — 188

9   Striking a chord in the reader: On metaphor as a constituent of the
    grammar of verbal art
    Timo Lothmann — 211

10 Openings in fiction: An approach to verbal art based on Hallidayian,
    cognitive and Hasanian Principles
    Peter Wenzel — 232

11 'That's not normal rabbit behaviour': On the track of the grammar
    of fictional worlds
    Rebekah Wegener and Timo Lothmann — 250

12   Future directions in the study of verbal art   278
     Wendy L. Bowcher

Author Index   314
Subject Index   316

Introduction: Ripples in a timeless world

Rebekah Wegener, Stella Neumann and Antje Oesterle

> To explore these universal themes of human existence bracketed between being and not being, to articulate artistically the sense of such a vast universe of feeling, longing, action and emotion as a coherent metaphor, verbal art relies most on these two indispensable matrices as its sources of energy – the powerful semiotic system of language and the intricately woven fabric of the semiotically shaped culture. (Ruqaiya Hasan 2011)

Sometimes people motivate you, sometimes they challenge you, sometimes they inspire you, and sometimes they do all three at once. Ruqaiya Hasan falls into the last category. It is impossible to capture the huge impact that her work has had and will continue to have on a wide range of people and areas of research. In this volume, we attempt to represent just a small snapshot of her impact on the study of verbal art.

Hasan devoted a large portion of her career to the study of verbal art and one of the reasons for this is that literary texts are important socio-cultural artefacts that give us valuable and long-lasting insights into humanity. As Hasan (2011: xix) argued, 'in my experience research on verbal art lays a foundation of respect for what is most central to the humanities and the social sciences, i.e., for the far reaching effects of language and culture on the formation of human history.' In this sense, it is easy to see them as different from other forms of language use and in some way special and distinct. Instead Hasan chose to challenge linguistics with literature and in so doing, to raise two fundamental questions: what is it about literature that makes it so different and so special? and how does this relate to other forms of language use?

Hasan also highlights the importance of context in studying language in general, but more specifically in studying verbal art. Because literary texts are about creating a fictional world and hence contain in them a sample of the complexity of contexts that we see in the world at large, it becomes necessary to make a clear distinction between the different contexts at play in a text and those at work in the writing and reading of a text.

It is in the nature of written language that it transcends the here and now and reaches beyond the lifespan of an individual to create new and dynamic forms of knowledge that may develop in directions that the original author might never have imagined. Because in writing something down we share our individuality both now and into the future, we do not have to know an individual to be touched and influenced by their individuality. As Hasan (2011) writes 'individual life is finite; knowledge is infinite'.

One of the lasting insights emerging from Hasan's work on verbal art is the extent to which it informs analysis and theory. This volume brings together chapters that offer a detailed account of Hasan's contribution to the study of verbal art, chapters that pay tribute to Hasan by adopting some of her central notions such as foregrounding, symbolic articulation, theme, secondary semiosis, etc. to inform their analyses, chapters that take Hasan's thinking as a starting point to explore new methodological approaches for the investigation of verbal art, and finally chapters by scholars who are new to Hasanian thinking and afford fresh perspectives and build bridges to related approaches.

Amongst the contributors in this volume are some of her closest collaborators and friends, some that knew her only through a long connection with her work and some that are new even to her work. The volume opens with papers by two of Hasan's closest collaborators. **Annabelle Lukin** starts out by giving a comprehensive overview and appraisal of Ruqaiya Hasan's work in verbal art. She takes stock of what it means to approach literature as a linguist working in a sociologically informed theoretical framework, in a framework that characterizes language as a social semiotic. Lukin reiterates Hasan's positions of and contributions to the study of literature and specifically the language of literature, which are also taken up in most of the other chapters collected in this volume. In this sense, Lukin's chapter serves as the actual introduction to this volume.

Rather than tracing Hasan's work directly, **David Butt** in his chapter picks up some of the questions close to the work of his close friend and mentor and offers a variation on these questions contributing his thoughts on what it means to teach literature from a language-based perspective. Drawing on a trove of literary examples, Butt discusses the inextricable link between community habits, i.e. the unselfconscious use of language in everyday life, and new thoughts crafted in verbal art. He refers to Hasan's claim that the importance of literary study in the classroom and at university needs to be explained and points out that the principled analysis of the language of literature provides evidence that, as Butt writes in his chapter, 'set[s] you free to think without the weight of some dominant critical authority'.

In their analysis of notions of truth in the novel *Foe* by J. M. Coetzee, **Donna R. Miller** and **Antonella Luporini** draw on the relationship between systemic functional linguistics and corpus linguistics. They use a corpus-assisted approach to analyse lexical items based on the morpheme {true} adopting Hasan's systemic socio-semantic stylistics framework. Miller and Luporini thus embark on a quantitative analysis of verbal art focusing on evaluative meaning – both aspects favouring in-depth qualitative scrutiny. The authors convincingly show that it is possible to get to the symbolically articulated theme of the novel in its evaluative context with the help of careful corpus analyses.

A tribute is paid to Hasan by **Kathryn Tuckwell** who reprises Hasan's 'The analysis of a poem' (1985/1989) as an exercise in literary stylistics. Tuckwell presents a meticulous metafunctional linguistic analysis of a sonnet by W. H. Auden and thus highlights the relationship between SFL – and especially Hasan's take on SFL – and literary form. With her analysis Tuckwell shows the lasting relevance of Hasan's approach to the analysis of literary language.

Delving more deeply into literary analysis and theory, **Martin Tilney** offers an analysis of strategies of foregrounding and defamiliarization in a story by Peter Carey. Tilney adopts a Hasanian approach to the analysis thus demonstrating the use of a linguistic toolbox that is ideal for a rich literary interpretation.

Analysing Simone de Beauvoir's autobiographical writings, **Alice Caffarel-Cayron** takes a linguistic approach to tracing Beauvoir's formation as a writer. Caffarel-Cayron applies her own account of transitivity in French to the analysis in order to capture Beauvoir's experience and interaction with literature which helps to understand the linguistic reflection of Beauvoir's stance as a writer who uses literature as a tool for change. The author thus links patterns in Transitivity choices to stages of growth and interaction with literature in Beauvoir and shows how, in a Hasanian perspective, the construal of agency and transcendence is symbolically articulated through these Transitivity patterns.

Fang Li, in her chapter on a corpus-linguistic analysis of Jane Austen's novels, shows how Austen's language represents a departure from the fairly abstract writing style of male predecessors of the likes of Johnson and Gibbon shifting from a linguistic focus on the narrator to the characters. Li links this to gender-related questions in the context of the transition towards universal literacy, i.e. literacy extending to women. By adopting this more general perspective, Li aligns with Hasan's approach to the study of verbal art – and language in general – which crucially links the analysis of individual texts to more general social questions.

Anna Espunya adopts a cross-linguistic perspective and analyses translations into English and German of a novel by the Spanish author Manuel

Vázquez Montalbán. Focusing on Appraisal phenomena she shows how emotions such as anger and nostalgia are subject to change in translation partly due to the culture-specific character of the value-laden social stereotypes alluded to by the writer and partly due to a more general tendency in translation to standardize the text. These phenomena are linked to Hasan's ideas of context and especially how literature re-contextualizes everyday-life experience.

Moving beyond a strictly systemic-functional analysis, **Timo Lothmann** takes up Hasan's notions of symbolic articulation and related concepts and links them to core ideas of cognitive linguistic frameworks, more specifically to conceptual metaphor and blending. Taking us all the way back to Beowulf and the metaphors deriving from it, Lothmann discusses the contribution of conceptual metaphors to foregrounding and symbolic articulation.

As a literary scholar engaging with the Hasanian – and Hallidayian – approach, **Peter Wenzel** also examines points of contact between Hasan's systemicist approach to the analysis of verbal art and a structuralist literary approach that draws extensively on cognitive ideas. This appears to be a fertile combination to capture patterns of structure in beginnings of narratives.

Miller and Luporini as well as Li use corpus-linguistic methods for their analyses and **Rebekah Wegener** and **Timo Lothmann** add experimental methods to the methodological tool box. They explore the relationship between author-reader context and intra-text context by analysing fictional worlds that take symbolic articulation into fantastic secondary worlds. They adopt Hasan's idea of second order semiosis as an indicator for the analysis of magical worlds in well-known fantastic novels and use a state-of-the-art empirical methodology combining linguistic analysis with an eye-tracking experiment. Their empirical study provides evidence that readers react differently to different strategies of introducing a magical context to the story world.

Finally, **Wendy Bowcher** not only reviews the previous chapters, linking them to Hasan's conceptualization of the language of literature, but crucially opens up a view to future directions of research on verbal art drawing on the pathway laid out by Ruqaiya Hasan and systemicists who have already taken her ideas further.

In putting together this volume, we have chosen to include authors who are themselves new to Hasan's work in a number of different ways. It is our hope that this will lead to a coverage of some aspects of Hasan's work to which those who are familiar with her may have become habituated. It is also hoped that this volume will encourage new research and promote the reading or re-reading of Hasan's tremendous work in this area. We look forward to new challenges, arguments, extensions and applications.

Dedication

Ruqaiya Hasan passed away on 14 June 2015, just a few weeks away from what was supposed to be a tour of Europe that was to include attending the International Systemic Functional Congress at our university, RWTH Aachen University, in July 2015. Many delegates took the opportunity to address and honour the influence Ruqaiya's work had on their research. One of the sessions dedicated to the topic of verbal art focused in particular on Ruqaiya's work and, when preparing the conference proceedings (Neumann *et al.* 2017), it appeared sensible to collect the papers on verbal art together with other related papers as a way of showcasing Ruqaiya's work on verbal art and demonstrating the influence it has had and will continue to have. The conference turned out to be a place for remembering Ruqaiya as a mentor and friend, as a brilliant mind, an astute critic and a supporter for young linguists from around the world. We dedicate this volume to the memory of this rare scholar and friend, who left such a deep impression in every-one who had the opportunity to meet her and who will inspire generations through her work as she continues to make not just ripples, but waves in a timeless world.

Acknowledgements

We would like to thank the team at Equinox and our reviewers Tom Bartlett, Alexanne Don, Lise Fontaine, Elma Kerz, Kim-Sue Kreischer, Timo Loth-mann, Paula Niemietz, Ben Neurohr, Bianca Schüller, Tatiana Serbina, Peter Stockwell, and Julia Vaeßen for providing reviews and feedback on all of these chapters. We would also like to thank our students Tobias Becker and Thomas Durst for their assistance in putting together this book.

References

Hasan, R. (2011). A timeless journey: On the past and future of present knowledge. In *Selected Papers of Ruqaiya Hasan on Applied Linguistics*, xiv–xliii. Beijing: Foreign Language Teaching and Research Press.

Neumann, S., R. Wegener, J. Fest, P. Niemietz, and N. Hützen (Eds) (2017). *Challenging Boundaries in Linguistics. Systemic Functional Perspectives*. Frankfurt a.M.: Peter Lang.

1 Language, linguistics and verbal art: The contribution of Ruqaiya Hasan to the study of literature

Annabelle Lukin*

1.1. Introduction

At the beginning of his best-selling, 700-page tome *Capital in the Twenty-First Century*, Thomas Piketty, Professor at the Paris School of Economics, defers to the power of literature to portray the human dimensions of social inequality, well beyond what disciplines such as economics, sociology, history or philosophy can offer. Novels, such as those of Jane Austen and Honoré de Balzac, provide us with 'pain-staking portraits of the distribution of wealth in Britain and France between 1790 and 1830'. These novelists, he argues, were 'intimately acquainted with the hierarchy of wealth in their respective societies'. They 'grasped the hidden contours of wealth and its inevitable implications for the lives of men and women, including their marital strategies and personal hopes and disappointments'. Their novels 'depict [ ] the effects of inequality with a verisimilitude and evocative power that no statistical or theoretical analysis can match' (Piketty 2014: 2). While Piketty's book provides a truly comprehensive statistical and theoretical analysis of wealth and income distribution of the world's major economies, it is instructive that he grants to literature a special wisdom on this topic.

It was the understanding of this particular kind of wisdom, through the lens of linguistics, that motivated Hasan's nearly 60-year fascination with texts of literature. Hasan, like Piketty, recognized that the themes in

*   Annabelle Lukin is Associate Professor of Linguistics in the Department of Linguistics, Macquarie University. She analyses media, political and literary texts, and more recently, healthcare communication (particularly in cancer treatment and end-of-life care). Her theoretical interests include the inter-relations of language and ideology, and language and context.

verbal art were also the concern of other disciplines. One might reasonably argue, for example, that 'the picture of the Elizabethan view of the universe that [Shakespeare's] writings build for us' are 'better elaborated and more explicitly debated in some specialist domain' (Hasan 1985: 100). So what does literature offer that other accounts do not? And, in answering this question, what are the implications for our understanding of the nature of language, and for the teaching of literature? These questions motivated Hasan's initial decision to undertake research on literature for her PhD thesis, a decision she has described as, academically, 'the most important decision of my life' (Hasan 2011a: xv). The problem of teaching literature – of 'how to teach literature to enable the learner to produce an independent reasoned "reading" of some existing work in literature' – was, she believed, important 'socially, morally and pedagogically' (Hasan 2011a: xv). At the time she began her formal Ph.D. research into this problem, she had 'no inkling of the many aspects of language which I would have to explore … in pursuit of this problem'. The problem 'opened unimagined vistas' and took her into 'multiple new domains of the study of language in its socio-cultural context'. Over the next fifty years of her life in linguistics, 'no matter what aspect of language I was engaged in … the challenges raised by the verbal art were never far from my mind' (Hasan 2011a: xv–xvi).

Having begun her academic life in the study of verbal art, Hasan was never to work professionally as a linguist in this specialist area of the discipline. The study of literature had almost the status of a hobby, while, in her institutional position, she diversified into studies of children's stories, mother-child talk across distinct class settings, the language of globalization, and discourse in educational settings. She studied and wrote on discourse from two languages, her mother tongue Urdu, and her second language, English, in which she lived most of her academic career. She worked on every linguistic scale: on sound patterns, lexis and grammar, on semantic units, and contextual phenomena. The bibliographies of her published works show she read into various neighbouring disciplines, such as sociology (Marx, Durkheim, Bernstein, Bourdieu), anthropology (Malinowski, Bateson, Douglas, Geetz, Hsu), psychology (Vygotsky, Bühler, Trevarthen), neuroscience (Edelman, Greenfield, Deacon, Damasio), and philosophy (Wittgenstein, Popper, Rorty). This cross-disciplinary experience – driven by her sense that human minds are the locus of processes that are psychological, sociological, cultural, and linguistic – led her into discussions on the nature of knowledge, and the nature of theories. She was also widely and deeply read across the discipline of linguistics, and directly engaged with the work of scholars in speech act theory and pragmatics (Levinson, Mey, Verschueren), in sociolinguistics (Labov, Gumperz, Goffman), and stylistics (Jakobson, Mukařovský, Chatman, McIntosh). And still she found time for the passion that first brought her into linguistics.

1.2. Reading Hasan on 'verbal art'

Hasan's published work on verbal art appeared over a span of 40 years: from 1967 to 2007. Her published works on verbal art are: 'Linguistics and the study of literary texts' (Hasan 1967), 'Rime and reason in literature' (Hasan 1971), 'The place of stylistics in the study of verbal art' (Hasan 1975), 'Language in the study of literature' (Hasan 1979), 'The nursery tale as a genre' (Hasan 1984), *Linguistics, Language and Verbal Art* (Hasan 1985), 'The analysis of one poem: Theoretical issues in practice' (Hasan 1988), 'Teaching literature across cultural distances' (Hasan 1996), and 'Private pleasure, public discourse: Reflections on engaging with literature' (Hasan 2007). From the notes for the as-yet unpublished final volume of her Collected Works, dedicated to verbal art, it is clear Hasan had planned to write a further four papers: a paper each on the poets Kenneth Slessor (from Australia), Robert Frost (from America), Wilfred Owen (from England), and Faiz Ahmed Faiz (from Pakistan). These were poets whose work she had analysed and presented on over many years. The notes to her analyses survive, but the full articles were not found among her papers after she died.

Her formal research in the field dates back to 1964, with the completion of her Ph.D. dissertation at the University of Edinburgh under the title *A linguistic study of contrasting features in the style of two contemporary English prose writers*, and under the supervision of M. A. K. Halliday, though her first foray into the field can be dated to a 1961 dissertation for a Diploma in Applied Linguistics (*The Linguistic Study of a Literary Text*, an analysis of Angus Wilson's short story 'Necessity's Child'). The Ph.D. thesis examined extracts from *Free Fall* by William Golding, and *Anglo-Saxon Attitudes* by Angus Wilson. The extract from *Free Fall* was 125 pages in length (5,276 clauses); the extract from *Anglo-Saxon Attitudes* was 73 pages (4,896 clauses). This corpus of over 10,000 clauses was analysed with respect to a number of grammatical systems, and some lexical patterns were also explored (in the pre-computer era!). The thesis shows, even at this early point in her career, Hasan's interest not simply in the analysis of literary works, but in the whole problem of what constitutes the field of 'stylistics', of what precisely can be encapsulated by the term 'style' if it is to be a theoretical term in the discipline. In this thesis, Hasan also began to elucidate the challenges for general linguistics presented by the analysis of literary works.

In her thesis there are also critiques of literary criticism, and its use of 'ad hoc, impressionistic categories for referring to language' (Hasan 1964:

3) – the critics she used as the basis of her rejection of traditional criticism included Yvor Winters, T. S Elliot, and J. M. Murry. She diagnosed the basis of 'the obscurity and elusive quality of the term "style"' as 'a logical consequence of taking a second step prior to the first, of stating conclusions without analyzing the relevant evidence available from the text' (Hasan 1964: 7). Her dissatisfaction with literary criticism was something that remained a live issue in her writing up until her final published paper in 2007, where she continued to argue against the ad hoc analysis of language in literature. Hasan argued throughout her career that literature was art crafted in language. It was artistic, because of how language was being used. In literature, she wrote, language 'is not as clothing is to the body; it *is* the body' (Hasan 1985: 91; emphasis in original).

Hasan's dissertation also shows the genesis of Hasan's thesis concerning the 'levels of meaning' in literature. This idea of levels of meaning in literature was not her own: Hasan refers for instance to Wellek and Warren's 1955 *Theory of Literature* (Hasan 1964: 16). But Hasan brought the concept into sharper relief, drawing on the linguistics of Firth (who saw meaning at all levels of the linguistic system, a concept that was clearly influential in Hasan's approach to literature) and Halliday's model, a linguistic theory with influences from Saussure, Malinowski, Firth, Whorf, and Hjelmslev (for a discussion of how these scholars influenced Halliday's stylistics, see Lukin 2015a). Hasan described 'the interpretation and scope of stylistics in this study' as 'very largely consistent with that envisaged by McIntosh and Halliday, and generally anticipated by Firth', even if 'the specific treatment of the subject' developed in the thesis was her own (Hasan 1964: iii). Because literature was art crafted in language, stylistics, she argued, needed a robust linguistic theory and description. She drew on Halliday's general linguistic framework, because of its socio-semiotic orientation (see e.g. Halliday 2003, in which he defends the key assumptions of his linguistic model).

In her Ph.D., Hasan set out her account of the levels of literature (see Figure 1.1), in terms of the stratum of 'internal meaning' or 'linguistic execution' ('which may be further subdivided into levels of language as set up within the linguistic sciences' (Hasan 1964: 16)), which literary works share with all other kinds of text. Here already this stratum included reference to 'textual context', glossed as 'context of situation'. The stratum of 'external meaning' was divided into the 'time dimension stratum', the 'authorship stratum' and the 'place stratum' (Hasan 1964: 16). These concepts evolved into her thesis about language in literature, elaborated in most detail in Hasan (1985), and her conception of the notion of context as it pertains to literature, explored in Hasan (1996). I discuss both of these developments in her work below (the 'internal stratum' is 'symbolic articulation', discussed

Figure 1.1: Hasan's early stratal model of the literature text (Hasan, 1964)

29

1. The Stratum of Internal meaning.

2. The Stratum of External meaning.

The stratum of internal meaning is approached through what we may call the stratum of linguistic execution which includes the following sub-divisions

<pre>
Phonology)
Grammar   )   Stratum of style
Lexis   )

Context and)
Situation)   Stratum of textual context
</pre>

Stratum of textual context is further subdivided into:

a) the stratum of organic structure.

b) the stratum of Psuedo Register situations.

b) above can be more delicately sub-divided to nth degree as the aim of study may require.   a) is sub-divided into 'character', 'plot', 'theme' and other aspects referable to organic structure.

The stratum of external meaning is sub-divided into:

a) Time Dimension Stratum.

b) Authorship Stratum and

c) Place stratum.

9a.   Strata in literary texts are not conceived of as a hierarchy, here; either of the strata (external/internal) may be studied first according to the aim of the study.   Any statement regarding strata composing the internal meaning <u>must</u> refer to the language of the text. No statements about any of these, unsupported by at least some utterances in the text may be made.   As each stratum is analysed it draws upon the analysis of another stratum, at the same time contributing to it.[1]   Though

---

1. Consider 'style' and 'inferred situation' or 'style and character' or inferred situation' and 'theme'.

in section 1.3; the 'external stratum' in section 1.4 on 'Text and context in verbal art'). 'Theme', a central concept in her stylistic model, did not appear as a separate stratum in the early model, though Hasan suggested at that time that literary texts have the potential to produce not only a 'transparent' thesis, but another thesis available only via inference (Hasan 1964: 17).

At the time that Hasan was writing her Ph.D., the work of the Prague School on literature was not easily available. Hasan cites some concepts from the Prague School through S. R. Levin's *Linguistic Structures in Poetry* (Levin 1962), which references a 1958 edition of Garvin's Prague School reader, published by the Washington Linguistic Club. Garvin's translations brought the concept of 'foregrounding', from the Czech term *aktualisace*, into English stylistics. Hasan's access to Garvin's book came only after the submission of her PhD (Hasan 2007: 37), when it was republished in 1964 by Georgetown University Press. The concept of 'foregrounding', from Mukařovský, would become particularly influential in her later work, though in its combination with Halliday's SFL, Hasan would produce an account with a 'tighter syntax' than that of Mukařovský (Hasan 1985).

Interwoven with discussions on the nature of 'stylistics' and 'verbal art' are Hasan's questions about what it means to teach literature, her conception of what makes verbal art distinct as a form of language use, and her analyses of various instances of literature, including short stories ('Necessity's Child', by Angus Wilson (Hasan 1967; 1985)), poetry (Anne Sexton's 'Old' (Hasan 1988)), W. B. Yeats' 'Old Men Admiring Themselves in the Water' (Hasan 1971), Les Murray's 'Widower in the Country' (Hasan 1985)), drama (Shakespeare's *As you Like It* (Hasan 2007)), as well as nursery tales (Hasan 1984). Across this spectrum of works are discussions of literary treatments of themes such as mutability, isolation, the continuity of 'death-in-life-in-death', the nature of talk in the formation of self, and the restoration of interpersonal equilibrium. Her passing references to other works of literature in her writings are extensive: she clearly read literature with attention and passion, an orientation which began at home (personal communication), but which was certainly shaped and developed in her education in Pakistan, at University College Lahore where she experienced 'brilliant teachers' such as Safdar Mir, Kwaja Manzoor, and 'Siraj Saheb', whose teaching ranged from the importance of ideology in the creation and evaluation of literature, to interpretations of the intricate meaning structures in Shakespeare (Hasan 2011a).

While never rejecting the value of non-linguistic accounts of literature – understanding the milieu in which the author was writing, as well the rise and fall of genres and styles of literary production, were of particular value – Hasan reserved a particular antipathy for unsystematic observations about language or language patterns in literature. In her early work, this antipathy was focused on traditional critics. In her later work, she voiced similar frustrations with the style of criticism in 'critical theory', which she saw as 'almost synonymous with "politically correct", legitimized by the fame of certain intellectual leaders' (Hasan 1996: 56). One of the many off-shoots of this early thinking on the problem of teaching about literature was Hasan's work on education (Hasan 2011b), and specifically literacy educa-tion. A key paper, not widely read in educational linguistics as far as I am aware, describes literacy pedagogies as essentially of three types. The first type is 'recognition literacy' are pedagogies concerned with letter-sound correspondence. Hasan's second type is 'action literacy', Hasan's term for pedagogies oriented to developing pupils' discursive abilities in uncritically reproducing the registers of education. Hasan does not reject either of these forms of literacy pedagogy, though she is clear on their limitations. What she advocates in this paper is a third type of pedagogy she called 'reflection literacy' – the ability to 'reflect, to enquire, to analyse and to challenge' (Hasan 2011c: 198) – which she valued over the other two because 'the endpoint of education has to be the production of new knowledge' (Hasan 2011c: 193). Only reflection literacy 'frees the reader from unquestioningly following the opinions of "authorities"' (Hasan 2007: 34); when done suc-cessfully 'it should ideally produce in the pupils a disposition to distrust doxic knowledge. i.e. knowledge whose sole authority is the authority of someone in authority' (Hasan 2011c: 199).

1.3. 'Style' versus 'verbal art'

In an approach that came to define her scholarship, Hasan started her inquiry into the study of literature from first principles, asking the question of what constitutes 'style'. In the opening paragraphs of her Ph.D. research, she writes:

> Each generation of critics has tended to modify the concept [of style – AL] in some respect, but one thing is common to nearly all such definitions: in spite of the repeated efforts to define it, the term style behaves much as if it had never been subjected to the restraints of any formal delimitation. (Hasan 1964: 1)

Among the aims of the first chapter of her thesis was achieving a tractable definition of the term 'style', and producing an outline of a 'total framework of the technique for studying literary texts with a view to establishing the place of the study of style in this modified sense' (Hasan 1964: 1). The idea of stylistics as simply the study of the language of literature, she suggested, was 'trivial and impracticable' (Hasan, 1971: 299) – it suffered from a lack of a conception of what aspects of the language of literature might be studied. The concept required some explicit notion of what language is, what its internal organization is like, and what the consequences might be of certain patterns of linguistic choices, and in particular, the interaction of patterns of linguistic choices. At the same time, it suffered from a lack of a theory of how the patterns in a literature text relate to the aesthetic work the text is doing. To undertake stylistics without a hypothesis on the nature of language is, she argued, 'a delusion' (Hasan 1971: 302). At the same time, linguistic analysis of literature without a concept of literature as a work of 'verbal art' was problematic. This is because 'there is almost no single language pattern at any level or rank which could be said to be crucially characteristic of literature' (Hasan 1971: 303).

Stylistics had to recognize 'the unity of "verbal-ness" and "art-ness"', since 'in literature, art is language, language is art' (Hasan 1971: 300). Hasan's model of this unity of verbal-ness and art-ness is set out in Figure 1.2. At the level of 'verbalization', literature shares the same characteristics as any other form of text. Its 'substance' is shared by all uses of language, and it can be subjected to the same kind of linguistic analysis as any other text. But unlike other types of text, literature produces a distinct order of meaning. As in existing accounts of the nature of literature, Hasan recognized this as the text's 'theme' or 'theme-constellation', and defined it as a 'hypothesis regarding the nature of the universe and man's [sic] relation to it' (Hasan 1971: 375). It is 'that which "explains" coherently the majority of the linguistic selections and their function in the text' (Hasan 1967: 115); it is 'what stays in the reader's consciousness long after the pleasure of encountering the "artistic turn" of phrases has dissipated itself' (Hasan 2007: 24). Because the stratum of theme is 'closest to a community's ideology', verbal art 'can never be dissociated from the community in which it was created' (Hasan 1985: 99).

The concept of theme in verbal art is recognized in all approaches to literature. But for Hasan, between 'verbalization' and 'theme' is the stratum of 'symbolic articulation', the key level which produces that unity of 'verbal-ness' and 'art-ness' which defines the literature text. Thus, in literature there are two layers of 'symbolization' or 'semiosis'. Hasan describes the first level as the product of the use of natural language, and the second as 'the product of the artistic system through foregrounding and repatternings of the first order meanings' (Hasan, 1985: 98). It is because of the two layers of symbolization that paraphrase can never adequately describe the meanings of a literature text. The art of verbal art, she argues, 'consists of the use of language in such a way that this second order semiosis becomes possible'

Figure 1.2: Verbal art and language (Hasan 1985)

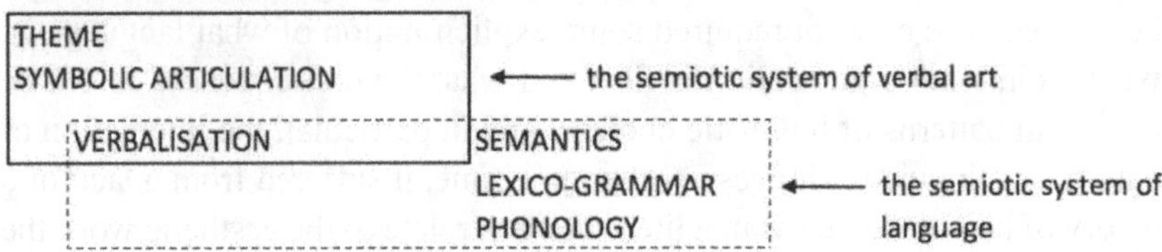

(Hasan 1985: 98). In the process of symbolic articulation, 'the meanings of language are turned into signs having a deeper meaning' (Hasan 1985: 98). One level of semiosis 'acts as a metaphor' for a deeper level of semiosis (Hasan 1985: 100).

The implications of Hasan's model for the study of literature texts are both theoretical and methodological. Theoretically, Hasan makes a case for the defining characteristic of literature. The argument that literature is simply that which a community regards as literature, is, she writes, of no use, since this is equally true of other varieties of language use (Hasan 2007: 22). This recognition of the particular function of language in literature not only produces a definition of literature: it entails a certain kind of concept of language. This fact of Hasan's inquiry was never out of her sight: she argued from Chapter 1 of her Ph.D. that, given the variety of registers that can be recruited to literature, the analysis of literary texts requires 'a model of linguistics which has the greatest competence in handling texts of a large variety, using the same theories, methods and categories' (Hasan 1964: 34). Hasan understood that the complexity of literature demanded a robust linguistic theory: the very notion of what linguistic patterns were available to be re-patterned, under the force of the regulative principle of theme, was entirely dependent on one's concept of the nature of language. In her reflections on her career, written in 2011, she began to use the term 'social-semiotic stylistics', and argued that verbal art relies on 'two indispensable matrices as its sources of energy … the powerful semiotic system of language and the intricately woven fabric of the semiotically shaped culture' (Hasan 2011a: xvii). These two 'engines of power' work together in the instantiation of a piece of verbal art. Their interaction is not only defining of the essence of this form of artistic activity, but also 'throws light on both its production and its reception' (Hasan 2011a: xvii). The socio-semiotically shaped culture provides the terrain for the germination of the 'poet's divine madness' (Hasan 2011a: xvii).

What are the methodological implications of Hasan's model? If the theme or themes of the work must be related to forms of linguistic patterning, what patterns are relevant? Here Hasan recruited the notion of foregrounding, a status achieved by a pattern when it 'stands out against an established tendency' (Hasan 1985: 94). Foregrounding depends on contrast, but given that contrast between two linguistic structures is easy to find and turns up in all texts, we need to understand how contrast becomes significant, such that it contributes to the construal of a work's deeper themes. Hasan's answer was that foregrounding 'becomes noticeable because of its consistency' in 'semantic direction' ('the various foregrounded patterns point toward the same general kind of meaning') and 'textual location' ('significant patterns of foregrounding have a tendency to occur at a textually important point') (Hasan 1985: 95). In summary, 'it is not the patterns per se that are artistic; it is the mode of their utilization that creates an important parameter of artfulness in verbal art' (Hasan 1985: 96).

Hasan's discussion of Angus Wilson's short story 'Necessity's Child' is the most detailed and comprehensive of her analyses of verbal art: it thus provides a good example of the method implied by her theoretical position. 'Necessity's Child' has young Rodney at its centre, a child with parents much more interested in each other than in their offspring. Let us consider Hasan's steps in her analysis of this story:

- Hasan first divides the story into eight movements, each centred around a discrete event or state based on distinct stylistic shifts.
- She explores the stylistic variation in these movements based on extracts from the story, variation which comes from grammatical patterns in logical relations, the use of rank-shifting to create complex things, choices in tense and modality, the absence of finiteness, etc.
- Hasan then observes/explains the function of the deployment of patterns from these systems, and explains their semantic consequences, such as distinctions in the construction of actualized/actualizing time versus imaginary time, the use of projection to construe dream-sequences, and the contrasts between Rodney in his dreams, and how he is construed in the talk of his parents.
- Hasan makes her hypothesis about the themes of the work – noting the difficulty of having to conduct analysis of distinct features separately, 'because they run into each other being part of the same general picture; and together they produce an effect that cannot be attributed to any one individual feature by itself' (Hasan 1985: 47).

From the variations in the text, Hasan argues that the stylistic shifts draw our attention to three 'parameters of contrast': the real versus the imaginary, Rodney as narrator versus Rodney as the observed, and talk versus non-talk. Each of these parameters is elaborated and related to specific linguistic features. With regards to the second of them, Hasan presents, albeit briefly, her concept of 'planes of narration' (Hasan 1985: 68), the 'objective plane' – where the narrator is a character outside the story – and the 'subjective plane' – where the narrator is a character within the story. Each of these two planes is subject to the distinction between 'direct' and 'indirect' narration: A narrator, whether inside or outside the story, can directly narrate events, the mode of 'direct narration' can be through either third or first person narrator. When the voices and points of view of characters in the story are brought in, via mental and verbal projection and/or other linguistic features that create the illusion that readers are in direct communication with one or more characters in a story, this constitutes 'indirect narration'. Indirect narration, be it on the objective or subjective plane, 'neutralizes the primary orientation of the corresponding plane' (Hasan 1985: 73). Indirect narration on the objective plane compromises the objectivity of the narration; indirect narration on the subjective plane – the introduction of the sayings and thought worlds of other characters – creates a more objective orientation to the narration, because the sayings and musings of the character-narrator are calibrated against the perspectives of other characters. 'Necessity's Child' recruits both planes, in both their direct and indirect modes, for its exploration of Rodney's struggle to understand his place in the world. Hasan sums up the interplay of these planes of narration in the following way:

> The four delicately balanced planes of narration become a powerful strategy for examining the ambiguities between the real and the imaginary, the subjective and the objective, exposing structures of parental communication that banish Rodney to a world, in which, surrounded by people, he must still be always alone, afraid and insecure. (Hasan 1985: 89)

This analytical move from the grammatical patterns to a thesis about the key, interweaving semantic strands of the story is complex, not only in her analysis of 'Necessity's Child', but in all the texts of literature which Hasan has analysed. The basis for Hasan's arguments about the themes of the works she analyses is always explicit. But the process of unpacking what has been subject to 'symbolic articulation' undoubtedly requires the analyst to have a deep knowledge of the grammatical systems of the relevant language, and some sense of their aesthetic potential.

1.4. The text and context in 'verbal art'

Hasan is known among systemic linguists for her long-standing interest in the problem of text-context relations, though it is perhaps not so well known that this theoretical problem captured her attention because of her interest in verbal art. As she wrote in her reflections on her career: 'with an interest in verbal art, it was no accident that very early research on the concept of text came to occupy a central place in my working life' (Hasan 2011a: xx). The nature of context in verbal art appears as part of her inquiry in her Ph.D. research, including the distinction between the inner and outer contexts of a literary text. And though it became a central question in her thinking – a problem with implications for the general architecture of Halliday's socio-semiotic account (see Lukin (2015b) for an account of Hasan's contributions to theorizing context in the systemic functional model) – she continued throughout her career to return to the specific issue of 'context' as a problem in the study of verbal art. With the typical Hasanian ability to see continuities in apparently disparate problems and theoretical issues, Hasan related the problem of context in literature to that of 'cultural distance' (Hasan 1996), a concept that at once brings together the meanings of a given text, in relation to the socio-cultural frames, languages and ideologies of both a writer and a proximal or distant reader. Figure 1.3 reproduces Hasan's visualization of the literature text as mediator, between writer and reader, of cultural distance, whether the distance is in time, space, or social location. This bundle of inter-relations she put, once again, into the problem of teaching literature, as well as the question of what makes a literature text survive over time. This, she argued, was 'neither entirely rationally determined nor just a matter of chance' (Hasan 1996: 56). In the simple act of wondering what it means to teach a literary text to some group of students, Hasan makes visible (particularly in Hasan 1996) the various dimensions she sets out in Figure 1.3. As Hasan notes, the text, via its author, is grounded in a particular context of construction. The author is, like the reader, a product of the socio-cultural frames, and semiotic systems through which s/he is socialized. In many cases, 'the socio-cultural frames for the author and his [sic] readers are very often not isomorphic' (Hasan 1996: 57). And, as Hasan has so brilliantly demonstrated, the socio-cultural frames for students within the same community can vary in a consequential fashion (Hasan 2009). Children are fashioned by their local culture, which is historically a function of the group's social position. Consequently, she argues, local affiliations produce cultural distance, and by extension, provide the basis for alternative readings of the same event, the same text, the same rule. This cultural distance is a feature of all societies (Hasan 1996).

The literary text has both inner and outer contexts – a point Hasan observed when writing her PhD, but most developed in Hasan (1996). The outer contexts are those of its context of creation, and of its context of reception, a distinction which fills out the nature of the relationship between author and actual reader. The text is the mediator of this tenor relation between writer and actual reader, and understanding how to calibrate the spatio-temporal distance between them is crucial to the pedagogics of teaching literature. Hasan rejects clearly any suggestion that the task is for the reader to 'find' the meaning the author intended, or to claim that there is some singular meaning 'in the text'. She does argue, however, that the reading is likely to be more gratifying if the reader works at understanding the particulars of the author's 'speaking position' (Hasan 1996: 53), that is, the cultural milieu and the artistic conventions in which the author was writing.

The inner context of the work also recruits cultural distance. Thus, the text has tenor values internal to it – its 'as-if' interactant relations – fictional portraits of people and modes of living which show to readers deep truths about human experience. These internal tenor values are, like all features of literature, subject to 'double articulation': they are 'readable' as tokens to the theme-constellation of the literary work. With the enormous complexity of tenor relations through such vectors of interactant relations as AGENTIVE RELATIONS (the roles derived from the social practice in which interactants are engaged), TEXTUAL RELATIONS (the relations construed by the production of text, e.g. roles as speaker and addressee), and SOCIAL RELATIONS (the interactants' biographies and social positioning, as they are relevant to a specific interaction – see Hasan 2014), and with language the central construer of these meanings, the possibilities for internal tenor values to be recruited to aesthetic ends are infinite. When we turn to the SFL notion of field, the 'as-if' character of literature and its propensity for double articulation are relevant here also: the events and actions of a literary work – its transitivity patterns – lead us towards some deeper meaning that the work is trying to explore or convey. It is here that the paradoxical character of literature – a work of fiction seeking to make overt and coherent some aspect of human experience – can be appreciated. With respect to mode, literary works are typically monologic, and lack the quality of 'process-sharing': that is, the reader receives the text without having been involved in its construction. But a literary work recruits various registers, to evoke various contexts. The selection and interweaving of these various contexts, in a work of literature, is subject to the regulative principle of theme. This variety of contexts come out of the intricate fabric of our semiotically shaped cultures. These contexts may be ones shared by all members of a community – though, as already mentioned, they are subject to the distinct interpretations that differently positioned members of society bring to them – or be restricted to certain members of a society. One further dimension of mode is that the variety of contexts artistically construed within an artistic work have to be somehow interwoven for the work to 'hang together'. There is much to be understood about the aesthetic qualities of mode, since, as Hasan has noted 'the principle for the integration of the many sub-texts in verbal art' is complex (Hasan 2011a: xxxi).

Figure 1.3: The text, the writer, the reader and the language in the context of culture (Hasan 1996)

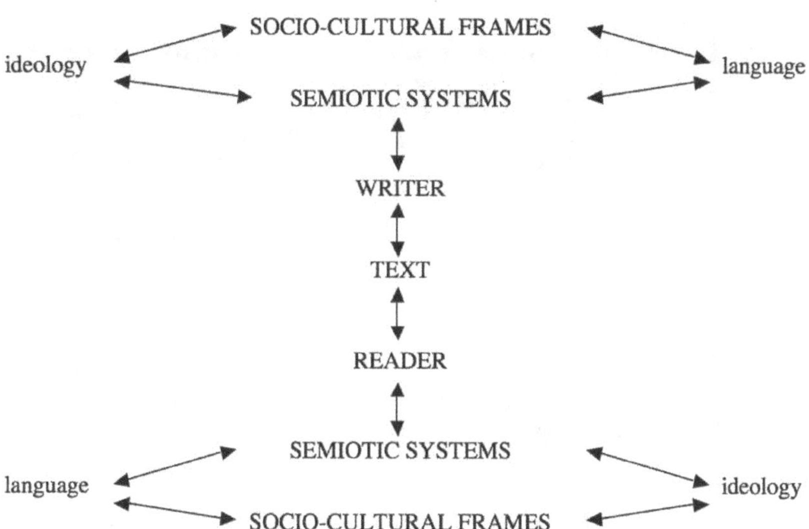

1.5. Characterization: The cline of dynamism

Hasan's exploration of literature's use of ordinary language for aesthetic ends led her to develop her 'cline of dynamism'. The cline is an echo of a proposal from Halliday's first paper in stylistics. In a discussion of Yeats's 'Leda and the Swan', Halliday proposes a 'cline of verbness', from the most 'verbish' selection at one end (the finite verbal group in a free clause) to the least 'verbish', where 'verbness' has become so attenuated the verb is 'subordinated altogether to the nominal element without even the formality of rankshift' (Halliday 2002). Hasan's cline developed out of her analysis of a poem by the Australian poet, Les Murray, which depicts a widower alone and isolated in the Australian bush. Recognizing that a key dimension of the man's experience depicted by the poem was his ineffectuality, Hasan proposed a means to investigate the relative grammatically-construed dynamism of an entity in a text, which she called a 'cline of dynamism' (see Figure 1.4). On a cline from 'dynamic' to 'passive', Hasan locates various transitivity roles, some as roles on their own, some as roles relative to a co-selected feature. Hasan explains the cline in the following way:

> If we define effectuality – or dynamism – as the quality of being able to affect the world around us, and of bringing change into the surrounding environment, the semantic value of the various –er roles

Figure 1.4: Hasan's cline of dynamism (Hasan 1985)

```
DYNAMIC
   1  ↑     (Actor  +  Animate Goal)      John took Harry to London
   2  |     (Actor  +  Inanimate Goal)    John took the books with
                                          him
   3  |     (Sayer  +  Recipient)         John told Harry ...
   4  |     (Sayer  +  Target)            John praised the system
   5  |     (Sayer)                       John talked
   6  |     (Phenomenon + Senser)         John/the picture attracted her
   7  |     (Senser)                      John recognised the house
                                          Mary was attracted by it/him
   8  |     (Actor  – Goal)               John went away
   9  |     (Behaver)                     John woke up
  10  |     (Carrier)                     John was sleepy
  11  |     (Goal/Target...)              John took Harry with him.
  12  |     (Range)                       I watched the house
  13  ↓     (Circumstance/...)            I have a sister
PASSIVE
```

must be seen as distinct. This distinction correlates with two factors: (1) the nature of the Process configuration into which the –er role enters, i.e. what other transitivity functions there are within the same clause; and (2) the nature of the carriers of roles, other than the –er role under focus. It may be added as a generalization that a human carrier of –er role appears more dynamic than a non-human animate, and the latter appears more so than an object. (Hasan 1985: 45)

The most dynamic selection is for an entity to be made Actor with an animate Goal; the least dynamic, i.e. most passive, is to turn up as a nominal group within a Circumstance. Hasan applied this cline to the roles of the widower in Murray's poem, quantifying the distribution of the transitivity roles of the character, so that she is able to conclude, empirically, that the widower describes his life through 'a catalogue of the desiderata of a bare existence' (Hasan 1985: 47).

This cline has been applied to other registers. Lukin (2008) draws on it for the study of media reporting of the 2003 Coalition invasion of Iraq, to show the relative dynamism in the representation of Coalition versus Iraqi forces in news from Australia's public broadcaster. Lukin shows that despite far fewer bombings committed by Iraqis, and much less effectiveness in the actions by Iraqi troops against the American invasion, the ABC construed Iraqi actions as if they were much more consequential and potent for the events of the invasion than the large scale bombing of Iraq by American and British forces. Garcia used the cline in a study of the depictions of violence by guerilla and para-military groups in the Colombian press. This analysis also showed a paradox. Despite many more killings by paramilitary forces than guerrilla forces in the 'internal conflict' in Colombia, the press made the various guerrilla groups appear much more powerful over the lives of Colombians (García 2008; García-Marrugo 2013). Ingold (2014) applies the cline of dynamism to religious discourse, specifically to the analysis of an excerpt from a sermon delivered by Brian Houston, the senior pastor of the Australian Hillsong megachurch. Drawing on a slightly adapted version of the cline (from Thompson 2008), Ingold shows the relative dynamism of the individual human compared with the invoked deities contrued through a 'traditionally Christian conception of the difference between subordinate humanity and omnipotent deities' (Ingold 2014: 105). Don (2007) used the cline to examine the projection of identity in an email discussion group, set up for the purpose of exploring online dynamics in what was at the time a newly emerging mode of communication.

1.6. Explicit appraisal: Engaging with literature

Hasan was over and over drawn to comment on what it meant to give a public appraisal of a work of literature. Hasan's final published paper on verbal art made this problem visible even in its title: 'Private pleasure, public discourse: reflections on engaging with literature' (Hasan 2007), and she argued here, again, about the problem of what it means to produce explicit appraisals of literary works, especially 'as part of the pursuit of a recognized discipline within the framework of official pedagogy', an issue that so captured my attention in my reading of Hasan that it became the focus of my own Ph.D. research (Lukin 2002). Official pedagogy, she argued, homogenizes the learner – it 'represents a negation of the heterogeneity of human culture' (Hasan 1996: 41). The focus of the 'teaching' of literature was the reproduction of 'received wisdom'. The principle underlying such teaching, she argued is '"doxic", not analytic', and 'a recipe for fundamentalist fervour' (Hasan 2007: 20). But Hasan's answer was not to favour the production of some kind of individual reading of a literature text. Our private responses to literature, she argued, are fundamentally social. Our individual identities, habits of mind and personalities are formed and shaped in and by the innumerable small momenta of daily living. Though our experiences are private, the meaning that we give them are 'at their very source, socially nuanced', since 'our value systems are ... essentially social artifacts' (Hasan 2007: 18). Readers of Hasan would know that the social nature of mind has been a deep theme in her work (see e.g. Hasan 2009; and cf. my earlier comment about her reading across disciplines). In the context of appraising literature, her point is that the individual reader is socially situated, and that even apparently personal responses to literary texts are learned. What makes a response 'subjective', she argues, is not its apparent individuality, but that it has no analytical framework:

> What makes a judgement subjective is not that is 'given' by nature, or that it is the manifestation of a mythical 'authentic self' not contaminated by the social: rather, the subjectivity of judgement lies in its not having been subjected to careful analysis – perhaps because there does not exist an argued theoretical framework, or because in certain non-specialist contexts we leave many things unanalysed, allowing their bases to remain unarticulated. (Hasan 2007: 18)

Where learners are subject to evaluation of their readings, she argued that the teaching of literature as a discipline must 'go beyond the retailing and recycling of personal reactions' (Hasan 2007: 19). Only an explicit framework – one with 'the widest possible application … which is maximally applicable to the genre, irrespective of variations in time, sub-genre, and the critic's response' (Hasan 1985: 90) – could enable criticism to become a robust discipline, one where a reader's interpretation of the themes of work was founded on explicit, and reproducible, analysis.

1.7. Conclusion: Linguistics and verbal art

Hasan's devotion to this topic, despite never having the 'luxury' of an institutional position through which to teach and research the language and literature interface, has produced not only reflections on the nature of verbal art from a linguistic point of view. She has, at the same time, shown why linguistics needs to rise to the challenge of analysing literary texts. Perhaps most interesting to me reading Hasan on literature is the insights she has given me about grammatical meaning. In literature, one has to see the aesthetic potential in grammatical patterns, and the ways in which patterns of grammatical meaning can, in relation to some particular set of co-selected features, draw attention to some of the deepest concerns of human communities. While analysis requires that distinct systems be considered on their own, it is in their inter-relation that their real aesthetic – semantic – power comes to the fore. Hasan, together with the stylistics of Halliday, shows in the footsteps of Whorf how deeply metaphysical are the grammars of human languages. The special and unique character of literature is that it treats themes dear to human communities via linguistic patterning, showing the particular beauty of the themes when construed through the process of symbolic articulation. This beauty is a function of the profound interconnection between language and culture. It is fitting to conclude with Hasan's own words:

It is by using language that the artist is able to explore some set of fundamental cultural elements that have become – or on their way to becoming – part of our consciousness/our mental habits, and these foreground for us the deepest concerns of humanity: how in the time that is ours for living, we humans act, react, relate to others, living for a brief moment without perhaps raising the tiniest of ripples in a timeless world, and how we must depart alone with or without pomp and glory, often leaving the world seemingly unimpressed; the artist thus explores the deep meaning of human history, and/or philosophy, and/or sociality, and/or ethics and morality. To explore these universal themes of human existence bracketed between being and not being, to articulate artistically the sense of such a vast universe of feeling, longing, action and emotion as a coherent metaphor, verbal art relies most on these two indispensable matrices as its sources of energy – the powerful semiotic system of language and the intricately woven fabric of the semiotically shaped culture. (Hasan 2011a: xvi–xvii)

References

Don, A. (2007). *A framework for the investigation of interactive norms and the construction of textual identity in written discourse communities: the case of an email discussion list.* Unpublished Ph.D, University of Birmingham.

García-Marrugo, A. (2013). What's in a name? The representation of illegal actors in the internal conflict in the Colombian press. *Discourse & Society*, 24 (4), 421–445. https://doi.org/10.1177/0957926513482063

García, A. (2008). 'As hard as it gets': A preliminary analysis of hard news reports of the internal conflict in the Colombian press. *Linguistics & the Human Sciences*, 4 (1), 5–30.

Halliday, M. A. K. (1964/2002). The Linguistic Study of Literary Texts. In H. Lunt (Ed.) *Proceedings of the Ninth International Congress of Linguistics.* Reprinted in J. J. Webster (Ed.) *Linguistic Studies of Text and Discourse. The Collected Works of M. A. K. Halliday, Vol. 2,* 5–22. London/New York: Continuum.

Halliday, M. A. K. (2003). On the architecture of human language. In J. J. Webster (Ed.) *On Language and Linguistics. Collected Works of M. A. K. Halliday, Vol. 3,* 1–29. London/New York: Continuum.

Hasan, R. (1964). *A linguistic study of contrasting features in the style of two contemporary English prose writers.* Unpublished PhD, Edinburgh University.

Hasan, R. (1967). Linguistics and the study of literary texts. *Études de Linguistique Appliquée* 5: 106–121.

Hasan, R. (1971). Rime and reason in literature. In S. Chatman (Ed.) *Literary Style: A Symposium*, 299–326. New York: Oxford University Press.

Hasan, R. (1975). The place of stylistics in the study of verbal art. In H. Ringbom (Ed.) *Style and Text: Studies Presented to Nils Erik Enkvist*, 49–62. Amsterdam: Skriptor.

Hasan, R. (1979). Workshop Report No. 6: Language in the Study of Literature. *Working Conference on Language in Education: Report to Participants*, University of Sydney.

Hasan, R. (1984). The nursery tale as a genre. *Nottingham Linguistic Circular*, 13, 71–102.

Hasan, R. (1985). *Linguistics, Language and Verbal Art*. Geelong: Deakin University Press.

Hasan, R. (1988). The analysis of one poem: Theoretical issues in practice. In D. Birch and M. O'Toole (Eds) *Functions of Style*. London: Pinter.

Hasan, R. (1996). Teaching literature across cultural distances. In J. James (Ed.) *The Language-Culture Connection*. Singapore: SEAMEO.

Hasan, R. (2007). Private pleasure, public discourse: Reflections on engaging with literature. In D. R. Miller and M. Turci (Eds) *Language and Verbal Art Revisited: Linguistic Approaches to the Study of literature*, 13–40. London: Equinox.

Hasan, R. (2009). *Semantic Variation: Meaning in Society and Sociolinguistics. The Collected Works of Ruqaiya Hasan, Vol. 2*, edited by J. J. Webster. London: Equinox.

Hasan, R. (2011a). A timeless journey: On the past and future of present knowledge. In *Selected Papers of Ruqaiya Hasan on Applied Linguistics*, xiv–xliii. Beijing: Foreign Language Teaching and Research Press.

Hasan, R. (2011b). *Language and Education: Learning and Teaching in Society. The Collected Works of Ruqaiya Hasan, Vol. 3*, edited by J. J. Webster. London: Equinox.

Hasan, R. (1996/2011). Literacy, everyday talk and society. In R. Hasan and G. Williams (Eds) *Literacy in Society*. London: Longman. Reprinted in J. J. Webster (Ed.) *Language and Education: Learning and Teaching in Society. The Collected Works of Ruqaiya Hasan, Vol. 3*, 169–206. London: Equinox.

Hasan, R. (2014). Towards a paradigmatic description of context: Systems, metafunctions, and semantics. *Functional Linguistics* 1 (1): 9. https://doi.org/10.1186/s40554-014-0009-y

Ingold, R. (2014). God, the Devil and you: A systemic functional linguistic analysis of Hillsong. *Literature and Aesthetics*, 24 (1), 85–116.

Levin, S. R. (1962). *Linguistic Structures in Poetry. Janua Linguarum, 23.* The Hague: Mouton.

Lukin, A. (2002). *Examining poetry: A corpus based enquiry into literary criticism.* Unpublished Ph.D, Macquarie University, Sydney.

Lukin, A. (2008). The explanatory power of the SFL dimensions for the study of news discourse. In *Proceedings from ISFC 35: Voices Around the World*, Sydney, 106–111. Macquarie University.

Lukin, A. (2015a). A linguistics of style: Halliday on literature. In J. J. Webster (Ed.) *The Bloomsbury Companion to M. A. K. Halliday*, 348–366. London and New York: Bloomsbury.

Lukin, A. (2015b). Language, context and text: The contributions of Ruqaiya Hasan.' In W. Bowcher and J. Y. Liang (Eds) *Society in Language, Language in Society*, 143–165. Basingstoke: Macmillan Palgrave.

Piketty, T. (2014). *Capital in the Twenty-First Century*. Cambridge, MA: Harvard University Press. https://doi.org/10.4159/9780674369542

Thompson, G. (2008). From process to pattern: Methodological considerations in analysing transitivity in text. In C. Jones and E. Ventola (Eds), *From Language to Multimodality: New Developments in the Study of Ideational Meaning*, 17–33. London: Equinox.

Wellek, R. and Warren, A. (1955). *Theory of Literature*. New York: Harvest Books.

2 On being a literature teacher: A language based perspective

David G. Butt*

2.1. On teaching language and literature

There are challenges, and opportunities, that are peculiar to the teaching of literature. These challenges – and the academic rewards – are what I wish to illustrate and reflect upon in this opportunity to write on topics in arts and humanities, particularly in relation to my teacher and career mentor, Ruqaiya Hasan.

I will set off from a summary statement that I have arrived at through my experiences working in literature and linguistics. I will then work more directly through examples to bring my initial claims about literature 'down to earth'. Many scholars have been brought to linguistic specializa-

---

*   David Butt is associate Professor in linguistics at Macquarie University and for more than a decade has been the Director of the University Research Centre for Language in Social Life (CLSL: now a Research Network). This Centre has conducted projects across communities and institutions for which functional linguistics provided significant evidence about the management of change. Through the Centre, he has been actively engaged with professionals in medicine (surgery and psychiatry), counselling, care for people with disabilities, intelligent systems design and brain sciences, cultural analysis (literature, theatre, world Englishes), complexity theory and 'smart spaces', Vygotskian approaches to education and training, financial reporting, courtroom explanations and forensic evidence, media and journalism, and child language development (in the traditions of Trevarthen and Halliday). The Centre has also investigated the interrelations between linguistics, verbal art (especially poetry), philosophy and the arguments of natural sciences (viz. biology; genetics; and physics). The Centre has actively promoted educational developments in various cultures beyond Australia – Singapore, India, and especially with Timor and in Indonesia. David has published extensively on verbal art and has conducted many research projects and classes on the subject.

tions by the questions surrounding the crafting of literature and verbal arts more generally: how do human minds make new thoughts out of community habits (i.e. out of languages)? how do verbal arts – these 'figments of mind' – direct our day by day experience in the way that I will argue they do? Ruqaiya Hasan was one such scholar drawn to the power of language to create the unique semantic consequences of verbal art; semantic consequences which both relied on the particularities of cultural patterns and on the apparent power to transcend any cultural specificity. We arrive at an impasse – we do not find the same meanings in verbal art, yet we do so often find relevant meaning and value within and across cultural traditions of valued texts. Hasan illustrated her fascination with the motif of mutability: a theme of many traditions of poetry. In English traditions, the theme was typically cast in the form of mournfulness and diminution of life, illustrated by the sub-genre of 'Ubi Sunt' poems (approximately: 'Where are they now?'). In Urdu, however, the image of ripened and dropped fruit has not been, traditionally, an image of loss, but of a life cycle being fulfilled, perhaps closer to the 'Ripeness is all' that seems hard won in Shakespeare's *King Lear*. Another great scholar for whom literature was the 'air beneath his wings' was Vygotsky (1896–1934). This 'Mozart of psychology' found many of the terms of his own enquiry from the debates raised around the Russian Formalist group of linguist investigators of literature, for example Shklovsky, Jakobson, and Tynjanov (Kozulin 1990; see also Kellogg 2014; and Toulmin for the comparison to Mozart). Vygotsky was preoccupied by the power of *Hamlet* to offer an experience of the potential of the human self beyond the actual.

Teaching about language is always more abstract than the teaching of other subjects because your topic is not only out there in the world; rather, it is also the very basis by which you see and sort your experiences in the world. This is the case whether we are referring to first language or foreign language teaching. It is like studying the eye in order to understand what can or cannot be seen – we study language in order to understand what can or cannot be meant. Verbal arts and literature take this situation one step further into difficulties: the artist takes our habitual patterns of speaking and combines them in such a way as to carry us to insights beyond our habitual ways of thinking. The artist offers us intimations of the previously 'unmeant' in a given community. The artist brings a disturbing message in her or his work, namely: that the experiential order taken on through childhood as an implicit 'consensus' with our speech community – our contract as to how the world will be construed – could have been drawn up according to other forms of symbolic practice. And an alternative texture in life might have led to quite different ways of experiencing the world, different ways of making sense of the human strivings that communities express through their language in verbal art (Whorf 1956).

2.2. Paradoxical claims about language arts and the task of stylistics

Stylistic analysis, in line with general principles of scientific enquiry, involves arguments against randomness. Unlike many recent fashions in semantics, pragmatics, and cognitive theory, however, stylistics does *not* depend on such non-randomness being intentional, conscious, sub-conscious, or even unconscious. Linguistic patterning in verbal art is a linguistic phenomenon. It needs to be addressed linguistically, and not via categories that first accommodate speech act philosophers, nativist psycholinguists (note the Ohmann hypothesis of the 1960s!), or experimental evidence in cognitive science that derives from any artificial isolation of human rewards and actions. While I remain open to the findings of every discipline – for instance, to the relevance of neuroscience and its current evidence concerning emotional and interpersonal structures, typically related to older systems of the brain (viz. Porges 2011; Panksepp and Biven 2012) – it would surely be irrational to reorganize the sub-discipline of stylistics on the basis of terms outside of the literary and linguistic categories within which the notion of style has evolved. Loaded terms such as intention, illocution, conversational maxim, cognitive relevance, and truth function are of dubious practical value in relation to meaning, and do not offer a 'sine qua non' in stylistic argument. Psychological notions risk returning the analysis of style to a theory of transmission: as if the signified message is 'back there' in the illocution awaiting shipment through the locutionary act out to a receiver's 'theory of mind'. While notions like 'stream of consciousness', personality and self, defamiliarization/'making strange', foregrounding, marked and unmarked selection, will continue to be invoked in the study of style, they do not set or restrict the agenda. In the same way, we could not accept a theory of literary response according to any rigid theory of social class or of 'social realism'. On the other hand, one might expect that stylistic analysis could produce results that could be compared with other academic disciplines in order to establish congruence, or signs of mutual support. Examples here could include psychological theories or theories of class and group differences in speech. Consider in this regard the recent status of corpus linguistics: the approaches of 'big data' and especially of corpus linguistics are liberating additions to stylistic methods, but they do not subsume and neutralize the work and theoretical problems of those working in the discipline. Corpus linguistics assists in establishing, and checking on the degree in, claims of non-randomness; but it does not interpret or give the value of such findings of regularity.

To open up debate somewhat, I would suggest here that literary stylistics, from the point of view of many writers, is fundamentally concerned with what has *not* been hitherto intended; with what is *not* expressed so much as 'found' through traditions of form; with what may be categorically at odds with declarations of the poet or writer; with what is distinguished in the totality of an oeuvre (i.e. not by the number and character of metaphoric enunciations in a specific work); and that even the terms we utilize commonly in discussing verbal art (e.g. fiction: non-fiction; verse; genre ...) hide more than they illuminate.

Let us move on, then, to illustrate some of the paradoxical features of literary traditions, the aspects that can present difficulties and opportunities for teachers and students of literature. I will set out from texts that cultures have held in high esteem. For my purposes here, we need to refer to Figures 2.1–2.14, Texts 2.1–2.4 and Tables 2.1–2.4, which I will refer to sometimes one by one, sometimes as a set. The figures and texts I use are all for the academic purposes of: (1) illustrating the paradoxical character of what we call literature; (2) demonstrating how productive the analysis of literary texts can be; (3) showing that contexts of culture and situation can be managed systemically when we are trying to bring together evidence from many levels in a text; and (4) arguing that verbal art derives its powers from the latent patterns in a text, patterns which, whether unconscious or conscious, create a higher degree of textual organization, and a new order of semantic 'ensemble' in the community. I take this view to be the result of a tradition of linguistic scholarship which includes the Russian Formalist critics (especially Jakobson 1978; 1987, and Tynjanov 1978, and their 'systemo-functional' approach of around 1928: (see Steiner 1984; Striedter 1989; and the original texts in translation by O'Toole and Shukman 1977; 1975–1981); the Prague School work of the 1940s (viz. Mukařovský 1977); and the development of Systemic Functional methods of comparing the instance of text against its system. See the work of Halliday 1964; 1971; 1984; Hasan 1964; 1971; 1975; Matthiessen 1993; 1995; and Martin 1992; Hasan's work devotes particular attention to the distinctive 'symbolic articulation' of verbal art: see the study of 1985 which sets out the issues pursued in this discussion.

Let us consider three of the most celebrated works of what is typically referred to as 'fiction'. The Russian novel *War and Peace* is an account of fictional characters, and historic figures, in the very much attested facts of Napoleon's invasion of Russia 1812–1813. This ultimate novel closes with an extended critique of the military strategies of Napoleon; and certainly gives a multitude of ethnographic perspectives on experiences and conditions in

Figure 2.1: *The Figurative Map* (Minard 1869)

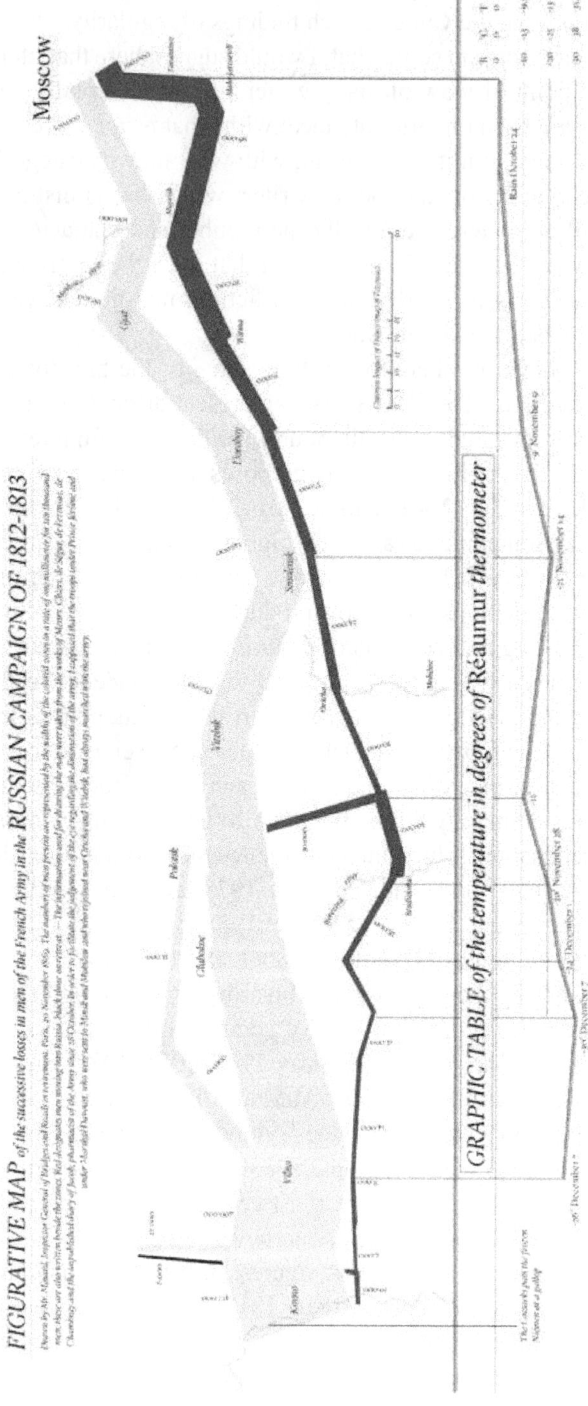

Russia during that war – the fires in Moscow; the social milieu; the details of battle (which Tolstoy experienced first-hand in the 1850s). The text is also pre-occupied with detailed representation of the discourses and tribulations of a single privileged class, reflecting the social position and domestic experience of Tolstoy himself (viz. his own relative is cited in the work). One needs to ask then: wherein lies the fiction?

The 'Figurative Map' (1869) by Minard (Figure 2.1) is a brilliant instance of multimodal innovation – a representation of the French Army as it diminishes from leaving Paris (heavy line: 440,000) to its return (thin black line = 10,000). These losses can be read off against date, place, and temperatures below zero. The map is 'figurative' (a 'figura' or metaphor), like the word we use for tropes and figures of speech in writing. This novel and the map were astounding developments of representation in Western culture. Both are imaginative, metaphoric, and faithful to experience or fact.

More disturbing is the novel by Joseph Conrad: *Heart of Darkness*. Conrad's attack on colonialism and European hypocrisy is narrated by a character, Marlow.

Marlow is not Conrad; yet how many details of Conrad's own trip up the Congo River, as a riverboat captain, are constitutive of the narration? This relationship between the world and the fiction has become the source of controversy: has Marlow's version of the world deepened prejudice about African people in its dramatic presentation of the veneer of civilization in the European characters (viz. the imagery of darkness; Kurtz's vision of 'The horror …', etc.)?

James Joyce's *Ulysses* is an account of one day in Dublin: supposedly 16 June 1904. It is totally dependent on the particularities of living in specific streets and under carefully enumerated conditions – from affairs of the heart to functions of the body! It is an ethnography of voices; it is an archive of registers – from pub quarrels to academic debates; parodies of bardic genres to a woman's soliloquy on sexual encounters. As suggested by the title, this sprawl of actual living is viewed against heroic tradition: the living persist. It is the heroic in a new key. But one can ask once more: what is the meaning of 'fiction'? what is the nature of the art in verbal art? how is it different from the representations of ethnographers or social scientists and psychiatrists, or of theologians and philosophers?

The poet Sappho (she lived on Lesbos in the sixth century BCE) is esteemed as the inspiration for much of Greek lyric poetry. Fragments still extant are widely regarded in classical eras of both Greece and Rome as the greatest lyric voice (Homer being 'Epic'). One notable poem gives a forensically accurate account of the human body struck by an infatuation. The Roman poet Lucretius (died by suicide c. 50 BCE) wrote a 7,000-line account *De Rerum Natura*: 'on the nature of things'. This remarkable poem I have studied for a number of purposes; but it is its surprising relation to science that I will mention here. This work, which stands in the front rank of Latin literature (a tradition almost as continuous as Chinese literature!), re-construed the Greek science of Epicurus (including atomism and infinite space) into a scientific text which was not surpassed by modern science until the nineteenth century.

Pasternak's novel, *Dr. Zhivago* offers a 'fictional' account of the Russian Revolution at the scale and complexity of Tolstoy's treatment of *War and Peace*. It deals with the great social and personal tumults of the period, and brings so much observation of fine detail, even the linguistic observation that the Party Officials increasingly talk in 'nouns'. It is a version of the world – one that was banned in Russia. Were it only 'fictional', the banning would seem unnecessary.

We can identify still more issues pertaining to verbal craft, representations of actual events; social value, and even prescience concerning international events, for example, Grahame Greene's intuitions about Americans and their catastrophic influence in Vietnam: viz. *The Quiet American*.

2.3. The discipline of literary enquiry: What is its object?

What is astonishing is that any choice of texts that a teacher of literature might make will produce a related spectrum of paradoxical effects. The terms *literature, fiction*, and *verbal art*, all serve loosely to get us talking; but they are ever being interpreted and re-valued in the culture. This is fine – verbal art is a participatory activity; or it should be.

But if we purport to teach a subject, we are obliged to explain the subject matter of our endeavours; the benefits of our practice; the reasons for the teaching to be included in the training of those in our institutions. Even if we all enjoy literature and verbal artistries, the rationale for teaching to this enjoyment should be sought and made public. This challenge as to the *techne* of the language teacher goes back to the life of Socrates, and his opposition to the teaching of rhetorical arts (Roochnik 1996).

What factors, then, can we be clearer about when discussing verbal art and its evaluation? In Figure 2.2, a number of concepts are set out that need to be kept in view when the interpretation of a text is being discussed: why is it that the Anglo-Irish texts of Yeats and Joyce are not seen as variant forms of English, one of the World Englishes, while many other writers with fewer local assumptions in their work will be classified as such? There are overt signals of difference that will generate classifications; and other, covert, differences that remain under explored in our analyses.

Figure 2.2: Rites of passage

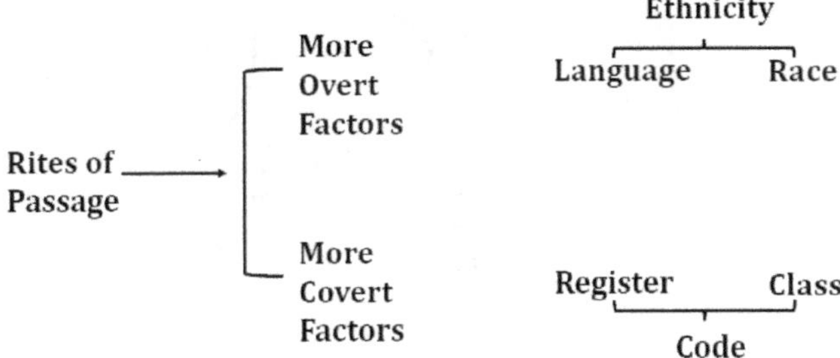

An example might be how much the individuation of point of view in contemporary literature in English (in the UK, USA, and Australia) has meant the values of collectivized social units – families and workers' unions, for instance – rarely carry kudos. No one is persuaded to grow up to be a union leader; although this may not be the case in the literatures of South America, or of China and India, for that matter.

The latent patterns of organization in a text (see Figure 2.3) can be thought of first, as the connections for which we currently have no clear account in linguistic theory (although we all may respond to the semantic consequences of the link); and second, as the connections which we can name, but which cannot be tracked by our reading over extended text (although, again, we may sense the consequences of the patterning 'subliminally' as Jakobson's suggested).

The poem of Robert Frost, 'The Silken Tent', is set out for the purpose of clausal analysis. It is a much anthologized sonnet; yet it appears to be a whimsical and clever comparison between a silken tent and the persona of a woman. The clause structure (in Figure 2.4) shows how the whole poem

Figure 2.3: Latent patterns of organization

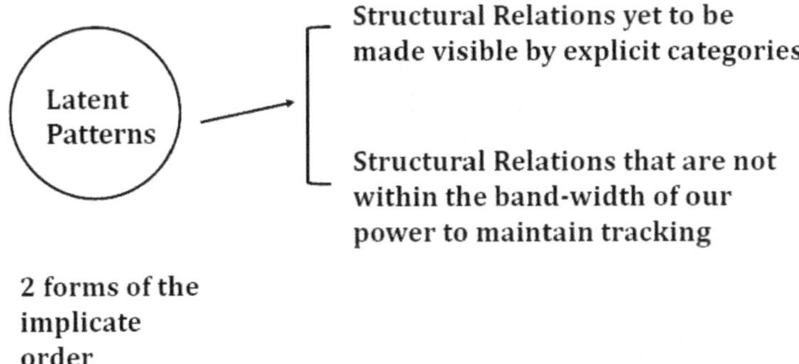

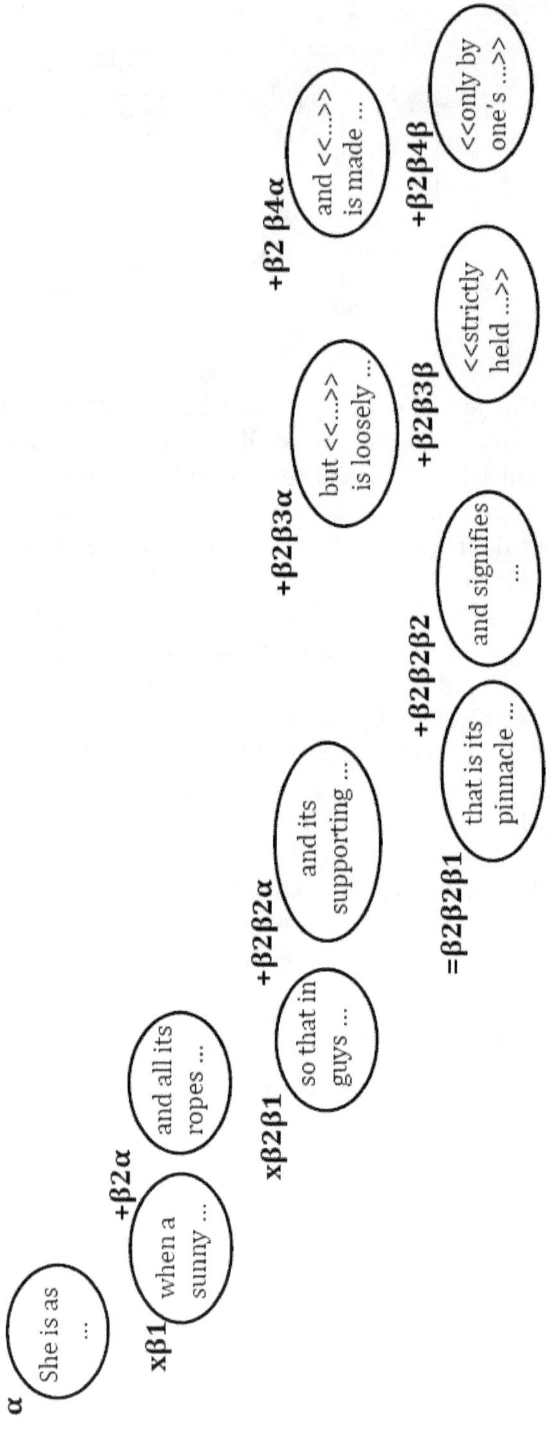

Figure 2.4: Clausal taxis in 'The Silken Tent'

Figure 2.5: Inner/outer contexts (Hasan 1979)

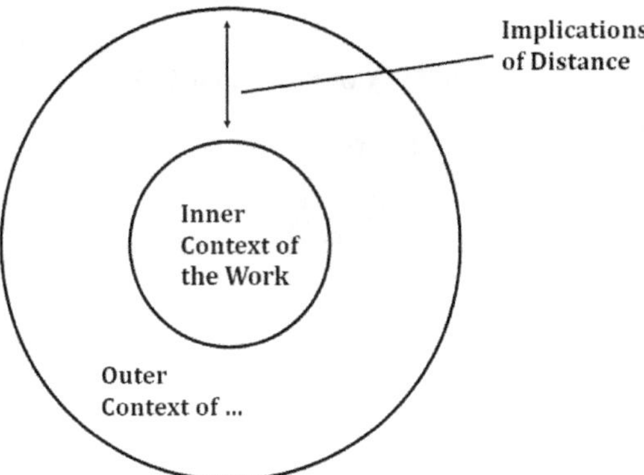

resolves itself into a single, balanced, periodic sentence. We will see in later examples how such organization can be put to various textual effects, particularly when combined with other resources for raising and lowering the textual visibility of a motif e.g. moving words in and out of the roles of agent, subject, and theme (see also Webster 1998; 2001).

2.4. Semiotic distances, semiotic differences

The distance between the inner context of a work, that constructed by the author's language, and the outer context of the reader's world is another semiotic distance that needs to be analysed systematically, as Hasan has pointed out (see Figure 2.5).

I think this idea of contexts can be extended to a nine cell matrix by which the investigation of literary topics and texts examines three kinds of context against three types of milieu: see Figure 2.6. There are contingencies that

Figure 2.6: Matrix of change (Hasan 1996)

<table>
<tr><td rowspan="2"></td><td colspan="3"></td><td>Matrix of
Change</td></tr>
<tr><td></td><td></td><td></td><td></td></tr>
<tr><td>Context of
Creation</td><td></td><td></td><td></td><td></td></tr>
<tr><td>of
Construction</td><td></td><td></td><td></td><td></td></tr>
<tr><td>of
Reception</td><td></td><td></td><td></td><td></td></tr>
<tr><td></td><td>Cultural
Systems</td><td>Linguistic
Systems</td><td>Aesthetic
Systems</td><td></td></tr>
</table>

Figure 2.7: Extrinsic and intrinsic in evaluating verbal art

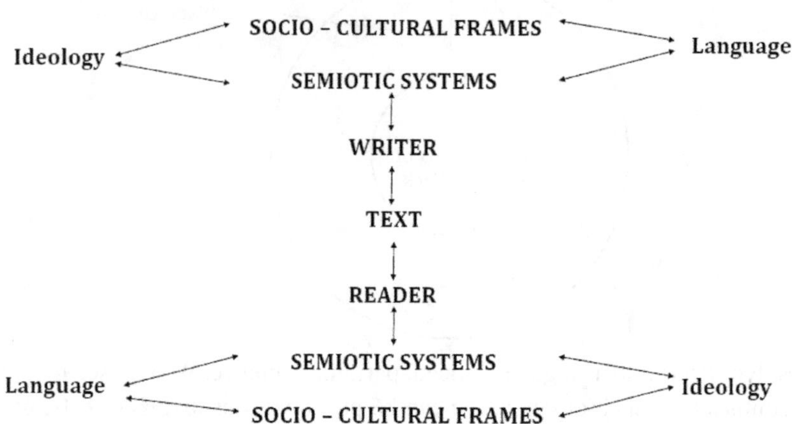

direct a work from the particularities of an author's experience (context of creation); there are those that are derived from the artistic expectations of the era (context of construction); and those that control the context of reception – how works can be heard or read.

All these have to be seen against the significance of changes in the cultural, linguistic, and aesthetic systems of a community. See also Hasan's diagram (Figure 2.7) for a more abstract overview of the pressures on a semiotic context. Think here of rhyme as a regularity and a resource in English poetry: different eras, and different influential poets of those eras have held to opposing views on the use of rhyme: e.g. Milton (seventeenth century) and Eliot (twentieth century) against; Browning (nineteenth century) and Frost (twentieth century) requiring it of their verse. We now hear all about us successful, popular song lyrics which use rhyme almost invariably, and yet, on the other hand, we see a growing tendency for poets, in Australia for example, to associate rhyme with outmoded, constraining aesthetic values.

2.5. An instance from Dr Ee

Many of these issues are relevant to the consideration of the crafting of the poem 'Dejection', by the Malaysian – Australian poet, Dr Ee Tiang Hong (1933–1990) (see my article at http://onlinelibrary.wiley.com/doi/10.1111/j.1467-971X.2009.01598.x/pdf). In Figures 2.8–2.10, the beguilingly simple poem is explored in a series of rudimentary linguistic steps. The orthography is examined to settle the clause boundaries and dependencies; the lexis is

Figure 2.8: Linguistic analysis of 'Dejection' (Step 1)

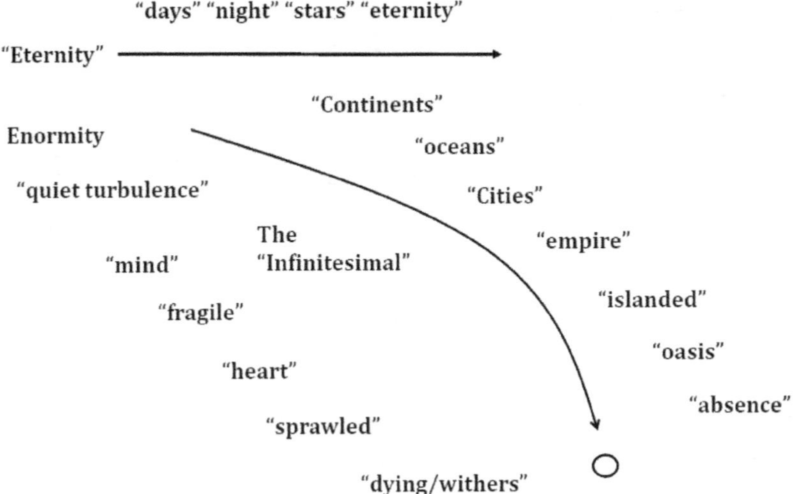

spread out around its most overt chains of similarity; and the lexis is seen against the depths of clause to clause organization.

First of all, the two overt motifs (semantic preoccupations) appear to be: extension in time: days that 'drag on' and 'eternity'; and extension in space, the movement from 'continents' and 'oceans' to 'island' and 'absence'. The topic of time changes to that of 'enormity' in the switch in the verse paragraph; and 'suggest' with 'eternity' changes to a series of geological terms that have psychological overtones: 'turbulence', 'fragile', 'withering', etc.

We now see an ensemble effect in the lexicogrammatical organization of this poem: the text sets out with a paratactic, additive clausal design. This changes with the shift to space: we follow hypotaxis which ultimately has as many depths of complexity as the Frost poem, but which gives little overt signal of that underlying complexity (again in contrast to 'The Silken Tent', which appears to be an exhibition of the virtuoso powers of the poet). The poem has a definite but latent gestalt – it begins as additive extension in time and then appears to move to enormity in space; but the latter becomes a form of graduation, with hypotactic 'telescoping' from large down to 'absence' (negative space). This diminuendo of scale moves also from the impersonal – 'continents'/'empires' – down to intimate and personal ('infinitesimal' and 'fragile'). The overall drift of the text is to surprise us with its transformation from orthographic and lexical simplicity to a complexity uncovered … and this gives realization to the 'quiet turbulence' that

Figure 2.9: Linguistic analysis of 'Dejection' (Step 2)

is foregrounded at the end of line 5: due to its appearance as an oxymoron. The third opposition becomes that between cosmic process and the 'mind' and 'heart' of the humans, challenged by their 'absence' and 'dejection'.

Crucially, it is the forms of counterpoint set up in the poem – between time and space, between scales of infinite and infinitesimal, and between geophysical and personal – that carry the reader into a complexity that the 'quiet' lexical surface of the text had not itself suggested (Figure 2.9).

But this subtle movement of structure, from parataxis to extending hypotaxis, is a gestalt I have found latent in a number of modernist poems – it appears to be one of the yet-to-be named, unconsciously absorbed and devised text plans that constitute a bank of semantic designs for poets who prepare themselves for their craft. It is like a grammatical form of the old notion, from Anglo-Saxon poetry of a thousand years ago, that poets carried a memorized 'word hoard'. This hoard was closer to lines organized to metrical/alliterative formulas – it was not based on words alone or by text patterns in a gestalt. Still, it is important not to discount that units of many ranks may have been latent in the craft of ex-temporizing poets. The unconscious design I have set out for 'Dejection' (Figure 2.10) was just one of the ensembles of patterns I discussed with Dr Ee when we met by chance one afternoon at a tea stall in Singapore. His reaction to my mentioning these semantic ensembles – what I saw as purposive, 'motivated' selections – was neither surprise nor rejection: he referred to them accurately, I believe, as part of a poet's 'syntactic training'; though he had not noticed the consistencies in his own work.

Figure 2.10: Linguistic analysis of 'Dejection' (Step 3) from the 'Eternity' perspective (1= 'The days drag on, and the nights,'; 2= 'the stars suggest eternity']

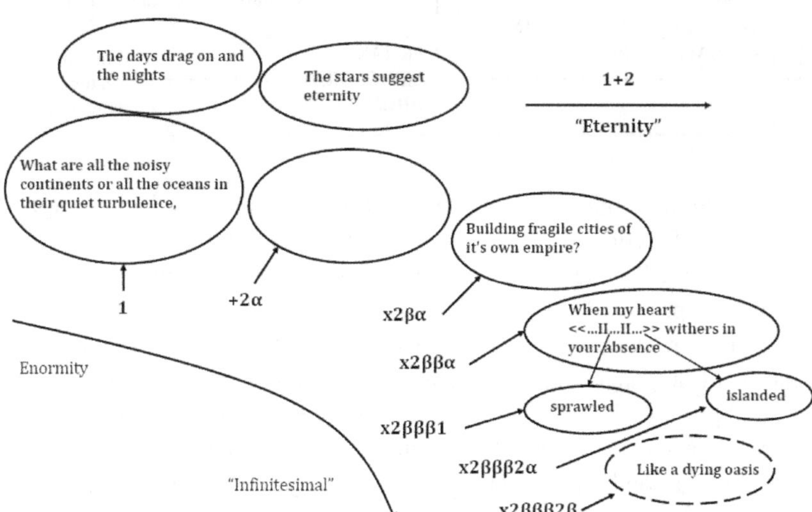

2.6. The order of language

All language is ordered; and the degrees of order are difficult to bring out for people who have been socialized into thinking of them as 'nature'. Literature takes the orders of language and directs them to an integrated purpose to which diverse areas of the grammatical system are recruited to a degree that cannot be explained away as chance, as random. There is, however, no implication of conscious planning in this form of artistic creativity; but there is no reason to dismiss explicit recognition of opportunity and planning by an artist either. It is like other skills taken on by humans in culture: a renewal of nature in the direction of mindfulness.

The level of hyper-organization in the language of the poem is theorized and set out diagrammatically by the diagram by Hasan (1985: 99) in Figure 2.11. According to Hasan, this extra level of 'symbolic articulation' sets the verbal art apart from registers which have a more direct transaction with the conditions of living. All patterns of language make up the level of verbalization in the artistic meaning; and, of course, aesthetic functions appear to have been as early as any communicative purpose in human interactions. The Russian Formalists made a similar claim about the differences between transactional language and language in its aesthetic mode: they called the

Figure 2.11: Hasan's schema (Hasan 1985)

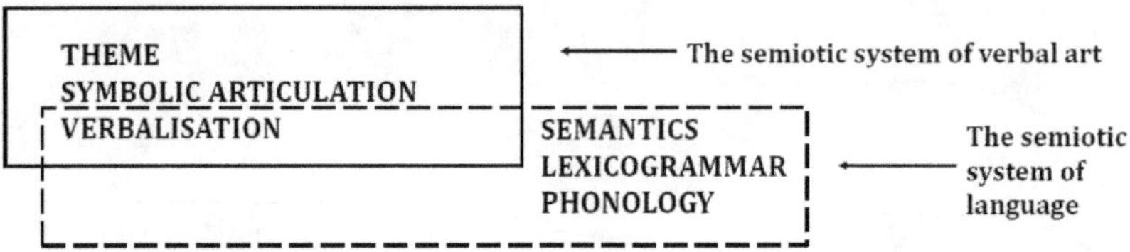

language of quotidian (everyday) transactions 'causal', and the language in its aesthetic function as 'teleological'. By the latter they meant that it is as if the language is patterned to some organizing purpose, even if the purpose can only be proposed *after the author sees* what has been written.

Where, however, is the teacher placed in this convergence of challenging patterns of language and other meaningful behaviours; that is, in cultures past and present? Reading literature can be an experience of choosing, and following leads … you take to this and not to that. But teaching literature is fulfilling a bond with students: namely, that you will be of professional assistance.

2.7. A workbench for linguistic enquiries

Here, the language based approach sets up the situation of teaching and learning quite productively. You will have noticed that the poem 'Dejection' was not, on first appearance at least, a challenging text. But the orthography created some points of equivocation: do the nights 'drag on' like the days, or do they go with the 'stars' and 'eternity'? why the question mark after 'empire' given that the 'when …' clause runs on …? The poet seems to leave any reader in 'two minds'. Such ambivalence can be fertile. But there is a need to establish the organization of a text in reading; and this is a good point for the teacher to assist without neutralizing the student's chance for interpretation – sorting out the linguistic demands of the text while leaving the global interpretation open to exploration. Perhaps this is like setting up one's work bench in a reliable way, checking the accuracy of your tools and measures, etc.

It was remarkable how much potential came from this relatively straightforward series of steps with 'Dejection': seeking the sentence boundaries; seeing these against the clause boundaries; noticing whether the clauses pile up additively or as subordination; looking for a run of related words. These tasks are not sophisticated steps of linguistic theory, but they did make for a sophisticated view of the artist's role in organizing the poem. In fact, we start to find evidence of why the text is valued as it is, why we cannot merely toss off another poem on loneliness and expect that it will merit the same need for preservation and passing on in a tradition as has occurred in the case of Dr Ee's poem (though that possibility should not be dismissed out of hand, either). The initial steps involved reflections on grammar and other language matters that are in the range of a student in early high school. In fact, as we step up in knowledge, so too our ability to judge what is special to an instance of text steps up, along with our range of registerial experience. For example, if we look briefly at poems by Ee (Text 2.3) one can see the way one might build up a sense of the strategies that poets, or particular poets, use in their craft. There are two poems about Bougainvillea – the beautiful flowering plant of tropical Asia and Australia (see http://onlinelibrary.wiley.com/doi/10.1111/j.1467-971X.2009.01598.x/pdf).

One might ask: why two poems on the one topic? But that is leaping ahead. As we examine the poems for their rudimentary organization, it is clear that 'Thoughts in a Garden' is quite distinct from 'To a Shrub': for example, there is no major clause in the first. There is one finite verb, but in an embedded clause (viz. a restricted relative clause): 'that would swell …'. The second poem is an inversion of this non-finiteness: it sets out from a Vocative to the 'shrub' and the first person Subject in a mental process clause. The poem about thoughts in a garden does not directly tell us of thoughts, but 'To a Shrub' does. The organization becomes clear even from this opening observation about Subject and Finite in the two poems: in 'Thoughts in a Garden' you are in the experience of the thoughts   it is soliloquy. And this is dramatically communicated by the moodless expressions: 'How refreshing … What relief … How crisp …'. One could write this in a diary, as if it needed not to engage with others. 'To a Shrub' is a comparison addressed out to the shrub, following the Renaissance convention for describing a woman from brow to foot. But we uncover this contrastive allocation of roles by the simplest of grammatical enquiries in English: where are the finite verbs? Knowing the register conventions of diary or Renaissance poem are another kind of teacherly input. But these emerge from following up the initial, simple question of where do the clauses begin and end.

2.8. Interpretive potential

The approach to literature through the language proves to be an authentic form of pedagogical assistance: it extends the interpretive potential by extending the students' vision of the meaning potential. It provides a platform from which to view the semiotic value of what has been selected in a poem, for instance, against what might have been selected, the value of the instance against how the text might have been otherwise. It assists in establishing what might be 'marked' in a text (i.e. what is a less expected arrangement in the language, and which, for this reason, demands a specific explanation for its selection). Any particular tendencies in the grammar might be seen as a *dominant* in the text: a term used by Jakobson and other Russian theorists for the domain of language which controls the selections made in other systems of the grammar. The poem 'Dejection' has a dominant in the shift of clause complexing, and in its subordination down to four depths in the poem; then, across this structure, the lexical rendering from great to small, and from absolute to personal utilizes the hypotaxis. Of particular concern in this kind of careful linguistic setting out and thoughtful inferencing is the comment from some literature specialists that all linguistic analysis must be inherently 'reductive'. This is a baffling claim. The linguistic approach adopted here only opens up possibilities; it does not preclude interpretations of any kind; but it does respect the decisions the artist has made with respect to the craft under discussion, namely, verbal art. With verbal art one might expect that, as a reader, one ought to defer to the verbal arrangements! We do not discuss music by interpreting the dress of the musicians or the kind of curtains over their stage. But, of course, in the 'attention-getting' overstatements of some academic environments, one theme that did become fashionable was the idea of 'reader response' criticism (influential in the 1980s). In the utterances of a few ostentatious proponents, this potentially useful examination of how the reader interacted with texts (recall the contextual matrix that we reviewed in Figure 2.6) became a self-advertising theory of the reader, and a diminution of any craft in the author. The approach to literature through language restores balance to this academic vertigo (see Melrose 1996 for an interesting reconciliation of contemporary practices; and Lukin and Webster 2005 for a summary of SFL approaches to stylistics).

2.9. Semantic consequences and translating literature

Another angle from language to literature teaching can be found in the use of translations. This may appear to be a foreign language teaching strategy only. Not at all. Nor does it require bilingualism across the students, or in the teacher. What is crucial is the commitment to learning and pursuing interpretations with your students … It can be a situation of peculiar opportunity in which members of the class become the primary sources of grammatical and aesthetic judges from another culture. The point is to compare the semantic consequences of different translations of poems or prose or drama, or even of modalities of artistic expression. Let us begin where we are, however, with verbal art, and poems.

Figure 2.12: Multiple translations of Li Po's 'Silent Night Thoughts' (He 2000)

JING		YE		SI
SILENT NIGHT			THOUGHTS	

Chuang	**Qing**	**Ming**	**Yüe**	**Guang**
Bed	front	bright	moon	light
Yi	**Shi**	**Di**	**Shang Shuang**	
Suspect	is	ground upon	frost	
Jü	**Tou**	**Wang**	**Ming**	**Yüe**
Raise	head	watch	bright	moon
Di	**Tou**	**Si**	**Gu**	**Xiang**
Lower	head	miss	native	land

In Figure 2.12, you can review a selection of different translations into English of Li Po's celebrated 'Silent Night Thoughts' (Wenli He 2000).

In her Master's thesis, Wenli He was able to select a wide span of translations over more than 200 years of English literary tastes (see selective sample: Table 2.1). The findings were not only about the rendering of the Chinese original, but about how individual translators, from specific cultural trainings and eras, responded to their task. The comparison of versions is taken up energetically by 'mother tongue', bilingual, or students for example from Korea and Japan, who have their interest in English and who may not be at all readers of Chinese, but who do have a sense of the Confucian values that might guide cultural and aesthetic decisions in a poem.

Using multiple translations for comparison of effects is an underutilized resource in the English literature classrooms of Australia, and in other places, I suspect. This is unfortunate as so many literature teachers have been trained in language work, including their familiarities with the translation work required of moving through the radical reformations of English from Anglo Saxon (of 1,000 years ago) to the various forms of Middle English (somewhat settled by Chaucer's choice to write in a southern English dialect, c. 1380), to the Renaissance forms of Spenser, Wyatt and Shakespeare (sixteenth century), and on to Early Modern and contemporary forms. The development of a future tense out of the modal system of Middle English, and the blurring or loss of the subjunctive, are but two of the 'dramas' that play out in this history, and which have deep consequences for how we read English writers (including Shakespeare) and the semantic strivings of their evolving communities.

Translators / Titles	Texts
Sun Yü 'Silent Night'	The moonlight lies bright before my couch; I wonder if it were frost on the ground? I raise my head and gaze at the bright moon; I hang my head, thinking of my native land.
Herbert A. Giles 'Night Thoughts'	I wake, and moonbeams play around my bed, Glittering like hoar-frost to my wandering eyes; Up towards the glorious moon I raise my head, Then lay me down – and thoughts of home arise.
Amy Lowell 'Night Thoughts'	In front of my bed the moonlight is very bright. I wonder if that can be frost on the floor? I lift up my head and look at the full moon, The dazzling moon I drop my head, and think of the home of old days.
Shigeyoshi Obata 'On a Quiet Night'	I saw the moonlight before my couch, And wondered if it were not the frost on the ground. I raised my head and looked out on the mountain moon, I bowed my head and thought of my far-off home.
Witter Bynner 'In the Quiet Night'	So bright a gleam on the foot of my bed – Could there have been a frost already? Lifting myself to look, I found that it was moonlight. Sinking back again, I thought suddenly of home.
Wong Man 'Night Thoughts'	On bed bright moon shone, Thought frost on ground formed, Raised head faced bright moon, Lowered head dreamed of home.

Table 2.1: Sample of Translated texts of Li Po's 'Silent Night Thoughts': Thesis by Wenli He

For a second example, in Table 2.2 there is the much anthologized *tanka* of Fujiwara no Teika (1162–1241). These show how selections of a first person pronoun, of the imperative mood over indicative or over a non-finite ('Looking about'), all set up quite different poems and quite distinct poetic effects.

Students can be encouraged to seek their own versions, perhaps even going on to question fellow students as to the verb elements by contrast with the nominal in the source and target languages, and so on. The result is like a student 'gymnasium' for poetic and grammatical exercises. There is also the benefit gained through starting into contrastive linguistics, even in a primary school class – students quickly notice that English is the odd language in its consistent demand for the speaker to offer something explicit

Source text	Translators / Translated texts
	W. LaFleur Gaze out far enough beyond all cherry blossoms and scarlet maples, to those huts by the harbor fading in the autumn dusk.
Fujiwara Teika (1162–1241) miwataseba hana mo momiji mo nakarikeri ura no tomaya no aki no yugure	Kenneth Rexroth I look around, No cherry blossoms, No maple leaves, Only a narrow inlet A thatched hut, In the Autumn evening
	Okakura Kakuzo (1906) I look beyond; Flowers are not Nor tinted leaves On the sea beach A solitary cottage stands In the waving light Of an Autumn eve.

Table 2.2: Translated texts of *Fujiwara no Teika* (Butt and O'Toole 2003)

in the Subject slot (a decision with wide semantic consequences, as shown in the attempts to accommodate the implicitness of Subject role in the Japanese of the Teika poem).

2.10. Textural visibility as linguistic evidence

To round off the claims of pedagogical challenges and opportunities in the teaching of literature, a number of the textual strategies so far discussed are exemplified in the poem set out with clause numbering and analysis of 'Sonnets from China XII' by English poet W. H. Auden (1907–1973) (see http://desertedcities.com/china12.html).

I often use this as a teaching text because it first intrigued me as a student of history and English poetry when I was in high school: why was it so 'effective'? but to what purpose? and why is it so much more significant than the prose report by fellow poet Christopher Isherwood from the same visit to a battle field, and written up as *Journey to a War* (1938)?

If we consider the poem and make some provisional, exploratory generalizations about the meanings involved, we then need to return to the 'workbench' to test our explorations for textual plausibility. Naturally, we could eschew the need for linguistic evidence; but that would only be consistent with relinquishing the role of a teacher in that environment. If the poem only acts as a stimulus for a reader to create a text, any text, in response (and this seems a not unreasonable activity), we should refrain from judging and examining student efforts as a discipline of study, or rational enquiry. Linguistic 'evidence' and 'plausibility' do not tell you what to think; rather, they set you free to think without the weight of some dominant critical authority that creates a 'canonical' account of possible interpretations. We can all learn from a Harold Bloom, or from (the very different) Frank Kermode; but we can hardly consign our interpretive responsibilities over to such culturally distant cardinals of literature, especially when the language of authors is analysed with such 'hit and miss' technique (as in the work of Bloom, for example, in his treatment of Wallace Stevens 1879–1955).

After analysing the Auden poem, we will arrive at this developed list of points.

- Expunge human control or volition.
- Relational process 'gambit'.
- Reverse agency; or occlude it.
- Semantic dissonance: action grammar?
- Put 'men' … in the Qualifiers of the Qualifier or in lower impact hypotactic clauses

The human participants appear to be without much agentive responsibility – they do not exercise volition in the verbs; and they are sometimes occluded from whatever is happening in the poem. In relation to the clause to clause taxis/combinations, men seem to be in subordinated or embedded structures; not in main clauses. This diminution of the role of humans is exemplified in Figure 2.13.

Figure 2.14 confirms the low textural visibility of the 'men' with the diagrammatic version of the clause structure around 'There is a plan …' It shows us how the static relational clauses are deployed in the poem.

Table 2.3 reminds us of the traditional distinction between material verbs that affect a following 'object' and those that do not. The latter might be best referred to as verbs or processes in *middle voice*, emphasizing the happening or emergence of an event by contrast with its being brought about by an agent.

Figure 2.13: Humans in Auden's 'Sonnet XII'

- **'men' are subordinate to 'plan':**

   There is a plan [for living men in terror of their lives, [[who thirst

   at nine || who were to thirst at noon ||

   who can be lost || and are, || who miss their wives ||

   and, unlike an idea, can die too soon]]].

- **Typically human activities (verbal & near-verbal processes) are not performed by humans:**

   - a telephone is talking

   - flags on a map declare ...

Figure 2.14: Clausal taxis in Auden's 'Sonnet XII'

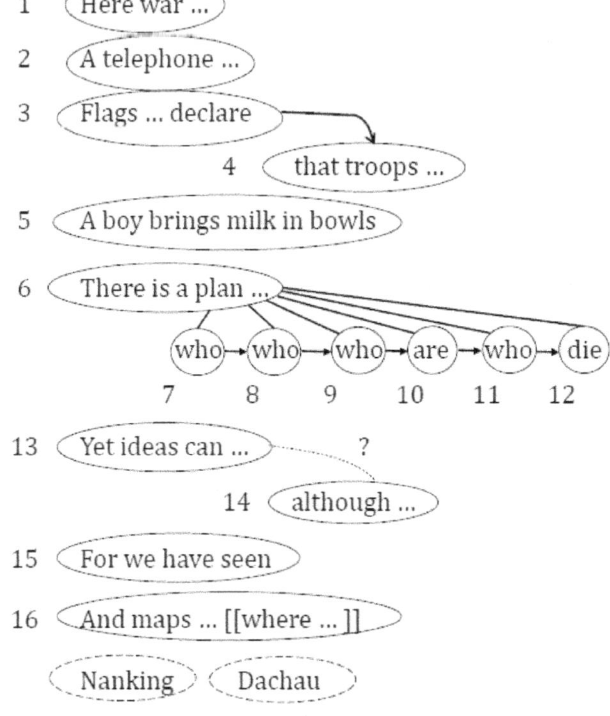

'Doing' Clauses in Auden's 'Sonnet XII'	Transitive/Intransitive Verbs
2 A telephone <u>is talking</u> to a man 3 Flags on a map <u>declare</u> 4 that troops <u>were sent</u> 5 A boy <u>brings</u> milk in bowls 7 who <u>thirst</u> at nine 8 who <u>were to thirst</u> at noon 11 who <u>miss</u> their wives 12 And, unlike an idea, <u>can die</u> too soon 14 although men <u>die</u> 15 For we <u>have seen</u> a myriad faces ecstatic with one lie 16 And maps <u>can</u> really <u>point</u> to places [[where life is evil now]]	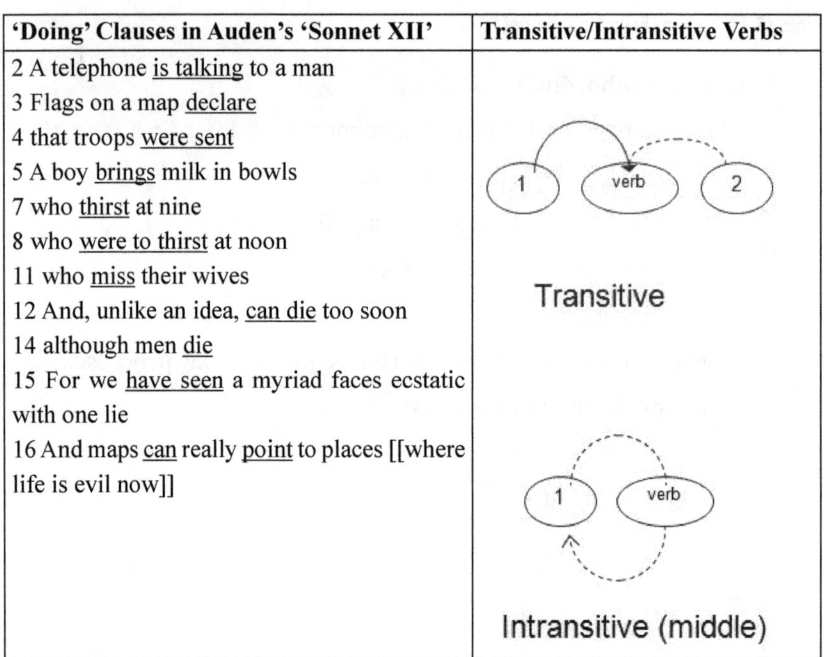

Table 2.3: Analysing material verbs in Auden's 'Sonnet XII'

Table 2.4 shows how little role the human agents are given in the poem – in fact, they are grammatical 'patients' (those that suffer the process rather than do anything). There is an exception in the boy who 'brings milk in bowls'. This strangeness is like many literary strategies that draw attention to the typical pattern in the text by foregrounding a singular exception to that pattern (viz. a way of the artistry drawing attention to itself: an observation originally made by Mukařovský 1977).

Functions	Examples
As Circumstance	a telephone is talking to a man
As Goal	that troops were sent
As 'Do-er'	who, unlike an idea, can die too soon (Actor) who thirst at nine (Actor / Behaver) who miss their wives (Senser)

Table 2.4: Limited role of human agents in Auden's 'Sonnet XII'

Personally, and as a student of history, I have learnt much about the circumstances of the war in China, and the specifics of the lives and journey of the two poets – Auden and Isherwood – to East Asia in 1938. All extremely absorbing, but as a result of the linguistic approach sketched out here, I have much to work through with literature students. They can sort out their own judgements and interpretations; but together we can see what are some of the principles of construction that make Auden's effort a unique text that the culture needs to retain and pass on. The poem extends the experience of communities of readers by extending the potential of systems that we hold in a collective (if we take up those systems in variable ways, there is just more to discuss 'systemically'). The craft of poetry makes for novelty in what is latent in our habitual practices of meaning. This paradox eludes many students and, sadly, many teachers. It should not. As emphasized by Hasan, if we purport to promote verbal art as a focus of study, we need to be able to explain why we give the activity its formal status in school room and university, and how we are to go about the process of that teaching. In such an explanation, it is the artistry of verbal art with which we can start. As a phenomenon realized in language, the disciplined analysis of the language in relation to the cultural contexts of its creation and of its current reception offer rational issues from which to set out. Being better informed about the craft of verbal art may also clarify for us all – students and teachers together – the role of our collective imagination in assigning value to human experience.

Notes

The valuable translations of Russian Formalists by O'Toole and Shukman (volumes 1–10) can be obtained on a memory stick (A$30) by writing directly to Professor O'Toole at 20a Holmes St. Shelley, W.A. Australia 6148.

References

Auden, W. H. and Isherwood. C. (1939/1973). *Journey to a War* (Revised Edition). London: Faber and Faber.

Birch, D., and O'Toole, M. (eds) (1988). *Functions of Style*. London: Frances Pinter.

Butt, D. G. (1983). Semantic 'Drift' in Verbal Art. *Australian Review of Applied Linguistics* 6 (1): 38–48. https://doi.org/10.1075/aral.6.1.04but

Butt, D. G. (1988). Randomness, order and the latent patterning of text. In D. Birch and M. O'Toole (Eds), *Functions of Style*, 74–97. London: Pinter.

Butt, D. G., and O'Toole. M. (2003). Transactions between matter and meaning: A functional theory for the science of text. In M. Amano

(Ed.) *Creation and Practical Use of Language Texts*. Nagoya: Nagoya University.

Butt, D. G. (2007). Thought experiments in verbal art: Examples from Modernism. In D. R. Miller and M. Turci (Eds), *Language and Verbal Art Revisited: Linguistic Approaches to the Study of Literature*, 68–96. London: Equinox.

de Saussure, F. (1916/1978). *Course in General Linguistics* (Eds C. Bally and A. Sechehaye in collaboration with A. Riedlinger). Glasgow: Fontana, Collins.

Halliday, M. A. K. (1971/2003). 'Linguistic function and literary style: An enquiry into the language of William Golding's *The Inheritors*. In S. Chatman (Ed.) *Literary Style: A Symposium*, London: Oxford University Press. Reprinted in J. J. Webster (Ed.) *Linguistic Studies of Text and Discourse. The Collected Works of M.A.K. Halliday, Vol. 2*, 88–125. London/New York: Continuum.

Halliday, M. A. K. (1964/2002). The linguistic study of literary texts. In H. Lunt (Ed.) *Proceedings of the Ninth International Congress of Linguistics*. Reprinted in J. J. Webster (Ed.) *Linguistic Studies of Text and Discourse. The Collected Works of M. A. K. Halliday, Vol. 2*, 5–22. London/New York: Continuum.

Halliday M. A. K. (1981/2002). 'Text semantics and clause grammar: How is a text like a clause?' In J. J. Webster (Ed.) *On Grammar. Collected Works of M. A. K. Halliday, Vol. 1*, 219–260. London and New York: Continuum.

Halliday, M. A. K. (1982/2002). The de-automatization of grammar: From Priestley's 'An Inspector Calls'. In J. M. Anderson (Ed.) *Language Form and Linguistic Variation: Papers Dedicated to Angus MacIntosh*, 129–159. Amsterdam: Benjamins. Reprinted in J. J. Webster (Ed.), *Linguistic Studies of Text and Discourse; Volume 2 in the Collected Works of M. A. K. Halliday*, 126–148. London/New York: Continuum.

Hasan, R. (1964). *A linguistic study of contrasting features in the style of two contemporary English prose writers*. Unpublished PhD, Edinburgh University.

Hasan, R. (1967). Linguistics and the study of literary texts. *Études de Linguistique Appliquée* 5: 106–121.

Hasan, R. (1971). Rime and reason in literature. In S. Chatman (Ed.) *Literary Style: A Symposium*, 299–326. New York: Oxford University Press.

Hasan, R. (1975). The place of stylistics in the study of verbal art. In H. Ringbom (Ed.) *Style and Text: Studies Presented to Nils Erik Enkvist*, 49–62. Amsterdam: Skriptor.

Hasan, R. (1985). *Linguistics, Language and Verbal Art*. Geelong: Deakin University Press.

Hasan, R. (1988). The analysis of one poem: Theoretical issues in practice. In D. Birch and M. O'Toole (Eds) *Functions of Style*. London: Pinter.

Hasan, R. (1996). Teaching literature across cultural distances. In J. James (Ed.) *The Language-Culture Connection*. Singapore: SEAMEO.

Hasan, R. (1999). Speaking with reference to context. In M. Ghadessy (Ed.) *Text and Context in Functional Linguistics*, 219–328. Amsterdam, Philadelphia, PA: John Benjamins. https://doi.org/10.1075/cilt.169.11has

He, (Linda) Wenli (2000). *The Moon Shines Everywhere: Translating Ideas Beyond Form – a brief comparison of Li Po's 'Silent Night Thoughts'*. Masters Thesis, Macquarie University.

Jakobson, R. (1978). Realism in art. In L. Matejka and K. Pomorska (Eds) *Readings in Russian Poetics: Formalist and Structuralist Views*. Cambridge, MA: MIT Press.

Jakobson, R. (Ed.) (1987). *Language in Literature*. Cambridge, MA: The Belknap Press of Harvard University Press.

Kellogg, D. J. (2014). *The Great Globe and All Who It Inherit. Narrative and Dialogue in Story-telling with Halliday, Vygotsky, and Shakespeare*. Rotterdam: Sense Publishers.

Kozulin, A, (1990). *Vygotsky's Psychology: A Biography of Ideas*. Cambridge, MA: Harvard University Press.

Lukin, A., and Webster, J. J. (2005). SFL and the study of literature. In R. Hasan, C. M. I. M. Matthiessen and J. J. Webster (Eds) *Continuing Discourse in Language: A Functional Perspective. Vol. 1*, 413–456. London and Oakville: Equinox.

Martin J. R. (1992). *English Text: System and Structure*. Philadelphia, PA and Amsterdam: John Benjamins. https://doi.org/10.1075/z.59

Matthiessen, C. M. I. M. (1993). Register in the round: Diversity in a unified theory of register analysis. In M. Ghadessy (Ed.) *Register Analysis. Theory and Practice*, 221–292. London: Pinter.

Matthiessen C. M. I. M. (1995). *Lexicogrammatical Cartography*. Tokyo: International Language Sciences Publishers.

Melrose, R. (1996). *The Margins of Meaning: Arguments for a Postmodern Approach to Language and Text*. Amsterdam and Atlanta, GA: Rodopi.

Miller, D. R. and M. Turci (Eds) (2007). *Language and Verbal Art Revisited: Linguistic Approaches to the Study of Literature*. London: Equinox.

Mukařovský, J. (1977). *The Word and Verbal Art*. New Haven, CT: Yale University Press.

O'Toole, L. M. (1982). *Structure, Style and Interpretation in the Russian Short Story*. New Haven, CT: Yale University Press.

O'Toole, M. (2001). Russian literary theory: from the Formalists to Lotman. In N. Cornwell (Ed.) *The Routledge Companion to Russian Literature*, 163–173. London and New York: Routledge.

O'Toole, L. M. and Shukman, A. (1975–1981). *Russian Poetics in Translation,* Volumes 1–8. Oxford: Holdan Books Ltd.

O'Toole, L. M. and Shukman, A. (eds) (1977). *Russian Poetics in Translation*, Volume 4: *Formalist Theory*. Oxford: Holdan Books Ltd.

Panksepp, J. and Biven, L. (2012). *The Archaeology of Mind: Neuroevolutionary Origins of Human Emotions*. New York: WW Norton & Company.

Porges, S. W. (2011). *The Polyvagal Theory: Neurophysiological Foundations of Emotions, Attachment, Communication, and Self-regulation (Norton Series on Interpersonal Neurobiology)*. New York: WW Norton & Company.

Roochnik, D. (1996). *Of Art and Wisdom: Plato's Understanding of Techne*. University Park, PN: The Pennsylvania State University Press.

Shklovsky, V. (1925/1990). *Theory of Prose*. Elmwood Park, IL: Dalkey Archive Press.

Steiner, P. (1984). *Russian Formalism: A Metapoetics*. Ithaca, NY: Cornell University Press.

Striedter, J. (1989). *Literary Structure, Evolution, and Value: Russian Formalism and Czech Structuralism Reconsidered*. Cambridge, MA: Harvard University Press. https://doi.org/10.4159/harvard.9780674418677

Tynjanov, J. (1978). On literary evolution. In L. Matejka and K. Pomorska (Eds) *Readings in Russian Poetics: Formalist and Structuralist Views*. Cambridge, MA: MIT Press.

Webster, J. (1998). The poet's language: Foregrounding in Edwin Thumboo's 'Gods can die'? *World Englishes*, 17 (3), 359–368. https://doi.org/10.1111/1467-971X.t01-1-00108

Webster, J. (2001). Thumboo's *David*. In T. C. Kiong, A. Pakir, B. K. Choon, and R. B. H. Goh (Eds) *Ariels: Departures & Returns. Essays for Edwin Thumboo*. Oxford: Oxford University Press.

Whorf, B. (1956). *Language, Thought, and Reality: Selected Writings* (Ed. John Carrol). Cambridge, MA: MIT Press.

3 Software-assisted systemic socio-semantic stylistics – Appraising *tru** in J. M. Coetzee's *Foe*[1]

Donna R. Miller[*] and Antonella Luporini[†]

> [...] without linguistics, the study of literature must remain a series of personal preferences, no matter how much the posture of objectivity is adopted [...]. (Hasan 1989[1985]: 104)

3.1. Introduction

This chapter reports recent findings in ongoing research on the interface between Systemic Functional Linguistics, henceforth SFL (cf. Halliday 1985 and subsequent editions), and Corpus Linguistics, henceforth CL (on such interface see, e.g. Thompson and Hunston (Eds) 2006; Bednarek 2010). More specifically, it investigates the potential limits of applying the

---

[*]   Donna R. Miller holds the Chair of English Linguistics at the Department of modern languages, literatures and cultures of the University of Bologna, where she coordinates its English Language Studies Program and heads the Department's Centre for Linguistic-Cultural Studies (CeSLiC). Her research has largely focused, in a Systemic Functional Linguistics perspective, on register analysis, in institutional text types and verbal art; her corpus-assisted investigations having specifically explored the grammar of evaluation in terms of APPRAISAL SYSTEMS.

[†]   Antonella Luporini works as a researcher in English Language and Linguistics at the Department of modern languages, literatures and cultures of the University of Bologna. She is a member of the Department's Centre for Linguistic-Cultural Studies (CeSLiC), where she is currently involved in two research projects, one on computer-mediated communication and English language teaching (COMETS), the other on Hasan's Systemic Socio-Semantic Stylistics (formerly Social Semiotic Stylistics, SSS) and the corpus.

methods of CL to the analysis of 'verbal art', using Hasan's Systemic Socio-Semantic Stylistics framework (hereafter SSS), a knowledge of which is in part presumed but also accessible in other papers in the volume.[2]

The text investigated is the novel *Foe*, which was published in still Apartheid times by South African writer, Coetzee. It is a rewriting of *Robinson Crusoe* (RC), the story now re-told by a woman named Susan Barton to a professional writer, Mr. Foe – the name clearly playing upon Defoe. More will be said about the story in Section 3.3 below.

Focus is on the text's evaluation of the notions of silence and truth in *Foe*, the first of which was the core concept probed in our pilot study (Miller and Luporini 2015), whose key findings will be cursorily summarized, as they are the basis for the subsequent stage presented here. We concentrate on relevant lexical items emerging from corpus investigation with WordSmith Tools (Scott 2012): in the first stage, 'silence'/'word'/'story', and in the second, *tru** ('truth'/'true(r)'/'truly'*)*. These were probed in extended concordances for meaningful clause as exchange/interaction patterns, in the second part using APPRAISAL SYSTEMS (Martin and White 2005), through carefully developed annotation schemes tested by significant inter-rater reliability. Analysis proceeds by means of 'shunting' (Halliday 2002[1961], 45; Miller 2006, 248), from clause or concordance line, to text, context(s) and intertext(s), and back, using the corpus as an 'echo-chamber' (Introduction to Thompson and Hunston (Eds) 2006: 13).

The chapter begins in section 3.2 with a brief overview of Hasan's SSS model.[3] In section 3.3, it proceeds to defining our research questions and methodology and pointing up the major problematic issues involved. Section 3.4 presents select significant findings of the stages of our analyses and, in closing, we make some brief extra-textual considerations and offer some tentative conclusions.

3.2. A brief overview of SSS

The essential premise of SSS is that literature is '[...] *created by languaging in a particular way*' (Hasan 2007: 16, original emphasis). In short, literature is a *special* text type, not a register like any other, essentially because the context-language connection in verbal art is fraught with complexities which other registers are simply not heir to (Hasan 1975: 54; 2007: 22–23). There are multiple contexts in play: the fictional context created by the text; a 'real' context of creation comprising the language, world view and artistic conventions of the time/place of writing, and a context of reception of the reader, all of which impact on the text and its interpretation and require the analyst's close attention (Hasan 1989[1985]: 101–103; cf. Hasan

1996: 50–54). Most importantly, however, this special text type requires a special theoretical and methodological take, one positing a *second order* of meaning, where first order meanings are *re*patterned as the symbolic articulation of theme, to be better explained below. Indeed, 'The art of verbal art consists of the use of language in such a way that this second order semiosis becomes possible' (Hasan 1989[1985]: 98).

3.2.1. The model

Hasan's descriptive and analytical model of SSS is one of 'double-articulation' (Hasan 2007, 33), visually represented as in Figure 3.1.

The first stratum of the higher semiotic system is labelled 'verbalization' and comprises all of the first order of semiosis; hence the broken line in the figure. At this level, the analysis of literature is identical to that for any text (Hasan 1989[1985]: 92).

With verbalization, however, all that can be said is what the text is 'about', through an inventory of isolated language patterns, which are insufficient for characterizing literature (Hasan 1989[1985]: 93–94). What is needed, says Hasan, is an emphasis on the *patterning of patterns* (1989[1985]: 91, passim), or, as Miller argues (2012; 2013; 2016a), on what Jakobson (1966) has called 'Pervasive Parallelism'.

But such patternings must be demonstrated, at the higher order, to be 'significant'. Such significance is akin to Mukařovský's (1964) notion of 'foregrounding' as consistent and motivated contrast with an established grammatical tendency (cf. Halliday's concept of the 'de-automatization of

Figure 3.1: The overlapping semiotic systems (based on Hasan 1989[1985]: 99)

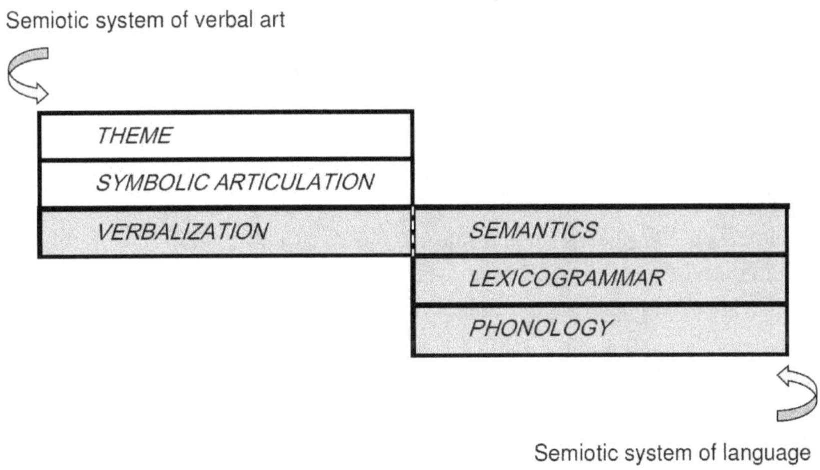

Semiotic system of verbal art

THEME

SYMBOLIC ARTICULATION

VERBALIZATION | SEMANTICS

LEXICOGRAMMAR

PHONOLOGY

Semiotic system of language

grammar', 2002[1982]: 131; for more on foregrounding see also chapters by Tilney and Wenzel, this volume, and Miller 2017. Foregrounding takes place in the middle stratum of the higher order, that of 'symbolic articulation': where the meanings at the first order of language are turned into signs having a deeper meaning, thus allowing us access to the literature text's 'theme'. Indeed, the same relationship of realization between strata that there is at the level of the semiotic system of language also holds among the strata of the semiotic system of verbal art. It is this second order of semiosis that is the critical criterion of the literature text.

The theme is tantamount to a generalization on some aspect of human existence; it '[...] can be viewed as a hypothesis about some aspect of the life of social man' (Hasan [1989]1985: 97). Without this theme, or reflection on humanity, and its symbolic articulation, there is, for Hasan, no verbal art (1989[1985]: 100). This is perhaps as good a description of what literature is as any other, but it is beyond question a vital feature of the 'specialness' principle, and in direct contrast with what Fowler famously claimed back in 1981: 'No plausible essentialist or intrinsic definition of literature has been or is likely to be devised. For my purpose, no such theory is necessary' (1981: 81).

Hasan would disagree.

3.3. Research questions, issues and methods

3.3.1. With reference to Part One

Our overall research question concerned the possibility of incorporating the methods and tools of CL in the SSS analysis of verbal art. That is, we asked how do-able an automated analysis of verbal art is in the Hasanian perspective. The proposal in itself is not unproblematic: when espousing a framework that is so scrupulous in its precepts, categories, and in the very definition of its object of inquiry, the question of the extent to which automated techniques can be effectively deployed must be posed.

Our past studies had already shown (e.g., Miller 2016b; Luporini 2016), that: (1) automated analyses alone don't at present enable all desired/required findings at the levels of semantics and context (cf. Halliday and Matthiessen 2004: 48–49), and that (2) systematically tracing the symbolic articulation of theme in verbal art is a question of analysis at precisely those levels. They had also shown that contextualized meaning analysis requires labour-intensive manual scrutiny, and close attention to logogenesis, i.e., to text '[...] in which the potential for creating meaning is continually modified *in the light of what has gone before* [...].' (Halliday and Matthiessen 1999: 18, our emphasis).

On the other hand, with reference to verbal art, the extent to which fore-grounding (seen as contrast with an established textual tendency) is quantifiable, at least in longer texts, seemed to us to be inscrutable without the assistance of CL methods. Indeed scholars, including Toolan (2009) and Biber (2011), show how using corpus evidence to support qualitative analysis of literature can be useful, even necessary. Halliday warns that mere statistical frequency is no guarantee of significance (2002[1971]: 102–103), but does see 'counting' patterns as a step towards determining what features may deserve further investigation. Hasan (2011) warns that practitioners of CL are '[…] not as sensitive to the notion of context as you'd wish they were'; as a generalization this is not untrue. But a distinction must be made between studies that are corpus-driven or -based and those, like our own, which are corpus-*assisted* and purposefully mindful of the complexities of context in verbal art.

On the methodological plane, well-known limitations inherent in using CL techniques for text analysis include the time-consuming task of corpus construction, if the text analysed isn't available in electronic format, and related copyright issues, especially when aiming to create a retrievable and reusable resource, one which would also make results replicable. Even when the text comes in ready-made electronic format, as in our case (the full-text version of the novel being available on scribd.com), it needs careful cleaning to avoid spelling mistakes or formatting problems which may affect results. Compiling ad hoc stop- and lemma-lists – or adapting existing ones to the text under scrutiny, as we did for our study – is also a delicate and labour-intensive task. A further advantage of using CL, however, is that one needn't worry quite so much about the permitted length of the text segments being cited!

So we asked: does CL have its part to play in the ongoing development of a rigorous SSS aimed at revealing the 'special' function of language in verbal art? We believed so. In our pilot study on *Foe*, we found that it plays an important *supporting* role, one of guaranteeing an empirical and statistical significance that cannot be manually achieved, especially when dealing with lengthy complex texts (Miller and Luporini 2015). At that stage, counting patterns was unquestionably instrumental in deciding where analysis had to go. And indeed it was the combination of software-gleaned quantitative data and manual analysis that led us to identify 'truth' as a keyword in the text, using RC as a reference corpus, and also to reveal its prominent tendency to occur in negative and/or interrogative lexicogrammatical environments (cf. section 3.4. below).

The finding re 'truth' was of course serendipitous (Leech *et al.* 2009: 31 n21), and opportune, allied as it is to what this 'difficult' novel is very schematically 'about':

A female protagonist, Susan, is shipwrecked while returning from a long unsuccessful search for her daughter. She is cast up on Cruso's island, where he lives with 'his man' Friday, now mute and unrecognizable from his namesake in RC. All three are rescued, but Cruso dies before they reach England, and Susan becomes obsessed with telling their 'true' story. Mr. Foe, the writer to whom she turns for help, has other ideas.[4]

3.3.2. With reference to Part Two

To include all lexical items having to do with 'truth' we examined node lemma *tru**. In order to demonstrate the validity of our choice, we first created the lemmatized word list for *Foe* (45,299 tokens), which established its significance. Then we compared the data on *tru** with those for RC, and also for a large reference corpus (the BNC available on SketchEngine (Kilgarriff *et al.* 2014), 112,289,776 tokens), as well as for its so-called 'Written Domain_Imaginative' sub-corpus (19,764,434 tokens). These results, presented in Table 3.1, were even more striking than hypothesized, amply confirming the extensive patterning of these patterns in our text, or their pervasive parallelism, and so also that they are likely to be symbolically articulating the theme of the novel. This was tentatively posited in our pilot study as being connected to the conflict which emerged there between silence and words, these last evincing a power, or impotence, to (re)shape history, and so, manipulate veracity. Part Two is dedicated to testing the hypothesis.

BNC (112,289,776 tokens)		BNC Written_domain_imag (19,764,434 tokens)		RC (121,779 tokens)		FOE (45,299 tokens)	
Raw freq.	Relative freq.	Raw freq.	Relative freq.	Raw freq.	Relative freq.	Raw freq.	Relative freq.
29,412	0.03 %	6,739	0.03%	38	0.03%	96	0.21%

Table 3.1: Comparative data for *tru**

Against this background – but also considering the novel's context of creation/reception, and the fact that the notion of truth in Apartheid South Africa surely deserves careful scrutinizing (Louw 2005) – in this second stage of the research we also specifically asked if the cumulative instances of *tru** could be said to construe the notion's relativity in the novel, as also already hypothesized in the first stage of our study.

Our research thus fast became a corpus-assisted SSS *appraisal study*, which undeniably set higher hurdles. As Hunston categorically puts it, evaluation analysis is '[…] by no means open to automation' (2004: 169). In addition, it is by now axiomatic that '[…] evaluation tends to be found throughout a text rather than being confined to one particular part of it' (Introduction to Hunston and Thompson (Eds) 2000: 19). This calls for the analyst's close attention to what SFL means by semantic prosody – the way that interpersonal meaning spreads or diffuses across clauses and across longer phases of discourse (Halliday 2002[1979]: 66–67). What is needed is to trace that 'cumulative groove of semantic patterning' (Coffin and O'Halloran 2005: 143; see also Hood 2006), which necessarily goes beyond the classic nine-word concordance window used, for instance, to assess collocational strength (cf. Louw 2007: 159; Sinclair 1991: 175). Though manual analysis of text segments, however extended, cannot be compared to a full text analysis, we once again considered reliable the features deserving of further investigation that quantitative analysis pointed up. And, though manual appraisal scrutiny itself comes at a cost, being naturally subject to bias and inconsistency, a risk that analyst(s) '[…] can only be *a*ware, and *be*ware, of – and, of course, declare' (Miller 2007: 178, original emphasis) – such risks can be counterbalanced through the development of rigorous annotation systems guaranteeing that the coders consistently adopt the same criteria for classification and thus significant levels of inter-rater reliability, as pointed out above.[5] Having preliminarily done this, close to 90% agreement for coded instances was achieved; in doubtful cases, consensus was reached through discussion.

So then, as in part one of our study, methodology once again involved a combination of CL and 'armchair' scrutiny (Fillmore 1992: 35). First, all instances of *tru** in the text were automatically retrieved in sentence-length concordances. Next, the instances were sub-divided into their word-classes: NG 'truth'; attitudinal epithet 'true(r)' and AG 'truly'. Then, in order to further minimize the inbuilt indeterminacy of appraisal studies, in our subsequent qualitative analysis we paid close attention to a number of additional interrelated elements, among which:

- the need to widen co-text to identify evaluative mechanisms as well as appraisees/appraiseds, sometimes going beyond the boundaries of already much extended concordances;
- assessing semantic prosody extending over longer stretches of text as identified through bi-, tri-, etc. colons;
- examining the 'coupling' (Martin 2010; 19) of ideational meanings and appraisal enacting attitude (Martin and White 2005; 62 ff.; Miller and Johnson 2013; 2014);

- probing appraisal categories tokening other categories, one inside the other, much like 'Russian Dolls' (Thompson 2014);
- hypothesizing individual/socio-cultural subjectivity, or repertoires/ reservoirs (cf. Martin 2010: 23), spelling voice and value orientation distinctions, not dissimilar to what Hasan called characteristic (individual/cultural) 'semantic styles' (1984);
- investigating the semantic location of relevant items in the text according to the 'part' of the novel in which they appear;
- and, finally, always taking into account the various contexts of the literature text impacting (re which cf. Section 3.2 above).

3.4. Analytical findings

3.4.1. Getting started

The lemmatized word list for *Foe* in Table 3.2 offers substantial evidence with reference to our research questions.

Rank	Freq	Lemma	Rank	Freq	Lemma
1	1685	I	16	138	*know*
2	737	**no** [no 198, nor 13, not 526]	17	134	Foe
3	610	You	18	132	come
4	562	He	19	130	she
5	512	It	20	113	*see*
6	388	Friday	21	111	*think*
7	340	**<u>But</u>**	22	110	day
8	319	We	23	108	take
9	304	*Say*	24	108	**word** [word 38, words 70]
10	217	Cruso	25	100	they
11	185	will	26	99	life
12	177	Would	27	99	*tell*
13	164	Island	28	96	**tru*** [true 39, truer 1, truly 21, truth 35]
14	149	**<u>If</u>**	29	94	time
15	142	**story** [history 11, stories 19, story 112]	30	94	*write*

Table 3.2: *Foe*: lemmatized wordlist

To be noted is, first, **tru***, ranking 28th, with a total of 96 occurrences – a relevant finding as noted above. We used a specially compiled stoplist to exclude some of the most common grammatical words, irrelevant to our analysis. However, we decided to include **no** (comprising 'no', 'nor' and 'not') in the wordlist, as negativity had emerged as prominent in the environment of 'truth' in part one of our study, as also noted. Its 737 occurrences signal a clearly marked negative prosody being enacted over the text, giving us a remarkably stable and staple finding. **Story** – a keyword emerging from part one – ranks 15th, with 142 instances (including those of 'history', invariably synonymous with it). **Word**, another key item, comes in 24th, with 108 occurrences.

Additional phenomena, also noted as significant from the start of our research, are manifest here as well: (1) those mental and verbal processes in italics in the Table (**know, see, think, say, tell**), plus the material but communicative process **write**; and (2) the conjunctions **but** and **if**, underlined in the Table, also excluded from the stoplist, because felt to be evidence of significant heteroglossic engagement mechanisms which we also aimed at investigating. We will come back to these below.

Noticeably, there is no sign of **silen***, which comes in only 92nd in the wordlist, but – despite its lower frequency – *is* important to the meanings of the novel, as shown in part one of our study: a demonstration that not everything that counts emerges from counting. We return to just how below.

On the basis of findings with reference to negativity, we were naturally curious about its collocation with *tru** and two other lexical items emerging as relevant from part one of the study (Table 3.3).

Not is number one collocate with both **true** and **truth**, and fifth with **story**; it does not collocate with **truly**, unless one widens the window span to 15R–15L, nor with **silence**, where only a very wide window (20R–20L) gives us **not**.[6] Also to note here are those significant mental and verbal processes once again, not surprisingly collocating – *coupling* – with all relevant items except **silence**: i.e., **know** and **said** with **true**; **tell** with **truth**, **felt** with **truly**, and **told** and **tell** with **story**.

In addition, once more we note the conjunctions **but** and **if**, collocating with all items except **silence**. Among the words in italics in the table, there is **story**, which is the single-most appraised element in our data, whereas **mother**, **Friday** and **Cruso**, also in italics, emerge as the predominant appraisees. Unsurprisingly, recalling his muteness, **Friday** is number one collocate with **silence**.

True (39)		Truth (35)		Truly (21)		Silence (31)		Story (112)	
T-score	Word	T-score	Word	T-score	Word	T-score	Word	T-score	Word
3.65058	**not**	2.91783	**not**	2.30313	I	2.45486	*Friday*	5.24519	you
3.45388	I	2.17457	I	2.03417	it	2.21045	child	4.97613	I
3.22207	It	2.14231	it	1.99552	you	1.81677	I	4.40749	it
2.81441	**but**	2.10594	**no**	1.85010	**but**	1.79239	we	3.46014	**but**
2.56529	she	1.96179	**tell**	1.72136	**felt**	1.71401	fell	3.23429	**not**
2.47526	you	1.86994	would	1.68114	they	1.66678	it	3.09117	island
2.22142	*mother*	1.83516	you	1.65620	**if**	1.60300	you	2.96449	Foe
2.16943	**know**	1.76560	we	1.62158	*Cruso*	1.41237	holds	2.93737	*Friday*
2.10498	**said**	1.75017	**but**	1.40673	flesh	1.40961	providence	2.75693	**told**
1.99672	grief	1.71169	give	1.40050	letters	1.40961	helpless	2.71000	will
1.90830	*story*	1.63702	*story*	1.39925	stood	1.39304	live	2.55332	**tell**

Table 3.3: Collocates (5R-5L) for relevant items in *Foe*

3.4.2. Appraisal findings

Table 3.4 shows the main Appraisees/-eds in the environment of our focus words.

Note that these are not exhaustive of all appraisees/-eds in the environment of our focus words, but that they do account for: in the case of **true**, 70% of them all; in that of **truth**, a full 91.4%, and in that of **truly**, 71.4%. In the environment of **true** and **truer**, the central appraised is **story**, closely followed by **mother** and what we have called **mother/child 'debate'**. This last is a key strand of the plot and involves the total ambiguity around Susan as mother to a child who presents herself as her lost daughter. Susan resolutely denies the truth of the child's version, but Foe questions the truth of her own. Here there are fewer instances of **Cruso**. In the environment of **truth**, the main appraiseds, which we consider together, are **story**, **history** and **tale**, followed closely by **Friday** or things strictly related to him. With an equal number of fewer instances, follow **Cruso** and **mother** (and **mother/child 'debate'**). In the co-text of **truly**, no appraisee or appraised is noticeably dominant, though once again the same elements can be found: coming in first is **Friday** (or **Friday**-related things), then **Cruso**, after which **story**, figuring as number one in the former environments, comes in – and finally **mother** (and **mother/child 'debate'**). The main appraisees/-eds are substantially uniform across the data, if with varying frequency. Among the additional evaluated entities, we find one sole instance of **freedom**, in connection with **truly**. Infrequency, as seen, is not the same as irrelevancy; we will be coming back to it below.

The main appraiser in our data is Susan herself, in 74 to 86% of all cases, depending on the focus word: for 'truth', 86%; for 'true': 74% (as well as for the only instance of 'truer'); for 'truly': 81% – with the caveat that analysis is of much extended concordances, and takes account of their 'cumulative groove'. This is evidence of the fact that *Foe* is truly Susan's story.

Tables 3.5, 3.6 and 3.8 report findings concerning the main APPRAISAL SYSTEMS that are enacted in the analysed concordances.

As we expected, the category of appreciation dominates in 30 of the 40 occurrencesof true(r). Most of these are instances of inscribed +ve reaction: quality – but, as implied above, identified appraisal categories are also very often tokening others; these have not been calculated here. As a result, however, we get the layering of categories which Thompson (2014) thinks of in terms of 'Russian Dolls'. In the following illustrative segment, Susan is defending her demand for detail in an imagined recount of Cruso's experience:[7]

Appraisees/ -eds					
True/ Truer (39+1)		**Truth (35)**		**Truly (21)**	
#s	**Who/ what**	**#s**	**Who/ what**	**#s**	**Who/ what**
12	**story** (of castaway/ Friday/ child)	12	**story/ history/ tale** (of castaway/ Friday/ child)	6	**Friday/ Friday-related**
11	**mother (& child 'debate')**	10	**Friday/ Friday-related**	4	**Cruso**
5	**Cruso**	5	**Cruso**	3	**story** (of Cruso/ Susan/ Friday)
		5	**mother (& child 'debate')**	2	**mother (& child 'debate')**
Tot.	**28/40** **(70%)**	Tot.	**32/35** **(91.4%)**	Tot.	**15/21** **(71.4%)**

Table 3.4: Main appraisees/-eds compared

True (39) + Truer (1)									
Inscribed Appreciation: Reaction: quality		**Invoked Appreciation: Reaction: quality**		**Invoked Appreciation: composition**		**Inscribed Judgement: SS: veracity**		**Invoked Judgement: SS: veracity**	
+ve	**-ve**	**+ve**	**-ve**	**+ve**	**-ve**	**+ve**	**-ve**	**+ve**	**-ve**
17	3	8	1	-	1	2	2	3	3
Tot. 20		Tot. 9		Tot. 1		Tot. 4		Tot. 6	

Table 3.5: Main APPRAISAL SYSTEMS enacted with 'true(r)'

(1)   Touches like these will one day persuade your countrymen that it is all **true**, every word, there was indeed once an island in the middle of the ocean where the wind blew and the gulls cried from the cliffs and a man named Cruso paced about in his apeskin clothes, scanning the horizon for a sail. (Concordance no. 1 for 'true', unsorted)

The inscribed +ve appreciation of 'every word' as **true** we see as also tokening the appreciation category of valuation, as it ultimately deals with 'truth'. Indeed, Susan begins her argumentation in the previous sentence by saying 'The **truth** that makes your story yours alone […] resides in a thousand touches which today may seem of no importance' (*Foe*: 18). In addition, it can be said to further token the appreciation category of the balance and complexity of composition, in speaking of the necessity for using 'touches like these' (i.e. small details that may seem irrelevant, but give substance to the story). Moreover, also tokened is +ve judgement on the propriety of using such touches for the purpose of telling the truth.

Evaluation in the environment of our search words is predominantly of abstractions – and irrealis. Table 3.6 provides details re this highly idealized abstraction, 'truth'.

Truth (35)					
Inscribed Judgement: SS: veracity		**Invoked Judgement: SS: veracity**		**Inscribed Judgement: SE: normality**	
+ve	**-ve**	**+ve**	**-ve**	**+ve**	**-ve**
7	2	18	7	1	-
Tot. 9		Tot. 25		Tot. 1	

Table 3.6: Main APPRAISAL SYSTEMS enacted with 'truth'

As can be seen, judgement is the category which is exclusively enacted, for the most part on veracity (34 out of 35), and largely by invoking (25 out of 34), 18 times with +ve polarity. A significant example of the only seven occurrences of invoked -ve judgement on veracity follows.

(2)   Dear Mr Foe, I am growing to understand why you wanted Cruso to have a musket and be besieged by cannibals. I thought it was a sign you had no regard for the **truth**. I forgot you are a writer who knows above all how many words can be sucked from a cannibal feast, how few from a woman cowering from the wind. (Concordance no. 29 for 'truth', unsorted)

The above is the only time that Susan admits that, for the writer, it could possibly be 'right' to want to embellish the truth. She is casting 'truth' as a debatable, and veracity as a questionable, value. That speaker's stance – or illustration of the repertoire of the individual – belongs, in all other instances in the text, to Foe. Perhaps this may also be seen as ultimately casting doubt on the truth of the novel *Foe* itself. So veracity, so clearly evaluated as an absolute value in and by the text – Susan's overriding obsession, remember – is ultimately – if but once – questioned by Susan herself.

At this point our analysis began to show how this novel often challenges a clear-cut distinction between +ve and -ve appraisal, setting up a continuum across which Susan, in particular, moves, uncertainly. This fuzzy polarity can be seen in the next example, also a good illustration of the relativity of truth.

> (3)   Return to me the substance I have lost, Mr Foe: that is my entreaty. For though my story gives the **truth**, it does not give the substance of the **truth** (I see that clearly, we need not pretend it is otherwise.) (Concordances nos. 13–14 for 'truth', unsorted)

So, on one hand, Susan evaluates her veracity as positive, but, on the other, as negative, somehow wanting.

And here we also see enacted the novel's – and unequivocally Susan's – major overreaching evaluative thrust, or our outer-most/biggest 'Russian Doll', so to speak: desperately wanting truth to be known, and told (+ve veracity of 'truth' as the 'ideal'), but at the same time despairing of ever being able to know and tell it (-ve veracity of what is said and/or capacity to say it).

In analysing longer segments of 'truth' concordances, we also discovered that 'silence' indeed couples with it, despite not collocating (see Table 3.3), and in a semantically two-fold way. First, 'silence' is what we'd seen in part one of our study, i.e., Friday's imposed silence:

> (4)   What is the **truth** of Friday? […] what he is to the world is what I make of him. Therefore, the **silence** of Friday is a helpless **silence**. He is the child of his **silence**, a child unborn, a child waiting to be born that cannot be born. (Concordance no. 32 for 'truth', unsorted, followed by concordances nos. 18–20 for 'silence', unsorted, generated for part one of our study)

But 'silence' is also a requisite for full truth-telling, as Susan tells Foe:

(5) The room is barely furnished. The **truth** is, it is not a room but a part of the attic to which you remove yourself *for the sake of silence.* [...] *To tell the **truth in all its substance*** you must have *quiet*, and a comfortable chair away from all distraction, and a window to stare through. (Concordances nos. 12 and 15 for 'truth', unsorted, our emphasis)

And again Susan's concern with substantial truth is enacted.

Before having a look at data concerning 'truly', we present Table 3.7, comparing the interrogative environments of our focus words, as further evidence of their indeterminacy in the text.

Focus words: interrogative environments					
True(r) (40)		**Truth (35)**		**Truly (21)**	
Tot. 14/40 (35%)		Tot. 13/35 (37.1%)		Tot. 13/21 (61.9%)	
Rhetorical	**Not rhetorical**	**Rhetorical**	**Not rhetorical**	**Rhetorical**	**Not rhetorical**
5 (35.7%)	9 (64.3%)	1 (7.7%)	12 (92.3%)	1 (7.7%)	12 (92.3%)

Table 3.7: Interrogative environments of focus words compared

As is evident in the table, the findings show, first, that the interrogative environment for all focus words is appreciably high, but that the phenomenon is highest, indeed with a nearly twice as high relative frequency, in the environment of 'truly'. Second, Mood: interrogative is for the most part genuine, i.e., not rhetorical – a significant 92.3% relative frequency in the environment of 'truly', but also in that of 'truth'; in short, a great deal of real questioning is – unsurprisingly we suggest, given results as presented so far – going on. One example, having to do with that 'mother/child debate' discussed re Table 3.4, is:

(6) I gripped her tight and pressed my fingers into her shoulders. Was this **truly** my daughter's flesh? (Concordance no. 14 for 'truly', unsorted)

For all her constant denial of the child as hers, here we have the only instance of Susan doubting that disavowal in the environment of our focus words.

But now for a closer look at appraisal in concordances with 'truly' (Table 3.8).

Truly (21)							
Invoked Affect: un/happiness		Invoked Judgement: SS: veracity		Inscribed Judgement: SS: propriety		Invoked Judgement: SS: propriety	
+ve	-ve	+ve	-ve	+ve	-ve	+ve	-ve
-	1	13	1	-	1	1	2
Tot. 1		Tot. 14		Tot. 1		Tot. 3	
*** + 2 irrelevant instances							

Table 3.8: Main APPRAISAL SYSTEMS enacted with 'truly'

As with 'truth', again +ve invoked Judgement on veracity-as-an-ideal overwhelmingly dominates. All 13 instances – of which example 6 above is one – enact the novel's major overreaching evaluative prosody as described above.[8] Another brief example, which also illustrates genuine interrogative with 'truly', follows:

> (7)   Who but Cruso, who is no more, could **truly** tell you Cruso's story? (Concordance no. 3 for 'truly', unsorted)

And an example with that only-once appraised Thing, 'freedom', metalingually brings indeterminacy once again to the fore:

> (8)   There is an urging that we feel, all of us, in our hearts, to be free; yet which of us can say what freedom **truly** is?' (Concordance no. 19 for 'truly', unsorted)

And at this point we feel we have the answer to our specific research question posed above: cotextual and cumulative instances of *tru** can indeed be seen to construe the notion's relativity in the novel; interestingly, in *Foe*, this seems to work to 'destabilize' both the character-character and the author-reader relationship, defying bonding by consistently questioning the possibility of identifying (and the very existence of) a shared set of values (cf. the contrasting effect emerging from Espunya's analysis, this volume).

3.4.3. How the data crunch distributionally

It also became clear that mapping the distribution of the focus words with reference to the clearly discernible parts of the novel was needed for a more complete view of how the semantic prosody is enacted across the text.[9] The parts are four, are clearly signalled graphically with roman numerals, and consist of: I, 40 pages/12,569 running words; II, 64 pages/19,141 running words; III, 40 pages/12,230 running words, and IV, a mere five pages/1,359 running words. These parts can be glossed as:

I.   Susan's recount of life on the island she was shipwrecked onto, as well as of the rescue, ending with Cruso's death on the ship, written on Mr. Foe's request;

II.   Susan's letters to Mr. Foe (epistolary novel style), starting with the sending of the recount above and touching upon myriad topics;

III.   Susan's recount of days spent with Mr. Foe (extensive conflictual dialogue);

IV.   Final highly enigmatic closing, having no clear narrative voice, yet being narrated by an omniscient 'I' who, however, is not the protagonist; Friday is. In contrast to the first three parts, this is written in the present tense. Indeed, tense is the only feature distinguishing the opening line of this part from that of Part three: 'The staircase was/is dark and mean.' (*Foe*, 113; 153).

Table 3.9 gives an overview of the raw data and relative frequency of the focus words in the text, according to these parts.

	True(r) (40)		Truth (35)		Truly (21)	
Part of text	**Raw freq.**	**Relative freq.**	**Raw freq.**	**Relative freq.**	**Raw freq.**	**Relative freq.**
1 (12.569 tokens)	6/40	0.05%	11/35	0.09%	2/21	0.01%
2 (19.141 tokens)	18/40	0.09%	19/35	0.10%	8/21	0.04%
3 (12.230 tokens)	16/40	0.13%	5/35	0.04%	11/21	0.09%
4 (1.359 tokens)	Ø	Ø	Ø	Ø	Ø	Ø

Table 3.9: *Foe*: Distribution of focus words in the text

In terms of raw data for **true(r)**, part two emerges as highest, closely followed by part three, which is highest in relative frequency. **Truth** dominates in part two, both in raw and relative frequency, but particularly in the first of these. **Truly** is predominant in part three, again in terms of both raw and relative frequency. All focus words disappear from part four, once again highlighting its very different nature.

Recalling that the main appraiser in our data is Susan herself, some comments can tentatively be made. As we have said, the first three parts are clearly Susan's story, but – as emerges from the description of those parts above – there are divergences. It is perhaps unsurprising that **true(r)** and **truth** are highest in part two, which is the longest part and consists in Susan's letters to Foe which, indeed, deal with the truth of her story. It is to us even less surprising that **truly** would dominate in part three, characterized as it is by the conflictual dialogue of Susan and Foe, as well as being the locus of the highest percentage of Mood: interrogatives. Also to be recalled is that **true(r)** is also considerably in evidence in this part as well.

Although 'silence' has not been included in Table 3.9, which deals only with the focus words of part two of our study, neither does this node word emerge from part four of the text – whereas 'no', 'but' and 'if' do emerge, and strongly. We will have more to say about these presently.

But first, an observation. We have argued that Friday's muteness is to be paired with the notion of silence (see also Table 3.3, with **Friday** as no. 1 collocate with **silence**) and have shown Friday represented as a stillborn, helpless silence in example 4 above – recall that **helpless** is also a collocate of **silence** (cf. again Table 3.3). And yet Susan, throughout the text, is obsessed with the effort '[…] to bring Friday to speech, or to bring speech to Friday' (*Foe*, 142), even musically, explicitly because his silence obstructs her search for truth: 'The **true** story will not be heard till by art we have found a means of giving voice to Friday' (*Foe*, 118). In part four, it is said '[…] this is not a place of words […] This is a place where bodies are their own signs. It is the home of Friday' (*Foe*, 157). And yet, despite being the home of Friday, and not being a place of words, this is not a place of total silence either: ultimately, it is from Friday's mouth that some sort of non-verbal, even non-human, communication, for the first time, and twice in these five pages, comes to the narrating 'I'. What is being meant is anyone's guess. But it is said to travel '[…] to the ends of the earth' (*loc. cit.*). Eschewing the lit-crit's lure, we will leave it here.

3.4.4. Engagement

When commenting the wordlist in Table 3.2, we'd noted the significant recurrence of the elements **but**, **if** and **no**. Though space considerations preclude lengthy comment on their engagement functions, something can be said.

First, as can be seen in Table 3.10, these elements are distributed over all parts of the text, but, in terms of relative frequency, especially in part three, which, recall, is marked by conflictual dialogue between Susan and Foe.

The function of conjunction **but** in the environment of our focus words is invariably to entertain (rather than to contract) ideas which are then

Part of text	But (340)		If (149)		No (737)	
	Raw freq.	Relative freq.	Raw freq.	Relative freq.	Raw freq.	Relative freq.
1 (12.569 tokens)	92/340	0.73%	30/149	0.24%	198/737	1.58%
2 (19.141 tokens)	135/340	0.71%	66/149	0.34%	312/737	1.63%
3 (12.230 tokens)	106/340	0.87%	48/149	0.39%	213/737	1.74%
4 (1.359 tokens)	7/340	0.52%	5/149	0.37%	14/737	1.03%

Table 3.10: Distribution of select engagement mechanisms in the text

countered by the suggestion of entertaining others. Conjunction **if** serves the purpose of hypothesizing what is also often countered and replaced. Negation – **not** and **no** markedly – often function to disclaim: deny and/or counter within these same stretches of text. Indeed, all three mechanisms often function together. The following extended example from part three, featuring a series of tortured intermeshed interrogatives, is illustrative.

> (9)   **If** he [Friday] was **not** a slave, was he nevertheless **not** the *help-less* captive of my desire to have our story told? How did he differ from one of the wild Indians whom explorers bring back with them, in a cargo of parakeets and golden idols and indigo and skins of panthers, to show they have **truly** been to the Americas? And might **not** Foe be a kind of captive too? I had thought him dilatory. **But** might the **truth not** be instead that he had laboured all these months to move a rock so heavy **no** man alive could budge it; that the pages I saw issuing from his pen were **not** idle tales of courtesans and grenadiers, as I supposed, **but** the same story over and over, in version after version, *stillborn* every time: the story of the island, as lifeless from his hand as from mine? (*Foe*, 150-151, our emphasis)

Friday is once more associated with helpless-ness, this time as the victim of Susan's obsession with their story. Ideational meanings and lexical meta-phors, tokening attitude, repeat themselves. Clearly the overwhelming evaluative thrust of the text is again enacted: +ve judgement on veracity as an ideal but -ve judgement on the possibility of telling THE story/THE truth, again being stressed. Truth-telling miscarries. Much like Friday in example 4 above awaited an impossible birth, it gives birth to mere lifeless (because UN-true) renditions, one after another. Typically, it is Susan who is the tormented 'entertainer' of possible ways of thinking here – another sign of her individual repertoire or semantic style, we suggest. Many other relevant examples could be offered, but it is time to conclude.

3.5. In closing

Our central research question for part two of our study was to what degree *tru** is related to the text's theme. The answer is to a great degree, as we feel has amply emerged above. Our findings convincingly demonstrate that instances of *tru** – in addition to the indeterminacy of the concept itself – are related to what was proposed in part one as theme – i.e., Friday's silence vs. Susan and Foe's words – *vis-à-vis* their power, or impotence, to (re)shape (hi)stories, and so, veracity. But in this second part of the study they have also shown us a semantically hybrid notion of silence which, beyond Friday's imposed muteness, is also actually construed as a requisite for truth-telling (examples 4 and 5 above). And now the possibility of ever doing so is seriously subverted – for Susan and Foe and perhaps also for Coetzee – in fiction and also, maybe, in history.

We maintain that the foregrounded patterning of patterns which has emerged from our investigation are consistent in the two ways Hasan specifies they must be (1989[1985]: 95): (1) in the stability of their semantic direction, so that 'The meanings which are being highlighted by the foregrounded patterns converge toward the same direction' (Hasan 1989[1985]: 95) – towards, i.e., what has emerged as our overreaching evaluative thrust; and (2) consistent in the stability of their textual location, meaning significant patterns of foregrounding tend to take place in textually significant places, as we have especially seen in our analysis of their distribution over the text. And so now we propose a reformulation of the consistently motivated theme of *Foe* which such patterns can be said to be symbolically articulating: *that the essential human condition is fraught with the precarious, because mutable and indeterminate, connection between silence and words, between narration and truth-telling.*

To further verify this, we revisited the context of creation (cf. 3.2 above). Even without a full comparative investigation of the novel in terms of its language, the contrastive corpus work presented in Section 3.3.2 has shown us that the use of *tru** in *Foe* was certainly *sui generis*. With reference to artistic conventions, *Foe* obviously links up to a milestone in the history of English literature (RC), but does so contratextually, deconstructing it, by, among other things, entrusting its story to a female narrator who despairs of the truth of her narration – thus better fitting into the hybrid and conflictual nature of contemporaneous postcolonial literature.

Concerning the writer's world view, on which much could be said, we will only note that in an interview from 1987, the year after *Foe* was first published, Coetzee asks if '[…] "the nature and processes of fiction" may also be called the question of who writes? Who takes up the position of power, pen in hand?' (Morphet 1987: 462). His intriguingly enigmatic Nobel Prize lecture of 2003 speaks of the original Robinson Crusoe's consternation in the face of '[…] the first bands of plagiarists and imitators [who] descended upon his island history […]', seeing them as '[…] *figures of a more devilish voracity, that would gnaw at the very substance of truth*' (original emphasis). That, however, is not the final word. The lecture continues, 'But now, reflecting further, there begins to creep into his breast a touch of fellow-feeling for his imitators. For it seems to him now that there are but a handful of stories in the world; and if the young are to be forbidden to prey upon the old then they must sit for ever in silence.' Our reformulation of the theme of *Foe* would appear to be further supported.[10] And dare we add that such a theme might also be seen as foreshadowing the South African Truth and Reconciliation Commission's impossible task (1995–2002; see Louw 2005)?

A brief word about the context of reception: Hasan concedes that the role of the reader (Eco 1979) is a vital one. But she insists that no reader is a 'free agent' (1989[1985]: 103). In short, readers are not free to make a text mean whatever they want it to mean. As she puts it:

> To arrive at the truth – the theme(s) of literature text – we must go through the time demanding exercise of meticulous linguistic analysis; it is this alone that can show what is being achieved in the work and how. And until we can do this, it is meaningless to talk about evaluation, for what we are evaluating in the absence of such careful analysis is more likely to be our inexplicit impressions against our equally accidental preconceptions of what an artist should or should not do. (1989[1985]: 103)

Notes

1. Even though this paper is the fruit of constant research collaboration, sections 3.1, 3.2, 3.3. and 3.5. were written up jointly, section 3.4.2 was written up by Miller and sections 3.4.1, 3.4.3 and 3.4.4, by Luporini.
2. Hasan provides us with this name for the practice of doing SFL stylistics, i.e., Systemic Socio-Semantic Stylistics, her last formulation before her untimely passing (personal communication to Miller, 1 January 2015).
3. For a more detailed survey of Hasan's lifelong research on verbal art, see Lukin's chapter, this volume, where she also rightly stresses Hasan's concern with teaching it, the subject of Miller and Luporini (forthcoming)

4.   *Cruso* is the spelling of Robinson's surname in Coetzee's novel.
5.   As Taboada and Carretero (2012, 278) put it, 'Appraisal in fact has been criticized for the arbitrariness of the labels and the difficulties that it poses for inter-rater reliability. However, we believe that it is still possible to design a system that guarantees this kind of reliability, even if some of the decisions made will unavoidably have some degree of arbitrariness.'
6.   For **truly**, T-score in 15R-15L span is 2.26 (**not**) and 2.16 (**no**). For **silence**, 20R-20L only gives **not** as significant (2.95) – plus **cannot** (2.22).
7.   Imagined, because Cruso keeps no journal, in marked contrast with the original Crusoe.
8.   The two irrelevant instances cited in the Table are: (1) of 'truly' as intensifier, enacting appreciation: impact, re a meteorological process type; and (2) 'truly' as again intensifying a hypothetical relational one.
9.   Although working within an albeit much-diversified and debated traditional CL perspective on semantic prosody, as well as being concerned with text segments rather than whole texts, Stubbs (2001: 202), speaks of 'prosodic' connotation, defined as connotation that is '[…] distributed prosodically across a textual sequence' (cited in Bednarek 2008: 133).
10. Of course a concern, an angst one might call it, over the constraints of language is a widespread postmodern complaint, to which Coetzee is not immune. How to create something 'other', speak what is as yet unspoken or even unspeakable, as a typically Coetzee-esque preoccupation, has been the subject of much criticism, as Clarkson (2009) points out.

References

Bednarek, M. (2008). Semantic preference and semantic prosody re-examined. *Corpus Linguistics and Linguistic Theory* 4 (2): 119–139. https://doi.org/10.1515/CLLT.2008.006

Bednarek, M. (2010). Corpus linguistics and Systemic Functional Linguistics: Interpersonal meaning, identity and bonding in popular culture. In M. Bednarek and J. R. Martin (Eds) *New Discourse on Language: Functional Perspectives on Multimodality, Identity, and Affiliation*, 237–266. London: Continuum.

Biber, D. (2011). Corpus linguistics and the study of literature: Back to the future? *Scientific Study of Literature* 1 (1): 15–23. https://doi.org/10.1075/ssol.1.1.02bib

Clarkson, C. (2009). J. M. Coetzee and the Limits of Language. *Journal of Literary Studies* 25 (4): 106–124. https://doi.org/10.1080/02564710903226817

Coetzee, J. M. (1986). *Foe*. London: Martin Secker & Warburg Ltd. (1987). London: Penguin.

Coetzee, J. M. (2003). Nobel lecture: He and his man. *Nobelprize.org*,

Nobel Media A B 2014. Last accessed 8 March 2016. http://www.nobelprize.org/nobel_prizes/literature/laureates/2003/coetzee-lecture-e.html.

Coffin, C., and O'Halloran, K. (2005). Finding the global groove: Theorising and analysing dynamic reader positioning using APPRAISAL, corpus, and a concordancer. *Critical Discourse Studies* 2 (2): 143–163.

Eco, U. (1979). *The Role of the Reader: Explorations in the Semiotics of Texts*. Bloomington, IN: Indiana University Press.

Fillmore, C. J. (1992). 'Corpus linguistics' or 'Computer-aided armchair linguistics'. In J. Svartvik (Ed.) *Directions in Corpus Linguistics. Proceedings of Nobel Symposium 82*, 35–60. Berlin: Mouton de Gruyter.

Fowler, R. (1981). *Literature as Social Discourse: the Practice of Linguistic Criticism*. London: Batsford.

Halliday, M. A. K. (1985). *An Introduction to Functional Grammar*. 1st ed. London: Arnold.

Halliday, M. A. K. (1961/2002). Categories of the Theory of Grammar. *Word* 17 (3): 241–292. Reprinted in J. J. Webster (Ed.), *On Grammar. Collected Works of M. A. K. Halliday, Vol. 1*, 37–94. London/New York: Continuum. https://doi.org/10.1080/00437956.1961.11659756

Halliday, M. A. K. (1971/2003). Linguistic function and literary style: An enquiry into the language of William Golding's 'The Inheritors'. In S. Chatman (Ed.) *Literary Style: A Symposium*. London: Oxford University Press. Reprinted in J. J. Webster (Ed.) *Linguistic Studies of Text and Discourse. The Collected Works of M. A. K. Halliday, Vol. 2*, 88–125. London/New York: Continuum.

Halliday, M. A. K. (1979/2002). Modes of meaning and modes of expression: Types of grammatical structure and their determination by different semantic functions. In D. J. Allerton, E. Carney, and D. Holdcroft (Eds) *Function and Context in Linguistic Analysis. A Festschrift for William Haas*, 57–79. Cambridge: Cambridge University Press. Reprinted in J. J. Webster (Ed.) *On Grammar. The Collected Works of M. A. K. Halliday, Vol. 1*, 196–218. London/New York: Continuum.

Halliday, M. A. K. (1982/2002). The de-automatization of grammar: From Priestley's 'An Inspector Calls'. In J. M. Anderson (Ed.) *Language Form and Linguistic Variation: Papers Dedicated to Angus MacIntosh*, 129–159. Amsterdam: Benjamins. Reprinted in J. J. Webster (Ed.) *Linguistic Studies of Text and Discourse; Volume 2 in the Collected Works of M.A.K. Halliday*, 126–148. London/New York: Continuum.

Halliday, M. A. K., and Matthiessen, C. M. I. M. (1999). *Construing Experience through Meaning. A Language-Based Approach to Cognition*. London: Cassell.

Hasan, R. (1975). The place of stylistics in the study of verbal art. In H. Ringbom (Ed.), *Style and Text: Studies Presented to Nils Erik Enkvist*, 49–62. Amsterdam: Skriptor.

Hasan, R. (1984). Ways of saying: Ways of meaning. In R. P. Fawcett, M. A. K. Halliday, S. M. Lamb, and A. Makkai (Eds), *The Semiotics of Culture and Language*, vol. 1, 105–162. London: Frances Pinter.

Hasan, R. (1985). *Linguistics, Language and Verbal Art*. Geelong: Deakin University Press.

Hasan, R. (1996). Teaching literature across cultural distances. In J. James (Ed.) *The Language-Culture Connection*. Singapore: SEAMEO.

Hasan, R. (2007). Private pleasure, public discourse: Reflections on engaging with literature. In *Language and Verbal Art Revisited: Linguistic Approaches to the study of literature,* D. R. Miller and M. Turci (Eds), 13–40. London: Equinox.

Hasan, R. (2011). Context in linguistic analysis. Paper delivered at *Register and Context* 2011, Macquarie University. Last accessed 5 April 2016. http://www.annabellelukin.com/ruqaiya-hasan.html.

Hood, S. (2006). The persuasive power of prosodies: Radiating values in academic writing. *Journal of English for Academic Purposes* 5 (1): 37–49. https://doi.org/10.1016/j.jeap.2005.11.001

Hunston, S. (2004). Counting the uncountable: Problems of identifying evaluation in a text and in a corpus. In A. Partington, J. Morley, and L. Haarman (Eds) *Corpora and Discourse*, 157–188. Bern: Peter Lang.

Hunston, S., and Thompson, G. (Eds) (2000). *Evaluation in Text. Authorial Stance and the Construction of Discourse*. Oxford: Oxford University Press.

Jakobson, R. (1966). Grammatical parallelism and its Russian facet. *Language* 42 (2): 399–429. https://doi.org/10.2307/411699

Kilgarriff, A., Baisa, V., Bušta, J., Jakubíček, M., Kovář, V., Michelfeit, J., Rychlý, P., and Suchomel, V. (2014). The Sketch Engine: Ten years on. *Lexicography* 1 (1): 7–36. https://doi.org/10.1007/s40607-014-0009-9

Leech, G., Hundt, M., Mair, C., and Smith, N. (2009). *Change in Contemporary English. A Grammatical Study*. Cambridge: Cambridge University Press. https://doi.org/10.1017/CBO9780511642210

Louw, B. (2005). Dressing up waiver: A stochastic collocational reading of 'The Truth and Reconciliation Commission (TRC)'. In D. R. Miller (Ed.) *Quaderni del CeSLiC. Occasional Papers*. Bologna: AMS Acta ALMA DL, 1–78. Last accessed 22 February 2016. https://doi.org/10.6092/unibo/amsacta/1142

Louw, B. (2007). Collocation as the determinant of verbal art. In D. R. Miller and M. Turci (Eds) *Language and Verbal Art Revisited: Lin-*

guistic Approaches to the Study of Literature, 149–180. London and Oakville, CA: Equinox.

Luporini, A. (2016). Grammatical metaphor through the lens of software? Examining 'crisis' in a corpus of articles from *The Financial Times*. In S. Gardner and S. Alsop (Eds) *Systemic Functional Linguistics in the Digital Age*, 260–275. London: Equinox.

Martin, J. R. (2010). Semantic variation – Modelling realisation, instantiation and individuation in social semiosis. In M. Bednarek and J. R. Martin (Eds), *New Discourse on Language: Functional Perspectives on Multimodality, Identity, and Affiliation*, 1–34. London/New York: Continuum.

Martin, J. R., and White, P. R. R. (2005). *The Language of Evaluation. Appraisal in English*. Basingstoke: Palgrave Macmillan. https://doi.org/10.1057/9780230511910

Miller, D. R. (2006). From concordance to text: Appraising 'giving' in *Alma Mater* donation requests. In G. Thompson and S. Hunston (Eds) *System and Corpus: Exploring Connections*, 248–268. London: Equinox.

Miller, D. R. (2007). Construing the 'primitive' primitively: Grammatical parallelism as patterning and positioning strategy in D. H. Lawrence. In D. R. Miller and M. Turci (Eds) *Language and Verbal Art Revisited: Linguistic Approaches to the Study of Literature*, 41–67. London: Equinox.

Miller, D. R. (2012). Slotting Jakobson into the social semiotic approach to 'verbal art': A modest proposal. In F. Dalziel, S. Gesuato, and M. T. Musacchio (Eds) *A Lifetime of English Studies: Essays in Honour of Carol Taylor Torsello*, 215–226. Padua: Il Poligrafo.

Miller, D. R. (2013). Another look at social semiotic stylistics: Coupling Hasan's 'Verbal Art' framework with 'the Mukarovsky-Jakobson Theory'. In C. A. M. Gouveia and M. F. Alexandre (Eds) *Languages, Metalanguages, Modalities, Cultures: Functional and Socio-Discursive Perspectives*, 121–140. Lisbon: BonD.

Miller, D. R. (2016a). Jakobson's place in Hasan's social semiotic stylistics: 'Pervasive parallelism' as symbolic articulation of theme. In W. L. Bowcher and J. Y. Liang (Eds) *Society in Language, Language in Society: Essays in Honour of Ruqaiya Hasan*, 59–80. Basingstoke: Palgrave Macmillan. https://doi.org/10.1057/9781137402868_3

Miller, D. R. (2016b). On negotiating the hurdles of corpus-assisted appraisal analysis in verbal art. In S. Gardner and S. Alsop (Eds) *Systemic Functional Linguistics in the Digital Age*, 211– 228. London: Equinox.

Miller, D. R. (2017). Language and verbal art. In T. Bartlett and G. O'Grady (Eds) *Routledge Handbook of Systemic Functional Linguistics*, 506–519. Abingdon: Routledge.

Miller, D. R., and Johnson, J. H. (2013). 'Register-idiosyncratic' evaluative choice in Congressional debate: A corpus-assisted comparative study. In L. Fontaine, T. Bartlett and G. O'Grady (Eds) *Systemic Functional Linguistics: Exploring Choice*, 432–453. Cambridge: Cambridge University Press. https://doi.org/10.1017/CBO9781139583077.026

Miller, D.R., and Johnson, J. H. (2014). Evaluative phraseological choice and speaker party/gender. A corpus-assisted comparative study of register-idiosyncratic meaning in Congressional debate. In G. Thompson and L. Alba-Juez (Eds) *Evaluation in Context*, 345–366. Amsterdam and Philadelphia, PA: John Benjamins.

Miller, D. R., and Luporini, A. (2015). Social Semiotic Stylistics and the corpus: How do-able is an automated analysis of verbal art? In A. Duguid, A. Marchi, A. Partington, and C. Taylor (Eds) *Gentle Obsessions: Literature, Linguistics and Learning. In Honour of John Morley*, 235–250. Rome: Artemide.

Miller, D. R., and Luporini, A. (forthcoming). Systemic Socio-Semantic Stylistics (SSS) as appliable linguistics: The cases of literary criticism and language teaching/learning. In A. Sellami Baklouti and L. Fontaine (Eds) *Perspectives from Systemic Functional Linguistics: An Appliable Theory of Language*. Abingdon: Routledge.

Morphet, T. (1987). Two interviews with J. M. Coetzee, 1983 and 1987. *TriQuarterly* 69: 454–464.

Mukařovský, J. (1932/1964). Standard language and poetic language. In P. R. Garvin (Ed.) *A Prague Reader on Esthetics, Literary Structure, and Style*, 17–30. Washington, DC: Georgetown University Press.

Scott, M. (2012). *WordSmith Tools Version 6*. Liverpool: Lexical Analysis Software.

Sinclair, J. McH. (1991). *Corpus, Concordance, Collocation*. Oxford: Oxford University Press.

Stubbs, M. (2001). Texts, corpora, and problems of interpretation: A response to Widdowson. *Applied Linguistics* 22: 149–172. https://doi.org/10.1093/applin/22.2.149

Taboada, M., and Carretero, M. (2012). Contrastive analyses of evaluation in text: Key issues in the design of an annotation system for attitude applicable to consumer reviews in English and Spanish. *Linguistics and the Human Sciences* 6: 275–295. https://doi.org/10.1558/lhs.v6i1-3.275

Thompson, G. (2014). Affect and emotion, target-value mismatches, and Russian dolls: Refining the appraisal model. In G. Thompson and L. Alba-Juez (Eds) *Evaluation in Context*, 47–66. Amsterdam and Philadelphia, PA: John Benjamins. https://doi.org/10.1075/pbns.242.03tho

Thompson, G., and Hunston, S. (Eds) (2006). *System and Corpus: Exploring Connections*. London: Equinox.

Toolan, M. (2009). *Narrative Progression in the Short Story, A Corpus Stylistic Approach*. Amsterdam and Philadelphia, PA: John Benjamins. https://doi.org/10.1075/lal.6

4 The analysis of a sonnet

Kathryn Tuckwell*

4.1. Introduction

The very simple and non-specific title of this essay is chosen in homage to Hasan's chapter 'The analysis of a poem' from *Language, Linguistics and Verbal Art* (1985: Ch. 2). To me, there are two ways (at least) of reading Hasan's title. First, it suggests that what will follow is an instance of literary stylistics – an analysis of a single poem, for the purpose of elucidating the meanings of that poem, and how that poem makes those meanings. Second, it suggests an outline of some aspect of a theory of literary stylistics – the system, as it were – an outline of the method for analysis any poem – 'here is how to analyse a poem'. Hasan's chapter fulfils both of these interpretations: it obviously provides the analysis of a single poem (Les Murray's 'Widower in the Country'), but it also, because it lays out so clearly the components of the analysis and Hasan's interpretation of literary meaning based on the 'patterning of patterns' (Hasan 1985: 96) displayed by that analysis, serves as a guidebook for others to perform similar careful analyses and interpretations.

Despite the parallelism in the title, the current chapter is unlikely to answer these two meanings in quite the same way that Hasan's chapter does. While it does present an analysis of a particular sonnet – Auden's 'Who's Who' – and does so in enough detail that it could serve, as Hasan's analysis and interpretation does, as a model for how to analyse a poem using the methods of systemic functional linguistics, it will not specifically function as a methodology for how to analyse a sonnet, in particular. One reason for this is that a sonnet does not require a particular methodology over and above the methods of literary analysis already provided by systemic functional linguistic theory – it is a text like any other, a piece of 'meaning in

*   Kathryn Tuckwell studied systemic functional linguistics at Macquarie University, Sydney, Australia, and now works as a freelance editor. Her interests include systemic functional grammar and grammatics, multimodal semiotics, textlinguistics and verbal art.

context' (Halliday and Hasan 1976: 293) construed and constructed through the system of language, and can be analysed as such. On the other hand, the literary form of the text – the fact that the text is considered a sonnet – cannot be completely irrelevant to how it makes meaning, and analysing a series of sonnets might begin to elucidate how the notion of literary form might interact with the dimensions of systemic functional linguistics. However, while the current analysis might serve as the beginning of a series of analyses of sonnets, it is nevertheless an analysis of just one sonnet, so can only touch the relationship between SFL and literary form.

This chapter will start by briefly outlining the central concepts drawn from SFL writings on verbal art, and the reasons for the selection of this sonnet for analysis. It will then move on to a detailed consideration of the findings of the metafunctional linguistic analysis of the sonnet, followed by an interpretation of these findings in relation to the meanings of the sonnet. Before launching into the theoretical detail and analytical findings, however, the sonnet is presented below.

T   Who's Who
I.   A shilling life will give you all the facts:
II.   How Father beat him, how he ran away,
III.   What were the struggles of his youth, what acts
IV.   Made him the greatest figure of his day:
V.   Of how he fought, fished, hunted, worked all night,
VI.   Though giddy, climbed new mountains; named a sea:
VII.   Some of the last researchers even write
VIII.   Love made him weep his pints like you and me.
IX.   With all his honours on, he sighed for one
X.   Who, say astonished critics, lived at home;
XI.   Did little jobs about the house with skill
XII.   And nothing else; could whistle; would sit still
XIII.   Or potter round the garden; answered some
XIV.   Of his marvellous long letters but kept none.

4.2. Method of analysis

The analysis performed here follows fairly closely the type of analysis presented by Hasan in *Linguistics, Language and Verbal Art* (1985) as well as Halliday's papers on text analysis, collected in the volume *Linguistic Studies of Text and Discourse* (2002a). It uses the categories of systemic functional grammar, as outlined in Halliday and Matthiessen (2004) and Matthiessen (1995), and a familiarity with these is assumed.

The central concepts employed in a stylistic analysis of this type are those of deautomatization and foregrounding, drawn from the literary tradition of

Russian formalism and the Prague School; for a discussion of these schools and concepts and their relationship to systemic functional stylistics, see Lukin and Webster (2005). Deautomatization is the idea that the language of literature draws attention to itself, such that everyday linguistic features and patterns are 'made strange'. Foregrounding is one method by which deautomatization is achieved, and is defined by Halliday (2002a [1971]: 98) as 'prominence that is motivated'. By 'motivated', he means relevant to the overarching meaning of the text, and he points out that prominence may either be an establishment of a norm, or a deviation from that norm, within a particular text (Halliday, 2002a [1971]: 98–107). That is to say, there may be a pattern of features that is numerically dominant in the text (and thus constitutes a norm for the text, whether or not that pattern of features is typically dominant in the system of language in general), and this is one type of prominence; if this pattern is then broken, even by one or two instances, then these deviations from the pattern are notable against the norm of the text overall, and this is another type of prominence.

The determination of what is foregrounded is dependent on the general principle of contrast and comparison that is significant in modern linguistics generally, and in SFL in particular. Saussure (1966: 115) pointed out that the value of a linguistic sign – a word, for example – rests not just with the fact that it 'can be exchanged for something dissimilar, an idea' but also with the fact that it can be 'compared with something of the same nature, another word', so that to determine the meaning of a word:

> one must also compare it with similar values, with other words that stand in opposition to it. Its content is really fixed only by the concurrence of everything that exists outside it. (Saussure 1966: 115)

Similarly, in SFL theory, the meaning of a grammatical feature is not just a function of its realization of semantic and contextual features, but also a function of its location in the network of grammatical choice – what is the significance of this choice (e.g. declarative mood) against the other choices that could have been made, but were not (the other options in the system of mood)? And Halliday (2002a [1964]: 6) points out that the same principle of comparison and contrast applies also to whole texts, saying:

> … a text is meaningful not only in virtue of what it is but also in virtue of what it might have been. The most relevant exponent of the 'might have been' of a work of literature is another work of literature. Linguistic stylistics is thus essentially a comparative study.

The interpretation of the analysis is thus a constant process of comparison and contrast in a number of dimensions, to answer questions such as these: What grammatical features are present, and in what proportions, and how do these proportions compare with the proportions in the grammatical system of the language as a whole, and within relevant 'subsections' of that system, such as comparable registers or comparable texts? Is one pattern of features so dominant that it is the norm for this text, and is that norm then broken, such that there is a contrast between the background pattern and the 'foreground'? Within the text, are there divisions or distinctions or categories present ('physical' divisions of the text such as stanzas, or categories drawn from culture, such as gender, or distinctions set up by the text itself, such as the two human entities in the sonnet under consideration here – the 'greatest figure of his day' and the 'one … who lived at home') that allow further comparison of sets of grammatical patterns associated with those divisions or categories? And with each of these questions, the answer is being compared, or tested, for relevance to the deeper meanings of the literary work, which are of course simultaneously emerging from the patterns being noted in the analysis. Thus there is a necessary shuttling back and forth between the observation of grammatical patterns and the interpretation of their relevance. This shuttling is essentially how the discussion in this chapter will proceed.

4.3. Selection of the poem

While the selection of an Auden sonnet needs no defence in terms of it being a 'valued text' (Halliday 1994: xxix; 2002b [1981]: 229) worthy of stylistic analysis, it is worth briefly noting the circumstances under which it was chosen here, since they will be referred to occasionally in the course of the discussion. The sonnet appears in a volume edited by Don Paterson, *101 Sonnets from Shakespeare to Heaney* (1999). Paterson takes a very straightforward approach to defining a sonnet for inclusion in the volume: 'The only qualification for inclusion in this book is that the poem should have fourteen lines' (1999: x) since, as he puts it, among

> all the po-faced or bloody asseverations on what constitutes the 'true' sonnet ... *no one* can agree on anything but the fact that it has fourteen lines. (Paterson 1999: x) [emphasis in original]

Each author in Paterson's volume is represented by a single sonnet, and the sonnets are not arranged in chronological order, nor by any other specified classification. However, there does seem to be an implicit thematic ordering of the sonnets, with the one appearing immediately before Auden's sonnet being Simon Armitage's 'Poem' – which, like 'Who's Who', references the idea of how a person's life is briefly summed up, for example in a eulogy.

The sense of a deliberate but implicit thematic ordering of these poems is strengthened by the fact that the six or more poems preceding Armitage's in the volume reference funerals, elegies, epitaphs, and so forth – the two sonnets that immediately precede the Armitage and Auden ones, for example, are Milton's 'On his deceased wife' and Brooks's 'Rites for Cousin Vit'.

Thus Auden's sonnet was originally chosen for analysis on the basis that it appears as part of a 'set' that could be used to look, in a larger project, at different constructions of the sonnet form. The Armitage sonnet in particular seems useful for comparison, not only because, as noted above, it seems to deal with similar topic matter to 'Who's Who', but also because its grammatical patterning is in some ways quite different to the Auden sonnet. While it is not possible to present the analysis of the Armitage sonnet here, this analysis has been done, and some of the striking differences will be referenced in discussing the analysis of the Auden sonnet, by way of pointing out that certain choices made by Auden are not governed by the literary form or what might be seen as the most general subject matter – the summing up of a life in some form of biography.

Turning now to initial impressions of the sonnet itself, we can see that the title, 'Who's Who', points to the idea of a short biography of a person's achievements, as might be contained in the reference publication of that name. This is echoed in the opening words of the sonnet, 'A Shilling Life' – presumably referring to a cheap and basic biography in the form of a 'Life of [famous person]' book or pamphlet. Without any linguistic or literary analysis, the poem can be seen to match the expectation set up by the title, in that each stanza is basically a short biography: the octet briefly chronicles a man's life and deeds, that ostensibly lead to him being listed in *Who's Who* and being the topic of a 'shilling life'; and the sestet is also a brief chronicle, this time of an individual whose quiet domestic activities we would probably not even think of as 'deeds' – we might rather think of them as 'doings' – let alone deeds worthy of an entry in *Who's Who*.

Clearly, however, Auden has not written the sonnet for the purpose of elucidating the life of two barely specified individuals. At the very least, he seems to be making a comment on the nature of biography, and it seems likely, given Auden's reputation as a poet and sonneteer, that this comment would be the tip of the iceberg as far as the theme of the sonnet is concerned – 'theme' being Hasan's term for the deeper level of meaning in a literary work, which is construed by consistency of foregrounding (1985: 99). The next section will attempt to elucidate this deeper level of meaning through a detailed systemic functional analysis of Auden's sonnet. The various findings of the metafunctional analyses will be presented first, followed by a discussion of how the various patterns work together to construe the meanings of the sonnet.

4.4. The analysis

The first step in any grammatical analysis is to break the text into the basic unit of grammatical constituency, the clause. The clause breakdown for 'Who's Who' is shown in Table 4.1 and, as is often the case, is immediately revealing with respect to how the patterns in the text contribute to the meaning of the sonnet. Including the title, there are a mere six ranking clauses in the poem, arranged as just two clause complexes, one in the octet and one in the sestet (for comparison, there are 18 ranking clauses in the Armitage sonnet, arranged as 12 clause complexes). In addition, there are 20 embedded clauses, indicated in Table 4.1 (and throughout this chapter) by '.1' etc. after the number of the ranking clause in which they are embedded. Initially it is not entirely clear that clauses 2.1 to 2.4 are actually embedded – it is tempting to treat them as a ranked apposition to what would then be the entirety of clause 2, i.e. 'A shilling life will give you all the facts', as is suggested by the colon after facts. However, the form of clauses 2.1 to 2.4 – each of them beginning with an actual or ellipsed 'how', functioning here as a relative pronoun of sorts – makes it hard to treat them as ranked; and then at 2.5, the 'of' makes it clear that the remaining embedded clauses are embedded as the nominal group of a prepositional phrase that modifies 'facts' (i.e. 'facts [of [[how he fought ...]]]'), which then makes it difficult to treat the intervening clauses as ranked rather than embedded. There's a further ambiguity caused by the colon at the end of clause 2.4, which again suggests that what follows will be a list, this time of the 'acts' just mentioned, but the 'of how' breaks this expectation and sends us back to the list of 'facts' already listed in this 'how' form. The embedding in the sestet, on the other hand, is unambiguous, being a clause complex that postmodifies 'one' via the relative pronoun 'who'. So in the octet, there are 11 clauses that define 'facts', and in the sestet, nine clauses that define 'one'. In other words, all of the 'deeds' and 'doings' that are described for the two individuals in the poem are downranked in the grammar – they are treated as subordinate to the surrounding happenings – which matches the initial understanding, mentioned above, that this poem is not primarily about the deeds (or doings) of the two individuals.

T	1. Who's who
I	2. A shilling life will give you all the facts:
II	[[2.1 How Father beat him, 2.2. how he ran away,
III	2.3. What were the struggles of his youth, 2.4. what acts
IV	Made him the greatest figure of his day]]:
V	Of [[2.5 how he fought, 2.6. ^HE fished, 2.7. ^HE hunted, 2.8. ^HE worked all night,
VI	2.9. Though giddy, 2.10 ^HE climbed new mountains; 2.11. ^HE named a sea]]:
VII	3. Some of the last researchers even write
VIII	4. Love made him weep his pints like you and me.
IX	5. With all his honours on, 6. he sighed for one
X	[[6.1 Who, <<6.2 say astonished critics>>, lived at home;
XI	6.3 ^WHO Did little jobs about the house with skill
XII	6.4 And ^WHO ^DID nothing else; 6.5 ^WHO could whistle; 6.6 ^WHO would sit still
XIII	6.7 Or ^WHO WOULD potter round the garden; 6.8 ^WHO answered some
XIV	Of his marvellous long letters 6.9 but ^WHO kept none]].

Table 4.1: The clauses in 'Who's Who

4.5. Interpersonal meanings

Some of the features of the interpersonal analysis are outlined in Table 4.2. As noted above, most of the clauses in the poem are rankshifted, and therefore do not select for mood. Nevertheless, they can all be considered to be 'giving information', and all but one of the embedded clauses does so using either simple past tense or a modal finite that also encodes past tense ('could' and 'would' in 6.5, 6.6 and 6.7). In the embedded clauses of the octet, the Subject of the embedded clauses is either 'he' or something closely associated with 'he' – 'Father' in 2.1, 'the struggles of his youth' in 2.3, and the acts that made him the greatest figure of his day in 2.4. In all except one of the embedded clauses in the sestet, the Subject is the relative pronoun 'who'. Thus the interpersonal grammar that attends to the two human individuals and their doings is that of a chronicle – a report of various activities in past tense – and this contributes to the sense of 'biography' noted among the initial impressions of the sonnet.

The single embedded clause in the sestet that does not have 'who' as subject is also the one that is not in past tense. It in fact forms a set with two of the ranked clauses in the octet – clause 2 and clause 3 – neither of which is in past tense. All three of these clauses has a Subject that might be classified as either a biography or the type of person who might contribute to a biography – 'A shilling life' in clause 2, 'researchers' in 3, and 'critics' in 6.2. Clause 3 is also the only clause, ranked or embedded, that has a modal Adjunct, and it is one that encodes counterexpectancy: 'even'. However, another member of this set, clause 6.2, also encodes counterexpectancy, but in this case it is in the form of an adjective in the nominal group serving as Subject: 'astonished critics'.

Of the remaining four ranked clauses, clause 1 is the title, which is in present tense and has 'Who' as Subject. It can be read as interrogative, asking 'which one is which?', but it is not punctuated as an interrogative. It can also be read as a declarative, which is essentially its function in the title of the famous reference book: it is introducing the idea that the poem, like that book, will tell you who is who. Two of the ranking clauses fit, interpersonally speaking, into the set formed by the embedded clauses in the octet: clause 6 is declarative past tense clause with 'he' as Subject, and clause 5 is a verbless minor clause that is dependent on clause 6, so 'he' as Subject and past tense are implied by association. This leaves a single clause that does not fit into any of the other sets in the body of the poem: clause 4, which is a past tense declarative like many of the other ranked and embedded clauses in the text, but which has a unique Subject, i.e. one that does not fit into the semantic sets of Subject already discussed ('he', 'who' and 'sources of information'): 'Love'.

At this point, then, we already begin to see overlapping grammatical and semantic patterns that make certain sets of grammatical features prominent. Numerically, clauses featuring 'he' or 'who' as Subject are most common, and these are also nearly all embedded clauses, nearly all in past tense, and nearly all declarative in structure, forming a background that is congruent with our conception of the register of 'biography'. There are then two further patterns that are minor in numerical terms, but which are thrown into contrast – foregrounded – against this background. The first is the set of three clauses (2, 3 and 6.2) that have as their Subject a human or human-generated entity that can be glossed as a 'source of information'; these clauses are also the only three in the sonnet where past tense is neither selected nor implied (the first has a modal finite of probability, 'will', and the other two are in simple present tense). There is also a thread of counterexpectancy in two of the three clauses in this set. Finally, there the clause that forms its own 'set', clause 4, which while fitting into the 'biography' set in terms of tense selection, falls out of this set both because it is a ranking clause, and because its Subject is neither 'he' nor 'who' but the unique item 'Love'.

Cl #	proc	Mood	Subject	Tense	Modality
1	be	interrogative	Who	present	
2	give	declarative	A shilling life	modal	Finite: probability: certain
2.1	beat		Father	past	
2.2	ran		he	past	
2.3	be		the struggles of his youth	past	
2.4	make		what acts	past	
2.5	fight		he	past	
2.6	fish		^HE	past	
2.7	hunt		^HE	past	
2.8	work		^HE	past	
2.9	(none)	verbless			
2.10	climb		^HE	past	
2.11	name		^HE	past	
3	write	declarative	Some of the last researchers	present	Adjunct: counterexpectancy
4	weep	declarative	Love	past	
5	(none)	verbless			
6	sigh	declarative	he	past	
6.1	live		who	past	
6.2	say		astonished critics	present	
6.3	do		^WHO	past	
6.4	do		^WHO	past	
6.5	whistle		^WHO	modal	Finite: inclination: ability
6.6	sit		^WHO	modal	Finite: usuality
6.7	potter		^WHO	modal	Finite: usuality
6.8	answer		^WHO	past	
6.9	keep		^WHO	past	

Table 4.2: Interpersonal features of 'Who's Who'

4.6. Textual meanings

Table 4.3 displays the textual choices made in the ranking clauses of the sonnet. Just as was noted above with respect to grammatical mood, rank-shifted clauses do not select for Theme, and so do not fully enter into the textual meanings in the poem. Thus, as there are just six ranked clauses in the poem, there are just six selections of Theme, and in all but one of the ranked clauses the Theme consists of a simple unmarked topical Theme. The exception to this, clause 5, will be considered in a moment. Looking first at the octet, the Theme selections and thematic progression, they are mostly so straightforward that they have essentially already been discussed in the outline of the first impressions of the poem at the beginning of this chapter. While the title has been analysed into Theme and Rheme in Table 4.3, it is probably best treated simply as a kind of hyper-Theme or macro-Theme (Martin 1992: 437) for the sonnet, since as a whole it mimics the title of the bibliographic reference work *Who's Who* and therefore sets up the idea that what follows will somehow be 'about' biography. The next Theme, 'A shilling life' in clause 2, progresses directly from this, referencing another kind of biography – a cheap book or pamphlet telling the life story of someone notable. Although there is quite a lot of content before the next Theme – the long embedded clause complex comprising 11 clauses, 2.1–2.11, which draws us into the details of the subject of the biography – the Theme in clause 3, 'Some of the last researchers' reminds us that the poem is thematizing biography as a concept, not the actual subject of a particular biography.

The next Theme, the last in the octet, is another simple unmarked topical Theme, 'Love' in clause 4, which obviously breaks the pattern of thematic progression set up so far. As noted above with respect to choices of Subject, this item is its own 'set' in the sonnet – whereas other entities serving as Subject can be categorized as being related to 'he' or 'who' or 'sources of information', this entity cannot. Similarly, in the thematic progression, 'Love' as Theme is a disruption to the pattern set up thus far in the poem.

The following set of clauses, clauses 5 and 6, also disrupts the thematic progression, but in another way. I have analysed clause 5 as a verbless minor clause with 'With' functioning as a kind of conjunction, and the rest of the clause functioning as a verbless circumstantial attributive clause (as will be seen in the experiential analysis), with the clause as a whole being a hypotactic clause that elaborates clause 6 – hence referring to these two clauses as a 'set'. As a non-finite clause, clause 5 does not select for Theme, so that here it is divided into textual Theme ('with') and Rheme ('all his honours on'). Some analysts might treat this 'clause' instead as a prepositional phrase functioning as a Circumstance in the clause that follows, in which case it would be serving as a marked topical Theme in the textual meanings, and even in my analysis, as a dependent clause opening a clause complex, it can be seen to serve as a kind of marked topical Theme to clause 6 (Martin, Matthiessen, and Painter 1997: 36). However one analyses it, there is a break in the pattern of simple unmarked topical Themes at the start of the sestet, even though the content of these clauses is the familiar 'life of he' drawn from the Rheme of previous clauses. So the disruption here is a change in the grammatical patterning of the Theme, in contrast to the disruption in clause

4, where the thematization of 'Love' broke the chain of reference to 'biography' that had been set up by previous simple unmarked topical Themes.

The final Theme, in clause 6, is 'he'. As already noted, this entity, while new in the thematic progression, is not new in the text, since it links back to the Rheme of previous clauses. However, it is worth noting that there is still a potential foregrounding here, since it is the only time in the sonnet that its most frequent Subject, 'he', appears in a ranked clause as Theme. The other most frequent Subject, 'who', does not appear at all as Theme in a ranked clause; the next most frequent, 'sources of information' appears twice (as well as in the macro-Theme of the title), and the least frequent Subject – the category of one, 'Love' – appears in Theme position just as frequently as the most frequent Subject, 'he', i.e. once.

Cl #	Textual	Inter-personal	Marked topical	Unmarked topical	Rheme
1				Who	is who
2				A shilling life	will give you all the facts
3				Some of the last researchers	even write
4				Love	made him weep his pints like you and me.
5	With				all his honours on
6				He	sighed for one

Table 4.3: Textual features of 'Who's who'

4.6. Ideational meanings

4.6.1. Logical meanings

Table 4.4 shows, in both symbols and wording, the logical relations between the ranking clauses of the sonnet. There are just three clause complexes; the first is the title and comprises just one clause. The fact that there are so few clause complexes means that there is not much that can be said about patterns at this point, but the hypotactic relations are worth noting before moving to look at the patterns within the embedded clause complexes. The first is between clause 4 and clause 3, which hypotactically projects it. Although clause 4 has been noted as one that is foregrounded by its unique choice of Subject, and by the fact that this Subject, 'Love', causes a disruption in the thematic progression of the octet, one can think of the hypotactic relation as 'downplaying' the experiential meanings of this clause in relation to the independent clause that projects it – clause 3, which is one of the set that has a 'source of information' as Subject. This will be discussed further in relation to experiential meanings, below.

The second hypotactic relation has also already been discussed in relation to its disruption of textual meanings – clause 5 hypotactically elaborates clause 6, and acts as a marked topical Theme to that clause. The significance of this relation will also be discussed further in later sections.

CC	*Clauses*	*Logical analysis*	
A	1. Who's who	1	independent clause
B	2. A shilling life will give you all the facts: [[...]]	1	independent clause
	3. Some of the last researchers even write	+2α	paratactic extension of 2
	4. Love made him weep his pints like you and me.	"2β	hypotactic projection of 3
C	5. With all his honours on,	=β	hypotactic elaboration of 6
	6. he sighed for one [[...]]	α	independent clause

Table 4.4: Logical relations between ranking clauses in 'Who's Who'

Table 4.5 outlines the logical relations within the long clause complex embedded in clause 2. None of the clauses are truly 'independent', but the first one has been designated as such, just to display the dominant pattern of paratactic extension: this is a list of the 'facts' that the shilling life will give you. There is one hypotactic relation, between a verbless minor clause and the clause that follows it, which essentially parallels the relationship between ranked clauses 5 and 6 – the clauses that were discussed as a 'set' with respect to textual meanings. This parallel carries through into the experiential meanings, as will be discussed below.

Table 4.6 displays the logical relations within the long embedded clause complex in clause 6. Again, the dominant pattern within the embedding is paratactic extension: there is a list of the 'doings' of the 'one who lived at home'. For the most part, this fits with our sense that the octet lists the deeds of the noteworthy entity 'he', and the sestet lists the 'doings' of the person for whom 'he' sighs, and the parallel structuring of the logical relations between the two embedded clause complexes invites a comparison of the two lists, which will be explored further with respect to experiential meanings below.

Clauses	Logical analysis	
[[2.1 How Father beat him,	1	"independent" clause
2.2 how he ran away	+2	paratactic extension of 2.1
2.3. What were the struggles of his youth,	+3	paratactic extension of 2.2
2.4. what acts Made him the greatest figure of his day]]:	+4	paratactic extension of 2.3
Of [[2.5 how he fought,	+5	paratactic extension of 2.4
2.6 ^HOW HE fished,	+6	paratactic extension of 2.5
2.7. ^HOW HE hunted,	+7	paratactic extension of 2.6
2.8. ^HOW HE worked all night,	+8	paratactic extension of 2.7
2.9. Though giddy,	x9β	hypotactic expansion of 2.10
2.10 ^HE climbed new mountains;	+9α	paratactic extension of 2.8
2.11. ^HE named a sea]]:	+10	paratactic extension of 2.9

Table 4.5: Logical relations in the embedding in the first stanza of 'Who's Who'

Clause	Logical relations	
[[6.1 Who, <<6.2>>, lived at home;	"β1	hypotactic projection from 6.2
6.2 say astonished critics	α1	"Independent" clause
6.3 ^WHO Did little jobs about the house with skill	+β2	paratactic extension of 6.1
6.4 And ^WHO ^DID nothing else ?WITH SKILL;	+β3	paratactic extension of 6.3
6.5 ^WHO could whistle;	+β4	paratactic extension of 6.4
6.6 ^WHO would sit still	+β5	paratactic extension of 6.5
6.7 Or ^WHO WOULD potter round the garden;	+β6	paratactic extension of 6.6
6.8 ^WHO answered some Of his marvellous long letters	+β7	paratactic extension of 6.7
6.9 but ^WHO kept none]].	+β8	paratactic extension of 6.8

Table 4.6: Logical relations in the embedding in the second stanza of 'Who's Who'

However, there is a difference here within the logical relations of the clause complex embedded in clause 6, in that the paratactic relations all follow from clause 6.1, but this clause is itself projected hypotactically from the clause that interrupts it, clause 6.2. This relationship is parallel to the relationship between ranking clauses 3 and 4 mentioned above. However, because in this case the rest of the embedded clause complex is related by paratactic extension to clause 6.1, the entire paratactic clause complex is hypotactic in relation to clause 6.2. Thus all of the 'doings' of the 'one' are subordinate to clause 6.2 through the mechanism of hypotactic projection, as well as subordinate to the main 'action' of the poem through the mechanism of embedding, as already discussed in relation to the clause breakdown. Clause 6.2 is one of the set of three clauses noted in the discussion of interpersonal meanings to have a 'source of information' as Subject; even though this clause is embedded, it is 'less subordinate' than the other clauses in the embedded clause complex, which emphasizes again the concept of biography over the content of the individual biographies, as it were.

4.6.2. Experiential meanings

This final section discussing the analysis of the poem deals with experiential meanings – who did what to whom, and under what circumstances. The findings of the experiential analysis have been split across Tables 4.7 and 4.8, with Table 4.7 displaying the features of the octet, and Table 4.8 displaying the features of the sestet. The findings are divided in this way mainly for neatness in presentation, because different features are relevant in the two stanzas: a quick comparison of the two tables shows that in the sestet, the columns for Initiator and Agent could have been left out altogether, since they are not used, whereas a column has been added for Circumstance – while Circumstances are not completely absent from the first stanza, there are certainly more of them in the second.

For simplicity in the display of the analysis, Tables 4.7 and 4.8 use as headings the roles in an ergative analysis of the text (Agent, Medium, etc.), while the transitive roles that correspond to and conflate with these ergative roles for each process type are mentioned in the surrounding discussion (see Halliday and Matthiessen 2004: Section 5.7.2 for a full discussion of the ergative model). While this form of display is 'neat' in any case because the ergative roles carry across different process types in the transitivity (so all clauses can be grouped and analysed under one set of headings), it is also relevant here because the ergative model is essentially a model of agency and causation – whether the process is caused by an agent (i.e. effective voice) or self-engendered (i.e. middle voice), and this seems particularly relevant to our expectations about how the life of 'he' might be construed, in that we might expect to be told how this great figure affected and changed the world around him: what processes he caused, as it were, that led to him being biography-worthy.

The analysis that follows will also draw on aspects of what Hasan (1985: 45–47) outlines as the 'cline of dynamism'. Hasan's ordering of Process-Participant configurations from dynamic to passive allows her to explain why the widower in Murray's poem seems ineffectual despite being first participant in many process configurations. This ordering also mostly corresponds to a cline of decreasing agency, i.e. the essential features of the ergative model are already implicit in the cline of dynamism. Added to this ergative perspective is the fact that Hasan makes explicit the cline of dynamism among the process types, with material processes being the most dynamic, then verbal, then mental, and finally, towards the passive end of the cline, relational attributive process configurations. The ergative model is overlaid, as it were, over this cline of process types, so that an Actor/Agent in a material process clause that also has a Goal/Medium is highest on the cline of dynamism, whereas an Actor in a material process clause that has no second participant falls about halfway between dynamic and passive. The cline of dynamism together with a more explicit ergative perspective is used in the discussion below to explain how 'he' follows a gradual trajectory of increasing agency in the embedded clauses of the octet. The discussion below will begin with an explanation of the patterns associated with 'he', including this trajectory of agentiveness, then move to the patterns associated with 'who', and finally to the less numerically dominant patterns in the text that are foregrounded against these dominant patterns.

The first thing to note about the patterns associated with 'he' are that the processes are mostly material and relational, which fits, superficially at least, with the idea of a biography telling us about a person's activities and characteristics. As shown by the cline of dynamism, material processes in particular provide the potential for 'he' to be fully agentive in the way we might expect someone from the pages of 'Who's Who' to be – changing the world in some way; performing monumental deeds in the material world. When we look at the detail, however, this is not the case – change occurs, as already noted, in the form of a trajectory of increasing agency across the clauses embedded in clause 2, but the trajectory begins with him being very much not the Agent of the activity, and ends before 'he' becomes fully agentive in the kind of monumental way we might expect.

The start of the trajectory of increasing agency is clause 2.1, 'how father beat him', which is the only effective material process clause in the poem in which 'he' is a participant; here 'he' is Medium/Goal rather than Agent/ Actor, and is clearly construed as powerless. The next material process clause is 2.2, 'how he ran away', which is a middle voice clause which shifts 'he' into the Actor role, but of course as Medium/Actor not Agent/ Actor. 'Run' is at least a self-engendered process which construes (along

Cl#	proc	Proc type	Voice	Initiator	Agent	Medium	Range
1	be	rel: id	eff		Who	who	
2	give	mat	eff		A shilling life	all the facts	*Beneficiary: you
2.1	beat	mat	eff		Father	Him	
2.2	ran	mat	mid			He	
2.3	be	rel: id	eff		What	the struggles of his youth	
2.4	make	rel: id	eff	what acts	him	the greatest figure of his day	
2.5	fight	mat	mid			He	
2.6	fish	mat	mid			^HE	
2.7	hunt	mat	mid			^HE	
2.8	work	mat	mid			^HE	
2.9	(none)	rel: att	mid			(he)	giddy
2.10	climb	mat	mid			^HE	new mountains
2.11	name	rel: id	eff	^HE	a sea	(none)	
3	write	verb: proj	mid			Some of the last researchers	
4	weep	mat: beh	cff		Love	Him	his pints

* Note that Beneficiary is not a type of Range, but has been listed in this column to save space.

Table 4.7: Experiential features of the first stanza of 'Who's Who'

with the Circumstance: location: spatial 'away') a definite, directed action, and one whereby 'he' removes himself from the situation of powerlessness. Thus between 2.1 and 2.2 there is a slight increase in 'agency', and a sense of a character who overcomes struggles, who is able to shift himself out of a position of powerlessness.

The next two clauses, 2.3 and 2.4, are both identifying relational processes that interrupt the series of material processes within the embedding, and to some extent interrupt the trajectory of agency. The first of these clauses construes 'he' obliquely (as part of 'the struggles of his youth') as Medium/Value, and in a way summarizes lexically the idea of 'struggle against adversity' that has just been construed grammatically in clauses 2.1 and 2.2. In the second of the two identifying relational clauses, 'he' is actually Agent/Token, but there is not a strong sense of his affecting the world in an agentive way, partly because relational processes are lower in the cline of dynamism than other process types, since they construe 'being' types of processes rather than 'doing' types of process, and partly because in this case the Agent is superseded, as it were, by an Initiator, 'what acts'. So at the same time as this clause lexically construes the idea that 'he' performed 'acts' that led to him being considered 'the greatest figure of his day', it grammatically construes the 'acts' rather than 'he' as the most agentive element in this process. Just as clause 2.3 lexically summarizes the previous two clauses, it seems as if clause 2.4 is a kind of summarizing preface to what follows, which we might gloss as 'I am about to tell you what acts made him the greatest figure' – with the colon at the end of this clause contributing to this expectation that what follows will be a list of great acts. But as already noted in the discussion of the clause analysis, this expectation is confounded by the form of the clauses that follows, and we shall now see that it is also confounded by the experiential content of those clauses.

After the intervening relational identifying clauses just discussed, the poem returns to material process clauses that describe the activity of 'he', and there is again a slight shift in agency. Clauses 2.5 to 2.8 are a series of middle voice material process clauses – 'how he fought, fished, hunted, worked all night'. All of the verbs in the series are of the type that could take a second participant – an object, in traditional terms – but since these are middle voice clauses, this second participant would be classified in SFL as a Range rather than a Medium – i.e. an entity that the process ranges over, rather than one it materially changes. Nevertheless, the presence of even a Range would give more of a sense of 'he' as a person who affects things around him; but the absence of a Range, or any other elaborating information such as Circumstances, leaves the status of 'fought, fished, hunted' somewhat ambiguous. It may be that these process configurations do refer to the 'acts' that made him a great figure – at least somewhat 'monumental' activities such as fighting a bully, fighting in a war or hunting big game in Africa. But as they stand, without a Range or Circumstances, these clauses read more like a reference to the pursuits of an English upper class country gentleman, typically characterized as 'huntin', shootin' and fishin'', than a chronicle of noteworthy deeds. Coming as it does at the end of this list of pursuits, 'worked all night' conjures an image of someone working at a lamplit desk in a private library or study, rather than, for example, someone working on the farm or at the mill all night. It may be that working all night at a desk might involve something more 'monumental' – plans for a big expedition, a battle, a world-changing invention, etc. But, taken together, clauses 2.5 to 2.8 seem to suggest not so much 'monumental deeds', as an idea that might be glossed, especially against the 'struggles' of clauses 2.1 and 2.2, as 'he became a gentleman despite his beginnings as a beaten child who ran away from home' – i.e. as another aspect of him overcoming 'the struggles of his youth', rather than the 'acts that made him the greatest figure of his day'.

Up to clause 2.8, then – coming towards the end of the 'facts' of his life as outlined in the long embedded clause complex – we have not really seen a hint of momentous deeds that might gain one a place in *Who's Who*. Finally, in 2.10 – the final material process clause within the embedding, we see such a deed: '^HE climbed new mountains'. This is still a middle voice clause, and 'he' is still Medium/Actor, but in this case a Range is present, so there is more of a sense of 'he' engaging with and affecting the world around him – although still not in a fully agentive role. Preceding this clause is one of the two relational attributive clauses in the poem that describe 'he': clause 2.9, 'Though giddy', which has already been noted to function as a marked topical Theme to clause 2.10. The experiential meanings of clause 2.9 and 2.10 set up another type of counterexpectancy: clause 2.9 construes 'he' as exactly the type of person who might not be expected to climb anything, and clause 2.10 counters this with the construal of him climbing an uncharted mountain. So although 'he' is not Agent, there is a strong sense of him being powerful here – not least because 'he' once again overcomes adversity, this time in the form of a medical condition.

The final clause in the embedding, 2.11, is another relational identifying process, and this time 'he' takes the 'most agentive' role in this process type – 'he' is Initiator, bringing about the identifying relationship between the Token/Agent, 'a sea', and the Medium/Value, its name – although the fact that the Medium/Value is absent reduces the agency somewhat. Nevertheless, clause 2.11, together with clause 2.10, unambiguously comprises the kinds of act that would indeed gain one an entry in *Who's Who*. It also completes the trajectory of gradually increasing agency set up by the material process clauses, where 'he' moves from being Goal, to being Actor in a series of unranged processes, to being Actor in a ranged process, and then Initiator in a relational identifying process.

Once the poem emerges, as it were, from the embedded clause complex, there are three ranked clauses that construe further activity of 'he': clause 4, which forms the last line of the octet, and clauses 5 and 6, which form the first line of the sestet (note that the analysis of clause 4 is part of Table 4.7, and that of 5 and 6 is part of Table 4.8). These are the only ranked clauses in which 'he' is construed as a participant. Two of these clauses, 4 and 6, are configurations of the behavioural subtype of material process, and they both construe emotionally loaded activities – weeping and sighing – and ones that suggest negative emotions at that. In addition, while behavioural process clauses are usually inherently middle, the first one here, clause 4, is rendered effective by the presence of an Initiator – 'Love'. So to the extent that 'he' is construed as a participant in the ranking clauses in the poem, 'he' is construed not only as a sufferer of emotions rather than a doer of deeds, but also as being under the control of an emotion – in this case one that is generally considered a positive emotion, but which causes a negative effect here. This is another point at which the ostensible biography of 'he' runs counter to what we might expect.

There are a couple of further points that are worth noting about these two clauses, on top of the fact that they have already been noted as foregrounded in the interpersonal, textual and logical patterns of the poem. First, clause 4, which in some ways is the most unique clause of the poem – in its choice of Subject, for example – is also marked out by the fact that is projected directly from one of the other foregrounded clauses of the poem, clause 3, 'Some of the last researchers even write'. It is not insignificant that clause 3 is the only clause in the poem that contains a modal Adjunct, and that this modal Adjunct construes counterexpectancy, and that this counterexpectancy therefore 'colours' our reading of the projected clause. While on one hand we know that everyone can potentially be brought to their lowest point by Love, the fact that this is mentioned as part of a biography of a great man is unexpected, and this is emphasized explicitly by the modal Adjunct in the projecting clause. This clause is also foregrounded by the presence of a Circumstance, in this case one of manner: comparison, 'like you and me', which introduces two essentially new participants into the poem: the reader and the writer/narrator of the poem. While there is an earlier instance of 'you', in the first line of the poem, that instance is ambiguous between a generic 'you' meaning 'one'; this instance of 'you' in clause 4 is unambiguously suggesting a comparison between the ordinary life of the reader and the life of 'he', the great man, as well as a general connectedness between the experience of the reader, the experience of the writer/narrator, and the experience of the great man. The explicit mention of reader and writer/narrator also draws attention to the poem as an act of communication and another 'source of information' beyond those that are explicitly mentioned in clauses 2, 3 and 6.2 of the poem.

Just as clause 4 forms a set with the projecting clause 3, clause 6 also forms a set with its preceding clause, as was mentioned in the discussion of textual meanings: clause 5, a verbless minor clause, functions as a marked topical Theme to clause 6, in the same way that clause 2.9 functions as a marked topical Theme to clause 2.10. Clause 5 also has parallel experiential meanings to clause 2.9, in that it is a relational attributive clause that describes 'him' – and it also functions in the same way to set up expectations that are countered by clause 6 (just as 'climbed new mountains' in clause 2.10 runs counter to the expectation set up by 'though giddy' in clause 2.9). Clause 5, 'With all his honours on' seems to describe someone in full regalia, who might be expected to maintain the emotionless veneer of office and to focus on the job at hand while ignoring worries of a personal nature; in clause 6, this notion is countered by 'he sighed for one …', i.e. his emotions are not held at bay by his regalia. As well as echoing the form of clauses 2.9 and 2.10, this pair of clauses echoes the counterexpectancy set up in clauses 3 and 4 – that even one bedecked with honours is just an ordinary person when it comes to the vagaries and difficulties of Love. It is also worth pointing out that like clause 4, clause 6 contains a Circumstance, which this time is one of cause: behalf, 'for one [[who lives …]]', which means that the rest of clause 6, the description of the one he sighs for, is actually embedded in the Circumstance of his sighing, and a construal of the cause of his sighing. This Circumstance also means that both of the emotive behavioural clauses, 4 and 6, construe causation, in what is normally a non-agentive clause type, so that while many of the material clauses describing the activity of 'he' were lacking in causation or directedness, both of the clauses that construe his emotions are not lacking in this way.

The final point to note with respect to the patterns associated with 'he' is that there are no mental or verbal process clauses involving this entity. Behavioural clauses that construe his emotion are the closest this sonnet comes to construing his mental life, and the relational: identifying clause where he 'named a sea' is the closest 'he' comes to creating meanings, verbally or mentally, in the poem, although 'his marvellous long letters' in clause 2.8 does obliquely construe this entity as a Sayer.

Moving now to the patterns associated with the entity that has been referred to so far as 'who': in this case all of the clauses with 'who' as participant are embedded; within the embedded clause complex they are also all dependent, being projected from the verbal process clause 6.2 'astonished critics say'. There are seven material process clauses, and 'who' is Medium/Actor in all of them; two of these seven are of the behavioural subtype, but in this case they are not emotionally loaded in the way that 'weep' and 'sigh' are. In clause 6.5 the process is 'whistle', which is almost a physiological activity, and might construe a joyful way of being, or simply a neutral, blasé one. The other behavioural process is 'sit' in clause 6.6, which is again a neutral kind of process that construes bodily position rather than any kind of activity. The other material processes associated with 'who' are similarly neutral and

Cl#	proc	Proc type	Voice	Initiator	Agent	Medium	Range	Circ
5	(none)	rel: att	mid			all his honours	On	
6	sigh	mat: beh	mid			he		for one (cause: behalf)
6.1	live	mat	mid			who		at home (loc: spat)
6.2	say	verb: proj	mid			astonished critics		
6.3	do	mat	mid			^WHO	little jobs	about the house (loc: spat); with skill (manner: qual)
6.4	do	mat	mid			^WHO	nothing else	??^WITH SKILL (manner: qual)
6.5	whistle	mat: beh	mid			^WHO		
6.6	sit	mat: beh	mid			^WHO		still (manner: qual)
6.7	potter	mat	mid			^WHO		round the garden (circ: loc)
6.8	answer	verb: non-proj	mid			^WHO	some Of his marvellous long letters	
6.9	keep	mat	mid			^WHO	none (of his marvellous long letters)	

Table 4.8: Experiential features of the second stanza of 'Who's Who'

relatively constrained: 'live' in clause 6.1, 'do' in clauses 6.3 and 6.4, 'potter' in clause 6.7 and 'keep' in clause 6.9. The most lexically rich of these verbs, 'potter' does describe movement, but it is small and undirected movement, in contrast to something like 'ran away' as appears in the octet. Three of these four processes have a Range, but in contrast to 'new mountains' in the octet, these Ranges are domestic and local, and two of them actually denote the absence of a Range: 'little jobs' in 6.3, 'nothing else' in 6.4, and 'none (of his letters)' in 6.9. Four of the material clauses have Circumstances that also constrain the locus of activity to the body or its domestic surrounds: 'at home' in clause 6.1, 'about the house' in clause 6.3, 'still' in 6.6 and 'around the garden' in clause 6.7. Even the Circumstance: manner: quality 'with skill' in clause 6.3 suggests narrowly focused attention on the jobs at hand.

In the clauses construing the activities of 'he', the division between ordinary material processes and the subtype behavioural was significant, but here they seem to form just one set, construing the local, bodily, constrained activities of 'who'. This set contrasts with the set associated with 'he', which are for the most part outdoor activities that involve movement into environments beyond the home. However, despite the 'astonished critics', the sense of 'who' is not of a person who is passive or lacking in ambition or whose life is limited, but instead of one who is happily self-sufficient and self-contained, who does not need to venture beyond the boundaries of their home to be fulfilled. This sense is strengthened by the fact that, first, there are no emotionally loaded processes that give any sense of dissatisfaction with life in general or the absence of 'he' – there is no sense of the weeping and sighing of 'he' being reciprocated. Second, against the pattern of material process clauses associated with 'who', there is a single verbal process clause, 6.8 '^WHO answered some of his marvellous long letters', with 'who' as Medium/Sayer, and 'some of his marvellous long letters' as Range/Target. As was noted above, this is one of the few places the sonnet comes close to construing 'he' as a Sayer, and the only clause that construes a two-way interaction between the two human entities who are the dominant participants in the poem. This clause begins halfway through line XIII of the poem, at the point where some sonnets might be part way into a summarizing couplet, but in this case it brings to light the likely cause of the earlier weeping and sighing: 'who' does engage with 'he', responding verbally to his verbal artefacts, but the fact that 'who' answers only some of the letters, and keeps none, indicates the extent to which they are immune to the attentions of the greatest figure of their time, despite the length and marvellousness of his letters. The sense of self-containment in the 'who' entity thus seems to reach its pinnacle in these final two clauses – the offer of human interaction is only partially responded to, and then discarded totally.

The last set of experiential meanings to be discussed in this section are those that attend to the 'set' of three clauses with Subjects glossed in the discussion of interpersonal meanings as 'sources of information' – clauses 2, 3 and 6.2. As noted in that discussion, these clauses are foregrounded by their choice of Subject, as well as by tense selections. They are also foregrounded experientially, in their construal of 'saying', against the background of construals of 'doing' and 'being' just described in relation to the human participants of the poem. The second two of the three clauses – clauses 3 and 6.2 – are very direct grammatical construals of saying – they are verbal process clauses of the projecting type, so that, as seen in the logical relations analysis, they 'project' much of the other content of the poem: clause 3 projects clause 4 ('Love made him weep his pints like you and me'); and clause 6.2 projects the rest of the embedded clauses in clause 6.

The remaining clause of this set, which comprises the first line of the sonnet, construes 'saying' not through a verbal process clause but a material process one. This is the most agentive of all of the material process clauses in the sonnet, since it includes three participants: not just the Agent/Actor 'A shilling life' and the Medium/Goal 'all the facts [[...]]', but also a Beneficiary of the giving, 'you'. While the process itself is not a projecting verbal clause, the embedded clause complex, as a defining relative clause complex that outlines the nature of the 'facts', can be considered a projection within the nominal group; and the presence of the Beneficiary, here construing a receiver of the 'facts', helps to emphasize the idea of 'transfer of information'. The fact that the Beneficiary is 'you', with its ambiguity between the generic 'you' meaning 'one', and the specific 'you' who is reading the poem, doubly emphasizes the idea of communication since it draws attention to the communicative nature of the sonnet itself, as well as of the 'sources of information' described in the poem. This brings us neatly to the underlying themes of the sonnet – a drawing of attention to the nature of communication of facts about other people – and a discussion of those themes in the next section.

4.7. The patterning of patterns: Counterexpectancy in 'Who's Who'

The first impressions of Auden's sonnet outlined towards the start of this chapter asserted that the poem is in some way 'about' biography, and certainly the majority of the content of the poem comprises what can be glossed as, if not biography, at least a chronicle of the activities of two people, who have been referred to throughout the discussion as 'he' and 'who'. Some of the features that contribute to this numerically dominant 'background' pattern are the simple past tense; the choice of 'he' or 'who' (often ellipsed) as Subject; the mostly simple thematic progression both within and outside of the embedding; the mostly paratactic relations between clauses (again both within and outside of the embedding) giving the sense of a list about each entity; the dominance of material and relational processes, and the involvement of 'he' and 'who' as participants in those processes, so that the text is mainly about those entities' activities in the material world. For the rest of the discussion here, this numerically dominant pattern will be referred to as the 'chronicle' pattern, forming the 'background' to the foregrounded patterns discussed below.

Against this 'background' forming the 'chronicle' pattern are several relatively subtle threads of meaning that I would characterize most generally as 'communication about other people's lives'. This characterization might seem at first to be synonymous with 'biography', but the more general definition obviously encompasses other genres, including trivial ones such as 'gossip' – and I think in a way Auden is playing with the idea that all communication about other's lives, even well researched biography, has the potential to take on the character of gossip, of the type that might open with 'you'll never believe what I heard', i.e. 'I'm about to tell you something that you're not expecting'. He achieves this through two main sets of overlapping patterns that will be discussed below: (1) patterns that are about communication – ones that foreground the communicative aspect of biography over the content of biography, and ones that foreground communication generally; and (2) patterns or features that are about 'counterexpectancy'.

The most obvious foregrounding of 'communication' is in the set of three clauses (2, 3 and 6.2) characterized as having Subjects that are 'sources of information'. As already noted in the discussions of the analysis, these three clauses are foregrounded against the 'chronicle' pattern in the different choice of Subject, the choice of present or modal (non-past) tenses, and the fact that they construe projection in some way. They are also foregrounded in that they, as a group, project most of the rest of the sonnet – the chronicle of 'he' is an embedded projection in clause 2, clause 3 projects clause 4, and clause 6.2 projects the rest of the embedded clause complex in clause 6 that is the chronicle of 'who'. The content that describes 'he' and 'who' – the actual biographic content – is thus framed and in a sense subsumed by the acts of saying that produce it.

There are also a couple of points in the poem where the communicative function of the poem itself is foregrounded, by the use of first and second person pronouns. The first of these is in one of the clauses just noted to foreground communication, clause 2. Here, both the presence of a Beneficiary – a receiver of the information – and the fact that the Beneficiary role is filled by the second person pronoun 'you' emphasizes the idea of transfer of information. There is some ambiguity here between whether the poem is directly addressing the reader or simply using 'you' generically to mean 'one' or 'everyone', but the general point still holds, that a third party, one who receives 'the facts', is invoked. The second time 'you' is used is in clause 4, as part of the Circumstance: manner: comparison 'like you and me'. Auden is using 'you and me' to represent 'ordinary people', i.e. 'great people weep over love the same way the ordinary people do', but the fact that he uses 'you and me' rather than 'everyone' or 'all of us' means that both the writer/narrator of the poem and its reader – the two participants in the current communicative act – are invoked. The use of 'like you and me' also falls into the patterns of meaning around counterexpectancy, which will be discussed further below.

Added to this emphasis on communication is the fact that even within the chronicle pattern, communication is foregrounded, in clauses 6.8 and 6.9, which comprise the last line and a half of the poem. Clause 6.8 is the only non-projecting verbal process in the poem, the only verbal process that does not fall into the 'sources of information' set described above, and the only clause in either part of the chronicle that is anything other than a material or relational process configuration. Added to this is the fact that it does not just construe communication as a verbal process, but that the Range/Target role in the clause is filled by a verbal artefact, 'his marvellous long letters', that is also the only representation, albeit an oblique one, of the verbal activity of 'he'. This verbal artefact is repeated, via the substitution 'none' in the last clause, and in fact the last word, of the poem.

These last two clauses also form part of the pattern of counterexpectancy in the poem, to which we will now turn. In the case of these two clauses, there has been no hint up to this point that the 'one who lived at home' was not fully reciprocating the affections of 'he'. Although 'he' is construed as weeping and sighing for the one at home, this is not necessarily because the love is unrequited; it may simply be that he misses his loved one at home. However, these two clauses make the lack of reciprocity clear; and the fact that, while they are distinguished from the rest of the chronicle pattern by their verbal content, they are otherwise simply part of the chronicle of the homely activities of 'who' (they are not distinguished by choice of tense or Subject, for example) makes this lack of reciprocity seem additionally shocking – a banal rejection and disposal of the letters (and presumably offers of affection) from 'the greatest figure of his day', slotted in among so many other everyday activities.

The alleged contrast between ordinariness and greatness, and the failure of this contrast, is another pattern that construes counterexpectancy in the sonnet, as evidenced in the Circumstance: manner: comparison in clause

4, 'like you and me'. The invocation of reader and writer/narrator as a representation of 'ordinary people' to which the great man is compared, also seems to impose on the reader the assumptions of counterexpectancy that the poem either construes both explicitly (in the modal Adjunct 'even' in clause 3, and the 'astonished critics' in clause 6.2) and more implicitly (such as in the two sets of clauses that have been noted already to set up an expectation and then counter it immediately – clause 2.9 'though giddy' followed by clause 2.10 'climbed new mountains', and clause 5 'with all his honours on' followed by clause 6 'he sighed for one [[who lived at home …]]'). In other words, the poem sets up the idea that great men behave in a certain way, and that it is surprising when they don't act that way, and the reader seems to be made complicit in the making of assumptions by their explicit inclusion in the poem; the poem seems to be saying 'Great men are just like you and me, you know', thus implying that the reader had asserted or assumed that great men are not like you and me. This is not to say that Auden is assuming that readers make this assumption; rather, that he is construing the rather complex relationship between the writer and reader of any text, whereby the writer typically has to take the expectations and assumptions of the reader into account.

The more explicit construals of counterexpectancy are also interesting in ways that have not been discussed yet. Although the modal Adjunct 'even' in clause 3 has been discussed above as 'colouring' the content of clause 4, i.e. construing the counterexpectancy in relation to the idea that a great man might be reduced to tears by love, just like ordinary people, as just discussed, the counterexpectancy actually occurs in relation to the writing of this idea: 'Some of the last researchers even write …'. So the counterexpectancy also suggests that we (or the writer/narrator) would not expect researchers of a biography to write such a thing, and indeed, in this case, it does seem that a serious biography would be unlikely to include such a personal detail; so there's a sense here that Auden is having a dig at biographers as being no better than gossip columnists. As already noted, in the very next set of clauses (5 and 6), which is not explicitly projected from such a dubious 'source of information', the poem continues to describe the emotional life of 'he', with the same sense of counterexpectancy between the greatness of the man ('with all his honours on') and his emotional behaviour ('he sighed …'), so that there seems to be a slide from the construal of the researchers' production of biography content as somewhat dubious (in clauses 3 and 4) to a direct construal in the poem of the same kind of 'gossipy' information, without any kind of mediating biographer to blame for the construal. This shift, along with all of the foregrounding already noted in relation to clauses 4, 5 and 6, also occurs between line VIII of the poem, the last line of the octet, and line IX, the first line of the sestet, which is also, in literary terms, the typical location of the turn or volta that is a feature of many sonnets, described by Paterson thus:

> ... a sudden shift in the development of the poem – a twist in the plot, the breaking of the argument into argument into proposition and counter-proposition, or something quieter: maybe just a shift in tone or rhetorical pitch. (Paterson 1999: xiv)

The other explicit expression of counterexpectancy, the 'astonished critics' in clause 6.2, also seems unusual for a couple of reasons. First, whereas the 'even' in clause 3 seems to relate to our (alleged) expectation that a great man would not be emotional and/or the fact that biographical researchers would write about this emotion, the counterexpectancy in 6.2 is not related directly to the construal of emotion in clause 6, but to the description of the object of that emotion, as is made very clear by the fact that the projecting clause 6.2 interrupts the first clause of the embedding, rather than projecting the main clause. The construal of counterexpectancy here seems distinctly odd: why would these characteristics of 'who', such as living at home and doing homely things, be cause for astonishment? This throws into relief the difference in quality between the items that have so far been grouped together as 'sources of information' – while 'researchers' and 'critics' in general might both be involved in the writing of a biography, the involvement of 'critics' seems less plausible and certainly both the content of their projection, and their overblown surprise at this content – as well as the fact that the researchers 'write' whereas the critics 'say' – marks the critics as being more towards the 'gossip' end of the spectrum of ways that one might communicate facts about another's life. Over the course of the sonnet, then, there is a shift in the quality of the 'sources of information'; from a named reference work in the title, to a cheap biography ('A shilling life') in clause 2, to the somewhat dubious 'researchers' in clause 3, to the outright gossipy 'critics' of clause 6.2.

The final source of counterexpectancy in the poem that will be discussed here has not been touched on at all so far, but relates to the construal of the object of a great man's affections as simply 'one who lived at home'. While the 'greatest figure of his day' is explicitly gendered, appearing in the poem as 'he', 'him' and 'his', the object of his affections is not explicitly gendered. Nor is 'who' implicitly gendered, as they might have been if they had been construed as knitting and baking, for example, or hunting and fishing, instead of pottering in the garden, doing small jobs around the house, and whistling. The lack of explicit gender in the sestet seems to play with what we might now call 'heteronormativity' – the assumption by most of society, even in current societies where sexuality is a much more open topic than it was in Auden's day, that if 'he' is weeping for the love of one who lives at home, that one is a woman. It is worth noting that while we could delve into Auden's own life and sexuality to discuss motivations for this lack of gender, this is not at all necessary: the absence of gender in the sestet is significant without such explanations, and operates as a demonstration of another failing of biographies and other communications about the facts of other's lives: that 'all the facts' are not knowable, or able to be told.

4.8. Conclusion

Thus the analysis of a sonnet – a close, systematic analysis of the language of a sonnet – brings us to the point, in the last section, where we were able to consider the patterning of patterns in the sonnet and how these contributed to the overarching Theme – the deepest level of meaning, in Hasan's terms. This Theme – the unknowability of facts about other's lives, and the necessary fallibility of sources that strive to tell us such facts – is a convenient point on which to conclude this chapter, because it is not just the crux of Auden's sonnet, nor just the crux of the analysis presented in this chapter, but in some ways the crux of all analyses such as these. As just noted in the last section, we do not need to make recourse to facts about Auden's life, or to literary criticism regarding Auden's works, in order to interpret the meanings of the poem – there is obviously a large body of late twentieth century literary and critical theory devoted to making this point, and there is not room to expand on it here (but Hasan does engage with some of this theory in Chapter 4 of *Linguistics, Language and Verbal Art*). Rather, as shown by Hasan, in her analysis of Murray's 'Widower in the Country' and many other analyses – and hopefully also in the analysis in this chapter – the meanings are available to us in the patterns of language (not just patterns of grammar, but patterns of meaning – of contrast – at every linguistic stratum) if we have a robust and coherent framework for analysing these patterns.

References

Fuller J. (Ed.) (2000). *The Oxford Book of Sonnets*. Oxford: Oxford University Press.

Halliday, M. A. K. (1964/2002). The linguistic study of literary texts. In H. Lunt (Ed.) *Proceedings of the Ninth International Congress of Linguistics*. Reprinted in J. J. Webster (Ed.) *Linguistic Studies of Text and Discourse. The Collected Works of M. A. K. Halliday, Vol. 2*, 5–22. London and New York: Continuum.

Halliday, M. A. K. (1971/2003). Linguistic function and literary style: An enquiry into the language of William Golding's `The Inheritors'. In S. Chatman (Ed.) *Literary Style: A Symposium*. London: Oxford University Press. Reprinted in J. J. Webster (Ed.) *Linguistic Studies of Text and Discourse. The Collected Works of M. A. K. Halliday, Vol. 2*, 88–125. London and New York: Continuum.

Halliday, M. A. K. (1994). *An Introduction to Functional Grammar*. 2nd ed. London: Arnold.

Halliday M. A. K. (1981/2002). Text semantics and clause grammar: How is a text like a clause? In J. J. Webster (Ed.), *On Grammar. Collected Works of M. A. K. Halliday, Vol. 1*, 219–260. London and New York: Continuum.

Halliday, M. A. K. (1987/2002). Poetry as scientific discourse: The nuclear sections of Tennyson's 'In Memoriam'. In J. J. Webster (Ed.) *Linguistic Studies of Text and Discourse. The Collected Works of M. A. K. Halliday, Vol. 2*, 149–168. London and New York: Continuum.

Halliday, M. A. K. (2014). *An Introduction to Functional Grammar*, rev. C. M. I. M. Matthiessen. 4th ed. London and New York: Routledge.

Hasan, R. (1985). *Linguistics, Language and Verbal Art*. Geelong: Deakin University Press.

Lukin, A. and Webster, J. (2005). Systemic functional linguistics and the study of literature. In R. Hasan *Continuing Discourse on Language*, 413–456. London: Equinox.

Martin J. R. (1992). *English Text: System and structure*. Philadelphia, PA and Amsterdam: John Benjamins. https://doi.org/10.1075/z.59

Martin, J. R., Matthiessen, C. M. I. M., and Painter, C. (1997). *Working with Functional Grammar*. London: Arnold.

Matthiessen C. M. I. M. (1995). *Lexicogrammatical Cartography*. Tokyo: International Language Sciences Publishers.

Paterson, D. (Ed.) (1999). *101 Sonnets from Shakespeare to Heaney*. London: Faber and Faber Limited.

Saussure de, F. (1916/1978). *Course in General Linguistics*. Edited by C. Bally and A. Sechehaye in collaboration with A. Riedlinger. Glasgow, Fontana: Collins.

5　Foregrounding and defamiliarization in Peter Carey's 'Conversations with Unicorns'

Martin Tilney[*]

5.1. Introduction

In a particularly revealing interview from 1977, fiction writer Peter Carey was asked how a reader should approach his stories, namely 'Conversations with Unicorns'. Carey replied:

> Well, I'd hope that the reader would approach them in a relaxed sort of way, hoping to be amused, or diverted. When he'd finished the story I'd hope he'd have found something new to think about. If I'd really done what I wanted to do he'd keep on thinking about the story for weeks, from time to time. If I was successful beyond my wildest dreams I would have given him (or her) something that would alter his (or her) perception of the world. (Ikin 1977: 38)

It is remarkable just how accurately Carey's comment seems to reflect the compelling nature of his short stories. Rubik (2005) has investigated the haunting effect of Carey's stories in terms of cognitive schemata and Coste (2003) has argued that the inherent ambiguity of 'Conversations with Unicorns' resists generic classification. A number of critical works mention the story (Ahearne 1980; Hassall 1994; Krstovic 2010; Pons 2001; Snodgrass

---

*　Martin Tilney is a PhD scholar at Macquarie University researching in the area of systemic functional linguistics and stylistics. Based in Australia, he has a background in literary studies and applied linguistics, specializing in TESOL. His research interests include literary stylistics, applied linguistics (EAP and critical discourse analysis), Australian literature, and language education. His current project focuses on systemic functional linguistics and the short fiction of Peter Carey.

2010; Turner 1988) but none deal with it in any significant amount of detail, and until now, there has been no attempt to conduct a stylistic reading of this fascinating and under-studied story. Approaching the text from a systemic functional perspective, I investigate the powerful aesthetic quality of the story in terms of prominent linguistic patterning occurring across various linguistic systems.

After outlining the development of foregrounding from Russian Formalism through to Prague School Structuralism and its culmination in Hasan's theory of foregrounding, I analyse Carey's text within Hasan's proposed framework. The results of this analysis suggest that the story defamiliarizes illusion in various ways. Finally, I conclude that by presenting an allegorical story about colonization and enlightenment, the author lays bare the illusions and lies that people live by on a daily basis. Discussing his stories, Carey once said, 'People often live in nightmares without knowing it. The nightmare creeps up on them and even when it's at its most intense it feels quite normal to them. Not nice, but normal. People come to accept their nightmares' (Ikin 1977: 33). Here, Carey seems to suggest that people tend to become unaware of unpleasantness in their lives through habitualization. 'Conversations with Unicorns' draws attention to the nightmare of colonial oppression that has become automatized over time.

5.2. Peter Carey's 'Conversations with Unicorns'

5.2.1. Background to the text

Carey is one of the most influential and innovative contemporary writers of fiction to emerge from Australia. To date, he has published 14 novels, four works of non-fiction, one children's book and two volumes of short stories. Carey is widely regarded as a postcolonial writer; many of his novels and stories explore the concept of colonialism, defined here as 'a label for the tendency of the settler populations … to disparage and exploit indigenous peoples' (Dominello 2001: 110). The story 'Conversations with Unicorns' is about colonialism, and was first published in a volume of short stories titled *The Fat Man in History* (Carey, 1974).

Carey is often identified with a generation of Australian authors known as the 'New Writers', who represented, as Kiernan (1977) points out, a self-conscious movement away from mimetic realism in Australian short fiction. Between 1958 and 1968 the Australian literary landscape was dominated by the realist novel. The writing of short stories, on the other hand, was regarded as an 'underground activity' (Clunies Ross 1981). By the mid-1960s writers such as Patrick White were challenging this tradition with short stories, and 'What had once seemed starkly realistic was beginning to look more like legend or dream' (Clunies Ross 1981: 166). It was this liberated perception of fiction that captured the imagination of a younger generation of writers who understood that prose fiction was capable of representing, as Clunies Ross points out, more than just common experience. Despite the popularity of their postmodernist American contemporaries, the New Writers were considered too alternative to be published in Australian literary magazines that were dominated by the 'Lawson gum-tree school' (Webby 1980) of realism in the 1970s.

The New Writers' movement away from conventional realism contextualizes Carey's preoccupation with the unreliability of history, which, he claims, is 'filled with denial and false consciousness' (Gaile 2005: 7). Carey's dissatisfaction with Australian history is addressed in many of his writings, perhaps most famously in the epigraph to his novel *Illywhacker*. He quotes Mark Twain's claim that Australian history 'does not read like history, but like the most beautiful lies … It is full of surprises and adventures, the incongruities, and contradictions, and incredibilities; but they are all true, they all happened' (Carey 1985: 19). While allegorical references to the real world are clear in some of Carey's novels, they are less certain in his short stories.

Carey's stories are often read as allegories of socio-political concerns and anxieties of Australian society in the 1970s. But as Bennett (2002) points out, the stories resist simple interpretation. Carey has admitted to deliberately obfuscating references to the real world in his fiction, mentioning 'a desire to locate the stories in places that cannot be immediately pinned down [...] simply so that I cannot be subjected to the trivial limitations placed upon me by geography or history or anthropology' (Ikin 1977: 37). Turner (1986: 434) also points out that 'Linkages [between non-realist forms and the real world] are rarely made systematically … but exist as correspondences with or inferences towards Australian society and mythology.' Even Carey claims that his stories are almost always relevant to the real world (Ahearne, Williams, and Brophy 1980). 'Conversations with Unicorns' is one such story, featuring a society of unicorns that are oppressed by an imperialist culture.

5.2.2. Unicorns and allegory

According to Strubel (1992), the history of unicorns in Western literature dates back to as early as the second century AD, when unicorns embodied Christian virtues in the Bible. Through the middle ages they came to represent various traits including strength, nobility and purity. In contemporary literature, unicorns retain some of these meanings but mostly symbolize the fantastic and the fabulous (Strubel 1992). The mythical value of the creatures conveniently allows Carey to endow them with an 'ambiguous immortality' (Hassall 1994: 22), just as in the works of Rainer Maria Rilke unicorns are 'infinite in time and space' (Strubel 1992: 1150). Carey's unicorns are also stubborn and unwilling to accept the ontological theories of an 'enlightened' outsider. The first-person narrator is from a colonial culture (the currency of British pounds and the specific type of colonial rifle reveal this) and the unicorns allegorically represent an unspecified subaltern other.[1] They do not have a specific real-world counterpart.

The story draws on other allegorical meanings. The naïve unicorns of the story consume milk and honey and live in caves. In Plato's famous allegory, he describes a group of people living in a cave, bound in such a way that they can only see the shadows of various objects created by firelight. Mistaking shadows for real objects, the prisoners, blind to reality, are content to live in an illusory world. The allusion to Plato is relevant in 'Conversations with Unicorns', in which the naturally immortal unicorns are unaware of the disturbing reality that they are hunted for sport by humans with guns. They do not know that the loud bang they hear when a unicorn dies is caused by guns, not God.

5.2.3. Synopsis of 'Conversations with Unicorns'

In the story, an unnamed narrator visits a community of unicorns and attempts to enlighten them about death in order to 'save' them. The male and female unicorns live in separate caves: a continuation of a tradition since 'heathen times' when according to legend, the unicorns were brought to the moor from a 'hot and strange land'. Unicorn trophies are lucrative and are greatly prized by industrialists, so the unicorns are shot by humans from behind 'the ridge' that separates the human and unicorn worlds. When a unicorn falls to the loud bang of a rifle, humans appear and remove the dead body. The religious unicorns believe that this removal is the rightful duty of humans; they believe that death is caused by God. During his first visit, the narrator is accused of blasphemy, attacked, and driven away. He is taken to a hospital by some hunters. Wounded but determined to accomplish his mission, he returns to the moor with a gun. He demonstrates the weapon to the unicorns, who remain unconvinced that it can kill. Eventually the unicorn leader named Moorav insists on being shot in order to prove the narrator wrong. At first, the narrator refuses, but Moorav claims not to be frightened of dying. The narrator shoots and kills Moorav, and the unicorns become silent and listless. The unicorn priest explains that the narrator has removed the 'gift of death' and also asks to be shot. The narrator loads his rifle, and the story ends. Finally, the narrator succeeds in enlightening the unicorns, but in doing so, imposes on them a foreign and irrelevant world view. The significance of this act of colonial violence is realized through the consistent foregrounding of various linguistic patterns.

5.3. Defamiliarization and foregrounding

Before continuing with my analysis of the text, I now outline some major developments in stylistic theory, beginning with foregrounding. The term foregrounding[2] is often thought to be central to many discussions of stylistics. The earliest roots of foregrounding, indeed of stylistics itself, date back to Classical poetics (see for example Burke 2014). Most discussions of foregrounding, however, begin with Russian Formalism. The Russian Formalists are often misunderstood as only having been interested in the 'form' of literature rather than meaning. They were a group of scholars who were active for roughly 15 years from around 1916 and were primarily interested in defining literariness as linguistic devices (techniques) that perform certain functions. Their aim was to differentiate literature from non-literature in terms of its raw material: language (Matejka and Pomorska 1971). By applying scientific methods to the analysis of verbal art, they addressed the question of whether the humanities could be considered a domain of science.

The rise of Russian Formalism is situated historically within the intellectual ferment and progressive thinking of the Russian Revolution. Early Formalist work by the likes of Viktor Shklovsky and Boris Eichenbaum established important conceptual foundations for stylistics. The term 'form' in the context of Formalism is often misinterpreted as an empty vessel that contains some kind of content. In fact, the Formalists were vehemently opposed to this idea. For them, form was the organizing principle of a work of art. 'The form of the work of literature is our own term for that totality of those of its elements which are capable of acting on our aesthetic sense (whether positively or negatively)' (Yarkho 1927, cited in O'Toole and Shukman 1977: 29).

The Formalists established that the correct object of study is not literature itself but literariness. No single device was characteristic of literature and different devices could share the same aesthetic function (Matejka and Pomorska 1971). In 'Art as technique' (1917), Shklovsky claimed that in everyday life, objects become habitualized so that people stop consciously noticing them. Thus, the purpose of art is to remove objects from this 'automatism of perception' by a process of defamiliarization (making the familiar seem strange). Shklovsky also posited that literature is like a machine, made up of various literary devices that manipulate form or highlight themselves in order to impede communication.

> The purpose of art is to impart the sensation of things as they are per-
> ceived and not as they are known. The technique of art is to make
> objects unfamiliar, to make forms difficult, to increase the difficulty
> and length of perception because the process of perception is an aes-
> thetic end in itself and must be prolonged. (Shklovsky 1917: 12)

Defamiliarization prefigured future developments in stylistics by establishing that art turns attention to the sign itself, or its own internal structure,
rather than its referent in reality. The Formalists also developed the idea
that there is no dichotomy between form and content; to change the form in
verbal art is to change the meaning. Hasan (1985: 91) echoes the Formalists
in her claim that in the study of verbal art, language 'is not as clothing to the
body; it is the body'.

With the influence of the Geneva school of linguistics and further important developments by Formalists including Roman Jakobson, the theory of
foregrounding was eventually developed by the Prague Linguistic Circle
(1926–1948). The Prague School structuralists extended the Formalist's conception of art to include not only a work's devices but also its function as
a whole system. Structure, in the context of Prague School poetics, is the
dynamic relationship between components in a work. A key member of the
Prague School was Jan Mukařovský, who saw poetic language as highlighted
against a background of standard language usage. For Mukařovský, automa-
tization is the schematization of an event, comparable to the 'automatism of
perception' mentioned by (Shklovsky 1917). Foregrounding, in contrast, is
the systematic violation of the scheme (Mukařovský 1932: 18).

Like the Formalist concept of defamiliarization, foregrounding draws attention to itself. Mukařovský claims that 'The esthetic gives man an ever renewed
awareness of the manifold and multivalued nature of reality, by making every
object in its power a center of attention for its own sake' (Mukařovský 1948:
33). The foregrounded element stands out against a background of the whole
system, and achieves maximum intensity when its self-reflexive expression
dominates other communicative functions. The background is simultaneously 'the norm of the standard language and the traditional esthetic canon'
(Mukařovský 1932: 22). Though both backgrounds are present at once, only
one of them is dominant at any given time.

Mukařovský recognized that the poetic function of language is more than
merely a sum of its foregrounded components. He claimed that in verbal art,
poetic language achieves maximum foregrounding when it demonstrates consistency and systematic character. The problem of defining such consistency
was addressed in later decades by linguists such as Leech (1965), Van Peer
(1986), Halliday (1971), and Hasan (1985). Unlike Mukařovský, Hasan did
not conceptualize foregrounding as the violation of an undefinable norm,

but as a contrast of linguistic patterning within the text. With recourse to the systemic functional model of language, Hasan proposed that the 'stability of semantic direction', comparable with Butt's (1983) 'semantic drift', is what is most important in foregrounding. In other words, relevant foregrounding that contributes to the artistic meaning of a work can occur through various formal realizations across different linguistic systems. Foregrounding theory has since been developed to include empirical literary studies (Van Peer, 1986; Miall and Kuiken, 1994; Van Peer, Zyngier, and Hakemulder, 2007) and cognitive stylistics (Stockwell, 2002; Shen, 2007). However, Hasan's earlier view of foregrounding allows the stylistician to elucidate the theme of a literature text without reliance on assumed mental processes that are involved in individual interpretation. Having thus outlined the literary and theoretical context of the story, I now turn to my analysis of the text. In this analysis, I will aim to show how a consistency of foregrounding is achieved through various instances of defamiliarization.

5.4. Text analysis

5.4.1. Tone

One of the most striking features of the text is its unique tone, which is achieved through its textual structure. Leech and Short (2007: 176) mention that complex sentences (composed of more than one clause) are 'to be preferred if the aim of the writer is to present us with a complex structure of ideas, a complex reading experience'. By extension, simple sentences (composed of a single clause) are generally used to construe simple ideas. In Carey's text, however, strange events and complex ideological conflict are expressed through simple sentences. The simplicity of the text is evident in the average length of the sentence. There are a total of 2,046 words, forming 122 sentences and 303 clauses in the text. This equates to an average of just 6.9 words per clause and 2.5 clauses per sentence. The text on average contains 16.8 words per sentence, which is shorter than the four authors studied by Leech and Short (2007) and shorter, even, than the average non-literature sentence (17.8 words) in the same study. As a result, the text achieves Carey's well-documented matter-of-fact tone, which contrasts with the bizarre fictional world that it conveys.

Further linguistic evidence for the simplicity of Carey's sentences can be seen in tactic and logico-semantic relations between clauses. Taxis, or degree of interdependency, is a relational structure between two clauses in a complex. The two functions of taxis are the 'linking' of clauses of equal status (parataxis) and the 'binding' of clauses of unequal status (hypotaxis).

The clause complexes in the text comprise 122 hypotactic (69.1%) and 56 paratactic (30.9%) relations.

Simultaneously, while being related tactically, the clauses within a complex are related logico-semantically, either through expansion or projection. Projection is the relation between locutions and ideas with the clauses that 'project' them. Expansion consists of three sub-types: elaboration (equals), extension (is added to), and enhancement (is multiplied by). The five types of logico-semantic relations are exemplified in the extract below, which highlight conflicting beliefs about death. The extract chosen is the opening of the story, which implies by virtue of homophoric reference that the unicorns being referred to are already known by the reader. This effectively brings the reader closer to the narrator, as there is a presupposition of familiarity through shared knowledge.

> (7) The unicorns do not understand. We have had long conversations (*expansion: extension*) but it is difficult for them. They insist (*projection: locution*) that I have come (*expansion: enhancement*) to collect the body of one of their number (*expansion: extension*) but at the same time they point out (*projection: locution*) that there is no body (*expansion: elaboration*) that it was collected by another man (*expansion: enhancement*) before I arrived. They continue to insist on these points (*expansion: elaboration*) laughing (*projection: locution*) that I have come for something that is not there.

As shown in Figure 5.1, the whole text contains 116 expansions (65.9%), of which 36 are elaboration (31 %), 47 are extension (40.5%) and 33 are enhancement (28.4%). Extension, which is the simplest type of enhancement, is the most common. Extension is typically construed by the word *and*. The relationship between clauses connected in this way is one of simple addition, contributing further to the unique tone. The conjunction *and* appears in thematic position 42 times, which is 62.7% of the total number of conjuncted Themes.

The hypotactic relations between clauses also demonstrate a strong preference for what Leech and Short (2007) describe as 'loose structure'. In a hypotactic clause complex, the independent clause construes the main information in the complex, while the dependent clause provides background. The order in which the clauses occur affects the meaning of the instance. When the hypotactic expansion trails the dominant clause in a thematically unmarked relation ($\alpha{\wedge}\beta$), the result is a looseness or lack of tension because the background information is presented at the end. 'Not surprisingly, loose structure is characteristic of a literary style which aims at natural simplicity and directness, rather than rhetorical effect' (Leech and

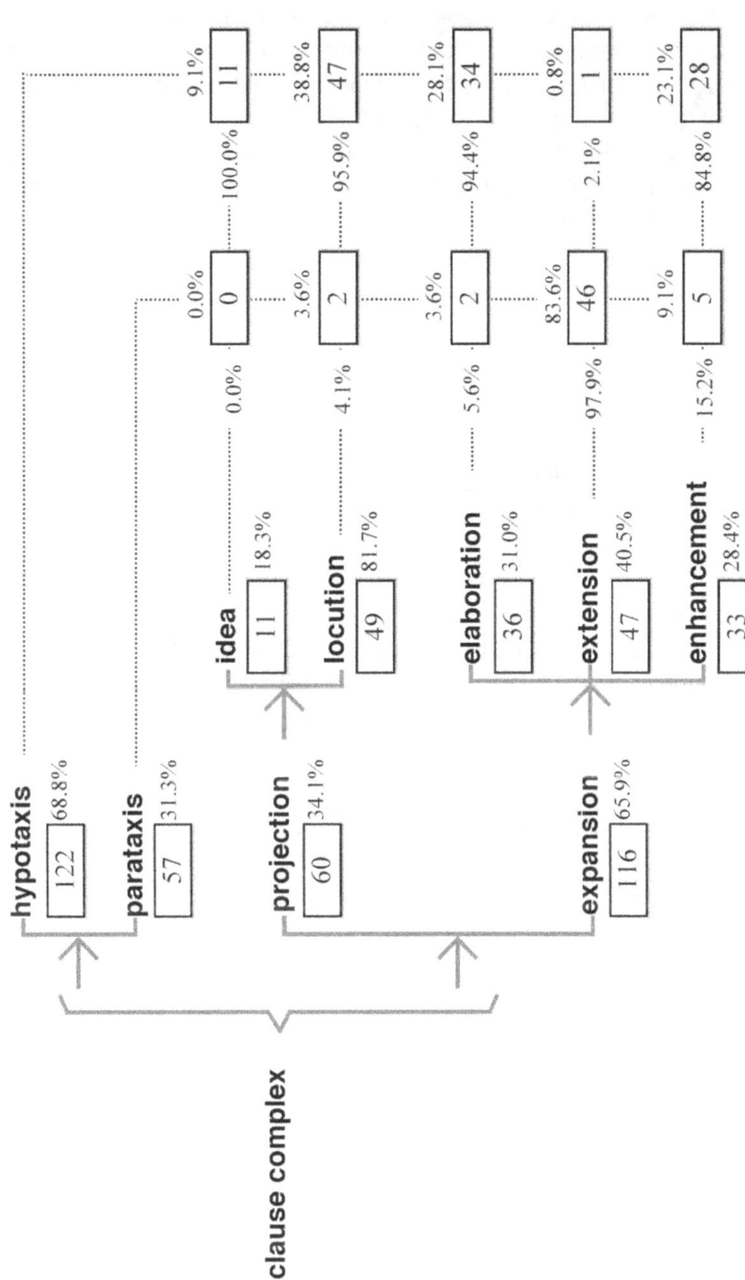

Figure 5.1: Tactic and Logico-Semantic Relations

Short 2007: 185). When the dependent element is not in final position (typically β^α or α<<β>>α, following standard systemic functional notation: see Halliday and Matthiessen 2004: 392), this thematically marked choice creates suspense because the subordinate information needs to be kept in mind until it is later resolved by the independent clause. Leech and Short (2007) call this device 'periodic structure'.

The overwhelming majority of hypotactic relations between clauses have loose structure. Of the 121 instances of hypotaxis, only 12 (9.9%) have the subordinate clause in non-final position. This includes parenthetical interrupting clauses. The preference for loose structure construes a sense of directness and simplicity in the narrator's tone, against which periodic structures are foregrounded.

Clause ID	*Clause*	*SFL analysis*
7.1	The men *they say* cannot be held responsible for the death of unicorns	α<<"β>>α
9.1	But they have no knowledge of guns, or *it turns out*, of weapons of any sort	α<<=β>>α
15.1	*When I return to the subject of guns* the unicorns laugh	xβ^α
19.1	God, *he informs me*, bestowed upon the unicorns (*and I use his exact words*) the gift of death	α<<"β>>α
24.3	and that God, *should he have any appearance at all*, would be most likely to have the appearance of a unicorn	α<<xβ>>α
31.1	(I say) *that if there is a God*, he certainly doesn't use a gun	xβ^α
40.1	*Mistaking this for a request*, they bring me a meal of wild honey brown bread and milk	=β^α
64.1	They also, *it would appear*, have become disenchanted with me	α<<=β>>α
73.2	*and unaware of my missionary activities*, treated me kindly	xβ^α
91.1	The bang, *they said*, was in no way like the bang of death	1<<"2>>1
101.3	I engaged in no calculations, for I knew that, *should I do so*, I would never prove my point	α<<xβ>> α
118.5	*and should he put his authority to the test*, they would not obey him	xβ^α

Table 5.1: Instances of Periodic Structure

Table 5.1 shows that periodic structure foregrounds certain notions, namely death, weapons, God, the narrator's condition after being attacked, and the breakdown of the unicorns' social structure. The most significant instance of foregrounding is the narrator's justification for shooting Moorav (101.3) because this is the act of colonial violence that is central to the story. The foregrounded structures in the table highlight key events in the plot and the ideological clash from which they derive and the narrator, through these choices, distances himself from the adverse impact of his actions.

5.4.2. Defamiliarization of setting

Despite the discursive implication of familiarity, the temporal and spatial location of the story world is unstable. This indeterminacy is linked to the function of deixis:[3] the semantic dependence on context. Definite reference is a predominant feature of the text, yet it is often the case that the referent is not identifiable. Halliday and Hasan (1976: 71) point out that 'The definite article has no content. It merely indicates that the item in question IS specific and identifiable; that somewhere the information necessary for identifying it is recoverable.' The information needed to resolve the definite item is either endophoric (cohesive) or exophoric (deictic). The function of exophoric reference differs according to whether the situation is specific or non-specific. If the identifying situation is non-specific, it implies that the addressee shares the addresser's knowledge of the world. This reference is called homophora, and is used aesthetically in the story. The use of the definite article *the* in *the cave* implies that the reader is familiar with *which* cave is being referred to. Similarly, other homophoric landmarks are *the ridge, the North knoll, the South knoll,* and *the moor.* In the following extract, homophoric reference creates the impression that the spatial location can be assumed to be known.

> (1) So I describe for them *the deep trench* that runs across the top of *the ridge.*

The attempt to resolve *the deep trench* ends with *the ridge,* which is also an instance of unresolved homophoric reference. Just as the text is spatially disorienting, it cannot be located in time. The references to cars and specific weapons suggest that the story could take place from as early as the last two decades of the nineteenth century, with the first patented motor car appearing in 1886 and the Lee Enfield rifle officially adopted by British and Commonwealth armies around 1888. However, the temporal setting is only vaguely familiar. The only indications of temporal location are present in certain grammatical systems.

The Theme[4] is a function in the clause structure 'which locates and orients the clause within its context' (Halliday and Matthiessen 2004: 64). The topical Theme of a clause is the departure point for presenting new information, and is defined as ending 'with the first constituent that is either participant, circumstance, or process' (Halliday and Matthiessen 2004: 79). An unmarked Theme, then, is one in which the topical Theme is conflated with the Subject of the clause, whereas a 'marked' Theme is one in which Subject and topical Theme are not the same entity. An example of unmarked Theme would be *The unicorns* in *The unicorns do not understand*. The text demonstrates an almost exclusive preference for unmarked Themes, which make up 257 (95.5%) of all instances. Of these unmarked Themes, over 70% of them are represented by animate participants in the story world, rather than spatial and temporal Circumstances.

The text has just 12 instances (4.5%) of marked Themes, which are highly foregrounded. Of these only five out of 12 are locative, with one Circumstance of place and four of time.

(2)   He tells me then *how in the early days* (Theme: temporal) the unicorns lived for ever

(3)   *At this point* (Theme: temporal) I find myself pinned on two sides by young unicorns

(4)   *Upon my release*, (Theme: temporal) my right leg in plaster and my ribs securely taped, I returned to the moor

(5)   *After the meal* (Theme: temporal) I persuaded them to come with me to the door of the cave

(6)   *Inside the cave* (Theme: locative) the unicorns lie quietly

Only examples 3, 4, and 5 above relate to the temporal dimension of the narrated story, none of which provide a stable temporal reference. The remaining Circumstances homophorically refer to a mythical time before the time of the narration (2) and the location of the unicorns' final resignation (6), neither of which can be resolved in the text. The foregrounded instability of time and place reinforces the allegorical quality of the story and defamiliarizes the reality of the story world.

5.4.3. Defamiliarization of neutrality

In any narrative text, the reader gains access to the fiction through the narrator. As a result, the values of the first person narrator are assumed to be shared by the reader (Leech and Short 2007). Although the tone suggests that the story is a neutral report, the narrator's personal values are foregrounded through various linguistic choices.

In past tense narration, the temporal distance between the occurrence of the event and the subsequent narration of that event is highlighted. On the other hand, present tense narration conveys an immediacy and directness that reads like the bare statement of fact, as if the reader were experiencing the events of the fictional world unfolding in real time. In discussions of tense switching in verbal narratives, Toolan (1988) refers to the present tense as 'the tense of direct experience' because it brings the reader discursively closer to the events being narrated. Carey's text switches between present and past tense, but the predominant choice is the present tense, comprising 61.9% of all free clauses. Most of the theological conversations are narrated in the present tense, but significantly, the shooting of Moorav is narrated in the past tense, effectively distancing the narrator from Moorav's death.

Yet another linguistic feature of the text that reveals the narrator's point of view is foregrounded modality. Modality is the area of meaning between positive and negative polarity, which opens up a space for ontological negotiation. In the system of modality, 'modalization' navigates the space between probability and usuality while 'modulation' spans the poles of obligation and inclination (Halliday and Matthiessen 2004).

Of the 303 clauses in the text, there are only eight instances of modality: four of probability and four of obligation. The rare modality in the text centres around the narrator and his perception of the events being narrated.

The modalization identified in Table 5.2 is concerned with the narrator successfully completing his task of 'enlightening' the unicorns (75.1, 75.2). The resulting rejection of authority within the unicorn society is modalized in 118.6, as well as the priest's 'enlightened' attitude towards death in 120.1. Whether a missionary, an anthropologist, or a lunatic, the narrator claims that his actions are performed with the best of intentions. Apart from the two rank-shifted instances of modulation (21.3, 21.4) the only obligations are for the unicorns to protect themselves (28.2) and for the narrator not to be surprised by the unicorns' 'ignorant' and violent responses to his preaching (77.2).

The lack of modality construes an emotional detachment in the story, which distances the narrator from the events he narrates. It also contributes to the neutral tone that is central to the text. To return to the discussion of hypotactic enhancement, the most frequently occurring enhancing relation in the text is concessive, with nine instances (27.3%). Table 5.3 shows that the concessive enhancements foreground the unicorns' lack of knowledge in 24.5 and 38.2, as well as their silence and fear following the death of Moorav, in 111.2 and 118.3. Clearly, this foregrounded clash of ideologies is significant.

Clause ID	Clause	Status	Modality Analysis
21.3	that the males *should live* together in the caves on the North Knoll	Rank-shifted	Obligation: Positive: Median: Implicit: Subjective
21.4	and the females ^*should live* in the caves on the South Knoll	Rank-shifted	Obligation: Positive: Median: Implicit: Subjective
28.2	that they *should guard* themselves against the men	Bound	Obligation: Positive: Median: Implicit: Subjective
75.1	I *would demonstrate* to the unicorns the nature of the gun	Free	Probability: Positive: Median: Subjective
75.2	and with luck ^*I would arrange* for them to make an exodus from the area to some remote part of the moor	Free	Probability: Positive: Median: Subjective
77.2	and I *could expect* no more	Free	Obligation: Positive: Low: Subjective
118.6	they *would not obey* him	Free	Probability: Positive: Median: Subjective
120.1	He *would regard* it as a great favour	Free	Probability: Positive: Median: Subjective

Table 5.2: Modality

Clause ID	Clause
24.5	*although* he [the priest] was no expert in these matters
27.2	*but* this only increases my desire to protect them from the wealthy industrialists who come
38.2	*although* the lion is described in one of their legends
44.2	*although* I stated, explicitly
68.2	*but* not caused by pain
88.2	*but* I was insistent
103.2	*but* then with the unicorns behind me still laughing, I pulled the trigger
111.2	*but* ^THEY do not talk
118.3	*but* they are frightened

Table 5.3: Concessive enhancing relations

Clauses 27.2, 88.2, and 103.2 all construe the narrator's attempts to justify his decision to shoot Moorav. Here, the foregrounded concession confirms his good intentions, his persistence, and the ridicule he faces while trying to prove his point. Clause 44.2 demonstrates an instance of communication breakdown. In each case, the hypotactic *but* clause means that the process that occurred was contrary to expectation. Thus, despite all the challenges the narrator faces, he appears determined to 'save' the unicorns from death.

In addition to a distinct lack of modality, the text also displays a lack of mood Adjuncts. A count reveals that there are four instances of *perhaps*, three of *still*, two of *always*, and one each of *almost, at all, certainly, eventually, ever, greatly, in fact, in no way, never, now, now surely*, and *surely*. There is largely no preference established for the choice of mood Adjunct in the text, except for the word *only*, which appears seven times. In systemic functional terms, *only* has the function of construing counterexpectancy (see Table 5.4).

Clause ID	*Clause*
5.3	that I could *only* have come for one reason
16.3	that *only* God has the power to take life
25.5	this is *only* natural
27.2	but this *only* increases my desire to protect them from the wealthy industrialists…
47.2	that I am *only* concerned [for their safety]
94.3	that we should *only* settle the matter

Table 5.4: Counterexpectancy

In Table 5.4, 16.3, 25.2 and 94.3 are concerned with the unicorns' religious beliefs about death. All of the other examples are about the narrator's justification to protect the unicorns from the so-called 'gift' of death by ironically killing the unicorn leader. By choosing *only*, the narrator counters the expectancy for the reader to doubt his good intentions, constructing a favourable self-image in a seemingly neutral report of events.

5.4.4. Defamiliarization of facts

The story is told by a homodiegetic narrator-observer in the first person, which draws attention to the narrator's reliability (Murphy 2012). Unlike third person narration, omniscience cannot be assumed for such a narrator. However, the unusual conversations and events of the story are told with 'a matter-of-fact tone' and 'a controlled treatment of suggestive, seemingly bizarre detail' by 'a narrator whose character is as ambiguous and shadowy as his experience is immediate and compelling' (Wilde, Hooton, and Andrews 1985: 145). In effect, the reader is obliged to adopt the narrator's point of view even if his trustworthiness is questionable. The narrator-protagonist is the focal character and 'knower' in the story; he is also the medium through which the reader can access the fictional world. The nameless narrator, despite his apparent proximity to the reader, is not identifiable. He reveals nothing about himself except for, at the level of discourse, an assumed intellectual superiority and claim to philanthropy. He is indeed a 'shadowy' narrator, as Wilde, Hooton, and Andrews (1985) point out, relaying assumptions about the unicorns as facts. The action of knowing is typically construed through mental Processes, but these make up only 8.5% of the processes in the text. This is an unusual choice, given that the story is concerned with the beliefs of the characters.

The unicorns are consistently portrayed by the narrator as ignorant and unknowing. Consider the following sentences that convey this:

(8)   The unicorns *do not understand*
(9)   We have had long conversations but *it is difficult for them*
(10) I mention guns. But *they have no knowledge* of guns or, it turns out, of weapons of any sort
(11) They *have no idea* of the nature of cars or of their purpose
(12) The unicorns are *beginning to appear stupid* to me
(13) Most of these animals, however, *are unknown to them*
(14) Their accents, at first pleasant, *seem to have become more rustic and so more stupid*

In most of the examples above (8, 9, 10, 11, 13), the narrator assumes superiority over the unicorns by declaring his observations as facts. The narrator also blocks direct access to his own inner world by expressing pain and emotion indirectly:

(15) *There are tears in my eyes*, but not caused by pain
(16) *There is a searing pain* in my side *and a dull blow* to my head

The above examples are significant because they blur the line between objective reality and sensory perception, thus disturbing the status of reality in the story world.

5.4.5. Defamiliarization of non-accountability

Despite the narrator's apparent philanthropy, certain textual choices reveal how he downplays his responsibility for the death of Moorav. It has been shown earlier (Figure 5.1) that 60 clauses (34.1%) are projections. Of these, only 11 (18.3%) are ideas and 49 (81.7%) are locution. Speaking, therefore is the dominant form of projection, which is not surprising given that the title contains the word 'conversations'. However, the text is a controlled monologue, with all instances of locution verbalized through the narrator. The narrator almost exclusively uses indirect speech, or hypotactic projection for presenting speech in the text. Through statistical analysis of a corpus of spoken texts, Nesbitt and Plum (1988) demonstrate that the occurrence of hypotactic locution is a marked form, since verbal clauses are most commonly construed through paratactic projection (direct speech). Direct speech is also confirmed as the unmarked choice in literature texts by Leech and Short (2007). In the text, Carey does not use inverted commas to mark speech, which as Leech and Short (2007) note, causes speech and narrative to run together. This is yet another device that creates the illusion of objectivity. There are only three clauses of direct speech in the whole story:

> (17) I say, *I have only come here to save you from death. I did not come to discuss theology, only facts.*

Although inverted commas have been omitted, the first sentence is a clear case of direct speech because the deictic *here* and the personal pronoun *you* clearly position the narrator as the direct addressor to the unicorns. The following sentence is also most likely direct speech due to its proximity to the previous instance, although its independent status as a clause further blurs the distinction between speech and narration. The highly foregrounded locution is consistent with other foregrounding I have highlighted in this chapter. The narrator draws attention to the category of speech presentation in which the speaker is held accountable for his words, and in this case the narrator's apparent philanthropy and rationality is highlighted. In addition to the basic indirect and direct speech structures, there are at least three other forms of speech presentation, which are described in Leech and Short (2007): the narrative report of speech acts (NRSA), free direct speech (FDS) and free indirect speech (FIS). The authors argue that FDS and NRSA are opposite poles on the cline of interference (see Figure 5.2). In other words, the narrator has no apparent control over an FDS report, but apparently has a large deal of control over an NRSA, which is closest to the mode of bare narration (the narrative report of action). Note that speech presentation need not be a verbal process, as in the following examples of FIS:

> (18) *There will be a return to the old times, and no one will die. The unicorns, without Gods or enemies, will slowly sink into a deep despair, and spend their hours in search of sleep, where, perhaps they will dream of dying. They will forget, eventually, that dying was ever possible.*

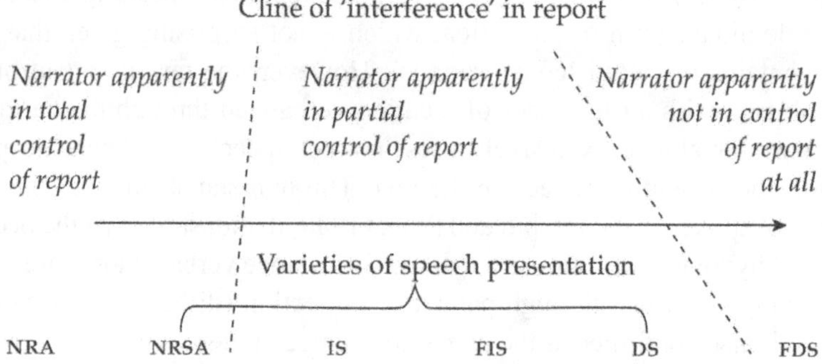

Figure 5.2: Cline of Interference. Reproduced from Leech and Short (2007: 260)

Here, the subjective voice of the narrator becomes blurred with an objective statement about the future. Free indirect discourse is a topic of considerable theoretical discussion in stylistics (see, for example Banfield 1982; Sotirova 2007; Short 2012), but I shall limit my discussion here to a brief overview of the speech presentation categories.

Table 5.5 shows the narrator's preference for IS and NRSA, revealing the extent of his control over the narrative. Every utterance is mediated through him so that individual speakers are hardly ever allowed to speak for themselves. Out of a total of 99 non-rankshifted clauses analysed here, there are 35 NRSA and 45 IS categories. In other words, 80.9% of all speech categories are the two most controlled types. On this level, the story demonstrates the power relationships inherent in colonial contact, with the colonizer exerting power over the subaltern other by controlling their voices. There is only one example of free direct speech, in which Moorav encourages the narrator to shoot him. The narrator appears to avoid responsibility for the reported utterance.

Speech Presentation Type	*Count*	*%*
NRSA	35	35.4
IS	45	45.5
FIS	11	11.1
DS	3	3
FDS	1	1
Ambiguous	4	4
TOTAL	99	100

Table 5.5: Overview of speech presentation

> (19) He said, it was only the unicorns in pagan times who did not die,
> *I am not frightened of dying.*

This single instance of FDS contrasts sharply with the dominant choice of controlled speech presentations. The first-person pronoun *I* in *I am not frightened* refers to Moorav. The present tense indicates that he is speaking directly but the clause is free from a projecting verb. This sentence emphasises Moorav's insistence to be shot, allowing the narrator to distance himself from the tragedy that silenced and displaced a whole community. The narrator thus constructs a pretence of innocence and non-accountability which contrasts with his appearance as the knower and hero.

5.5. Conclusion

In this analysis a number of tensions between predominant and foregrounded linguistic patterns have been identified. Locating these foregrounded patterns within various systems of language, I have attempted to demonstrate how a sense of familiarity is disturbed by laying bare the techniques used to represent the story world. From the very first sentence, the reader is thrust into a strange fictional reality without explanation. The reader is assumed to be familiar with the story world, but its spatial and temporal instability has an opposite, defamiliarizing effect. Through certain choices in tense and point of view, the reader takes on the perspective of an unreliable narrator-observer, who reports with a factual tone and claims to have knowledge that only an omniscient narrator would be privy to. Despite his fallibility, he controls the narration very closely, particularly by preventing the unicorns from speaking for themselves and presenting his observations as facts. At the same time, the narrator distances himself from his crucial act of colonial violence that devastates the community. A pretence of truth and a claim to humanity are upheld by the narrator, yet upon examining consistently foregrounded linguistic patterns, it becomes clear that the apparent reality of the story world is a clever fabulation, much like the 'beautiful lies' of Australian history.

The story is a colonial allegory, but through the lens of defamiliarization, it can also be viewed as a comment on the power of lies. The unicorns live in an illusory world, oblivious to the higher level of reality. The unicorns' understanding of death is based on a lie, perhaps one told to them long ago to ensure easy hunting. As the reader recognizes the instability of the unicorns' reality, he or she may also notice the power of lies at work in the real world, perhaps reflecting on the nature of neutrality, fact, and accountability in the stories that inform society. Although there is no definite allegorical link between Carey's fictional world and the real world, the artistic utilization of linguistic devices in the text may prompt the reader to think about the 'beautiful lies' of Australian history, particularly the oppression of certain people by more technologically advanced cultures. It is my view that this disturbing recognition is the artistic success of 'Conversations with Unicorns': the aesthetic effect that has the power to make the reader continue to think about the story from time to time. Since Carey's interview in 1977, he has indeed achieved a remarkable level of literary success. As Carey once suggested, perhaps it is because his stories, through the skilful patterning of language, have the ability to alter our perceptions of the world.

Notes

1. The term *subaltern*, coined by Antonio Gramsci, is used in the context of post-colonial studies (see Ashcroft, Griffith, and Tiffins 2007).
2. The original Czech term used by Mukařovský is *aktualisace*. The common term *foregrounding* comes from Garvin's (1964) translation. Other translators such as Galan (1985) and O'Toole and Shukman (1977) use the term *actualization*
3. The term *deixis* is here used in the sense of endophoric reference (Halliday and Hasan 1976) as a textual function and not as the interpretation of a referred entity as in cognitive stylistics.
4. Note the distinction between lower-case *theme* as the 'deepest' meaning of a literature text (Hasan 1985) and capitalized *Theme* as functional label.

References

Ahearne, K. (1980). Peter Carey and short fiction in Australia. *Going Down Swinging* 1: 7–17.

Ahearne, K., Williams, S., and Brophy, K. (1980). An interview with Peter Carey. *Going Down Swinging* 1: 43–55.

Ashcroft, B., Griffiths, G., and Tiffin, H. (2007). *Post-Colonial Studies: The Key Concepts*. 2nd ed. London: Routledge.

Banfield, A. (1973). Narrative style and the grammar of direct and indirect speech. *Foundations of Language* 10: 1–39.

Bennett, B. (2002). *Australian Short Fiction: A History*. St Lucia: University of Queensland Press.

Burke, M. (2014). Rhetoric and poetics: The classical heritage of stylistics. In M. Burke (Ed.) *The Routledge Handbook of Stylistics*, 11–26. Abingdon: Routledge.

Butt, D. G. (1983). Semantic 'Drift' in verbal art. *Australian Review of Applied Linguistics* 6 (1): 38–48. https://doi.org/10.1075/aral.6.1.04but

Carey, P. (1974/1994). *The Fat Man in History*. St Lucia: University of Queensland Press.

Carey, P. (1985). *Illywhacker*. London: Faber.

Clunies Ross, B. A. (1981). Some developments in short fiction, 1969–1980. *Australian Literary Studies* 10 (2): 165–180. https://doi.org/10.20314/als.e9a2780eb9

Coste, D. (2003). Peter Carey's 'Conversations with Unicorns': Allegory, Metafiction and Parable. Unpublished Manuscript.

Dominello, F. (2001). Colonialism. In T. Blackshield, M. Coper, and G. Williams (Eds) *The Oxford Companion to the High Court of Australia*, 110–113. Oxford: Oxford University Press.

Gaile, A. (2005). The 'Contrarian Streak': An Interview with Peter Carey. In A. Gaile (Ed.) *Fabulating Beauty: Perspectives on the Fiction of Peter Carey*, 3–16. Amsterdam: Rodopi.

Galan, F. W. (1985). *Historic Structures: The Prague School Project, 1928–1946*. Austin, TX: University of Texas Press.

Garvin, P. L. (1964). *A Prague School Reader on Esthetics, Literary Structure and Style*. (Trans. and Ed. P. L. Garvin). Washington, DC: Georgetown University Press.

Halliday, M. A. K. (1971/2003). Linguistic function and literary style: An enquiry into the language of William Golding's 'The Inheritors'. In S. Chatman (Ed.) *Literary Style: A Symposium*. London: Oxford University Press. Reprinted in J. J. Webster (Ed.) *Linguistic Studies of Text and Discourse. The Collected Works of M. A. K. Halliday, Vol. 2*, 88–125. London/New York: Continuum.

Halliday, M. A. K. and Hasan, R. (1976). *Cohesion in English*. London: Longman.

Halliday, M. A. K. and Matthiessen, C. M. I. M. (2004). *An Introduction to Functional Grammar*. 3rd ed. London: Arnold.

Hasan, R. (1979). 'Workshop report No. 6: Language in the study of literature. *Working Conference on Language in Education: Report to Participants*, University of Sydney.

Hasan, R. (1985). *Linguistics, Language and Verbal Art*. Geelong: Deakin University Press.

Hassall, A. J. (1994). *Dancing on Hot Macadam: Peter Carey's Fiction*. St Lucia: University of Queensland Press.

Ikin, V. (1977). Answers to seventeen questions: An interview with Peter Carey. *Science Fiction: A Review of Speculative Literature* 1 (1): 30–39.

Kiernan, B. (1977). Introduction. In B. Kiernan (Ed.) *The Most Beautiful Lies: A Collection of Stories by Five Major Contemporary Fiction*

Writers: Bail, Carey, Lurie, Moorhouse and Wilding, ix–xv. Sydney: Angus and Robertson.

Krstovic, J. (2010). 'Peter Carey.' *Short Story Criticism* 133 (2010): 1–72.

Leech, G. (1965/2008). 'This Bread I Break' – Language and interpretation. In *Language in Literature: Style and Foregrounding*, 28–36. Abingdon: Taylor & Francis.

Leech, G, and Short, M. (2007). *Style in Fiction: A Linguistic Introduction to English Fictional Prose*. 2nd ed. New York: Longman.

Matejka, L., and Pomorska, K. (1971). *Readings in Russian Poetics: Formalist and Structuralist Views*. Chicago, IL: Dalkey Archive Press.

Miall, David, and Kuiken, D. (1994). Foregrounding, defamiliarization, and affect: Response to literary stories. *Poetics* 22: 389–407. https://doi.org/10.1016/0304-422X(94)00011-5

Mukařovský, J. (1932/1964). Standard language and poetic language. In P. R. Garvin (Ed.) *A Prague Reader on Esthetics, Literary Structure, and Style*, 17–30. Washington, DC: Georgetown University Press.

Mukařovský, J. (1948/1964). The esthetics of language. In P. L. Garvin (Ed.) *A Prague School Reader on Esthetics, Literary Structure and Style*, 31–69. Washington, DC: Georgetown University Press.

Murphy, T. P. (2012). Defining the reliable narrator: The marked status of first-person fiction. *Journal of Literary Semantics* 41 (1): 67–87. https://doi.org/10.1515/jls-2012-0004

Nesbitt, C. and Plum, G. (1988). Probabilities in a systemic-functional grammar: The clause complex in English. In R. P. Fawcett and D. Young (Eds) *New Developments in Systemic Linguistics. Theory and Application*, 2: 6–38. Open Linguistics Series. London: Pinter.

O'Toole, L. M. and Shukman, A. (Eds) (1977). *Russian Poetics in Translation, Volume 4: Formalist Theory*. Oxford: Holdan Books Ltd.

Pons, X. (2001). Weird tales: Peter Carey's short stories. In J. Bardolph (Ed.) *Telling Stories: Postcolonial Short Fiction in English*, 391–407. Amsterdam: Rodopi.

Rubik, M. (2005). Provocative and unforgettable: Peter Carey's short fiction: A cognitive approach. *European Journal of English Studies* 9: 169–184.

Shen, Y. (2007). Foregrounding in poetic discourse: between deviation and cognitive constraints. *Language and Literature* 16 (2): 169–181. https://doi.org/10.1177/0963947007075983

Shklovsky, V. (1917/1965). Art as technique. In L. T. Lemon and M. J. Reis (Eds) *Russian Formalist Criticism: Four Essays*, 3–24. Lincoln, NE: University of Nebraska Press.

Short, M. (2012). Discourse presentation and speech (and writing, but not thought) summary. *Language and Literature* 21 (18): 18–32. https://doi.org/10.1177/0963947011432049

Snodgrass, M. E. (2010). *Peter Carey: A Literary Companion*. Jefferson, LA: McFarland and Company.

Sotirova, V. (2007). Speech and thought presentation: Historical transformations of free indirect style.' In D. Hoover and S. Lattig (Eds) *Stylistics: Prospect & Retrospect*, 129–141. Amsterdam: Rodopi.

Stockwell, Peter. (2002). *Cognitive Poetics: An Introduction*. London: Routledge.

Strubel, A. (1992). The Unicorn. In P. Brunel (Ed.) *Companion to Literary Myths, Heroes and Archetypes*, 1145–1150. London: Routledge.

Toolan, M. (1988). *Narrative: A Critical Linguistic Introduction*. London: Routledge.

Turner, G. (1988). Science fiction, parafiction, and Peter Carey. *Science Fiction: A Review of Speculative Literature* 10 (1): 15–21.

Turner, G. (1986). American dreaming: The fictions of Peter Carey. *Australian Literary Studies* 12 (4): 431–441. https://doi.org/10.20314/als.942c65340d

Van Peer, W. (1986). *Stylistics and Psychology: Investigations of Foregrounding, Croom Helm Linguistics Series*. London: Croom Helm.

Van Peer, W, Zyngier, S., and Hakemulder, J. (2007). Foregrounding: Past, present, future. In D. Hoover and S. Lattig (Eds) *Stylistics: Prospect & Retrospect*, 1–22. Amsterdam: Rodopi.

Webby, E. (1980). The long march of short fiction: A seventies retrospective. *Meanjin* 39 (1): 127–133.

Wilde, W. H., Hooton, J., and Andrews, B. (1985). *The Oxford Companion to Australian Literature*. Oxford: Oxford University Press.

6 Simone de Beauvoir's construal of language and literature in *Mémoires d'une jeune fille rangée* (1958): A Hasanian perspective

Alice Caffarel-Cayron[*]

> En hommage à Ruqaiya Hasan
> 'If language can be used to defend a reality, then by the same token,
> it can be used to examine the very reality created by it'
> (Hasan 199:34)

6.1. Introduction

This chapter retraces Simone de Beauvoir's experience with language and literature from childhood to adulthood as it is construed in the first volume of her memoirs *Mémoires d'une jeune fille rangée* (1958).[1] Using Systemic Functional Linguistics (SFL), it explores transitivity patterns in passages where Beauvoir talks about her experience of/with literature. It focuses in particular on experiential roles assigned both to literature and to Beauvoir as she interacts with literature. It also explores the processes in which literature and Beauvoir are involved. The aim is to show that Beauvoir's view of literature as an activity and a tool for change in the world is reflected in

---

[*] Alice Caffarel-Cayron has been teaching French and Linguistics in the Department of French Studies since 1996. Her main research interests are the grammar and semantics of French, Discourse analysis, stylistics and language typology. She has developed a systemic functional description of the grammar of French that she has applied to the teaching of French, linguistics, discourse analysis and stylistics in the Department of French Studies. Her *Systemic Functional Interpretation of French Grammar* was first published by Continuum in 2006 and republished as paperback in 2008. She is currently conducting research on the language of Simone de Beauvoir and the impact her writings had on readers.

her choice of linguistic patterns. In addition, the analysis reveals the growth of Beauvoir from a child with a passion for books to a writer who would become one of the most influential of the twentieth century. Hasan's (1985) model for the analysis of verbal art serves as point of departure to our analysis and gives us the means to discuss how the Theme of language as action is symbolically articulated by foregrounded experiential patterns in Beauvoir's memoires. Abstracts from letters to Simone de Beauvoir after the publication of the *Mémoires* will serve to illustrate its impact on readers.

Je me suis mise à lire et c'est captivant dès la première page. Sincère, et objectif cependant. Cela m'émerveille que l'on puisse être aussi près de ses sensations d'enfance et les avoir maitrisées, les voir du dehors, sans qu'elles perdent rien de leur acuité. Justement je pensais ces temps-ci que l'on a trop tendance à voir la jeunesse moderne comme un « phénomène social », en dehors, et cela ne nous apprend rien. C'est l'aventure intérieur qui compte: la vôtre, située dans une époque certes, vaut pour tous les temps. Et je me sens proche de vous par les réactions, et cela aidera aussi tant d'autres, cette conquête personnelle d'une liberté. [reader writing to S de B about the Mémoires: 5/11/58][2]

[Your memoirs were captivating from the first page. Sincere, but also objective. It amazes me that someone can be so in touch with their experience of childhood, have mastered it, considered it from a distance, and then succeed in not sacrificing any of the beauty or intensity of its description. I feel that these days we reflect on modern youth only from the exterior, as a social phenomenon, which teaches us nothing. It's the internal experience, which has value, and yours, although it is clearly situated in a specific era, has eternal value. I feel close to you as a result of your interpretation, and I'm sure your conquest of a personal freedom will help many others.]

Simone de Beauvoir was one of the most influential intellectuals of the twentieth century who through her various writings in multiple genres such as novels, memoirs and essays conveyed her experience and vision of the world. In 'La Force de l'âge' she wrote:

Whether it is a question of a novel, an autobiography, an essay, an historical work or no matter what, the writer attempts to set up communication with others by means of the uniqueness of his personal experience; his work must make the existence of his experience evident and it must bear the mark of that experience – and it is by means of his style, his tone of voice and his rhythm that he communicates his experience to his work. No particular kind of writing is on

> *the face of it privileged; none is condemned.* (Beauvoir, 1974, 115;
> translated by Patrick O'Brian)

Beauvoir's view on literary language and verbal art as a particular use of language, or style that can cut across genres is very pertinent and resonates with many ideas about language that systemic functional linguistics (SFL) encapsulate.

In the Introduction to 'Simone de Beauvoir: The making of an intellectual woman', Toril Moi (1994, 4) writes:

> The intertextual network of fictional, philosophical, autobiographical and epistolary texts that she left us is our Simone de Beauvoir.

The aim of this chapter is to explore how Simone de Beauvoir came to be Simone de Beauvoir/a corpus of texts. The approach taken is primarily a linguistic one: by exploring her writing about her earlier life experience of literature we aim to get a representation of the making of Simone de Beauvoir as a writer. In order to do that, I will analyse how she construes her experience of literature as a child, teenager and young adult in the first volume of her memoirs, *Mémoires d'une jeune fille rangée*. As the memoirs are full of references to the books that surrounded Beauvoir's childhood and document her first experiences with writing, it provides many insights into Beauvoir's relationship with literature from an early age. We will use Halliday's (1994) theory of transitivity as applied to French in Caffarel (2006) to analyse Beauvoir's experience of literature and the different roles assigned on the one hand to Beauvoir and on the other to 'literature'. We will also explore the types of processes in which Beauvoir and 'literature' are involved. This will give us a glimpse on how Beauvoir came to become *'un écrivain engagé'* (a committed writer), i.e. a writer that uses literature as a tool for change, as a mode of action. In order to analyse how Beauvoir's conception of literature is encoded in her *Mémoires*, we will use Hasan's (1985) model for the analysis of verbal art, which provides us with a model for the analysis of symbolic meanings, what Hasan calls 'second-order semiosis' (see section 6.2). To illustrate the impact of Beauvoir on her readers, we will intertwine our discussion with abstracts from letters sent to Beauvoir by her readers after the publication of the *Mémoires*. Hasan (1985: 103) was well aware of the role of the reader in promoting a text when she wrote: 'the context of creation and reception merge in the reading of a text. Readers are the medium for a text's achievement; and in a sense, the role of the reader is paramount'.

As mentioned above the *Mémoires* gives us amongst other things a window into Beauvoir's experience of books and literature from a young age till adulthood when she finally decides that her life project will be to write in order to have an impact on the world and transcends herself. As shown by some of the letters' abstracts below, there is ample evidence that Beauvoir succeeded in her life project in the wealth of letters from readers that can be found in the manuscript Department at the Bibliothèque Nationale de France in Paris (BNF: Cote NAF 28501; See also Caffarel 2013, Augras 2016).

On 8 November 1958, a reader of the *Mémoires* would write to Beauvoir:

Je viens de lire votre « jeune fille rangée » ; ce livre m'a, non pas intéressé ; il m'a passionnée ; et je me suis demandée, après tout, pourquoi je ne vous écrirai pas. Je suppose que c'est surtout pour moi que je le fais ; mais certains passages de votre livre m'autorisent à croire qu'il ne peut vous être indifférent d'apprendre que telle ou telle personne a été touché par ce que vous écrivez de vous-même et de votre vie. Je dis « touchée » au sens où le boxeur peut l'être.

[I've just finished your memoirs and it not only interested me, it filled me with passion, and I had to ask myself what good reason I had not to write you. I suppose it's primarily for myself that I am, but certain passages from your memoirs lead me to believe that you wouldn't be indifferent to learning a reader had been touched by your words and your life. I use 'touched' in the sense in which we might say a boxer was touched.]

Another reader, that same year, would write:

Mademoiselle

J'ai lu votre livre avec ravissement. Je veux parler des « Mémoires d'une jeune fille rangée ». Tout y est adorable : le style, l'allure, et surtout les choses dites, sans aucun fard, dans aucune retenue et cependant avec une pudeur et une discrétion touchantes.

Je ne sais si les « auteurs célèbres » reçoivent souvent des lettres d'éloges, mais il m'a semblé que c'est une « récompense » qui leur est due lorsqu'ils nous ont procuré d'agréables moments et surtout le sujet d'importantes méditations.

Ce « contact » que vous recherchiez furieusement à 19 ans, on le trouve très vite en lisant votre livre ; on a tellement besoin de contacts !

[Mademoiselle,

I read your book with great delight. Of course I refer to '*Mémoires d'une jeune fille rangée*'. I loved it all: the style, the allure of it all, but mostly the things you said, with such clarity and without hesitation, yet also with a modesty and discretion that was so very touching.

I'm not sure whether 'famous writers' often receive letters of praise,
but it seems a 'recompense' they are due when they have gifted us
such delightful moments and such important food for thought. The
'contact' you sought so fervently at the age of 19 is found in seconds
upon reading your book; and we are so in need of contact!]

And on 5 May 1959, another would write:

Madame,

...

*C'est merveilleux d'avoir réussi une œuvre aussi sympathique et
humaine. [...]. J'aime le ton de votre livre : vous ne vous étalez pas
sur vous même avec complaisance et c'est cela qui est plaisant. On
sent une quête sincère de la vérité en vous-même et autour de vous.
J'ai suivi vos hésitations, vos surprises, vos découvertes et vos déci-
sions avec autant d'intérêt à chaque page. [...]*

*Merci encore et avant tout de n'avoir pas « fait de la littérature »
mais de vous être racontée avec le souci de vous comprendre et, je
pense aussi, d'aider les autres à se comprendre.*

[Madame,

…

It is marvellous that you have succeeded in producing an oeuvre that
is so nice and human. [...]. I like the tone of your book: it is not
self-indulgent which is pleasing. It feels like a quest for sincerity and
truth within and around you. I followed your hesitations, your surprises, your discoveries and your decisions with as much interest on
each page. [...] Thank you again and above all for not 'making literature' but for telling us about you while trying to understand yourself
and, I think also, helping others to understand themselves.]

The reader's evaluative comment on Beauvoir's writing that she is 'not
making literature', alludes to some of the characteristics of Beauvoir's
style that go against traditional literary norms and can convey ideas and
experience in a very fluid and dynamic mode, which makes her philosophical ideas accessible to readers from different ages, background and social
status. Not many philosophers have been able to convey symbolic meanings
(social and philosophical meanings) in the way that Beauvoir did and that
is one of the many reasons why it is so interesting to study her language.
Furthermore, as Scholz (2000: 211) so rightly says:

Throughout her autobiographical, philosophical, political and literary works, Simone de Beauvoir displays a clear interest in language, both the spoken and the written word. This interest tends to focus not on language as a monolithic system but rather as what makes communication and participation in meaning possible – necessarily embedded in and embodied by a socio-historical context, inseparable from existence.

One of the objectives of this chapter is thus to analyse the way Beauvoir constructs her experience of language and literature so as to get a representation of the role of literature in her life as she was growing up. The other is to identify Beauvoir's linguistic choices and demonstrate that they correlate with her conception of the role of literature as she sees it within her philosophy of existence. In Section 6.2, I will outline some of Beauvoir's main ideas about literature as she discussed them in 'What can literature do?' a talk she gave in 1964 as part of a debate on the power of literature. In Section 6.3, I will give a brief overview of some of the main aspects of Hasan's approach to the analysis of literary texts, as most of her concepts are discussed in previous chapters in this book. In Section 6.4, I will present an analysis and interpretation of a number of passages from the *Mémoires* in terms of Halliday's transitivity models, the transitive and the ergative modes of participation, in the context of Hasan's approach to the analysis of verbal art. Halliday's transitivity models will also be briefly introduced at the beginning of Section 6.4.

6.2. Beauvoir on literature

On 9 December 1964, Simone de Beauvoir took part in a debate entitled '*Que peut la littérature?*' (What can literature do?) between proponents of 'the new novel' (*Le nouveau roman*) and those of 'committed literature' (*littérature engagée*). The debate focused in particular on the meaning of the act of writing as well as the social function and aim of literature. The contributions from each author (S. de Beauvoir, Jean-Pierre Faye, Jean-Paul Sartre, Yves Berger, Jean Ricardou, and Jorge Semprum were published in 1965 in a book titled '*Que peut la littérature*' presented by Yves Buin: L'Inédit 10|18.

In her contribution, which also appeared in *Le Monde* in 1965, Beauvoir defines literature as 'an activity carried out by human beings, for human beings, with the aim of unveiling the world for them, and this unveiling is an action' (Beauvoir 1965: 73; translated by Toril Moi 2009). Moi (2009: 189) points that '*another reason why this text has remained neglected is its unpretentiousness. Beauvoir's voice is clear and simple, her examples ordinary*'. Beauvoir's ability to construe complex ideas in ways that are clear is what makes her language so extraordinary and was also noticed by another reader of Beauvoir, Claire Cayron,[3] when she commented on something Beauvoir had written in the preface to Violette Leduc's *La Batârde*:

> *J'ai aussi lu votre préface pour Violette Leduc. Vous êtes une dangereuse préfacière. Je crois d'ailleurs que vous vous en rendez compte puisqu'en dernière ligne vous sentez le besoin d'inviter le lecteur à aller au delà de vous, dans le texte même...*

> *'Une vie c'est la reprise d'un destin par une liberté'. Comment trouvez-vous des phrases pareilles. Il me faudrait des pages pour exprimer ce que vous dites en 4 mots.* (Cayron : 3/12/64)

> [I also read your preface for Violette Leduc. You are a dangerous preface writer. Anyway, I believe that you are aware of this as in your last sentence you feel the need to invite the reader to go beyond you, in the text even.

> 'A life is taking back one's destiny with freedom'. How do you find such clauses. I would need pages to express what you say in four words. [My translation]]

In 'Que peut la Littérature, Beauvoir explains that within the philosophy of existentialism the world is seen as 'une totalité détotalisée' ['a detotalized totality']. It means that 'on the one hand there is a world that is the same for everyone; but that on the other hand we are all in a situation in relation to it, this situation implying our past, our class, our condition, our project, that is, all that makes our individuality' (Beauvoir, 1965: 76, my translation). We could think of the world as the overall potential of existence with each individual having only access to certain aspects of that world depending on each individual's situation. This is where literature finds its meaning according to Beauvoir: 'literature has the power to go beyond other modes of communication and allow us to communicate what separates us' (1965: 79) [My translation].

In *La Force des Choses (Force of Circumstance)* (1963: 679), **Words** *without doubt, universal, eternal, presence of all in each,* **are the only transcendent power** *I recognize and am affected by; they vibrate in my mouth, and with them I can communicate with humanity.* **They wrench tears, night, death itself from the moment, from contingency, and then transfigure them.** *Perhaps the most profound desire I entertain today is that people should repeat in silence certain words that I have been the first to link together.* (translated by Howard, *Force of Circumstance*: 1965: 650. My emphasis)

Sally Scholz (2008) points out that Beauvoir uses the concepts of 'immanence' and 'transcendence' to explain women's situation in *The Second Sex*

(1949). 'Immanence is stagnation within a situation, while transcendence is reaching out into the future, through projects that open up freedom.' Throughout her life Beauvoir's project was literature and she used literature to act in the world, to impact on her readers, to make them think and act beyond their own situation.

Madame

Au terme d'un long voyage en train je viens de fermer vos Mémoires d'une jeune fille rangée » sur leur dernier page, et, depuis je ne cesse de penser à ce livre.

Oui il m'a bouleversée comme aucun livre ne m'a bouleversée depuis longtemps. Pourquoi ? Parce que vous avez raconté votre histoire avec une « présence » extraordinaire... (6/2/1959)

[Madame,

At the end of a long train trip I have just closed your '*Mémoires d'une jeune fille rangée*' on their last page and, since, I cannot stop thinking about that book. Yes, it hit me like no book has hit me in a very long time. Why? Because you told your story with an extraordinary 'presence'.]

In this chapter we will on the one hand try to unravel the ways Beauvoir constructs her experience of literature, as a reader, and writer, across time; on the other hand, we will illustrate that Beauvoir's conception of the role of literature as a mode of action, of impacting on the world and as a means to transcends oneself beyond one's own situation is construed in her choice of experiential resources.

Before embarking into the analyses of passages from the memoirs, I will briefly point out some of Hasan's main ideas about the analysis of literature as she talks about them in *Linguistics, Language and Verbal Art* (1985) (see also Butt: chapter 2 in this volume).

6.3. Hasan on literature

Hasan (1985: 94–99) proposes that verbal art has a similar internal design to that of language itself, i.e. that it has three levels, corresponding to the levels of meaning, lexicogrammar and expression that are related to each other by realization. The three levels in verbal art are 'theme' (corresponding to the level of semantics in language), 'symbolic articulation' (corresponding to the lexicogrammatical level) and 'verbalization' (corresponding to the expression level). The 'lowest' level, the level of literary expression (i.e. verbalization) is realized by language itself – language is the means by which literary meaning is expressed. This is in why language should be central to the analysis of any literary text. The highest level, 'theme' is 'the deepest level of meaning in verbal art; it is what a text is about when dissociated from the particularities of that text' (Hasan 1985: 97). Hasan adds that 'in its nature, the theme of verbal art is very close to a generalization, which can be viewed as a hypothesis about some aspect of the life of social man' (Hasan 1985: 97). This aspect of Theme is very important in our research which aims to explore how Beauvoir's general ideas about literature are foregrounded through the 'symbolic articulation' of grammatical experiential patterns. Hasan (1985: 98) explains that 'the stratum of symbolic articulation is where the meanings of language are turned into signs having deeper meanings. Foregrounding and patterning of patterns play an important role in ascribing the second order meanings to the patterns of the first order meanings.' Hasan refers to the way that verbal art articulates symbolic meanings through consistency of foregrounding as 'second-order semiosis'.

Hasan (1995: 95) points out that foregrounding can be achieved through two types of consistency in the lexicogrammatical patterning:

1. A number of lexicogrammatical patterns that contribute towards 'the same general kind of meaning'; foregrounded patterns, in other words, are consistent with what Butt calls their 'semantic drift' (cited in Hasan 1985: 95).
2. 'Significant patterns of foregrounding have a tendency to occur at a textually important point', by which she means 'some significant point in the organisation of the text as a unity' (Hasan 1985, 1995–1996).

Throughout the analysis presented below we will see emerge on the one hand a pattern whereby literature carries agency throughout but in different process type environments depending on Beauvoir's stage of development and on the other hand a pattern whereby Beauvoir gains agency step by step as she becomes a user and creator of literature. We will see that changes in roles assigned to Beauvoir coincide with different stages of growth and interaction with literature.

6.4. The construal of Beauvoir's experience of literature in *'Mémoires'*

For the purpose of this analysis, I have selected eight passages from *Mémoires d'un jeune fille rangée*. All English translations are by James Kirkup, *Memoirs of a Dutiful Daughter* (1959).

In the first two passages Beauvoir is about six years of age and about seven in passage 3. In passage 4, she is about 12, whilst in passages 5, 6 and 7 she is between 14 and 18. Fourteen is the age when Beauvoir rejects God, and literature replaces religion in her life. In the last passage, Beauvoir is 21 and this is the age she decides her life project will be to be a writer and help change the world through her writings. A reader would write to her in 1959 quoting a line from the Mémoires:

> « *M'exprimer dans une œuvre qui aiderait les autres à vivre* » [quote from 'Les Mémoires]. *Quelle ambition ! Vous l'avez pleinement accomplie.* (A reader, 6 February 1959)

> ['To express myself in an oeuvre that will help others to live'. What an ambition! You have fully accomplished it.]

One of the main Themes foregrounded throughout the selected passages is that 'Literature is transcendent' and 'Literature has agency'. The notions of transcendence and agency which is a key concept in Beauvoir's philosophy of existence are themselves embodied in the transitivity models as put forward by Halliday (1994) and Matthiessen (1995):

> The root of the grammar of the nuclear transitivity of processes and participants are two simultaneous systems, **AGENCY** and PROCESS TYPE. They reflect two models of transitivity.

> (i) The first is highly generalized and cuts across the various process types. It is concerned with the variable of external cause or not (i.e., external to the combination of Process + Medium) – effective or middle. This is the ergative model …

> (ii) The second is process-type specific; the traditional representative is the material clause: the basic question is whether the combination of Actor + Process extends (**transcends** to another participant (Goal) or not. This is the transitive model. (Matthiessen, 1995: 20)

The Process Types system distinguishes between a number of processes such as Material, Behavioural, Mental, Verbal, relational (identifying and attributive) and existential processes. Material processes encompass the realm of doing and happening, Behavioural processes are in between material and mental/verbal processes but represent the mental and verbal as activities and cannot project; they also include physiological processes such as sneezing and crying. Mental and verbal processes have the potential to project another clause as Idea or locution. Relational processes put two functions into relation either an identity relation or attributive relation. Existential processes serve to bring a new participant into existence. (See

Caffarel 2006/2008, Caffarel 2016 for a more detailed account of transitivity in French.)

The AGENCY system distinguishes between middle and effective clauses. Middle clauses represent experience as self-engendered, whilst effective clauses represent experience as brought about by an Agent. In other words, effective clauses have the Agent function assigned to one participant whilst middle clauses do not have an agent. In some effective passive clause, the Agent can be elliptical but its trace is nonetheless important.

I will now turn to the analysis of the eight passages mentioned above where we will be able to see those two transitivity systems at work.

6.5. Foregrounded transitivity patterns across the eight passages selected

In this section, we will explore how Beauvoir's experience of literature is symbolically articulated at different stages of the first 20 years of her life.

As the analysis and summary of patterns in Table 6.1 show, in passage 1, books are represented as having agency over Beauvoir. However, as a pre-school child, books impact on Beauvoir, not in a material way, but in an affective way. They affect Beauvoir emotionally and mentally. The experiential resources foregrounded in this first passage are that 'Books and words' are Agent in Mental and Verbal processes, as well as Actors in Behavioural processes representing mental and verbal activities. Books bring comfort and meaning to the young Beauvoir in a similar way that her mother does. This passage has only one material process which represents the act of opening a book by Beauvoir. At this stage Beauvoir has the roles of Medium/Senser in effective mental clauses and of beneficiary of meaning. When she does not understand a word, her mother explains it to her. From a very young age, Beauvoir becomes aware of the way language impacts on her and what it can bring to her.

Transitivity analysis of passage 1: p.68 (Beauvoir is five years old); Translation, p.45.

(1a)

Les livres	me	rassuraient;
Agent/Penomenon	Medium/Senser	Proc: mental: effective

I found reassurance in books:

(1b)]

Ils	parlaient
	Proc: Behavioural

They said what they had to say

(1c)

Et	ne dissimulaient rien;
	Proc: Behavioural

and didn't pretend to say anything else;

(1d)

en mon absence,	ils	se taisaient;
Circ: Time	Proc:	Proc: Behavioural

When I was not there, they were silent;

(1e)

je	les	ouvrais,
Agent	Medium	Proc: Material: effective

if I opened one,

(1f)

et alors	ils	disaient exactement	[[ce qu'ils disaient]];
	Medium	Proc: verbal	Range

it said exactly what it meant:

(1g)

Si	un mot	m'	échappait,
	Agent	Medium	Proc: mental: effective

if there was a word I didn't understand,

(1h)

Maman	me	l'	expliquait.
Medium	Beneficiary	Range	Proc: verbal

Mama would explain it to me.

Clause No	Agent	Medium	Process Type	Beneficiary
(1a)	Les livres (**books**)	me (Beauvoir)	Mental	
(1b)		ils (**Books**)	Behavioural	
(1c)		[**Books**]	Behavioural	
(1d)		ils (**Books**)	Behavioural	
(1e)	Je (Beauvoir)	les (**Books**)	Material	
(1f)		ils (**Books**)	Verbal	
(1g)	Un mot (a **word**)	m' (Beauvoir)	Mental	
(1h)		maman	Verbal	Me (**Beauvoir**)

Table 6.1: Summary of experiential resources in passage 1

In the second passage, the same experiential semantic patterns are foregrounded: books, their author and characters in books continue to affect Beauvoir emotionally with books/stories being Agent in mental clauses. However, in this passage 'literature' is also constructed as Agent in a material clause, changing Beauvoir's perception of the world: Beauvoir becomes aware that reality is relative and does not equate truth.

Books also make her dream and think. In addition to being construed as Medium in effective mental and material clauses, Beauvoir continues to be represented as a Beneficiary in both verbal and material clauses. At this young age, in addition to being affected emotionally by books, Beauvoir benefits and learns from them.

Transitivity analysis of passage 2: p. 69

(1a)

Parfois pourtant	le livre	me	parlait	plus ou moins confusément	du monde [[qui m'entou-rait]] ou de moi-même ;
	Medium/ Sayer	Beneficiary/ Addressee	Proc:Verbal	Circ: Manner	Verbiage/ Range

But occasionally a book would speak to me more or less vaguely about the world around me or about myself:

(1b)

alors	Il	me	faisait rêver, ou réfléchir
	Agent	Senser/Medium	Proc: Mental

then it would make me wonder, or dream,

(1c)

et	quelquefois	Il	bousculait	mes certitudes.
	Circ: Time	Agent/Actor	Proc: material	Goal/Medium

and sometimes it would shake my convictions.

(2a)

Andersen	m'	enseigna	la mélancolie;
Agent/Actor	Beneficiary	Proc: material	Goal/Medium

Andersen taught me what melancholy is;

(2b)

dans ses contes,	les objets	pâtissent,
Circ: Place	Medium/Senser	Proc: Mental

in his tales, objects suffer from neglect,

(2c)

se brisent
Proc: Material

are broken

(2d)

se consument
Proc: Material

and pine away

(2e)

sans	mériter	leur malheur;
	Proc: Mental	Phenomenon/Rage

without deserving their unhappy fate;

(2f)

la petite sirène, <<...>>	souffrait	à chacun de ses pas

the little mermaid was in agony at every step she took

(2g)

<<avant de	s'anéantir>>
	Proc: Material

<<before she passed away>>

(2h)

comme si	elle	eût marché	sur des charbons ardents
	Medium/Actor	Proc: Material	Circ: Place

as if she were walking on red-hot cinders,

(2i)

et cependant	elle	n'avait commis	aucune faute:
	Agent/Actor	Proc: Material	Goal/Medium

yet she had not done anything wrong:

(2j)

ses tortures et sa mort	me	barbouillèrent	le coeur
Agent/Phenomenon	Medium/Senser	Proc: Mental	Range

her tortures and her death made me sick at heart.

Cl. No	Agent	Medium	Process	Range	Beneficiary
(1a)		le livre (**book**)	Verbal	the world around me or myself	me (**Beauvoir**)
(1b)	il (**book**)	me (**Beauvoir**)	Mental (dream and think)		
(1c)	il (**book**)	mes certitudes (**Beauvoir's certainties**)	Material		
(2a)	**Andersen**	la mélancolie	Material		m' (**Beauvoir**)
(2b)		les objets	Mental		
(2c)		[objects]	Material		
(2d)		[objects]	Material		
(2e)		[objects]	Mental	leur malheur	
(2f)		la petite sirène (the little mermaid)	Mental		
(2g)		(the little mermaid)	Material		
(2h)		elle (mermaid)	Material		
(2i)		elle (mermaid)	Material		
(2j)	ses tortures et sa mort (**mermaid's torture and death**)	me (**Beauvoir**)	Mental	le coeur	

Table 6.2: Summary of experiential resources in passage 2

In passage 3, Beauvoir recounts her first experience of writing a fictional story. There is a significant change in the patterns of foregrounding in that Beauvoir takes on the role of Agent. She is also for the first time represented as Senser in a non-agentive mental clause. Beauvoir is Agent in the process of writing which as a young child she interprets as a similar process to constructing objects with cubes when she was a toddler. At this stage, she plays with language as she used to play with cubes, and to her the power of language is like magic. By putting words together, she can create an imaginary world. By becoming a creator of stories Beauvoir comes to realize she can impact on the way her family views her and get attention. As she starts gaining agency and using language to impact on her inner world and create new worlds, literature, in parallel, continues to impact on her and Beauvoir continues to be constructed as Beneficiary: books provide models for her.

Passage 3: pp 70–71
Translation, p. 52

(1a)

Malgré leur conformisme,	les livres	élargissaient	mon horizon;
Circ:	Agent	Proc: Attributive/Attribute	Medium/Carrier

Despite their conventionality, my books helped to broaden my horizons;

(1b)

en outré	je	m'enchantais	en néophyte	de la sorcellerie [[qui transmute les signes imprimés en récit]];
	Medium/ Senser	Proc: Mental	Circ: Manner	Range/Phenomenon

besides, I was charmed to be an apprentice t the sorcery that transmutes printed symbols into stories;

(1c)

le désir	me	vint	[[d'inverser cette magie].
Agent/...	Medium/Senser	Proc: Mental	...Phenomenon

and it was natural that I would want to reverse the magical process.

(2a)

Assise	devant une petite table,
Proc: Material	Circ: place

Seated at a little table,

(2b)

Je	décalquai	sur le papier	des phrases [[qui serpen- taient dans ma tête]]:
Agent/Actor	Proc: Material	Circ: Place	Medium/Goal

I would transfer to paper sentence that were winding about in my head:

(2c)

la feuille blanche	se couvrait	de taches violettes [[qui racontaient une histoire]].
Medium/Actor	Proc: Material	Range

the white sheet would be covered with violet blotches which purported to tell a story.

(3a)

Comme	je	ne cherchais pas	dans la littérature	un reflet de la réalité
	Medium/Actor	Proc: Material	Circ: Place	Range

As I did not look to literature for a reflection of reality,

(3b)

je	n'eus jamais	l'idée [[de transcrire mon expérience ou mes rêves]] ;
Medium/Carrier	Proc : Attributive : Poss	Range/Attribute

I never had the idea that I might write down my own experiences or even my dreams ;

(3c)

[ce qui m'amusait],	c'	était	[[d'agencer un objet avec des mots]
	Medium/Token	Proc : identifying	Range/Value

the thing that amused me was to manipulate an object through the use of words,

(3d)

comme	j'	en	construisais autrefois	avec des cubes ;
	Agent/Actor	Medium/Goal	Proc : Material	Circ : Manner

as I once used to make constructions with building-blocks ;

(3ᵉ)

les livres seuls, et non le monde dans sa crudité,	pouvaient	me	fournir	des modèles ;
Agent/Actor	Proc : Modal^…	Beneficiary	…Material	Medium/Goal

only books, and not life in all its crudity, will provide me with models :

(3f)

Je	pastichai.
Medium/Actor	Proc : Material

I wrote pastiche

(4)

Ma première oeuvre	s'intitula	*les malheurs de Marguerite.*
Medium/Token	Proc : Identifying	Range/Value

*My first work was entitled **The Misfortunes of Marguerite.***

Cl. No	Agent	Medium	Process Type	Range	Beneficiary
(1a)	les livres (**Books**)	mon horizon (Beauvoir's horizon)	Proc : Attributive		
(1b)		je (**Beauvoir**)	Mental	the sorcery [[that transmutes printed signs into stories]]	
(1c)	le **désir**	**me**	Mental	[[to reverse the magical process]]	
(2a)		[**Beauvoir**]	Material		
(2b)	je (**Beauvoir**)	sentences [[that were winding about my head]]	Material		
(2c)		the white page	Material	violet blotches [[that told a story]]	
(3a)		je (**Beauvoir**)	Material	a reflection of reality	
(3b)		Je (**Beauvoir**)	Attributive : possessive	the idea [[to transcribe my experience or my dreams]]	
(3c)		c'[[What amused me]]	Identifying	to construct an object with words	
(3d)	je (**Beauvoir**)	objects	Material		
(3e)	**Books** and not the world in its crudity	models	Material		me (**Beauvoir**)
(3f)		je (**Beauvoir**)	Material		
(4)		My first work	Identifying	*Les malheurs de Marguerite*	

Table 6.3: Summary of experiential resources in passage 3

In passage 4, the power of literature is further foregrounded with language and the stories written by Beauvoir gaining greater agency: language can change nothingness into reality, ignorance into knowledge. This is the crucial moment when Beauvoir becomes aware that by writing things down she can make them more transparent for others to understand. She knows how to use language. She also feels that by writing her stories inspired by experience she brings them out of nothingness and give them an existence. In this passage, Beauvoir, her stories and the language she uses have the main roles either as Agent or Medium in middle clauses and are thematized. There is an increase in the use of material processes.

Passage 4: p. 93

(1a)

En revanche	je	savais	[[me servir du language]],
	Medium/Senser	Proc: Mental	Range/Phenomenon

In compensation, I knew how to use language, [in contrast with drawing]

(1b)

et puisque	il	exprimait	la substance des choses,
	Medium/Sayer	Proc: Verbal	Range

and as it expressed the essence of things,

(1c)

Il	les	éclairait.
Agent	Medium/Carrier	Proc: Attributive/Attribute

it illuminated them for me.

(2a)

j'	avais	tendance [[à raconter tout ce qui m'arrivait]]:
Medium/Carrier	Proc: rel: attributive: Poss	Range/Attribute

I had a spontaneous urge to turn everything that happened to me into a story:

(2b)

Je	parlais beaucoup,
Medium/Behaver	Proc: Behavioural

I used to talk freely,

(2c)

j'	écrivais volontiers.
Medium/Actor	Proc: Material

and loved to write.

(3a)

Si	je	relatais	dans une redaction	un episode de ma vie,
	Medium/Behaver	Proc: Behavioural	Virc: Place	Range/ Phenomenon

If I was describing in words an episode in my life,

(3b)

Il	échappait	à l'oubli,
Medium/Phenomenon	Proc: mental?	Circ: Place

I felt that it was being rescued from oblivion,

(3c)

il	intéressait	d'autres gens,
Agent/Phenomenon	Proc: Mental	Medium/Senser

that it would interest others,

(3d)

Il	était définitivement	sauvé.
Medium/Carrier	Proc: Attributive	Range/Attribute

and so be saved from extinction.

(4a)

J'	aimais aussi	[[inventer des histoires]];
Medium/Senser	Proc: Mental	Range/Phenomenon

I loved to make up stories too:

(4b)

dans la mesure [[où elle s'inspirait de mon experience	elles	la	justifiaient;
Circ:	Medium/Acteur	Range	Proc: Comportemental

when they were inspired by my own experience, they seemed to justify it;

(4c)

en un sens ,	elles	ne servaient	à **rien**,
Circ:	Medium/Actor	Proc: Material	Beneficiary

in one sense, they were of no use at all,

(4d)

mais	elles	étaient	uniques, irremplaçables,
	Medium/Carrier	Proc: Attribitive	Range Attribute

but they were unique and irreplaceable,

(4e)

Ells	existaient
Medium/Existant	Proc: existential

they existed,

(4f)

et	j'		étais	fière [[de les avoir tirées du néant]]
		Medium/Carrier	Proc: Attributive	Range/Attribute

and I was proud of having snatched them out of nothingness.

Cl. No.	Agent	Medium	Process type	Range
(1a)		je [**Beauvoir**]	Mental	[[to use language]]
(1b)	il (**language**)	the substance of things	Identifying	
(1c)	il (**language**)	les (things)	Attributive	
(2a)		j' (**Beauvoir**)	Attributive: Possessive	a tendency [[to tell everything that happened to me]]
(2b)		je (**Beauvoir**)	Behavioural	
(2c)		je (**Beauvoir**)	Material	
(3a)		je (**Beauvoir**)	Behavioural	an episode of my life
(3b)		il (**an episode of Beauvoir's life**)	Mental	forgetfulness
(3c)	il (**an episode of Beauvoir's life**)	other people	Mental	
(3d)		il (**an episode of my life**)	Attributive	saved
(4a)		j' (**Beauvoir**)	Mental	[[invent stories]]
(4b)	**elles** (The stories)	la (**Beauvoir's life**)	Material	
(4c)		elles (the **stories**)	Material	
(4d)		elles (the **stories**)	Attributive	unique and irreplaceable
(4e)		elles (the **stories**)	Existential	
(4f)		j' (**Beauvoir**)	Attributive	proud [[to have snatched them out of nothingness]]

Table 6.4: Summary of experiential resources in passage 4

In passage 5 the transcendence of literature is further foregrounded with literature being construed as giver of immortality to Beauvoir and in return Beauvoir gives books to humanity thus 'unveiling the world to them and this unveiling is an action'. This is where her ideas about literature as she discussed them in 'What can literature do?' are brought to the fore and a majority of material processes are selected to foreground literature as a mode of action.

Passage 5: p. 187
(Translation, p.142)

(1a)

Elle [La littérature]	m'	assurerait	une immortalité
Agent/Actor	Beneficiary	Proc: Material	Medium/Goal

[Literature] would grant me an immortality

(1b)

Qui	compenserait	l'éternité perdue;
	Proc: material	Medium/Goal

which would compensate for the loss of heaven and eternity;

(1c)

il n'y avait plus	de Dieu
Proc: existential	Medium/Existant

There was no longer any God

(1d)

Pour	m'	aimer
	Range/Penomenon	Proc: Mental

to love me,

(1e)

mais	je	brûlerais	dans des millions de coeurs.
	Medium/Actor	Proc: Material	Circ: Place

but I should have the undying love of millions of hearts.

(2a)

En écrivant	une oeuvre nourrie de mon histoire,
Proc: Material	Medium/Goal

By writing a work based on my own experience

(2b)

Je	me crérais	moi-même	à neuf
Agent/Actor	Proc: Material	Medium/Goal	Circ: Means

I would re-create myself

(2c)

et	je	justifierais	mon existence.
	Agent/Actor	Proc: Material	Medium/Goal

and justify my existence.

(3a)

En même temps	je	servirais	l'humanité:
	Agent/Actor	Proc: Material	Medium/Goal

At the same time I would be serving humanity:

(3b)

quel plus beau cadeau	lui	faire	que des livres?
Range/Attribute	Béneficiary	Proc: material: effective	Medium/Goal

What more beautiful gift could I make it that the books I would write?

Cl. No.	Agent	Medium	Process type	Range	Beneficiary
(1a)	Elle [**literature**]	immortality	Material		m' [**Beauvoir**]
(1b)	immortality	loss of eternity	Material		
(1c)		Dieu [God]	Existential (negative)		
(1d)		[God]	Mental	m' (Beauvoir]	
(1e)		je[**Beauvoir**]	Material		
(2a)		[**Beauvoir**]	Material (write)	a work based on my own experience	
(2b)	je [**Beauvoir**]	myself (**Beauvoir**)	Material (create)		
(2c)	je [**Beauvoir**]	my existence	Material		
(3a)	je	humanity	Material		
(3b)	[**Beauvoir**]	**Books**	Material	Present	lui [**humanity**]

Table 6.5: Summary of experiential resources in passage 5

Passage 6 continues with the theme developed in passage 5 and brings to the fore a crucial period in Beauvoir's life when she rejects religion and the idea of God which she replaces with literature as a means to gain transcendence. In this extract literature and Beauvoir have equal agency in material processes, emphasizing literature as a mode of action and the way it impacted on Beauvoir and changed her view of the world. She would later use literature in the same way to change the lives of her readers.

Passage 6: p. 245
Translation, p. 187

(1a)

La littérature	prit	dans mon existence	la place [[qu'y avait occupée la religion]]:
Medium/Actor	Proc: Material	CircL Place	Range

Literature took the place in my life that had once been occupied by religion:

(1b)

Elle	l'	envahit	tout entire
Agent/Actor	Medium/Goal	Proc: Matérial	Range

it absorbed me entirely,

(1c)

Et	la	transfigura.
	Medium/Goal	Proc: Material

and transfigured my life.

(2a)

Les livres [[que j'aimais]]	devinrent	une Bible
Medium/Carrrier	Proc: Attributive	Range

The books I liked became a Bible

(2b)

où	je	puisais	des conseils et des secours;
	Medium/Acteur	Proc: Material	Range

from which I drew advice and support;

(2c)

j'	en	copiai	de longs extraits;
Agent/Acteur	Medium/...	Proc: Material	...Goal

I copied out long passages from them;

(2d)

j'		appris	par coeur	de nouveaux cantiques et de nouvelles litanies, des psaumes, des proverbs, des prophéties
Medium/Actor		Proc: Material	Circ: Manner	Range

I learnt by heart new canticles and new litanies, psalms, proverbs, and prophecies

(2e)

Et	je	sanctifiai	toutes les circonstances de ma vie
	Agent/Actor	Proc: Material	Medium/Goal

and I sanctified every circumstance in my existence

(2f)

En	me	récitant	ces textes sacrés.
	Beneficiary	Proc: Material	Range

by the recital of these sacred texts.

(3a)

Mes emotions, mes larmes, mes espoirs	n'en étaient pas	moins sinceres:
Medium/Carrier	Proc: Attributive	Range/Attribute

My emotions, my tears, and my aspirations were no less sincere on account of that:

(3b)

les mots et les cadence, les vers, les versets	ne me	servaient pas à feindre:
Agent/Phenomenon	Medium/Senser	Proce: Mental

the words and the cadences, the lines and the verses were no aids to make-believe:

(3c)

mais	ils	sauvaient	du silence	toutes ces intimes aventures [[dont je ne pouvais parler à personne]];
	Agent/Actor	Proc: Material	Circ: Place	Medium/Goal

but they rescued from silent oblivion all those intimate adventures of the spirit that I could not speak to anyone about;

(3d)

entre moi et les âmes soeurs [[qui existaient quelque part, hors d'atteinte]],	ils	créaient	une sorte de communion;
Beneficiary	Agent/Actor	Proc: Material	Medium/Goal

they created a kind of communion between myself and those twin souls which existed somewhere out of reach;

(3e)

au lieu de	vivre	ma petite histoire particulière,
	Proc: Material	Range

instead of living out my small private existence,

(3f)

je	participais à	une grande épopée spirituelle.
Medium/Actor	Proc: Material	Range

I was participating in a great spiritual epic.

(4a)

Pendant des mois	je	me nourris	de littérature:
	Actor/Medium	Proc: Material	Range

For months I kept myself going with books:

(4b)

mais	c'	était alors	la seule réalité [[à laquelle il me fût possible d'accéder]].
	Medium/Token	Proc: Identifying	Range/Value

they were the only reality within my reach.

Cl. No.	Agent	Medium	Process Type	Range	Beneficiary
(1a)	**Literature**	the place [taken by religion]	Material		
(1b)	elle [literature]	l' [Beauvoir's existence]	Material		
(1c)	**[literature]**	la [Beauvoir's existence]	Material		
(2a)		**Books [[that I liked]]**	Attributive	**a Bible**	

Cl. No.	Agent	Medium	Process Type	Range	Beneficiary
(2b)		je [Beauvoir]	Material	advice and support	
(2c)	j' **[Beauvoir]**	long book extracts	Material		
(2d)		je [Beauvoir]	Material	new litanies, psalms, proverbs, profecies	
(2e)	je **[Beauvoir]**	circumstances of my life	Material		
(2f)	**[Beauvoir]**	these sacred texts	Material		me **[Beauvoir]**
(3a)		my emotions, my tears, my hopes	Attributive:negative	less sincere	
(3b)	**words, lines, verses**	me [Beauvoir]	Mental		
(3c)	**ils [words...]**	intimate adventures[I could speak to no one]	Material		
(3d)	**ils [words...]**	a kind of communion	Material		between myself and twin sisters that existed somewhere out of reach
(3e)		**[Beauvoir]**	Material	a small particular existence	
(3f)		je **[Beauvoir]**	Material	a great spiritual epic	
(4a)		je **[Beauvoir]**	Material	Literature	
(4b)		c' **[literature]**	Identifying	the only reality within my reach	

Table 6.6: Summary of experiential resources in passage 6

In passage 7, Beauvoir represents the moment when she decides to write her first novel. We see a variety of processes from relational to material via mental and behavioural processes. The use of an identifying relational process at the start serves to create a link between Beauvoir's writing and her existence. Then Beauvoir desire to write her experience and communicate with humanity is further specified through mental and behavioural processes. She also comes to realize that literature is art, and she begins to compose her first novel.

Passage 7: p. 272
Translation: p.208

(1a)

Ce que je rêvais d'écrire	c'	était	'un roman de la vie intérieure';
	Medium/Token	Proc: identifying	Range/Value

What I dreamt of writing was a 'novel of the inner life';

(1b)

Je	voulais communiquer	mon experience.
Medium/Actor	Proc: Behavioural	Range

I wanted to communicate my experience.

(2)

J'	hésitai.
Medium/Senser	Proc: Mental

I hesitated.

(3a)

Il	me	semblait sentir	en moi	'un tas de choses à dire';
	Medium/Senser	Proc: Mental	Circ: Place	Range/Phenomenon

I could feel within me 'masses of things to say;

(3b)

mais	je	me rendais compte
	Medium/Senser	Proc: Mental

but I realized

(3c)

qu'	écrire	est	un art
	Medium/Carrier	Proc: Attributive	Range/Attribute

that writing is an art

(3d)

et que	je	n'y	étais pas	expert.
	Medium/Carrier	Range/Attribute	Proc: Attributive	Range/Attribute

and that I was not expert.

(4a)

Je	notais tout de même	plusieurs sujets de romans
Agent/Actor	Proc: Material	Medium/Goal

All the same I jotted down a few subjects for novels

(4b)

et finalement	je	me décidai.
	Medium/Senser	Proc: Mental

and finally I made a decision.

(5)

Je	composai	ma première oeuvre.
Agent/Actor	Proc: Material	Medium/Goal

I composed my first work.

Cl. No.	Agent	Medium	Process Type	Range
(1a)		[[what I dreamt of writing]]	Proc: identifying	[[a novel of the inner life]]
(1b)		**je (Beauvoir)**	Proc: Behavioural	Beauvoir's experience
(2)		**J' (Beauvoir)**	Proc: Mental	
(3a)		**me (Beauvoir)**	Proc: Mental	'masses of things to say'
(3b)		**je (Beauvoir)**	Proc: Mental	
(3c)		*Writing*	Proc: Attributive	***Art***
(3d)		**je (Beauvoir)**	Proc: Attributive:negative	Expert
(4a)	je (**Beauvoir**)	few subjects for novels	Proc: Material	
(4b)		je (**Beauvoir**)	Proc: Mental	
(5)	je (**Beauvoir**)	my first novel	Proc: Material	

Table 6.7: Summary of experiential resources in passage 7

Passage 8 foregrounds the outcome of Beauvoir's interaction with literature through her childhood and the realization of its power to change one's view of the world. It is literature after all that made her challenge reality and reject religion as well as her situation of immanence. In this passage, Beauvoir gains full agency over her world and decides that her life project will be to write. Writing is further construed as inseparable from her existence. We have a majority of material clauses but also an existential clause foregrounding that her existence is ahead of her through writing, and her writing will serve to act on the world and empower others.

Passage 8: p. 453

Translation: p. 345

(1a)

Je	ne me demandais plus:
Medium/Senser	Proc: Mental

I no longer asked myself

(1b)

Que	faire?
Medium/Goal	Proc: Material

What shall I do?

(2a)

Il y avait	tout à faire; tout [[ce qu'autrefois j'avais souhaité faire]]:
Proc: existential	Medium/Existant

There was everything to be done, everything I had formerly longed to do:

(2b)

Combattre	l'erreur
Proc: Material	Medium/Goal

to combat error,

(2c)

Trouver	la verité,
Proc: Material	Medium/Goal

to find the truth,

(2d)

La	dire,
Range/Verbiage	Proc: verbal

to tell it

(2e)

Éclairer	le monde
Proc: Material	Medium/Goal

and expound it to the world,

(2f)

peut-être même	aider à	le	changer
	Proc: mat...	Medium/Goal	...erial

perhaps to help to change the world.

Cl. No.	**Agent**	**Medium**	**Process Type**	**Range**
(1a)		je (Beauvoir)	Mental	
(1b)	**[Beauvoir]**	que	Material	
(2a)			Proc: existential	everything [[I had wished **to do** in the past]]
(2b)	**[Beauvoir]**	error	Proc: Material	
(2c)	**[Beauvoir]**	truth	Proc: Material	
(2d)		**[Beauvoir]**	Proc: verbal	truth
(2e)	**[Beauvoir]**	the world	Proc: Material	
(2f)	**[Beauvoir]**	le [the world]	Proc: Material	

Table 6.8: Summary of experiential resources in passage 8

Going back to Hasan's model, the main themes from our analysis of the construal of literature in Beauvoir's memoirs is that of agency and transcendence that reflects the two models of transitivity proposed by Halliday (1994) and Matthiessen (1995). The transcendental nature of literature and 'doers' of literature are symbolically articulated through patterns of transitivity selections. Beauvoir's interpretation of her interaction with literature shows that at an early age, she assigns agency to books in the context of mental clause: they impact on her emotions and bring about consciousness to Beauvoir and teach her about the world. In 'What can literature do?', Beauvoir defines literature as a way of seeing the world and unveiling the world and this unveiling is an action. The agency assigned to literature in mental and material clauses in Beauvoir's childhood extends to Beauvoir as she becomes a user of literature and ultimately a creator of literature. As Beauvoir realizes that she can in turn use language to impact on her world, she starts gaining agency and ultimately impact on others and assign value to her own existence.

From childhood to adulthood, Beauvoir goes through an experiential/ existential transformation in interaction with literature: from beneficiary, to actor/user of literature and ultimately agent of change in the world through her literary work. This semantic drift towards action, agency and transcendence allows her to go beyond her own situation as a girl born in a conservative catholic and bourgeois environment destined to marriage and gain power over her existence.

By examining the reality constructed by Beauvoir in passages where she talks about literature, it becomes apparent that Beauvoir's linguistic choices are not arbitrary and contribute to realizing her conception of literature and philosophy of existence whereby, choice, action, agency and transcendence are key concepts.

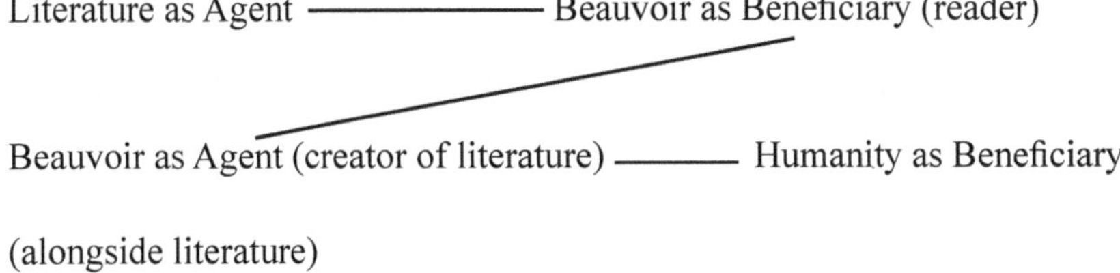

(alongside literature)

In conclusion, the themes encoded in the patterns of transitivity highlighted in the eight passages selected all lead to Beauvoir and literature becoming one: her existence as an individual cannot be dissociated from her existence as a corpus of text as the becomes 'the Textual Simone de Beauvoir' as Toril Moi (1994: 3) describes her.

6.6. Postscript

Simone de Beauvoir, Claire Cayron and Ruqaiya Hasan were the most influential women in my life and all three through their writings and thinking about literature motivated my work on verbal art. I am greatly indebted to them:

> *The objective through which I aim to transcend myself must appear to me as a point of departure towards a new transcendence. Thus develops fortunately, without ever immobilizing itself in unjustified facticity, a creative freedom. The creator relies on previous creations to create the possibility of new creations. ((Beauvoir, 1947: 39)*

> *I re-read your memoires at least once a year; I like to walk in your life. It is like one of those well kept gardens where it seems I breathe an air of immortality. The constant progression that you have followed as a writer and as a human being is to me like a tonic... there*

is not only a pen at the end of your fingers. There is a paintbrush, a scissor, and a hammer. To read you enchants me and stimulates me. (Claire Cayron, 1965 – Abstract from a letter to Beauvoir. My translation)

So long as some members of the community find the artistic structure worthwhile, the author has defied the oblivion imposed by death. (Hasan, 1985: 102)

References

Augras, J. (2016). 'Écritures de lecteurs: Beauvoir lue.' *La réception des Mandarins* (1954–1959), 387. Paris: RHLF Vol. 2, April–June 2016.

Beauvoir de, S. (1947). *Pour une morale de l'ambiguïté*. Paris: Gallimard.

Beauvoir de, S. (1958). *Mémoires d'une jeune fille rangée*. Paris: Gallimard.

Beauvoir de, S. (1959/2005). *Memoirs of a Dutiful Daughter*. Translated by James Kirkup. New York: HarperCollins Publishers.

Beauvoir de, S. (1965). *Que Peut La Littérature*. Edited by Yves Buin, L'INEDIT 10|18, 73–92. Paris: Union Générale d'Éditions.

Caffarel, A. (2006). *A Systemic Functional Grammar of French: From Grammar to Discourse*. London: Continuum.

Caffarel-Cayron, A. (2013). The influence of Simone de Beauvoir's writings on Claire Cayron's personal and creative life: A preliminary journey through their correspondence (1964–1984). *Simone de Beauvoir Studies*. Volume 29, 4–19. Oxford: Oxford Academic.

Caffarel-Cayron, A. (2016). Beauvoir and the Agency of Writing. In D. Banks and J. Ormod (Eds) *Nouvelles études sur la transitivité en français: Une perspective systémique fonctionelle*, 57–80. Paris: L'Harmattan.

Fallaize, E. (1988). *The Novels of Simone de Beauvoir*. London: Routledge.

Halliday, M. A. K. (1994). *An Introduction to Functional Grammar*. 2nd ed. London: Arnold.

Halliday, M. A. K. (2009). *The Essential Halliday*, J. J. Webster (Ed.). London: Continuum.

Hasan, R. (1985). *Linguistics, Language and Verbal Art*. Geelong: Deakin University Press.

Moi, T. (1994). *Simone de Beauvoir. The Making of an Intellectual Woman*. Oxford: Blackwell.

Moi, T. (2009). What can literature do? Simone de Beauvoir as a literary theorist. *PMLA* 124 (1): 189–198. https://doi.org/10.1632/pmla.2009.124.1.189

Rouch, M. (2017). 'Vous ne me connaissez pas mais ne jetez pas tout de suite ma lettre'. Le courrier des lecteurs et lectrices de Simone de Beauvoir. In F. Blum (Ed.) *Genre de l'archive: Constitution et transmission des mémoires militantes.* Paris: Codhos Editions.

Scholz, S. (2000). Simone de Beauvoir on language. *Philosophy Today* 44 (3): 211–223. https://doi.org/10.5840/philtoday200044331

Scholz, S. (2008). *The Second Sex. Philosophy Now, A Magazine of Ideas,* 69. https://philosophynow.org/issues/69/The_Second_Sex

7 Jane Austen's shapely sentence and the differentiation of dialogue from narrative: Towards a clause complex of her own

Fang Li[*]

7.1. Introduction: *A Room of One's Own*

In this chapter, I twist together two different strands of Ruqaiya Hasan's work: verbal art and the language of the home. We begin with Virginia Woolf's observation that in order to write the domestic fiction novels of naturalistic conversation and verbal thinking rendered as inner speech in free indirect discourse, Jane Austen could not simply appropriate the 'male' clause complex then in use by male writers like Samuel Johnson and Edward Gibbon. She had to develop a new kind of 'shapely' sentence for her own use. This raises three intriguing questions: Why did Woolf feel that Johnson and Gibbon wrote 'a man's sentence'? What exactly was this 'shapely' alternative that Jane Austen devised? Why do we value it the way we do today? I find that Johnson and Gibbon misappropriated an elaborated code of verbal science for literary purposes, that Austen did indeed laugh at their ponderous nominalizations – but that she also heavily appropriated them in framing narrative for lively dialogues. This meant the penetration

[*] Fang Li received an MA from King's College London in English Literature in 1997 and a PhD from University of Washington in 2009, and is currently an associate professor teaching in the Department of English Literature and Culture at Hankuk University of Foreign Studies. Fang Li has published articles and book chapters mostly on the works of nineteen-century British novelists such as Elizabeth Gaskell, Jane Austen, and Charles Dickens. Fang Li got to know Ruqaiya Hasan's work quite recently, after meeting her at the 40th ISFC in Guangzhou.

of the elaborated code by a homely restricted one, both a consequence and a cause of female literacy. This kind of merry table-turning with revolutionary implications animated the work of Ruqaiya Hasan throughout her career.

In *A Room of One's Own*, Virginia Woolf remarks that a woman writer at the beginning of the nineteenth century, having solved the problem of securing a room of one's own to write in and a modest income to write on, soon discovers that there is no readily available sentence to write with. She asks us to consider the following:

> The grandeur of their works was an argument with them, not to stop short, but to proceed. They could have no higher excitement or satisfaction than in the exercise of their art and endless generation of truth and beauty. Success prompts to exertion; and habit facilitates success.

Woolf doesn't give the source of the text – it is a quotation from William Hazlitt's essay 'On application to study' first published in 1823 – but she does tell us that the generic clause complex which underlies it 'is a man's sentence; behind it one can see Johnson, Gibbon and the rest'. While Charlotte Brontë, Woolf says, 'stumbled and fell' and 'George Eliot committed atrocities with it', 'Jane Austen looked at it and laughed at it and devised a perfectly natural, shapely sentence proper for her own use and never departed from it' (77). We do not need to accept Julia Kristeva's opposition of the childlike and female 'semiotic' to the adult and male 'symbolic' (1993) in order to feel, when Woolf offers this text as an example, that it is the hand of a nineteenth-century man writing to his contemporaries and not to us.

As Halliday and Matthiessen point out in the very first pages of their *Introduction to Functional Grammar* (2014), a grammarian may focus on a short text for two rather different reasons, which, with a little stretching, might fit perfectly two great passions of Ruqaiya Hasan's intellectual life. First of all, the grammarian may simply use a short text as a means for finding out about the system of language. But second, the grammarian can also focus on this text as an object of value in its own right – like a work of art. This gives rise to different questions: 'Why does the text mean what it does (to me, or to anyone else)? Why is it valued as it is?'

In what follows, we shall 'exapt', these quite general, grammatical questions – that is, we shall borrow structures developed for one function and apply them to a slightly different one, rather as the vocal tract itself, developed for breathing and eating, could be 'exapted' for speech (see Li and Kellogg 2012). We'll ask: why and how does the Hazlitt text suggest a masculine, and even a nineteenth-century masculine hand to Woolf, and to us? What is this 'shapely' sentence which Jane Austen devised as an alternative? And – at the risk of re-opening the demagogic debate over the desirability or otherwise of gendered sentences (Mills 1995) –why should we value Jane Austen's 'shapely sentences' as we do today, particularly since they were not so valued in her own time?

7.2. Why do we feel that Hazlitt's sentence is 'a man's sentence'?

John Barrell claims that what Woolf is objecting to is simply 'a certain brevity, crispness and clarity of statement' which the author assumes 'to be achieved by the deployment of binary, though not necessarily of antithetical, structures'. Barrell apparently has in mind paratactically arrayed groups such as 'not to stop short, but to proceed' or 'excitement or satisfaction'. Even 'the exercise', with its embedded phrase 'of their art' and 'endless generations' with its matching embedded phrase 'of truth and beauty' form a kind of binary structure (1988: 86). According to Barrell, these binary structures are intended to demonstrate on the one hand, a fine ability to discriminate, and on the other, a wholeness of vision.

This frankly subjective judgement can be illuminated by the simple use of the text annotations given in Halliday and Matthiessen's *Introduction to Functional Grammar*.

(1)
|||The grandeur [= of their works] | was | an argument [x with them]
$$[[= 1 \parallel \text{not |to stop short} \parallel$$
$$+ 2 \parallel \text{but | to proceed.]] |||}$$

(2)

||| They | could have | no higher 1 excitement
                                      + 2 or satisfaction
                               [x than [[x in 1 the exercise [of | their art]
                                           +2 and endless generation [of 1 | truth
                                                        + 2 | and beauty.]]]] |||

(3)

||| 1 Success | prompts | to exertion; ||
|| +2 and habit | facilitates | success.|||

However, one thing this annotation illuminates is that what Barrell says of the balanced pairs of the 'masculine' text is equally true of Woolf's own writing.

```
||| Jane Austen   1 | looked          | at it |
                 +2 | and laughed   | at it |
                            +3 |and devised  | a perfectly natural, shapely
                            sentence
                                       proper [x for her own use] |
                 +4 | and never departed | from it. |||
```

Here too there are binary but not necessarily antithetical structures, nice discriminations, and wholeness of vision. So where do the differences lie?

At the sounding level, Hazlitt re-uses ending syllables where Woolf re-uses the beginnings: Hazlitt has 'argument' and 'excitement', and 'satisfaction', 'exertion', and 'generation' but Woolf uses a gentle alliteration to tie 'looked at it' and 'laughed at it', and similarly ties 'devised' and 'departed'.

At the level of textual organization, while parataxis is used to generate rhythm and beauty in both, Hazlitt uses far more embedding. As David Tallentire (1976) has pointed out, Woolf does not use much hypotaxis in her work, preferring to link clauses paratactically. The apparently unnecessary reiteration of 'and' seems to emphasize the equality of the various parts in the whole. But a preference for parataxis is not necessarily a coded expression of a woman's striving for equality between genders. For one thing, as we can see in the analysis of the Hazlitt sentences, it can just as well express that fine discrimination and wholeness of vision which Barrell ascribes to male writers. For another, although Woolf does appear to eschew hypotaxis, she does make use of embedding ('proper for her own use'), and embedding is, arguably, an even more radical form of inequality between elements, since it involves rankshifting.

At the level of experiential meaning, where Woolf has a human Senser, Behaver, and Actor; Hazlitt's text is full of non-human abstract nominals ('grandeur', 'excitement', 'satisfaction', 'endless generation', 'exertion'), some of which are even Actors ('success', and 'habit'). Thus, through systemic-functional eyes, one can easily make out that Hazlitt is using grammatical metaphor: processes which are canonically realized as verbs (such as 'argue', 'excite', 'satisfy', 'exert', and 'generate') are instead realized as nouns ('argument', 'excitement', 'satisfaction', and 'generation'). This a-canonical realization corresponds in turn to imaginary entities: abstractions that end in '~ment' and '~tion'. This in turn explains the reused endings we noted above when we looked at sounding.

What the annotation cannot demonstrate is that these differences are general and not simply an artefact of our selection of short texts. Still less can it show that they are, as Woolf suggests, essentially male or female. But one thing we can say about all of these differences is that each one realizes a different textual mode and a different semantic orientation. The textual mode for Woolf is that of oral rather than written text, what Halliday (2002: 350) has called the 'choreographic', dynamic form of complexity that we tend to in speaking rather than the 'crystalline', static form used by Hazlitt. The semantic orientation for Woolf is that of everyday speech, where phenomena appear arrayed on a single 'plane' of generalization (as in a visual purview, where all objects in view are equally concrete) rather than budding or blossoming on a tree of hierarchically arranged abstractions, as we see in Hazlitt.

Basil Bernstein linked semantic orientations like these to code orientations. A restricted code orientation reflects what Emile Durkheim called an organic rather than a mechanical mode of social organization; what Ferdinand Tönnies would have called the *Gemeinschaft* orientation of people involved in low-autonomy professions doing interchangeable types of work. An elaborated code reflects a more *Gesellschaft* orientation in high-autonomy professions doing individual and non-interchangeable types of work. Ruqaiya Hasan (1985; 1991/2011) and Carmel Cloran (1999) demonstrated that these different code orientations apply not only to the persons actually involved in the work, but also to the women at home caring for children. This finding that the profession of parents have distal effects on the semantic orientations of the child should not surprise overmuch, for at least three reasons.

First of all, there is the prehistory of each family. As Deborah Cameron (2007) points out, many women marry men, often men of their own speech community and class background. Even if these women do not already share a code orientation with their husbands, they will soon require a shared code orientation for home use, and in a patriarchal society it is unsurprising that this will be, more often than not, that of the husband. Second, there is each family's current history: as Urie Bronfenbrenner (1979) points out, the most important context influencing the life (and even the lifespan) of the child is one which the child hardly ever even lays eyes on – the conditions under which parents work. In a class-ridden and class-riven society this will be either conditions in which people work with tools and are more or less replaceable (as tools are) and thus experience mechanical solidarity, or else conditions in which people work with signs and are more or less irreplaceable (as signs are). Finally, there is the family future history: as Thomas Piketty has pointed out, the social mobility of the twentieth century was rather more the exception than the rule under capitalism, and while there may be many outstanding exceptions, particularly on the borders of classes, there is always a strong 'washback' effect from the child's future employment possibilities: certain children and even their parents are bound to feel that a textual orientation towards the written mode does little for girls who are destined to spend their lives in housework, and a semantic orientation towards individualism can only handicap those bound for factory jobs. Hasan and Cloran found that one of the most important variables that predicts a restricted code orientation, for example, was the sex of the child, while another important variable was the profession of the parents (1986).

Somewhat mischievously, this finding has been criticized as a 'deficit' linguistics (e.g. Jones 2013), designed to show the restricted code was somehow incapable of creating true concepts. Yet a more careful reading of Bernstein, Hasan – and even Jane Austen – demonstrates that no such interpretation is required. Historically, since Newton, elaborated codes have been the means through which scientific and academic concepts are communicated, but it hardly follows that an elaborated code is the necessary precondition. Taking Halliday's three time-scales of semiohistory, it is easier to make the contrary argument: whether one is speaking sociogenetically (that is, in terms of how Newton and Galileo generated elaborated codes for writing scientific English in the first place), ontogenetically (that is, in terms of how children learn the elaborated codes in school), or even logogenetically (that is, in terms of how one explains elaborated codes in the course of a conversation), it is the restricted code which is the necessary precondition for the elaborated one: since what the elaborated code elaborates is the restricted code, we might refer to the latter as 'pre-elaborated'.

Both Bernstein and Hasan argued that the elaborated code orientation is not the unique path to higher concepts. The art of teaching might be defined as the art of constructing an elaborated code from a restricted one; a skilled parent or teacher knows how to semiotically mediate, to unpack the Greco-Latin words, the embeddings, and the nominalizations into familiar, everyday words, whole clauses and expressions that the child can recognize as the metaphors that they are. Without abandoning the more abstract, classifiable, and thematizable word meaning, the adult demonstrates a linguistically less dense way to reach the concept, a psychologically less steep path to the summit of thinking. In Vygotskyan terms, what was an intra-mental – and even intra-clausal, lexical – relationship in narrative then becomes externalized as an inter-mental relationship between turns in a dialogue. This may then be 're-internalized' as a new intra-mental, intra-clausal, lexical meaning in a new narrative. But this brings us to our second question: what happens when the semiotic mediator is not a parent or a teacher, but a woman novelist?

7.3. What is this 'shapely sentence' that Austen devised?

In order to answer this question comprehensively, we must analyse a whole novel. In their own work on verbal art, both Ruqaiya Hasan and Michael Halliday have criticized the circularity of textual analyses which simply support subjective aesthetic responses with examples carefully selected for that very purpose, Novels, which are very heterogeneous in their formal properties, are particularly open to this kind of cherry picking commentary; one can find material to support almost any judgement if one looks blindly enough. In this section, we take three alternative approaches. The first is to attempt to characterize the novelistic text type as a whole by looking at its sociocultural position in history. The second is to try to characterize the novel as a whole by examining statistically how much the author has succeeded in formally differentiating the dialogue from the narrative. The third is a form of simulation: it is to use these formal properties derived from the whole to construct our own imitation version of the authors in question.

First of all, whether or not one recognizes gendered sentences, the fact remains that two centuries ago when Jane Austen put pen to paper, text types were heavily gendered. The novel was an overwhelmingly feminine type of text, both in terms of its readership and its writers, and it would be surprising if this were not reflected in the code orientation, at least of the female characters. Gentlemen did not for the most part dabble in novels, but Samuel Johnson did write something that, although not quite a novel, is certainly a work of fiction.

Rasselas is a fable about an Abyssinian prince who is kept in a 'happy valley' while awaiting his accession to throne. Jaded, he decides that only the widespread observation of worldly suffering will bring him an understanding of happiness. With his mentor Imlac, and his sister Nekayah with her lady-in-waiting Pekuah, the prince tunnels his way out of the happy valley. They journey to Cairo and interview many people in various walks of life in order to decide which one is most conducive to human happiness. There is one brief episode of excitement, in which Pekuah is abducted by Arab bandits and ransomed by her companions, and then, in 'a conclusion in which nothing is concluded', the party gives up the search and returns to Abyssinia.

Let us compare this non-novel with Austen's first effort, *Northanger Abbey*. Austen's novels are sometimes called 'novels of conversation', but if one simply takes the material that appears between quotation marks as 'dialogue' and that which appears outside quotes as 'narrative', it is easy to show that the real conversation piece is *Rasselas*. *Rasselas* contains far more dialogue, at least as percentage (67.5% of *Rasselas* vs. 38.9% of *Northanger Abbey*). Similarly, if one looks at sheer sentence length and confines the analysis to the part of the story outside the quotation marks, it appears that Jane Austen's narrative sentences are, on average, not only longer than Johnson's, the individual clause-complexes are actually longer and on the whole more complex. So not only is Johnson more dialogic, Austen is more narrativistic – at least, to a first, superficial, and entirely quantitative, glance.

If, on the other hand, one turns that quantitative eye to what is inside the quotation marks, a somewhat different picture emerges. *Rasselas* contains only 222 turns of talk vs. *Northanger Abbey*'s 920 turns. So each of Johnson's turns is, on the average, nearly 110 words, more than three times as long as Jane Austen's. Table 7.1 compares the overall word count for each text as a whole, the words and proportion of total words devoted to narrative (as defined as being outside quotation marks), the words and proportion of total words devoted to dialogue (defined as being inside quotation marks), the mean length of clause in words, and the total turns of talk and mean length of turn in words.

Work and Author	Total Words	Total Words Outside Quotation Marks ("Narrative")	Mean Length of Narrative Clause Complex in Words	Total Words between Quotation Marks ("Dialogue")	Total Turns of Talk	Mean Length of Turn of Talk in Words
Rasselas, Samuel Johnson	35,949	11,682 (32.5%)	414/11,682 28.22 words	24,267 (67.5%)	222	109.3
Northanger Abbey, Jane Austen	74,756	45,731 (61.1%)	1,499/45,731 30.5 words	29,025 (38.9%)	920	31.5

Table 7.1: Bigger differences between narrative and dialogue in Austen than in Johnson: mean length of narrative clause in words and mean length of turn of talk in words.

While Jane Austen's narrative sentences may be quite close to the Johnsonian model, with perhaps even some slight exaggeration of Johnson's loquacity, her conversations sharply diverge from them. This would certainly reinforce a tendency towards parataxis, since conversation tends towards parataxis and away from embedding.

We saw that Hazlitt's selections were quite rich in nominalizations that end in '~tion', e.g. 'satisfaction', 'generation', and 'exertion'. If words which are not grammatical metaphors (e.g. 'question' and 'mention') are eliminated then the 'find and replace' function can be used to find exemplars, and the word count function will supply the total word count.

Table 7.2 shows the results of the comparison.

Corpus	Narrative in *Rasselas*	Dialogue in *Rasselas*	Narrative in *Northanger Abbey*	Dialogue in *Northanger Abbey*
Words ending in '~tion'	158/11,682 (every 73.9 words)	409/24,267 (every 59.33 words)	610/45,731 (every 74.9 words)	132/29,025 (every 219.9 words)

Table 7.2: Bigger differences between dialogue and narrative in Austen than in Johnson: '~tion'

We can see that once again the contrast between narrative and dialogue is far greater in Austen, particularly for '~tion' words (and that, curiously, Johnson's dialogue is actually richer in '~tion' words than his narrative!). But we can also see that once again Austenian narrative is very similar to Johnsonian, at least as far as the frequency of words ending in '~tion' are concerned.

Up to this point we have emphasized the accessibility and the replicability of our method: it is a backyard or basement analysis that hardly rises to the level of systemic-functional grammar at all; it is something a curious student with a word processor that has a 'search and replace' function and access to the Gutenberg.com text files can do very easily. As a result, the breakdown is purely quantitative rather than genuinely analytical. But thanks to the work of Mick O'Donnell, there is now a more sophisticated and more significant way: the UAM Corpus Tool. This free software not only allows the coding and comparison of a wide range of texts (as many other software packages do) it includes an automatic parsing function with a built-in version of systemic-functional grammar. While the automatic parsing process is far from perfect and the product does need to be proofread, particularly when small amounts of data are being used, the tool allows us, almost for the first time, to undertake grammatical comparisons of whole books without the necessity of a large research budget and a staff of willing and well-trained graduate students.

Table 7.3, for example, shows larger differences between the grammatical features of dialogue and narrative in *Northanger Abbey* than in *Rasselas*. The difference between the proportion of finite clauses in the dialogues between Catherine Morland and her friends and the proportion of finite clauses in the narrative commentary is more than 10% in Jane Austen – and less than 6% in Samuel Johnson. With Modality, Tense, Mood, Voice, and Polarity, the story is pretty much the same: Characters in Jane Austen talk differently from the narrator, while characters in Samuel Johnson talk more or less the same.

Can we move this analysis any further towards the lexical end of the lexicogrammatical continuum? Ruqaiya Hasan, after all, showed that lexical choices are really just the most delicate form of grammatical choice (1987). The UAM Corpus Tool contains a remarkable feature which will allow us

Clause Feature	Rasselas				Northanger Abbey			
	Dialogue		Narrative		Dialogue		Narrative	
	N	%	N	%	N	%	N	%
FINITENESS	N=3289		N=1492		N=4743		N=3975	
finite	2576	78.32%	1089	72.99%	3999	84.31%	2830	71.19%
nonfinite	719	21.86%	412	27.61%	753	15.88%	1149	28.91%
MODALITY	N=3289		N=1492		N=4743		N=3975	
Nonmodal	1984	60.32%	969	64.95%	3116	65.70%	2412	60.68%
Modal	592	18.00%	120	8.04%	883	18.62%	418	10.52%
TENSE	N=3289		N=1492		N=4743		N=3975	
Present	1161	35.30%	49	3.28%	1980	41.75%	147	3.70%
Past	553	16.81%	866	58.04%	764	16.11%	2149	54.06%
MOOD	N=3289		N=1492		N=4743		N=3975	
Declarative	1809	55.00%	812	54.42%	3243	68.37%	2355	59.25%
Interrogative	57	1.73%	0	0.00%	141	2.97%	34	0.86%
Imperative	226	6.87%	28	1.88%	356	7.51%	83	2.09%
VOICE	N=3289		N=1492		N=4743		N=3975	
Active	2960	90.00%	1325	88.81%	4536	95.64%	3611	90.84%
Passive	329	10.00%	167	11.19%	207	4.36%	364	9.16%
POLARITY	N=3289		N=1492		N=4743		N=3975	
Positive	3033	92.22%	1423	95.38%	4124	86.95%	3701	93.11%
Negative	256	7.78%	69	4.62%	619	13.05%	274	6.89%

Table 7.3: Differences in the number and proportion of various grammatical features in dialogue and in narrative: *Rasselas* compared with *Northanger Abbey*

to extend to this more delicate end of the lexicogrammatical continuum the observation of how a particular subtext such as 'narrative in *Rasselas*' distinguishes itself from 'dialogue in *Rasselas*' and from narrative and dialogue in Jane Austen. The 'Keywords' feature will calculate the propensity of particular words to occur in a sub-corpus when compared with the corpus as a whole. For example, the word 'prince' appears 41 times in the *Rasselas* Narrative sub-corpus, and only twice in all the other files in our corpus (*Rasselas* Dialogue, *Northanger Abbey* Narrative and *Northanger Abbey* Dialogue). UAM Corpus Tool then calculates 'keyness' or 'propensity' by comparing the relative frequency of the word in the subcorpus compared to other words in the subcorpus to the relative frequency of the word compared to other words in the corpus as a whole. In this way, we can see the lexical choices that make the narrative passages by Samuel Johnson stand out from the corpus and compare them to those which distinguish his dialogue, as well as to the lexical choices made by Jane Austen in her narrative and in her dialogue.

Table 7.4 shows the top ten most 'key' lexical choices for nouns.

Ten most 'key' nouns in *Rasselas*		Ten most 'key' nouns in *Northanger Abbey*	
Narrative	Dialogue	Narrative	Dialogue
'prince'	'nations'	'heroine'	'madam'
'astronomer'	'riches'	'gallery'	'heavens'
'banks'	'effects'	'affair'	'nonsense'
'princess	'earth'	'glance'	'stuff'
'palace'	'sea'	'examination'	'dear'
'music'	'qualities'	'colour'	'thing'
'lake'	'external'	'manuscript'	'creature'
'mountain'	'maids'	'size'	'lord'
'valley'	'mankind'	'visitor'	'fellow'
'sage'	'condition'	'whisper'	'sir'

Table 7.4: Key nouns for narrative and dialogue in *Rasselas* and *Northanger Abbey*

This table shows us how misleading an analysis based purely on turn length or sentence length can be, for here we can clearly discern a distinction between Johnsonian narrative and Johnsonian dialogue, and it's not at all what we might expect. The narrative passages are characterized by concrete words concerned with exotic scenery ('banks', 'palace', 'lake', and 'mountain') and romantic characters ('prince', 'princess', 'astronomer', 'sage'). The dialogues, on the other hand, are concerned with generalities (the 'effects' and 'qualities' of 'external' 'conditions', such as 'nations', 'riches', 'earth', 'sea', and 'mankind'). Where characters do appear as the objects of conversation they are abject and female ('maids' – but these are overwhelmingly part of the narrative of Pekuah, who is abducted with her maids by an Arab brigand).

In contrast, the key lexical selections in Austenian narrative seems much more concerned with giving the heroine's visual experiences and her response to them ('gallery', 'glance', 'examination'). The selections in dialogue are words which are centrally implicated in interpersonal meanings: 'stuff' and 'nonsense', and terms of address, such as 'madam', 'dear', 'lord', 'fellow', and 'sir'. Where there are abstractions, e.g. 'heavens' and 'creature', these too are mainly interpersonal Themes ('My dearest creature!' and 'Oh, heavens!').

Verbs present us with an even more counter-intuitive view. Speaking generally, we can say that the key selections made by Johnson for narrative are mostly verbal or mental processes, while those made by Austen are material processes. But dialogue presents a kind of mirror image: the Johnsonian selections are typically material processes, while the Austenian ones are mental and verbal (see Table 7.5).

Ten most 'key' verbs in *Rasselas*		Ten most 'key' verbs in *Northanger Abbey*	
Narrative	Dialogue	Narrative	Dialogue
'discovered'	'become'	'reached'	'signify'
'retired'	'live'	'conveyed'	'pray'
'observed'	'act'	'seated'	'says'
'entreated'	'fly'	'returning'	'hate'
'rose/arose'	'reason'	'quitting'	'assure'
'continued'	'cease'	'roused'	'dare'
'confined'	'content'	'flattering'	'persuade'
'approached'	'consider'	'pointed'	'ask'
'considered'	'fall'	'softened'	'got'
'resolved'	'suffer'	'catching'	'torment'

Table 7.5: Key verbs for narrative and dialogue in *Rasselas* and *Northanger Abbey*

Notice that the top ten most 'key' words in the narrative passages of *Rasselas* are all in the past tense, while those in the dialogue passage are all present simple. In contrast, four out of ten in *Northanger Abbey* are actually in some present form or non-finite form, e.g. 'Returning through the large and lofty hall, they ascended a broad staircase of shining oak, which, after many flights and many landing-places, brought them upon a long, wide gallery'.

So far we've tried to situate the Austenian novel historically and characterize it socioculturally, and we've attempted to get a sense of the overall quantitative differences between Austen's sentence and those of Johnson. But keyness allows us to go a step further in the qualitative direction and attempt a third strategy: simulation. To get a feel for how these differences create different narrative voices, we might make up a typically Johnsonian narrative passage using the lexicogrammatical features that we have found most distinctive.

> During these nightly perambulations in the valley at the foot of the great mountain, the prince one evening observed the astronomer retired by the bank of a lake. He resolved himself and approached the sage, so that the same might be entreated to consider why he and the princess should continue to be confined in this place.

Granted, the insertion of a '~tion' in the circumstantial theme seems somewhat gratuitous: 'perambulation' is not one of the key words. But the two clause complexes average out to just over the length required by a typical Johnsonian narrative sentence (28.5 words here, compared to 28.22 on average). For reasons of space, it is difficult to do this with a Johnsonian dialogic passage:

> 'No matter what external riches are ours from earth and sea and no matter what the qualities of their effects on nations,' said the Prince, 'mankind's condition suffers where we cease to reason and consider, and become like beasts of the air who merely fly or fall when we act.'

The average spoken turn in *Rasselas* would be roughly twice this length.

In contrast, we saw that a typical Austenian narrative clause-complex is somewhat longer than a Johnsonian one. Using all of the distinctive words we discovered, a reasonable facsimile might sound something like this:

> Returning through the gallery, our heroine was soon pointed by the oil lamps to her own apartment, where she reached for a large-sized manuscript with a most flattering leather binding. A softened whisper and a glance conveyed to her the presence of a visitor, and quitting the examination of her book, she coloured abruptly.

Here the second clause-complex is some six words too short, but the very shortness of the final matrix clause has a dramatic effect. We might simulate some of her short-turn dialogue thus:

> 'Good heavens, Madam! What stuff you dear creatures read! Pray try this volume of Gibbon instead.'

> 'Oh, I hate history. I am persuaded that it can only be nonsense! How is it that Mr. Gibbon can tell us what Caractacus, Agricola, or Alfred really said, still less what he thought?'

> 'Yes, we may assure ourselves that that the speeches and thoughts we read in histories have been invented. Yet I dare say that cannot mean they do not signify. Surely if novelists have got the right to torment us with made-up speeches, then historians may do likewise.'

If we average out the length of these invented Austenian turns we find that they come to less than one word over the average length of Austen's actual dialogue turns (31.5 words).

But perhaps the most important thing to keep in mind is that this typical Austen sentence is not typical at all: there is the rich variety in Finiteness, Modality, Tense, Mood, Voice, and Polarity that we observe in the general statistics. In Austen, not only are dialogic sentences different from narrativistic ones but there are different voices in dialogues, and they do differ along some of the lines we've been considering. By this very fact, however, the different voices interpenetrate each other, with some women's voices taking up the hypotaxis, grammatical metaphor, and even the hierarchical, esoteric and exclusive forms of discourse which were proper to men. And this brings us to the final question we wish to consider in this chapter, namely....

7.4. Why should we value this 'shapely sentence' the way we value it today?

We are now in a much better position to appreciate what advantages Jane Austen might have derived from formally differentiating narrative and dialogue and having the dialogue appropriate and speak through (Christie 2002) the narrative (e.g. through free indirect speech) rather than the other way around, as we observed in the work of Johnson. Let's consider the different structures and the different voices revealed by Hallidayan transcription of a short conversation between Catherine Morland and her new friend Eleanor Tilney, concerning the relationship of novels to histories. Catherine says:

(1)

||| 1 | I | read | it | a little | as a duty, |
|| + 2   but | it | tells | me | nothing [[[that does not either vex or weary me]] |||.

(2)

||| 1 [1 | The quarrels of popes and kings with wars and pestilences in every page; |
+2 | the men all so good for nothing, |
+3 | and hardly any women at all— |
    =2 it | is | very tiresome; |
+2 and yet | α   α | I | often | think |
              'β | it | odd x [[that it should be so dull]],
        x β for | a great deal of it| must be | invention.|||

(3)

|||1   1   [1 The speeches [[that are put into the heroes mouths]]
             +2 | their   1 thoughts
                        2 and designs— |
=2   the chief [of all of this] | | | must be | invention, |
+2 and | invention | is [[what delights me | in other books.]] |||

Like Virginia Woolf, Austen uses a good deal of paratactic extension ('+ but', '+and', '+ yet'). But there are some instances of hypotaxis ('I often think it odd' and 'for a great deal of it must be invention'), a good deal more embedding ('odd that it should be so dull', 'nothing that does not either vex or weary me', and 'invention is what delights me in other books'), and even some grammatical metaphor ('invention'). Above all, Austen sets a pattern of what Vygotsky (Выготский 1934/2005) would call переживания, or 'trans-experience' – the feeling of what happens followed by thoughts about what happened. Closer to Austen's own time, Wordsworth might refer to it as emotions reflected upon in tranquillity (1800/1914: 26).

How does Catherine reflect on her experience? It is not so much a process of thinking about feeling; rather it is a process of feeling about thinking. First there is first a clause complex (1) which describes her desultory readings in history. This is followed by a clause complex (2) which elaborates the experience as parallel nominal groups ('quarrels', 'men all so good for nothing', and 'hardly any women at all' and then sums up the nominal groups with 'it' and pronounces upon 'it' with 'tiresome'. The pattern is repeated and varied in clause complex (3), but this time with an innovation which brings her a decisive step nearer her interlocutor. The desultory reading experience is again unpacked into nominal groups ('speeches that are put into the heroes' mouths', 'their thoughts and designs' and then summed up, but this time in a grammatical metaphor ('invention'), which allows Catherine to place the summed-up material as theme for a more positive evaluation, a contrast which explains her perplexity at her own feelings. The complexity is choreographic indeed, acutely self-aware and even profound but not at all calculated and certainly not neatly balanced: two of these double patterns of experience and then appraisal (history and Catherine's reflection on it, then the speeches and Catherine's reflection on them) packed into three orthographic sentences instead of the more canonically realized four.

Catherine Morland's new friend, Miss Tilney, is quite charmed, but her response is thinking about feeling rather than vice versa. It is also much more measured in content and balanced in form.

(1)

||| 'β Historians, α you think, << said Miss Tilney>> are not happy in their flights of fancy.|||

(2)

||| They | α display | imagination
                +β without | raising | interest.|||

(3)

||| I | 1 | am | fond of history, |
             | + 2 and   α | am | very well contented |
              |xβ   to take | 1 the false
                              +2 with the true. |||

Here the complexity is much more crystalline and masculine; in fact, the structure is quite reminiscent of the Hazlitt quotation with which we began.

Miss Tilney projects Catherine's thought, then paraphrases without attempting to unpack it. She then responds with her own thought, reusing the categories that Catherine introduced ('the false' = 'invention'). In every clause complex there is hypotaxis in one form or another. Above all, there are nominalizations: 'flights of fancy', 'imagination', 'interest', 'the false' and 'the true' linked by unmodulated relational processes, just as was seen with Hazlitt's sentences. As with Hazlitt, grammatical metaphors are linked with unmodulated, mostly relational, processes, and much stricter parallelism.

In fact, Miss Tilney's views on history are much like those of her brother Henry and so it is not that surprising that the hypotactic constructions, the nominalizations, and the unmodulated relational processes are rather authoritative and even masculine – brothers and sisters are apt to share wordings as well as meanings. But Eleanor's role is not simply to parrot Henry's wordings to Catherine; more often she is Henry's foil and even his critic. Verily, the sharing of wordings and meanings goes both ways, and this explains why Henry, in turn, has the power to charm Mrs. Allen by sharing his thoughts and feelings about muslins and delight Catherine herself with feelings and thoughts about Mrs. Radcliffe's novels.

One element that makes Catherine's dialogue stand out from Miss Tilney's is Catherine's use of modulation ('should be', and 'must be') in contrast to Miss Tilney's more authoritative assertions; another is the greater parallelism and denser use of grammatical metaphor in the speech of the latter. Halliday claims that nominalizations and unmodulated relational processes arise in scientific writing in English with the work of Newton, who attempted to render in good English prose the kinds of abstractions and equations that he had expressed mathematically elsewhere in the *Opticks*. This style of 'prose equations' became so authoritative that it was soon 'exapted' for different purposes – e.g. the political economy of Adam Smith, the philosophy of John Locke and David Hume, the sentimental fables of Samuel Johnson and eventually the art criticism of Hazlitt, where it was seized upon as masculine by Virginia Woolf.

Together with Virginia Woolf, we can be quite certain of something about which both Samuel Johnson and Jane Austen had only the dimmest intuitions: the future of English literature. Dorrit Cohn points out (1992: 82) that one of the key distinctions between historical narratives and fictional ones is not so much the presence or absence of thought processes, but rather their mandatory modulation. Biographers, for example, are forced to say things like 'Napoleon must have reflected bitterly on the perfidy of his countrymen as the island of Saint Helena appeared out of the South Atlantic gloom'. Of course, the novelist is also entitled to say such things; as Paul Hernadi (1976) remarks, fictional narratives require, just as historical narratives forbid, a division of labour between the narrator and the author, and this division of labour makes it possible for the novelist to say more or less anything that a historian might say simply by reinventing the narrator as a historian. However, the novelist is not required to talk like this, and in fact one has grown accustomed, particularly since the work of Jane Austen and Virginia Woolf, to much more unmodulated access to the psychological processes of our characters.

As Halliday and Matthiessen (2014: 446–448) point out, quotation is a very strongly dispreferred option for reproducing thoughts (only 2.5% of clause nexuses projecting thinking were of this type in their sample of 6,832). So when the narrator claims to be able to tell us the exact words that a character is thinking, the reader interprets this not as mendaciousness but as fiction. In contrast, direct access to exact wording is at least theoretically possible, and this is precisely the claim that is being made whenever a narrator opens a quotation with quotation marks. Yet when one tries to reproduce even a very recent conversation word for word, the fictitiousness of our mental transcript is plainly apparent when one compares it with an actual transcript or even with someone else's account of the conversation. In practical terms, therefore, the reproduction of exact wordings by a narrator of the speech of characters, should be no less a hallmark of fiction than the reproduction of thinking as words, and if, as Cohn (1978) says, it is the borderline cases of her distinction between historicity and fictiveness that truly establish the borders, then the example of quoted speech should be, in the history of the genre, all the more determining and defining.

And so it was. Early epistolary novels (e.g. *Pamela*, *Evelina*, and even Jane Austen's earliest efforts) circumvented the problem of the reader's incredulity about the wording by the use of the form of personal letters, which seemed to offer a guarantee of the exact wording as far as the letter-writer was concerned, and then threw the onus of the reliability of transcribed conversations on the supposed correspondent. Richardson's novels were written without quotation marks, at least initially. *Northanger Abbey*, for example, has 19 instances of a use of quotation marks that would be distinctly non-standard today. For example, when Henry tries to scare Catherine with a lurid description of how she will be lodged when they arrive at the Abbey, Catherine's feelings and words are given thus:

> Catherine, recollecting herself, grew ashamed of her eagerness, and began earnestly to assure him that her attention had been fixed without the smallest apprehension of really meeting with what he related. 'Miss Tilney, she was sure, would never put her into such a chamber as he had described! —She was not at all afraid.' (p. 127 in the Oxford World's Classics edition)

The use of 'she' *within* the quotation marks to refer to the speaker herself is striking to us now (though similar examples can be found in the works of Elizabeth Gaskell and Charlotte Brontë). But by simply removing the quotation marks, one would get a fairly typical instance of one of the important technologies that Jane Austen and her novel of conversation made to the English novel: the use of free indirect speech.

The quotation mark, free indirect speech and the novel itself are literary technologies which seem to have co-evolved, at least in English, alongside an acceptance of what Cohn calls 'fictionality', that is, the understanding that fiction is not mendacious, but rather tells the truth about its own fictitiousness so that it can tell us truths about less observable matters with some authority. Among these less observable matters are unheard conversations and unspoken thoughts, and, as Woolf tells it, Jane Austen soon discovered that the heavily nominalized style got in the way of all that, found a better way, and stuck with it. Voloshinov (1973: 123) claims that free indirect speech is another milestone in the evolution of that narrative technology, a border which marks off our own era of 'relativistic individualism' from the 'realistic and critical individualism' of the nineteenth-century novel. In the same way, the 'pictorial style' of reported speech with authorial retort and commentary forms a river dividing the nineteenth-century novel from the current of the 'rationalistic dogmatism' of the age of Johnson. If so, Jane Austen marks the fording place.

7.5. Conclusion: A clause complex of our own

We set out to answer three questions: What makes the clause complexes typical of Johnson and Gibbon 'male'? How does the 'shapely' Austenian sentence stand out in contrast? What does this distinction signify for the exclusiveness of male discourse and the historic transition towards universal literacy that we see with the rise of female readers and female writers? Here's what we've found: Johnson (and also Gibbon) used an elaborated register developed for a code orientation towards the highly abstract, characterized by heavy nominalization, relational verbs, and paratactic units, often contrasting in polarity ('not this but that'). Austen made a clear – even slightly exaggerated – distinction between the narrator and the characters, using much shorter turns that foreground interpersonal meanings for the latter. We may speculate that the contrast between Austenian narrative and dialogue matters for two reasons. First of all, it casts a slightly parodistic light on the narrating historian and foregrounded and highlighted a lively and relatively authentic dialogue. Second, it allows the thoughts of the characters to penetrate the narration itself, and transform 'narrative' into intra-personal, self-directed dialogue. This penetration of the elaborated register by the restricted register – the permeation of the thoughts of the narrator by the thoughts of characters – enabled characters to 'appropriate and speak through' (as Frances Christie says) the narrator instead of having the narrator appropriate and speak through characters. In this way, it decisively placed a new semiotic means in the hands of women, as well as writers and readers everywhere. Jane Austen might have been personally conservative, but her differentiation of dialogue from narrative appears nothing short of revolutionary.

Or was it simply the continuation of an older subversive tradition? Bakhtin (1981) argues for a conception of the novel as a constant presence in literary history – the eternal fording place between everyday speech and literature, the place where the one crosses over into the other, through devices like the projection of a dialogue through a narrative, or the penetration of dialogue into narrative. This view of an ever-present novel that goes all the way back to Menippean satire and even Socratic dialogue stands very much in contrast to more historical accounts of the novel, such as that of Georg Lukács (1962), who argues that the novel is the 'epic' of our own time, or that of Ian Watt (2001), who associates the novel with the rise of the reading middle class. Yet these two contrasting views are not quite as irreconcilable as they may seem: it is possible to see the novel as evolving historically precisely through exaptations – borrowings from previous text types which take older textual resources and shunt them in the direction of entirely new literary functions. In order to bring about this type of specifically literary exaptation, however, the earlier textual resources need first to be detached from the functions they performed in earlier genres. For example, in order for Cervantes to devote the textual resources developed in chivalric novels of adventure into a meditation on senile dementia at the end of life, he had first to break the reader's attachment to the earlier genre. Cervantes managed this by placing the phraseology typical of chivalric novels in dialogue rather than narration; Austen, as we have seen, does this too (Miss Tilney) but mostly she works the other way around, allowing her characters' thoughts to seep into the narration (Emma).

As Genette (1982) points out, one way that the reader's attachment to a well-established genre is broken is through parody. Previous literary critics, exploring Jane Austen's penchant for irony, have concluded that her distancing herself from the omniscient, extradiegetic narrator is what allows her to get closer to the character point of view (Morini 2010; Pallarés-García 2012). But the sharp stylistic divergence we have observed between the clause complexes that Austen realizes as conversations and those she realizes as narrations might suggest that this ironic distance can be fruitfully examined from the other end. Instead of considering that the narrator is treating the characters with a certain detached sympathy, one might consider the hypothesis that the characters, by indulging in what one can read as fairly realistic but also rather trivial dialogue, suggest in the author's mind – and in that of the reader – a knowing, and ironic, commentary on the pomposity of historicizing narration.

Compare, for example, the following Austenism from near the end of the novel, with the quotation from Hazlitt at the beginning of this chapter. Catherine has been summarily dismissed from the Abbey by the General, who has been given an exaggerated notion of Catherine's impecuniousness by John Thorpe. She is on her way home, not in a stylish carriage driven by an expectant suitor, but using public transportation. Through Catherine's tears, the narrator observes:

> A heroine in a hack post-chaise is such a blow upon sentiment, as no attempt at grandeur or pathos can withstand.

It is not too much of a strain to hear the voice of Jane Austen chuckling gently at Johnson, Gibbon, and Hazlitt in this narration. If we listen carefully, with Ruqaiya Hasan's acute systemic-functional ears, to the subsequent dialogue, we may discern the voices of Virginia Woolf and the generations of future female novelists to follow. We may even – and it is in this that we see most clearly the realism of Jane Austen's verbal art – make out clause complexes that are recognizably our own.

References

Argaman, O. (2010). Linguistic markers and emotional intensity. *Journal of Psycholinguistic Research*, 39(2), 89–99.

Bakhtin, M. M. (1981). Epic and novel. In M. Holquist (Ed.) *The Dialogic Imagination*. Austin, TX: University of Texas Press.

Barrell, J. (1988). *Poetry, Language and Politics*. Manchester: Manchester University Press.

Bernstein, B. (1996/2000). *Pedagogy, Symbolic Control and Identity: Theory, Research, Critique*. (Revised Edition). Lanham, MA: Rowan and Littlefield.

Bernstein, B. (1973). *Class, Codes, and Control. Volume 1*. St. Albans: Paladin.

Bronfenbrenner, U. (1979). *The Ecology of Human Development*. Cambridge, MA and London: Harvard University Press.

Cameron, D. (2007). *The Myth of Mars and Venus*. Oxford: Oxford University Press.

Christie, F. (2002). *Classroom Discourse Analysis. A Functional Perspective*. London: Continuum.

Cloran, C. (1999). Contexts for Learning. In F. Christie (Ed.) *Pedagogy and the Shaping of Consciousness: Linguistic and Social Processes*, 31–65. London and New York: Continuum.

Cohn, D. (1978). *Transparent Minds*. Princeton, NJ: Princeton University Press.

Cohn, D. (1992). *The Distinction of Fiction*. Baltimore and London: Johns Hopkins.

Genette, G. (1982). *Palimpsestes*. Paris: Éditions du Seuil.

Halliday, M. A. K. (2004a). *The Language of Science. The Collected Works of M. A. K. Halliday, Vol. 5*, J. J. Webster (Ed.). London: Continuum.

Halliday, M. A. K. (2004b). *The Language of Early Childhood. The Collected Works of M. A. K. Halliday, Vol. 4*, J. J. Webster (Ed.). London: Continuum.

Halliday, M. A. K. (2014). *An Introduction to Functional Grammar*, rev. C. M. I. M. Matthiessen. 4th ed., London and New York: Routledge.

Hasan, R. (1985). *Linguistics, Language and Verbal Art*. Geelong: Deakin University Press.

Hasan, R. (1987). The grammarian's dream: Lexis as most delicate grammar. In M. A. K. Halliday and R. P. Fawcett (Eds), *New Developments in Systemic Linguistics: Theory and Description*, 184–212. London: Pinter.

Hasan, R. (2011). *Selected Works on Applied Linguistics*. Beijing: Foreign Language Teaching and Research Press.

Hasan, R., and Cloran, C. (1990). A sociolinguistic interpretation of everyday talk between mothers and children. In M. A. K. Halliday, H. Nichols, and J. Gibbons (Eds) *Learning, Keeping and Using Language: Selected Papers from the 8th World Congress of Applied Linguistics*, Sydney, 16–21 August 1987, 67–99. Amsterdam: Benjamins. https://doi.org/10.1075/z.lkul1.10has

Hazlitt, W. (1870). *In The Plain Speaker: Opinions on Books, Men and Things*. London: Bell and Daldy.

Hernadi, P. (1976). Clio's cousins: Historiography as translation, fiction, and criticism. *New Literary History* 7 (2), 247–257. https://doi.org/10.2307/468505

Jones, P. E. (2013). Bernstein's 'Codes' and the linguistics of 'Deficit'. *Language and Education* 27 (2), 161–179. https://doi.org/10.1080/09500782.2012.760587

Kristeva, J. (1993). *Les nouvelles maladies de l'âme*, Paris: Fayard.

Li, F. and Kellogg, D. (2012). Revoicings and devoicings: Requests, confessions, and acts of violence in three 'industrial' novels. *Scientific Study of Literature*, 2 (1), 108–127. https://doi.org/10.1075/ssol.2.1.07li

Lukács, G. (1962). *The Theory of the Novel*. London: Merlin.

Mills, S. (1995). *Feminist Stylistics*. New York: Routledge.

Morini, M. (2010). The poetics of disengagement: Jane Austen and echoic irony. *Language and Literature* 19 (4), 339–356. https://doi.org/10.1177/0963947010372955

Pallarés-García, E. (2012). Narrated perception revisited: The case of Jane Austen's Emma. *Language and Literature* 21 (2), 170–188. https://doi.org/10.1177/0963947011435862

Tallentire, D. (1976). Confirming intuition about style using concordances. In A. Jones and R. F. Churchouse (Eds) *The Computer in Literary and Linguistic Studies, Third International Symposium*. Cardiff: University of Wales Press.

Tönnies, F. (1887/1957). *Community and Society (English translation of Gemeinschaft und Gesellschaft)* East Lansing, MI: Michigan State University Press.

Voloshinov, V. N. (1973). *Marxism and the Philosophy of Language*. Cambridge, MA: Harvard University Press.

Watt, I. (2001). *The Rise of the Novel*. Berkeley and Los Angeles, CA: University of California Press.

Woolf, V. (1928/1970). *A Room of One's Own*. Harmondsworth, Penguin Books.

Wordsworth, W. (1800/1914). Preface to the Lyrical Ballads. In *Famous Prefaces, the Harvard Classics*. New York: P. F. Collier and Son, Co.

Выготский, Л. С. (1934/2005). Мышление и речь. Москва: Соцэкгиз.

8 Appraisal and master identities in contemporary Spanish crime fiction: The case of *Los mares del Sur* and its translations into English and German

Anna Espunya[*]

8.1. Introduction

This chapter explores the verbal reproduction of emotional states as a resource for the negotiation of master identities in fiction. The focus of interest is the role played by evaluative language as a bonding mechanism, one of the resources authors use to construe a community of shared values with their readership. The contemporary Spanish novel *Los mares del Sur* (Vázquez Montalbán 1979) has been chosen because one of its central themes is the constant negotiation of identity and identities (social and generational). The novel has been translated into English and into German; by comparing these new re-instantiations with the source text, we observe different approaches to preserving the indices of identity negotiation. In the two samples analysed, one recreating anger, the other recreating nostalgia, resources are different. The first one, characterized by judgement, presents social stereotypes, items that are value-laden, heteroglossic and culture-bound, hence difficult

[*]	Anna Espunya is Associate Professor of English Studies and Translation at Universitat Pompeu Fabra (Barcelona). Her research interests lie at the interface between linguistics, stylistics and translation studies. Her latest publications include the co-edited *The Translation of Fictive Dialogue* (Rodopi 2012), as well as several book chapters on the translation of fictive orality devices from English into Catalan, and on the role of fictive orality in the creation of narrative point of view. She is the principal investigator of project ValTrad ('Evaluation in Translation', funded by the Spanish government, reference FFI2013-42751-P), aimed at the study of evaluation in various registers of translated discourse (literary and legal translation).

to translate in their complexity both in English and in German. The second sample lexically creates a mood of heaviness that explicitly appraises objects in the protagonist's individual experience but implicitly links with the collective historic memory of the losing side in the Spanish war. In the English translation, the tendency towards textual standardization, through the editing of repetitions and the normalization of syntax, changes the fabric of nostalgia.

The aim of this contribution is twofold. In the first place, the chapter explores the representation of emotional states as a resource for the negotiation of affiliation, in particular of master identities (Martin 2010: 24). A discourse sample from the contemporary Spanish novel *Los mares del Sur* (Manuel Vázquez Montalbán 1979) has been selected where narrative technique and lexicogrammatical choices are used to represent a display of two of the main characters' recurring feelings, anger and nostalgia, both relevant for the overall meaning of the author's work. The second aim is to show the re-negotiation that takes place when translators render such fragments of discourse, taking as a case study the English and German translations. The methodology is qualitative and the main theoretical notions are drawn from affiliation theory and Appraisal Theory in systemic functional linguistics, and from translation studies.

We take fiction writing to be an asynchronous communicative act involving several potentially embedded levels of sender-addressee relationships. Thus, characters communicate with each other, the narrator communicates with an implicit addressee, and above all, the author communicates with the reader (for a development of the discourse situation in fiction, see Leech and Short 1981: 259–271). From the perspective of dialogism, 'even apparently monologic texts (e.g. a formal written novel) set up a dialogue and anticipate a response from the reader' (Bakhtin 1981, cited in Munday 2012: 12). Fiction appeals to the reader to agree or disagree with the ideas and values presented or constructed, and to recognize individual and collective identities with which to affiliate. I assume that the representation of an emotional state, particularly if it is done from the point of view of the experiencer, is a possible resource to engage the reader to sympathize with the character. Furthermore, familiarity of the reader with the situation triggering the emotion may enhance affiliation through shared knowledge and values.

Among the literary genres, detective fiction, particularly the hard-boiled version, has been considered the medium for performing social criticism and ideological analysis (Resina 1997; Krajenbrink and Quinn 2009). In Spain, journalist, poet, essayist and novelist Manuel Vázquez Montalbán (1939–2003) used the genre conventions of the detective novel for the purposes of historical and social chronicle (Bayó 2001) of the country's vicissitudes from the post-war period to the restoration of democracy in a series of

24 novels with private detective Pepe Carvalho as the main character. The Carvalho novels express the author's view that human beings (and fictional characters) are the product of their social background, their 'affective education' and their 'circumstances' (Bayó 2001: 7). The author achieves this by 'portraying the cultural, socio-political, and economic conflict between the classes as well as between the individual and the system' (ibid.: 7).

As regards literary technique, Vázquez Montalbán merges 'the prosaic with the poetic, realism with experimentalism, description with argument, the particular with the general, the personal with the collective' Bayó (2001: 8). Even if the predominant narrative form is third person narration with internal focalization (the narrator adopts Carvalho's point of view), direct speech is present in the form of conversations between Carvalho and his acquaintances and interviews with suspects. Characters display individual linguistic repertoires recreated vividly and richly through a range of language varieties, user-related (social, geographical), use-related (characters reflect many fields of activity: the gourmet, the literary aficionado, the political activist, the trade-unionist, the policeman, the war veteran, etc.) and hybrid (subcultures such as the suburban youths, criminals, prostitutes, etc.). Together these voices form a fabric that the reader can identify as a cultural reservoir.

Several of the books in the Carvalho series have been translated into a range of languages and awarded prizes for best detective fiction in European countries (mainly France, Germany and Italy). Translation involves a mediation process where an individual re-instantiates a given text exploiting the meaning potential offered by a new language system in a different culture. The question is to what extent a systemic parallel affiliation offer can be made to the new reader, given the role of linguistic resources in the negotiation of affiliation. The focus on the renderings of certain critical points allows the analyst to infer the closeness and mutual knowledge between societies, similarities and differences between reservoirs, linguistic resources for affiliation, and the role of translation.

The structure of this chapter is the following. In section 8.2, I situate identity as the concern of systemic functional approach to language, particularly within the frame of affiliation theory. Section 8.3 presents a brief overview of the main master identity traits in the Carvalho character and the novel *Los mares del Sur* according to the literature. Section 8.4 introduces the main research issues and goals of translation studies. Section 8.5 provides essential background on the novel and its translations. Section 8.6 presents an analysis of the discourse fragment displaying anger and its link with the negotiation of ethnic/class identity, in the Spanish source text and in the English and German translations; in section 8.7 I turn to the representation of nostalgia. Finally, section 8.8 is devoted to the conclusions.

8.2. Identity in SF linguistics, affiliation and bonding

Identity is strongly related to the hierarchy of individuation, i.e. specialization through social group, sub-groups and the individual (see Martin 2010: 22). In this model, communal identity is negotiated through language by means of two opposed trajectories called *allocation* and *affiliation*. Allocation is how a culture classifies identities, subdividing itself into smaller communities of users, which share given *master identities* (e.g. generation, gender, class, ethnicity and dis/ability) or a given subculture, to the personae that make up the repertoire of an individual user (cf. Martin 2010: 24). The opposite trajectory, affiliation, goes from persona to culture. Following Bernstein (1996, cited in Martin 2010: 23), a community possesses a set of semantic strategies, or *reservoir*, while an individual possesses a *repertoire*, his or her own set of coding strategies, part of which are shared with the rest of members of his or her community, and part of which are individual, a product of his own context and activities.

Among the linguistic resources to negotiate affiliation is evaluative language. Studies on affiliation in naturalistic conversation data have identified points in a conversation where identity or identities, and affiliation to the same group, are being negotiated between the interactants. These are called 'bonding moments' (Stenglin 2004). Bonding as a mechanism of affiliation is based on sharing (Bednarek 2010: 253). Both Martin and Bednarek identify many resources for bonding: appraisal (Martin and White 2005) and involvement (anti-language, swearing, technical terms and expert languages, naming); intertextual references and allusions, references to beliefs, and the sharing of personal experience. It is to be expected that the same resources will be used for bonding in fiction writing as well, not only in fictive dialogue but also in inner monologue and thought representation. After all, 'fiction seems to be designed to align readers, as well as ... characters by construing identities of characters' (Bednarek 2010: 252, citing Martin 2008: 56). I claim that the displays of emotion in the fragments invite bonding between reader and author.

8.3. Master identities in the Carvalho Series by Manuel Vázquez Montalbán

There is general agreement that contemporary Spanish detective fiction is as much about identity as it is about crime solving methods. Colmeiro (1994: 183) states that 'la encuesta policíaca sirve al investigador como excusa para la búsqueda de su propia identidad personal' ['the detective investigation serves as an excuse for the investigator's search for his own personal identity', my translation].

The scholarly literature on Vázquez Montalbán's fiction focuses particularly on national/cultural identity, the main issue during the historical context of its initial reception (in the late 1970s political and intellectual movements fought to vindicate the Catalan identity and to obtain the political instruments that would allow its development after decades of repression). Scholars agree that the character Carvalho, the detective, rejects straightforward national identification, as a Catalan, a Galician (as his last name suggests) or a Spaniard. He is the son of immigrant parents, although raised in Barcelona from a very early age. In various occasions throughout the series, he gives vague answers when asked about his national allegiance. For King (2013: 29) this lies at the basis of his characterization. Nevertheless, scholars disagree in their interpretation of this lack of definition. Some interpret it as a rejection of the concept of national identity altogether. Thus, Santana (2000: 542) states that 'the Carvalho series has traditionally shown an obvious contempt for nationalistic ideals and the gentrification of Spanish society, and a particular appreciation for the *mestizaje* [mix] imposed on Barcelona by the phenomenon of immigration.' Others see it as a proposal for the redefinition of the concept of national identity. Miranda and Pezzotti (2011: 81) observe that the Carvalho series 'reflect a renegotiation of national identity in a multicultural context', particularly 'the dialectic between national and regional, present and past'. In such a redefinition, the ideal nation is contrasted to the real nation, where citizens, including newly arrived immigrants, play a role. For a review of Vázquez Montalbán's stance on this issue, see King (2013). The issue of national identity is relevant for the interpretation of the first fragment, discussed in section 8.6.

Carvalho's identity is influenced by his individual chronology. He is a member of the post-war generation, children raised during the hard years of food rationing, authoritarian schooling and control of sexuality by the Catholic Church. As a middle-aged man he is a member of the *generación del desencanto* the 'disappointed generation' living in the realization that Spain's transition to democracy required perhaps too many political sacrifices, but at the same time aware that their own gentrification has left them unable to rebel, although this will not be reflected until the later Carvalho novels. His generational identity is reflected in nostalgia, the key emotion in the second passage, discussed in section 8.7. Nostalgia paves the way to the vindication of historical memory. Carvalho's flow of thoughts often includes flashbacks into his childhood and adolescence full of minute details about places and activities, many of them no longer existing. As with anger, memories shared with the reader enhance affiliation with a community of values the author is trying to build, particularly as the detective's memories are always highly loaded with evaluation:

'We don't after all simply affiliate with feelings; we affiliate with feelings about people, places, and things, and the activities they participate in, however abstract or concrete. (Martin 2008: 57–58, in Bednarek 2010: 253)

8.4. Translation

Translation is a form of re-writing a text across different language systems so that the new text bears a relation with the source text. The goal of (descriptive) translation studies is to find what types of relations are possible between target and source texts and to identify constraints on such relations.[1] The knowledge thus obtained can be applied to translation criticism and pedagogy (see Holmes 1972/1988).

In the publishing industry, the translator is usually a different individual from the original author; translation is a complex operation consisting of re-instantiation of a text so that it affords (identical/equivalent) readings,[2] inescapably coupled with a re-individuation operation, where the readership may expect – as is the case in literary translation – both the result of a creative act and a coherent glimpse of the instantiation choices of the original texts. In other words, the individual translator draws on his or her repertoire, although s/he must be particularly sensitive to the individuation axis of the source text author (cf. Farias da Souza's three-dimensional model of interlingual re-instantiation, Farias da Souza 2013: 581).

Analysing translated works involves 'reconstruing the translator's interpretive and translatorial steps from his/her choices in the TT (Target Text) and also contrasting his/her reading to alternative readings of the ST (Source Text) with the guidance of models of language and translation' (Farias da Souza 2013: 585). The focus on the renderings of certain critical points allows the analyst to infer the closeness and mutual knowledge between societies, similarities and differences between reservoirs, linguistic resources for affiliation, and the role of translation.

8.5. The novel *Los mares del Sur* and its translations

The source text was published in 1979, after winning the Planeta prize,[3] the Spanish Booker, according to Pluto Press, the first British publisher of the novel. The plot is set in 1977, two years into the restoration of democracy in Spain.[4] The body of Carlos Stuart Pedrell, construction businessman and poetry aficionado, is found at a construction site in Barcelona. He had been missing for a year during which he was thought by his family and friends to be in Polynesia fulfilling his escapist dreams. His widow hires detective Pepe Carvalho to find the killer. The detective's reconstruction of the victim's whereabouts for that lost year leads him to interviews with work associates, family, friends and lovers, including acquaintances from the 'satellite' neighbourhood of San Magín, built by Stuart Pedrell's company, where the killer is eventually identified.

Southern Seas, translated by Patrick Camiller, was first published in 1986 by Pluto Press in the Pluto Crime series, which was active between 1984 and 1987.[5] Nine years had gone by since its publication in Spain. According to Bayó (2001: 148), the author had enjoyed increased international literary prominence since 1981, the year that he was awarded the Prix International de Littérature Policière. The novel was republished in 1999 by Serpent's Tail in its crime fiction series, which features other Carvalho novels. In North America it is published by Melville House in its Melville Crime series.

According to the Index Translationum database, Patrick Camiller has translated mostly historical and political essays such as Volker Skierka's biography of Fidel Castro (Polity Press). Before tackling *Southern Seas*, he had translated *Asesinato en el Comité Central* (*Murder in the Central Committee*, 1984). Reviews of the translation were positive, as recorded in Bayó (2001: 152–153): 'Montalbán's style is grounded in sensory detail, and he writes with authority and compassion' (Blurb, *Publishers Weekly*); Christopher Wordsworth of *The Observer* remarked that it was 'highly readable … the gluttonous Barcelona sleuth is quite something'.

The German translation was first published in 1985 with the title *Tahiti liegt bei Barcelona* ['Tahiti is close to Barcelona'], translated by Bernhard Straub. In 1986, Vázquez Montalbán was awarded the 'Deutscher Krimi Preis' in the former Federal Republic of Germany for the next novel *Carvalho und der Mord im Zentralkomitee* [*Asesinato en el Comité Central*] and the Bunche prize of literary critics for *Manche gehen baden* [*El Balneario*]. The second edition by the same translator was published in 2013; it is in fact a retranslation, as reflected in the new title *Carvalho und die Meere des Südens*.

8.6. Analysis of a text fragment: Carvalho's reproachful speech

The fragment chosen is written in the narratological form of thought representation introduced by a narrator-experiencer. After a lively dinner party with friends, where the literary resonances of the South Seas are discussed, Carvalho finds himself home, thirsty and ill with an aching liver. He juggles several ideas in his mind and suddenly ties odd threads into a coherent hypothesis, namely that the site where the body was found must be the remotest place possible from the murder site, in the view of the killer. This leads him next to deduce that the victim never reached the South Seas literally, but rather that he escaped to the district of San Magín, a working-class neighbourhood built precisely by his company.

Carvalho reads from a reference book on urban development given to him over the course of the dinner earlier that evening. The fragment is presented as thought representation alternating facts with comment. To facilitate analysis, I have enclosed in brackets different voices present in the text. The parts numbered as '1' echo the contents of the reference book. The narrator lets the reader share the ideational contents, i.e. the list of construction deficiencies and lack of social services, through the voice of the detective. The selection of this ideational content indirectly affords negative judgement, not only by Carvalho but by the reader as well.[6] In Macken-Horarick's words (2003: 299): 'Evoked appraisal is important to analyse because it is a primary mechanism by which a text insinuates itself into reader attitudes.'

Following the presentation of facts, with no graphical or paratextual means of separation, we read Carvalho's imaginary reproachful address to the victim. The parts numbered as '2' represent his thoughts combined with his tirade at the dead man whom he addresses in the second person. From the narrative technique point of view, there are two distinct communicative acts, namely Carvalho's imaginary words targeted to Stuart Pedrell, whom we know to be dead, and the true communication from the author to the reader, who is allowed to 'listen in' so that Carvalho's emotional state and political stance is made known.

ST1: Spanish

[1/San Magín fue poblado mayoritariamente por proletariado inmigrante. El alcantarillado no quedó totalmente instalado hasta cinco años después del funcionamiento del barrio. Falta total de servicios asistenciales. Reivindicación de un ambulatorio del seguro de enfermedad. De diez a doce mil habitantes.] [2/Menuda pieza estabas hecho, Stuart Pedrell. ¿Iglesia? Sí.] [1/Se hizo una iglesia moderna al lado de la antigua ermita de San Magín. Todo el barrio sufre inundaciones cuando se desbordan las canalizaciones del Llobregat.] [2/ El criminal vuelve al lugar del crimen, Stuart Pedrell. Tú te fuiste a San Magín a ver tu obra de cerca, a ver cómo vivían tus canacos en las cabañas que les habías preparado. ¿Un viaje de exploración? ¿Tal vez de búsqueda de la autenticidad popular? ¿Investigabas usos y costumbres charnegas? ¿La caída de la d en posición intervocálica? Stuart Pedrell, ¿qué coño fuiste a buscar a San Magín? En taxi. O en autobús. No. En metro. Seguramente fuiste en metro para una mayor identidad entre forma y fondo del largo viaje a los mares del Sur. Y luego dicen que la poesía es imposible en el siglo veinte. Y la aventura. Basta coger el metro y puedes ir de safari emocional por un módico precio.] [1979: 139–140]

TT1: English

[1/San Magín was populated by a mainly immigrant proletariat. The sewage system was not properly completed until five years after they had moved in. Municipal services were completely lacking. There were angry demands for a health clinic. Between ten and twelve thousand inhabitants.] [2/A smart piece of work, Stuart Pedrell. Was there a church? Yes.] [1/A modern church was built next to the old San Magín hermitage. The whole development gets flooded when the Llobregat drainage system overflows.]

[1/Yes, Stuart Pedrell. The criminal returns to the scene of his crime. You went to San Magín to take a close look at your handiwork, to see how your coolies were living in their purpose-built hovels. A voyage of exploration? Researching true popular culture? What were you studying – the habits and customs of immigrants? The intervocalic pronunciation of the letter 'd'? Why the hell did you go to San Magín, Stuart Pedrell? Did you go by taxi? Or bus? No. Underground. You must have gone by underground, so as to achieve a closer identity of form and content on your long trip to the South Seas. And people say that poetry and adventure are impossible in the twentieth century! You only have to take the underground and you're off on a low-cost emotional safari.] [2012: 102]

Stuart Pedrell is negatively evaluated first of all through the accusation of responsibility for all construction deficiencies, and second through his allocation to the Catalan bourgeoisie by stereotypically attributing him attitudes and words that would alienate the inhabitants of the neighbourhood, mostly immigrants from the South of Spain. The reproaching tone is achieved by the use of the vocative 'Stuart Pedrell', the interrogatives addressed at him, and exclamations such as the judgement formula 'Menuda pieza estabas hecho', used ironically to evaluate someone who is shrewd, astute or vicious. Lexically, it contains the intensifying adjective *menudo, –a* [literally 'tiny'] meaning an exaggerated degree and the noun *pieza* [literally 'piece']. In Appraisal Theory terms, it is used for judgement of +capacity (social esteem) but also –propriety (social sanction). Its marked syntax (fronting of the predicator complement) requires the reader to recreate prosody and hence it is an element of fictive orality and involvement.

While *menuda pieza* is a popular idiom for passing judgement, *criminal* is a legal term, used here as an allusion to popular detective wisdom. With the generalization 'El criminal vuelve al lugar del crimen' Carvalho accuses the entrepreneur of social crime, that of building a low-quality estate (although later the character of Ana, the victim's lover and a social justice activist, will point out that conditions are much better in San Magín than they were in the actual shantytown of Somorrostro).

In the English translation the insertion of the paratextual separation between the contents of the book and Carvalho's comments facilitates the reading experience. The subjective analyst's perception is that the anger distilled by Carvalho is less intense in the translation than in the source text. While in Spanish both the syntax and the lexicon contribute to the representation of an outburst of anger, the sarcasm of the English version is more subdued. For example, the English translation of 'Menuda pieza estabas hecho' is 'A smart piece of work', which is ambiguous between the work done by Stuart Pedrell (the neighbourhood) and the man himself. The structure is elliptical, as only a clause fragment inscribing the judgement is uttered, instead of a full clause (e.g. 'what a smart piece of work you were/it was'). The lack of a verb contributes to its semantic ambiguity. Intensification is not explicit by comparable lexical means; however, the fact that *pieza* is translated as the four-word expression 'smart piece of work' may allow for the coupling of lexical with phonological information through an emphatic reading with a stress on each item: the adjective 'smart' lexically expressing the implicit meaning of *menuda*, 'piece' as the head noun, equivalent to Spanish *pieza*, and the complement 'work' (which evokes the idiom 'a nasty piece of work'). The expletive 'what the hell', translating the sexual taboo 'qué coño' expresses a similar degree of transgression and hence involvement.

In this address to Stuart Pedrell, two words uttered by Carvalho, namely *canacos* and *charnegas*, allocate people to a group. They are difficult to render and display variation in different translations, as will be discussed in the rest of the section.

The word *canacos* [literally 'Kanak' or 'the Kanak people'] is part of the lexical choices that build the South Seas allegory. *Canacos* live in *cabañas* ['huts'], a humble form of housing compatible with the natives of the Polynesia. Earlier in the novel an artist mentions the Polynesian theme through the introduction of *canacos*:

'Él quería que le pintara algo muy primitivo, con el falso candor de Gauguin cuando pintaba a los canacos, pero trasladado a todo lo aborigen del Empordá, donde está Lliteras.' [1979: 17]

'He wanted me to paint something very primitive. The faux-naif style of Gauguin's Canaques period, but transposed to the native life of Lliteras.' (published English translation [2012: 31])

Indeed, the South Seas were Stuart Pedrell's obsession, as everybody reminds Carvalho.[7]

The English translation renders *canacos* not as 'Kanak' or 'Canaque' (the French art term) but as 'coolies'. A slight change in appreciation takes place with the translation of *cabañas* as 'hovels', which may be coherent with 'coolies', but which foregrounds bad conditions more than the source *cabañas* ['huts'].

Although Martin and White (2005) do not propose a specific category, a term that stereotypes a group fits in the dimension of judgement, particularly of social esteem. The specific traits might be [-normality], since the essence of stereotyping is the identification of a relevant difference, and [-capacity], since in the case of 'coolies', it is the lack of specific skills that is significant.

The use of the derogatory 'coolies' as the correspondence for the attitudinally neutral *canacos* renders the anger in Carvalho, thereby compensating (as a translation technique) for the rendering of the explicitly derogatory *charnegas* with the neutral denotation 'immigrants'. However, the use of a term clearly associated with England's colonial past activates a different network of intertextual associations that may be confusing for an English reader not knowledgeable of the Spanish history and demography. A further disadvantage of 'coolies' is the loss of the intratextual link with the first occurrence of *canacos* linking the painter Gauguin with Stuart Pedrell's search for authenticity through contact with aborigines.

The ethnic stereotype that invokes attitude in Carvalho's reproachful address to Stuart Pedrell is the adjective *charnegas* (in 'usos y costumbres charnegas'). The noun *charnego* is a derogatory term to refer to 'an immigrant from a non-Catalan speaking region of Spain' (RAE Dictionary). Uttered by Carvalho, the word works on two different levels: as a reconstruction of the victim's speech, allocating him in the powerful Catalan bourgeoisie that would view the immigrants as second-class citizens; second, by daring to utter it, as a means to vindicate the social group in solidarity. In fact, Vázquez Montalbán had re-appropriated the term for himself in an interview conducted in 1996 with Georges Tyras (Tyras 2004: 63–64). This is interpreted in Ibarz (2006: 84) as revealing of 'the author's engagement with, and experience of, living in a multi-ethnic and bilingual society where symbolic imaginary structures are constantly in dialogue'.

Each language has its own set of ethnic and social stereotypes whose semantic multidimensionality – the denotation of the group that is being stereotyped, their identity indexical value, and their evaluative semantics – is difficult to preserve in translation.[8] They are 'value-rich', i.e. they are susceptible to value manipulation and frequently involve translation shifts (Munday 2012: 41). The adjective *charnegas*, for all its cultural specificity and ethnic/social identity associations, is a true 'critical point' in translation in the sense of Munday (2012: 41), i.e. that 'there exists the possibility that they will affect the reception of the text'.

In English it is solved with the denotative 'immigrants' without further specification of geographical origin. Carvalho's sarcastic allusion to the victim's research interests in the particularities of their accent may be lost to most English readers. In Appraisal Theory terms, in the English translation attitude is not directly inscribed nor indirectly provoked by the use of the derogatory word but rather indirectly afforded by the mention of immigrants as the object of the victim's curiosity ('a voyage of exploration'). The inference is that he must have viewed them as alien to his world rather than as his fellow citizens.

In reading the translation, one wonders about reader response. As far as the original readership is concerned, according to Santana (2000: 542), 'What Vázquez Montalbán offers his intended readers (who, in order for the spatial determinations of the novel to acquire full significance, are those familiar with the city of Barcelona) is a mirror on which they can see not what they consciously are, but rather what they do not recognize as part of their own beings.' In using 'coolies', the translation gets closer to the original intent (that of making the middle-class [Catalan] reader acknowledge their capacity for holding racist/classist attitudes). In translating the taboo *charnegas* as the descriptive 'immigrants', the reader's response is not targeted through a socially shocking use of language but through a process of inference.[9] The socially shocking use of language is compensated by the judgement-provoking 'coolies'.

Since the translation solutions are a reflex of the negotiation of identity in a new cultural environment, each language will provide a different set of resources. The case of German is particularly interesting as there are two versions, both by the same translator though separated by 28 years, but each displaying a different strategy. 'Translation, especially multiple translations, is a particularly promising scenario for the investigation of the relation between selected and unselected forms for the analysis of the value orientations that underlie these selections' (Munday 2012: 13).

TT2a: German (1985)

San Magín wurde hauptsächlich von zugewanderten Arbeitern aus Südspanien bewohnt. [...] Du bist nach San Magín gegangen, um dein Werk aus der Nähe zu betrachten, um zu sehen, wie die Kanaken in den Baracken hausen, die du ihnen gebaut hast. Eine Entdeckungsreise? Vielleicht die Suche nach der Ursprünglichkeit des Volkes? Wolltest du die Sitten und Gebräuche der Untermenschen erforschen?

TT2b: German (2013)

San Magín wurde hauptsächlich von zugewanderten Proletariern aus Südspanien besiedelt. [...] Du bist nach San Magín gegangen, um dein Werk aus der Nähe zu betrachten, um zu sehen, wie deine Südsee-Kanaken in den Hütten hausen, die du ihnen gebaut hast. Eine Forschungsreise? Vielleicht die Suche nach der Ursprünglichkeit des Volkes? Wolltest du die Sitten und Gebräuche der <u>xarnegos</u> erforschen? [hypertextual link on *xarnegos* offering the denotation: "katalanisch für Immigranten aus Südspanien", i.e., Catalan for immigrants from Southern Spain (196)]

In the first translation, *Kanaken* is a word with potentially three senses, one of which is derogative for workers from the south of Europe, including and particularly the Turkish. This sense provokes negative evaluation. In the second translation, the term is disambiguated by means of the pre-modifier 'Südsee' (i.e. South Sea), a precise denomination of the native people from Polynesia that does no longer provoke negative evaluation. The name of the dwellings varies accordingly, from 'Baracken' in the first to 'Hütte' in the second.

With regard to *charnegas*, the changes suggest a radical shift in the translation strategy. In the first translation, the taboo *Untermenschen* is a negative judgement on capacity. However, its intertextual associations are undoubtedly negative in the German society. In the second translation, the loanword *xarnegos* spelled with 'x' instead of 'ch', under the Catalan spelling norms, signals the presence of a foreign language and culture. The reader is helped paratextually through a footnote that provides the denotation (Immigrants from the south of Spain), but not the social implications of its use. It can contextually be reconstructed but the full meaning potential is accessible only to those with some knowledge of the Catalan social history.

The changes that take place in the retranslation are fully detailed in Espunya and Pavić Pintarić (2016), where they are interpreted as symptomatic of the evolving status of the work in the target society. The hypothesis is that the adscription to a genre of the Carvalho novels changed over time, from detective fiction, i.e. popular or 'middle-brow', commercial, etc. to 'contemporary Spanish literature', possibly as a consequence of the increase in appreciation of the non-detective aspects such as the social and political chronicle, historic memory and the literary merits. The German readership may have evolved as well in their knowledge of the Spanish reality.

8.7. A childhood trip: Nostalgia as bonding

The second text fragment follows the one that has been analysed in the previous section. Carvalho has finally fallen asleep and as he wakes up, the notion of San Magín reminds him of a childhood trip to a rural landscape that would later be transformed into a similar neighbourhood.

ST2: Spanish

Tenía un borroso recuerdo de casas de campo y albercas de cemento. Su madre caminaba ante él con la cesta llena de arroz y aceite comprados de estraperlo en alguna de aquellas casas. Cruzaban las vías del tren. A lo lejos, hacia ellos, venía la ciudad mellada de la posguerra, una ciudad delgada llena de palos grises y huecos. ¿Por qué había tantos palos grises sobre los tejados? Sacaron el aceite de un odre rancio. Cayó en el interior de la botella como un mercurio verde y lento. Esto sí que es aceite de verdad y no el de racionamiento. Él caminaba detrás. En su bolsa de hule había cinco barras, cinco de pan blanco, blanquísimo, como de yeso. Campos y campos, caminos pedregosos por los que pasaban ciclistas amalvados por el crepúsculo o carros movidos por percherones lentos y pesados como su mierda rotunda. Luego la ciudad empezaba insinuándose en un barrio de barracas en coexistencia con antiguas torrecillas y casas apresadas por la posguerra, cumpliendo condena de perdedoras de la guerra civil. Calles de tierra, luego adoquinadas, finalmente heridas por la espina de las vías de los tranvías al que subían cansados por la caminata, con la aventura en la cesta y en los ojos la promesa del hambre saciada. [1979: 140–141]

TT3: English

Hazy memories came back to him. Of country houses and cement reservoirs. His mother coming towards him with a shopping basket full of rice and oil bought on the black market from one such house. They crossed the railway tracks. In the distance loomed a sparse, raggedy post-war town, full of grey wood and empty spaces.

> They poured the oil from a musty wineskin and he watched it fill the bottle like a stream of green liquid mercury. This was real oil, not the stuff you got with ration coupons. He walked back. In his oilskin bag were five long loaves of white bread, as white as gypsum. Field after field. Stony tracks which bore cyclists coloured mauve by the setting sun, and carts drawn by horses as slow and heavy as their own manure. Then the streets of the town began to spread out into a suburb of dingy modern blocks which co-existed with little old turreted houses and homes expropriated by the Civil War victors to complete the punishment of the vanquished. Streets that changed from earth to paving stone, before finally being dissected by the splintering metal of tramlines. They trudged home, tired from the long walk, with adventure in their basket and the hope of a sated hunger in their eyes. [2012: 101–103]

Memories intrude in his train of thought as revealed to the reader through internal focalization (a third person experiencer narrator). In terms of the theory of text worlds (Werth 1999), this recollection creates a new conceptual space inside the text world of Carvalho's present day, i.e. a 'sub-world'. 'This projection forms a distinct situation of its own, because it sets up a reality outside the parameters of the existing text-world' (Simpson 2004: 91). Carvalho remembers accompanying his mother on one of her trips to the country to buy food from a peasant house and their walk back from the country to the city.[10]

This episode does not contribute to the advancement of the plot; it helps remind readers that Carvalho belongs to the post-war generation (there are two instances of the word *posguerra*) and that he is willing to mention the existence of a losing side ('perdedoras de la guerra civil'). These instances may serve as bonding cues for a whole generation of readers, also in acknowledging the changes undergone by those rural spaces as entire estates or 'satellite towns' were developed to house the waves of workers. Postwar hunger and immigration are presented simultaneously.

This passage is characterized by inscribed appreciation, the appraisal of things, and also the presentation of ideational content that may cause the reader to align with the writer's appraisal, i.e. provoked attitude. It is a factual description but one that draws heavily on perceptual details and poetic language. The syntactic choices that recreate the spoken variety provide the scaffolding for ideational content and appraisal. Most noticeable are the repetition figures ('stair figures' in López 2012: 175), such as 'la ciudad …, una ciudad'; 'cinco barras, cinco de pan blanco, blanquísimo, como de yeso') and the emphatic polar clause contrasting the purity of the bread from the peasant's with the bread from coupons.[11]

In the English translation the syntax has been manipulated to comply with the conventions of the written medium. One sentence is eliminated (the question as to why there were so many grey sticks on the roofs of houses). Stair figures are lost (as in 'In his oilskin bag were five long loaves of white bread, as white as gypsum') and traces of popular spoken Spanish are rendered closer to standard English. This is not an isolated instance but is a rather general phenomenon (see, for example, Espunya 2012 on the translation of Spanish post-war writer Martín Gaite). One possible explanation is that the copy-editor subjects the translator's manuscript to a standardization process.

Carvalho's recollection is rich in visual details. His gaze singles out some items encountered along the way: the town, the oil, the bread, the horses, the cyclists, the roads and the villas. Their descriptions include reference to their colour – the grey sticks, the green oil, the white bread, the mauve cyclists – and kinesic qualities: slowness and heaviness, which can be either positive or negative depending on what is appraised (the oil or the horses and cyclists).

The lexical choices in the translation render appreciation in similar ways as in the source text, although linguistic material is often deleted. Consider, for example, the oil and the bread, two *realia*. The adult Carvalho remembers how the oil fell into the bottle and then, as signalled by free direct discourse in the present tense, remembers the impact that the pouring of the oil had on the onlookers, probably his mother and himself. The present tense is rendered in English by a past tense, which transforms free direct into free indirect speech, foregrounding the narrator rather than the experiencer, and as consequence, distancing the reader from the experience.

The idiom *de verdad* (literally, 'in truth') inscribes positive valuation, as does the English counterpart 'real', in contrast with 'stuff', which reinforces the negative valuation of the alternative product. The thickness and low viscosity of the oil (positive composition properties) are invoked by means of a comparison with mercury 'como un mercurio verde y lento', rendered as 'a stream of green liquid mercury'. Arguably, the emphasis on the thickness, which is familiar to the Spanish reader as a test for high-quality olive oil, is weakened by the omission of *lento* ['slow'], and by the use of the noun 'stream' and the explicit adjective 'liquid'. On the other hand, the noun 'stream' affords a reading of abundance, which is positive in the context.

The description of the bread they had bought from the peasant inscribes positive appreciation of composition and reaction. The two terms of the repetition 'blanco, blanquísimo' contribute different meanings; the first term, *pan blanco* denotes the type of bread, whereas the second, *blanquísimo*, denotes its colour, intensified by the superlative morpheme, i.e. the impact of the bread approximates to the highest degree. In the context of post-war Spain, the whiteness of the bread is a positive quality, as it indicates that it is made of fine wheat flour, Spain's favourite variety. In contrast, bread available with the coupons was brown bread, often made with whole grain flour of cereals other than wheat. The comparison of the whiteness of the bread with the whiteness of gypsum, as rendered in the translation, is a means to invite positive appreciation. In the translation, the intensification of white is lost, left to the comparison with gypsum, i.e. graduation is indirectly provoked rather than directly inscribed.

Towards the end of the flashback, the boy and his mother are approaching the city walking on roads that they share with cycle riders and draught horses. The coinage *amalvados* (from 'malva', the colour mauve) describing the cycle-riders in the twilight is an example of the juxtaposition of the beautiful with the vulgar.[12] The cyclists share the road with the horses, described as *lentos* ('slow'), inscribing negative judgement of their capacity, and *pesados* ('heavy'), with a heaviness that extends to their own waste. In Spanish, *mierda* is a taboo item. By using it Carvalho may be signalling bitterness and 'covert prestige' (Edwards 2009, 68). The collocation of *mierda* with *rotunda* is unusual; *rotundo* is a property of the entire human body ('rounded and stocky') or of a speech act (*una negativa rotunda*, 'an emphatic "no"'). It inscribes negative appreciation, probably impact (a class of reaction) and contributes to the characterization of the overworked horses. Like the *palos grises* (the grey sticks), these heavy horses are details that help compose the physical and emotional landscape of the evening trip home.

In the English translation the juxtaposition of opposites is lost: *amalvados* is rephrased as the prosaic 'coloured mauve' while *mierda* is replaced with the neutral 'manure', with the ensuing loss of involvement.

The adjectives 'slow' and 'heavy' in the translation inscribe negative judgement of capacity; however, the semantic reiteration of heaviness is weakened by the loss of *rotunda*, perhaps an attempt to remove the unusual collocation. The potential for evocation is diminished.

The description continues with the last legs in their trip towards the city.[13] It contains instances of personification strongly contributing to the mood of weariness. According to Argaman (2010), the use of metaphor correlates with emotional intensity. Due to space considerations, I will focus on the personification of the houses, described as *apresadas* (literally, 'imprisoned') and 'cumpliendo condena de perdedoras' ('serving time as losers'). The transitivity pattern is unusual, since houses are not among the entities that can become imprisoned, and they can 'serve time' only metaphorically. The reader is forced to interpret this imprisonment as their demise linked to the outcome of the Spanish war, although in a non-specific way. In the English translation, this personification is not preserved; instead, we observe an attempt at providing a straightforward explanation 'expropriated by the Civil War victors to complete the punishment of the vanquished'. The source text does not assert that the houses had been expropriated. After the war, the owners of these presumably empty houses may have been sick or injured, may be dead or in exile, or indeed in prison. In terms of Appraisal Theory, the reader is guided differently. While the source text *provokes* through personification (the imprisonment of houses), the translation *affords* a reading (the expropriation of the houses) with the plain reconstruction of the ideational content. This phenomenon whereby the translator closes the range of readings has been recurrently observed in many different genres and language pairs; in fact it is considered one of the tendencies in translation, that of explicitation. Munday (2012: 147) notes the phenomenon in the translations of works by Jorge Luis Borges into English, seemingly triggered by the presence of 'creative colloca-tions, non-standard lexical primings, where the translator is forced to interpret the referent and the form of appraisal without being able to rely on a stock of ready-made translation equivalents'.

8.8. Conclusions

This chapter explores the use of appraisal resources in order to enhance bonding of the readers with the group identities created by Vázquez Mon-talbán through his detective Carvalho. The two passages analysed repre-sent, respectively, anger and nostalgia. The former draws on judgement of people (social esteem towards the immigrant people, i.e. normality and capacity, and social sanction towards the businessman, i.e. propriety/ethics) while the second draws on appreciation of objects (reaction, composition and valuation). Resources from different strata combine to represent emo-tional states (phonology and lexicogrammar to build a tirade, lexicogram-mar and discourse structure to build a text sub-world). Bonding is related to the sharing of values and evaluation; by means of social stereotypes, the character Carvalho builds for himself and for the explicit addressee a value system that is offered for the reader (the implicit hearer) to share.

The English translation tends towards standardization, probably to ensure readability. The mimesis of spoken discourse present in the Spanish text is modified to accommodate the planned end of the spectrum. Eliminating the disruptions in the linear order of sentences may be beneficial to rhythm and reading flow; however, together with the replacement of taboo items by neutral ones, the strategy may be detrimental to the representation of emo-tional states. Elimination of unusual collocations and of obscure ideational content seems to be aimed at the facilitation of the reading experience.

Nowhere are the challenges of crossing linguistic and cultural boundaries better reflected than in the translation of ethnic/social stereotypes. Even though the languages involved (Spanish, English and German) include stereotypes in their reservoirs, their multiple semantic dimensions render total equivalence impossible. The translator is faced with a choice between denotation and impact. If impact is chosen, many translation solutions will give rise to marked historical resonances. From the paraphrase of the denotation 'immigrants' compensated with 'coolies', in the English translation, to the widely different solutions of the German translations (i.e. *Untermenschen* and the loan word *xarnegos*), we can observe different social norms at work regarding acceptability in translation.

As regards the flashback, we observe in the English translation the same editorial tendency towards a standard written register. Poetic form and fictive orality are literary resources that seem to be undervalued. The episode is relevant for the negotiation of master identities: nostalgia goes hand in hand with the curating of historic memory, not just of the great collective events but also of the daily individual experiences shared by a whole generation.

Later books in the Carvalho series were translated into English by Ed Emery and Nick Caistor. One avenue for further work is to compare the translation solutions to identical or similar problems in those novels. Further work on social stereotypes can explore other Spanish writers whose fiction is set in the same background, such as Juan Marsé.

The focus on the renderings of certain critical points allows the analyst to infer the closeness and mutual knowledge between societies (for example, the English 'coolies' suggests an absence of expectation that the reader will know the Catalan society, in contrast with the German solution *xarnegos*; the description of olive oil foregrounds different qualities in Spanish – thickness – vs English – abundance – similarities and differences between reservoirs (comparable judgement formulae like 'a piece of', 'the criminal returns to the scene of the crime'), linguistic resources for bonding (different weight given to fictive orality), and the potential for impact of the translation on the reception of the author.

Appraisal theory provides tools for a fine-grained textual analysis, with the categories of the attitude system (judgement and appreciation) and especially with the integration of implicit forms of evaluation. This wider perspective is definitely applicable to the comparative work required for the analysis of translations. As the translation of 'casas apresadas por la posguerra' into 'homes expropriated by the Civil war victors' illustrates, it is often the case that translations render explicitly what the source text left as implicit. Further work will undoubtedly prove the interdisciplinary potential of the framework.

Notes

1. There are numerous sources of constraints both individual – e.g. a translator's background and education, which influence their repertoire, their cognitive abilities, and their conceptualization of the task – and social – e.g. the status of foreign, translated literature in the editorial system (see Toury 1995), the economic and cultural dominance of one society over the other (see Bassnett and Lefevère 1990) and the function of the translated text. One of the main goals of the Translation Studies discipline is formulate correlations between actual textual choices and these constraints.

2. Assuming that the translator intends a compliant reading, instead of tactical (i.e. interested) or resistive (opposing the reading position of the text) ones (see Martin and White 2005: 62 on types of reading, from an ideological perspective).

3. Planeta is a publisher based in Barcelona.

4. Pluto Press is an independent London-based publisher that defines itself as 'one of the world's leading radical publishers, specialising in progressive, critical perspectives in politics and the social sciences' (Pluto Press 2014). The Pluto Crime series was edited by Ronald Segal, but 'also bears the influence of Pete Ayrton who, at Serpent's Tail, republished some of the titles and other works by the authors' (Ridley 2014).

5. In Martin and White (2005: 67) a distinction is made between direct and indirect strategies for the realization of attitude. Affording is the most indirect, as it is a form of inviting evaluation through the presentation of facts.

6. The artist tells Carvalho about this obsession in the same visit, which is transcribed below in its English translation:

'The South Seas?'

'His obsession. I think he'd been reading a poem about Gauguin, and he started to pursue the myth.[...]' (p. 35)

7. Culture-specific lexical items are items designating either realities or constructs that can be virtually only understood in relation to the particular social and material environment of the source language. Such items tend to be considered marks of 'local colour', adding plausibility to the representation of the world where the plot develops. They undoubtedly contribute to affiliation.

8. Terms that denote group identities are indeed critical points in translation. Munday (2012: 117) discusses the renderings of the polysemous word *criollo* in the translations of several of the works by Peruvian Nobel Prize Laureate Mario Vargas Llosa.

9. As text worlds are defined referentially but also deictically, space is crucial for the reader to form this conceptual space. The English translation has several mistakes concerning deictic anchoring. For example, Carvalho remembers walking behind his mother. But the Spanish 'su madre caminaba ante él' is translated as 'His mother coming towards him' instead of 'before him' or simply 'in front'; the sentence 'él caminaba detrás' (i.e. 'he walked behind her' or 'he followed her'), closing the text world where the pouring of the oil takes place is translated as 'he walked back'. This leads the reader to reconstruct the episode

as the child walking to meet his mother on her way back and then walking along with her, which is incoherent given that he witnessed the pouring of the olive oil. This observation does not necessarily affect the bonding experience unless the spatial confusion puzzles the reader.

10. Stair figures involve splits of the speech chain that break up the linear continuity of linguistic units through paradigmatic axis interferences in the syntagmatic axis. Utterances are built incrementally (step by step, hence the name 'stair') with partial coincidences and/or repetition of lexical items.

11. Creation of new words is another of the traits of Vázquez Montalbán's style. Earlier in this novel, Carvalho is looking for a girl with 'cabellos mielados', literally 'honeyed hair' (i.e. honey-coloured hair).

12. Another spatial disruption in this episode concerns the iconic presentation of the roads with the child as the vantage point: first the dirt country roads, then paved roads and finally city streets with the tram rails. The translation suggests the opposite trajectory: 'Then the streets of the town began to spread out into a suburb of dingy modern blocks'. The verb 'spread out' indicates motion from a core to a periphery, here the suburban spaces, just the reverse of their actual trip from the country to the city. It is easy to predict a much more confusing experience of constructing a sub-world for the reader of the translation than it is for the reader of the source text.

References

Argaman, O. (2010). Linguistic markers and emotional intensity. *Journal of Psycholinguistic Research*, 39(2), 89–99.

Bassnett, S., and Lefevère, A. (Eds) (1990). *Translation, History and Culture*. London and New York: Pinter Publishers.

Bayó Belenguer, S. (2001). *Theory, Genre, and Memory in the Carvalho Series of Manuel Vázquez Montalbán*. Spanish Studies Series, 11. Lewiston, NY: Edwin Mellen Press.

Bednarek, M. (2010). Corpus linguistics and Systemic Functional Linguistics: Interpersonal meaning, identity and bonding in popular culture. In M. Bednarek and J. R. Martin (Eds), *New Discourse on Language: Functional Perspectives on Multimodality, Identity, and Affiliation*, 237–266. London: Continuum.

Bednarek, M. and Martin, J. R. (Eds) (2010). *New Discourse on Language. Functional Perspectives on Multimodality, Identity and Affiliation*. London and New York: Continuum.

Brumme, J. and Espunya, A. (Eds) (2012). *The Translation of Fictive Dialogue*. Approaches to Translation Studies 35. Amsterdam and New York: Rodopi.

Colmeiro, J. F. (1994). *La novela policíaca española: teoría y crítica* [The Spanish detective novel: theory and criticism]. Barcelona: Anthropos.

Depetris, I. (2011). Cartografía para los recuerdos: Barcelona y la(s) memoria(s) de la posguerra en *Los mares del Sur* de Manuel Vázquez Montalbán. *CONFLUENZE*, 3 (2): 99–109.

Edwards, J. (2009). *Language and Identity. An Introduction.* Key Topics in Sociolinguistics Series. Cambridge: Cambridge University Press. https://doi.org/10.1017/CBO9780511809842

Espunya, A. (2012). Sentence connection in fictive dialogue. In J. Brumme and A. Espunya (Eds) *The Translation of Fictive Dialogue*, 199–215. Amsterdam and New York: Rodopi.

Espunya, A. and Pavić Pintarić, A. (2016). Identität und Emotionalität in Vázquez Montalbáns Carvalho Roman *Los mares del sur* und seinen deutschen Übersetzungen. In A. Pavić Pintarić, Z. Sambunjak, and T. Zelić (Eds) *Sprachliche Konstituierung der Identität durch Emotionalität*, 127–143. Tübingen: Gunter Narr.

Farias da Souza, L. M. (2013). Interlingual re-instantiation – a new systemic functional perspective on translation. *Text&Talk*, 33 (4–5): 575–594. https://doi.org/10.1515/text-2013-0026

Holmes, J. S. (1972/1988). The name and nature of translation studies. In *Translated! Papers on Literary Translation and Translation Studies*, 67–80. Amsterdam: Rodopi.

Ibarz, A. (2006). Francoism and the Dialectics of Space: The Case of Manuel Vázquez Montalbán's *Angst-Ridden Executive. Journal of Catalan Studies*, 9: 83–109.

King, S. (2013). Carvalho y Cataluña: la subjetividad en los márgenes'. *Cuadernos de Estudios Manuel Vázquez Montalbán*, 1: 28–45.

Krajenbrink, M. and Quinn, K. M. (Eds) (2009). *Investigating Identities. Questions of Identity in International Crime Fiction.* Amsterdam and New York: Rodopi.

Leech, G. and Short, M. (1981). *Style in Fiction. A Linguistic Introduction to English Fictional Prose.* London and New York: Longman.

López S. A. (2012). Recreating spoken syntax in fictive orality: An analytical framework. In J. Brumme and A. Espunya (Eds), *The Translation of Fictive Dialogue*, 167–183. Amsterdam and New York: Rodopi.

Macken-Horarik, M. (2003). Appraisal and the special instructiveness of narrative. *Text*, 23 (2): 285–312. https://doi.org/10.1515/text.2003.012

Martin, J. R. (2010). Semantic variation – modelling realisation, instantiation and individuation in social semiosis. In M. Bednarek and J. R. Martin (Eds) *New Discourse on Language: Functional Perspectives on Multimodality, Identity, and Affiliation*, 1–34. London and New York: Continuum.

Martin, J. R., and P. R. R. White. (2005). *The Language of Evaluation.*

Appraisal in English. Basingstoke: Palgrave Macmillan. https://doi. org/10.1057/9780230511910

Miranda, C. and Pezzotti, B. (2011). 'Investigating society: The cases of Pepe Carvalho and Tito Ihaka. *Journal of New Zealand Studies*, NS 11: 81–92.

Munday, J. (2012). *Evaluation in Translation: Critical Points in Decision Making*. Abingdon and New York: Routledge.

Resina, J. R. (1997). *El cadáver en la cocina. La novela criminal en la cultura del desencanto* [The corpse in the kitchen. Crime novel in the *desencanto* culture]. Barcelona: Anthropos.

Ridley, M. (2014). Pluto Crime. In http://www.inf.brad.ac.uk/~mick/ (Accessed 25 February 2014).

Santana, M. (2000). Manuel Vázquez Montalbán's *Los mares del Sur* and the Incrimination of the Spanish Transition. *Revista de Estudios Hispánicos*, XXXIV (3): 535–560.

Simpson, P. (2004). *Stylistics. A Resource Book for Students*. London and New York: Routledge.

Stenglin, M. (2004). *Packaging curiosities: towards a grammar of three-dimensional space*. Unpublished PhD Thesis, University of Sydney, Sydney.

Toury, G. (1995). *Descriptive Translation Studies and Beyond*. Amsterdam: John Benjamins. https://doi.org/10.1075/btl.4

Tyras, G. (2004). *Entretiens avec Manuel Vázquez Montalbán*. Paris: La Renaissance du livre.

Vázquez Montalbán, M. (1979). *Los mares del Sur*. Barcelona: Planeta.

Vázquez Montalbán, M. (1985). *Tahiti liegt bei Barcelona*. Translated by Bernhard Straub. Reinbek bei Hamburg: Rowohlt.

Vázquez Montalbán, M. (1986). *Southern Seas*. Translated by Patrick Camiller. London: Pluto Press.

Vázquez Montalbán, M. (2005). *Los mares del Sur*. 2nd edition. Barcelona: Planeta. First ed., 1979.

Vázquez Montalbán, M. (2012). *Southern Seas*. Translated by Patrick Camiller. Brooklyn, NY: Melville House Publishing. First ed., 1999.

Vázquez Montalbán, M. (2013). *Carvalho und die Meere des Südens*. Translated by Bernhard Straub. Berlin: Klaus Wagenbach Verlag. (E-Book edition).

Werth, P. (1999). *Text Worlds: Representing Conceptual Space in Discourse*. London: Longman.

9 Striking a chord in the reader: On metaphor as a constituent of the grammar of Verbal Art

Timo Lothmann[*]

> exclamatio est: vitam brevem esse, longam artem.
>
> (Seneca 2009, I.2)

9.1. Introduction and scope

Hasan's framework of verbal art (cf. Hasan 1989; 2007) has provided a fresh perspective on literature as a dynamic variety of language use. Building on Halliday's semiotic system of language as a multiple coding array (cf. Halliday 1985), she has suggested an additional stratal system to operationalize the artistic in the literary media genre. On this basis, this article intends to show how metaphors and their patterning help construct deeper meaning and thus contribute to the art status of texts. By using examples of (lexicogrammatical) metaphorical instantiations in selected works which have been deemed literature for centuries, such as *Beowulf* and metaphysical poetry, it is argued that the *symbolic articulation* of the *theme*[1] has recourse to particular metaphorical conceptualizations, and their realization as sequences and layers in the text, respectively. To that end, an opening-up of the systemic-functional basis of Hasan's semiotic system to the cognitive approach of conceptual metaphor (cf. e.g. Lakoff and Johnson 2011) is proposed.

---

[*] Timo Lothmann is a researcher and lecturer of English linguistics at RWTH Aachen University where he completed his PhD on the Tok Pisin Bible translation in 2006. He has also taught at the universities of Münster and Paderborn. His research interests include reading and translation processing, pidgins and creoles, postcolonialism, and imaginary worlds. He lays particular stress on interdisciplinary perspectives. Recent publications comprise a metaphor approach to literary identity. Currently, he focuses on fields of application of conceptual metaphor and blending theory.

This article highlights the explanatory potential that stems from a convergence of the frameworks and thus corroborates the lack of boundaries between lexicogrammar and abstract conceptualizations of the mind. In this regard, it is confirmed that socio-temporal distance challenges the modern recipient in terms of *theme* identification. However, the analysis of underlying metaphors in the historical examples under concern shows that this distance can be bridged so that these texts can still be appreciated as 'Hasanian' works of art.

9.2. Theoretical background

What makes literature particular, or put differently in Hasan's words, what are the special attributes that make a text become part of literature as a variety of language (cf. e.g. Hasan 1975: 54)? Time has passed since the beginnings of her involvement with the topic (cf. Hasan 1967; 1975). Today, clearly fuelled by Hasan's 1985 volume on language and verbal art, linguistic approaches to literature and a linguistic view on stylistics and art within text in general still are, and continue to be, enriching text analyses and related academic debates across disciplines.

For Hasan, the interpretive assumptions of individual recipients are of secondary, if any, importance. Rather, it is the text (featuring language, and thus language functions) and the context of its creation that should be at the centre of the analyser's attention (cf. Miller 2010: 30). In this vein, language is means and end. Linguistic tools, according to Hasan, enable an objective and hence advisable approach to literature without having to rely on more traditional, seemingly arcane strategies to come to terms with literature as a type of discourse (cf. Hasan 1988: 72; 1989: 104). What is more, she continues, 'literature' is the fusion of discourse and art (cf. Hasan 2007: 16), while the elusive notion of 'art' is shaped by the particularity of language and its functioning in text (cf. Hasan 1989: 91).

Hasan found in Halliday's semiotic approach to language seen as a network of systemic relations based on choices (cf. e.g. Halliday 1985; Hasan 2013) a suitable foundation for a model of verbal art. She posits a second-order, artistic meaning on top of the Hallidayian first-order, natural language meaning (cf. Figure 9.1). She includes the first-order semiosis in a *verbalization* stratum where the wording, i.e. the linguistic execution, is located as the text recipient's access gate to verbal art. This stratum construes *symbolic articulation*, which Hasan sets up as an additional layer where normal, non-artistically motivated semiosis is augmented via the exploitation of language to such a (linguistically) observable extent that the result is art. Moreover, this layer has a mediating function: It links the

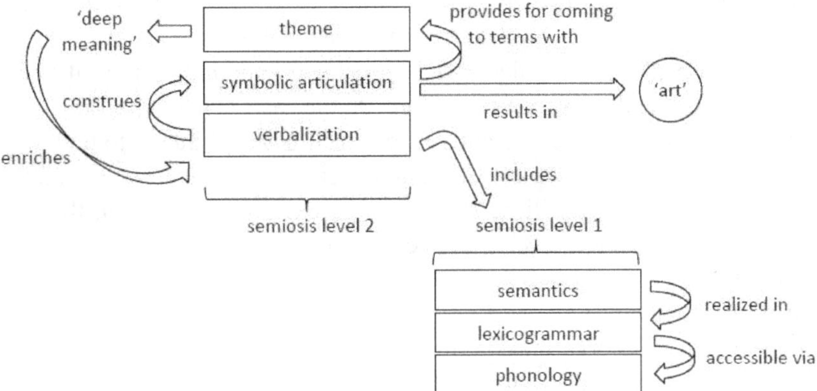

Figure 9.1: The tristratal framework of verbal art and its relation to Halliday's semiotic system (cf. Hasan 1989: 99, modified)

verbalization of the verbal artefact with its abstract, deeper meaning which Hasan labels *theme* (cf. Hasan 1975: 57; 1989: 97).

The *theme* is more than just an abstracted message. According to Hasan, the deeper meaning relates to an issue that is of relevance for the author's and the recipients' cultural community as a whole, including norms of social (co-) existence, philosophical reflections, and worldviews in general (cf. Hasan 1989, 100).[2] If literature is seen as a cultural value per se and in particular, it never 'acts' in a social void, i.e. it is and remains to be a matter of semiotic negotiation between authors and recipients, given that they share capabilities of relevant sociosemiotic exchange. The *symbolic articulation* of the *theme* may result in art within the cultural contexts of text creation, text reception, and text situation. Thus, in Hasan's terms, contexts always precede texts, and it is the language use that encapsulates these contexts, defines genres, and determines the relevant meaning potential (cf. Hasan 1996: 41; 2011: xxv). After all, it is the function of artistic language use to act meaningfully towards the *theme* which, in turn, as the highest meaning-organizational instrument, motivates and justifies according linguistic choices.

This brief reappraisal of Hasan's theoretical framework requires referring to *foregrounding* in particular as a tool to create art. Inspired mainly by Mukařovský,[3] Hasan stresses the consistent use of patterning of patterns, or *foregrounding*, for a second-order semiosis (cf. Hasan 1989: 101). According to her, such consistency makes first-order meanings transformable and reinterpretable (cf. Hasan 2007: 33). In the event of reinterpretation, this *double articulation* creates a higher-order significance (cf. Pagano and Lukin 2015: 93–94), with *foregrounding* as a main means. More specifically, *foregrounding* consistency is then a matter of the stability of its semantic direction and of its textual location (cf. Hasan 1989: 96; Miller 2010: 42). In what follows, the stress will be put mainly on stability of textual location.[4]

Hasan's modelling implies that a systematic patterning within the text fosters its perception as a coherent unit. On the basis of a text passage from *Beowulf* and two examples from metaphysical poetry, I intend to highlight such systematic patterning by referring to metaphors and their text-strategic clustering. Further, it will be of interest to examine the tension that the metaphor-based *foregrounding* creates when the author interweaves deliberate, *theme*-inspired breaks of the related patterning into the fabric of the story as a (potential) piece of verbal art. If the *theme* is 'what the text is about when being dissociated from the text' (Hasan 1989: 97), then it is the quality of the dissociation which is elusive. It becomes graspable via the identification of *foregrounding* and its possible consistency as a main carrier of verbal art. It is stated here that metaphors contribute to that consistency, and can hence form a part of the grammar of verbal art (cf. Hasan 2007: 27). In Hasan's words:

> language patterns such as [...] metaphor, simile, imagery, alliteration, assonance etc., are mentioned as important, [...] but when it comes to identifying what part they play in the make up of the text, no satisfying account emerges. (Hasan 2007: 23)

Her contributions have continuously attempted to close this perceived gap. In terms of my own Hasan-inspired analysis I have selected historical English poetical texts not only due to the assumed high metaphorical frequency, but also due to the additional area of conflict that the spatio-temporal and cultural distance of author and modern recipients represents. On the basis of historical recognition and linguistic impact, the texts rank among the so-called literary texts which qualify as artefacts in the Hallidayian sense (cf. Halliday 2014: 3).

Metaphors, and related lexicogrammatical instantiations, occur in all spoken and written registers. Here, I consider the Hasanian framework open enough to allow for a cognitive perspective that relies on the pervasiveness of metaphors as underlying structures of our conceptual system. The conceptual metaphor approach as suggested by Lakoff and Johnson (2011) and Lakoff and Turner (2009) is chosen here to work out the patterning of metaphors as a component of the configurations within the *symbolic articulation* stratum, and hence as a *foregrounding* element contributing to verbal art, in the texts under concern. As a side effect, the procedure is intended to show the complementarity of functional and cognitive approaches. In other words, abstract conceptualizations of the mind are seen as directly linked to lexicogrammatical choices and patterns.[5]

9.3. Example discussion: *Beowulf*

In its surviving form of 3,182 lines in alliterative verse, *Beowulf* represents an often-cited example of Old English epic poetry to which neither a direct text source nor a specific date of origin nor a particular author can be assigned. Among its diversified and complex strands of narration, *Beowulf* contains the most substantial account of a hero-versus-dragon confrontation in the Western medieval text tradition. For reasons of selection from this vast and narratively complex text, I want to focus on the dragon episode (ll. 2200–3182) which constitutes the crescendo part of the entire text. More particularly, I intend to zoom in on the construction of the dragon as a character and its antagonist relation to Beowulf himself by highlighting selected conceptual metaphor instantiations and, accordingly, their *theme-guided* patterning in the respective text passage.[6] The basis of the analysis, however, remain the author's linguistic choices that constitute the *Beowulf* text as it has been handed down to us. In order to approach the otherwise unspecifiable context of text creation, the discussed examples will be from the (presumably close-to-original) Old English text.[7]

Let us examine the domain FIRE first. The *Beowulf* dragon is a *fȳrdraca* and *līgdraca* (ll. 2333, 2689, 3040), i.e. a fire- and flame-dragon. In these compounds, the semantically interrelated modifiers *fȳr* and *līg* establish a character specification: dragon, fire, and flame are realized as inextricably linked and form a conceptual entity. The fire the dragon spits is harmful, as evidenced on several text occasions, and is negatively connoted with the fear it causes in man (cf. l. 2780: *līgegesan wæg*). Metaphors involved in the conceptualization of dragon-related fire, and hence of the dragon itself, can be clustered and exemplified as follows:

FIRE is (THROWABLE) WEAPON	– cf. *glēdum spīwan* (l. 2312); *wearp wælfȳre* (l. 2582)
FIRE is INSTRUMENT OF VENGEANCE	– cf. *wolde se lāða līge forgyldan* (l. 2305)
FIRE is ENCASEMENT	– cf. *fȳre befangen* (l. 2274); *landwara līge befangen* (l. 2321); *fȳrwylmum fāh* (l. 2671) [8]
FIRE is (PERSONIFIED) WAVE	– cf. *Līg ȳðum fōr* (l. 2672)
FIRE is (WARRING) ENTITY IN MOTION	– cf. *hioroweallende* (l. 2781); *strēam […] brecan* (ll. 2545-46)
DRAGON BODY is CONTAINER OF FIRE	– cf. *glēdum beswæled* (l. 3041)

Additionally, the personification of fire, i.e. here the use of domain-related vocabulary in subject position, is occasionally used with metonymic function. Fire thus becomes an actor in place of the dragon (cf. l. 2313, *brynelēoma stōd*).

The author exploits further domains to conceptualize the dragon. With regard to the domains GUARDIAN and TREASURE, the noun *weard* is frequently used in *Beowulf* as a synonym of the dragon, thus specifying its principal occupation: it guards and, later in the narration, actively defends a hoard previously hidden in a barrow. This treasure is semantically intertwined with the dragon, as is observable in the compound *wyrmhord* (l. 2221). The relevant conceptualizations in this context are:

DRAGON is GUARDIAN OF
OBJECT

    (i.e. OF TREASURE)   – cf. *hordwelan heolde* (l. 2344);   *Weard* [...]
                                                 goldmāðmas hēold (ll. 2413–2414); *hordweard* (l. 2554)

    (i.e. OF BARROW)   – cf. *beorges weard* (l. 2524)

TREASURE is (PERSONI-   – cf. *Sinc ēaðe mæg* [...] *oferhīgian* (ll. 2764–2766)
FIED) POWER

Beyond the dragon's main defining capacity (i.e. spitting fire) and task (i.e. hoard-guarding), the *Beowulf* author seeks to conceptualize the dragon as an antithesis to the hero. First of all, via the lexicogrammatical choices it is portrayed as a beast, i.e. a clearly non-human being:

DRAGON is (FAST) SERPENT   – cf. *stonc* (l. 2288); *hringbogan* (l. 2561);
                                          biteran bānum (l. 2692)

DRAGON'S BREATH is BATTLE   – cf. *oruð* [...] *hildeswāt* (ll. 2557–2558)
SWEAT

Its size (cf. l. 3042) and age (cf. l. 2278) are extraordinary and thus suggest power. Further, the dragon is a skilful *lyftfloga* (l. 2315): equipped with wings, it can perform airborne attacks (cf. ll. 2312–2315) with fire (cf. above). As a solitary, presumably uncivilized earth-dweller (cf. l. 2712, *eorðdraca*), it appears to have nothing in common with the human sphere against which it is mapped. The air and below the earth's surface are the dragon's natural habitats.[9] Further, as an *ūhtsceaða* (l. 2271), it is a night creature (cf. l. 2211) that is described as being dire, harmful and particularly hostile to man:

DRAGON is (VENOMOUS)   – cf. *þēodsceaða* (l. 2688);[10] *attorsceaðan*
ENEMY OF MAN   (l. 2839)

DRAGON is (WINGED ENEMY)   – cf. *gūðsceada* (l. 2318);   *gūðfreca* (l. 2414);
WARRIOR   *gūðflogan* (l. 2528)

DRAGON is DECEITFUL GUEST   – cf. *inwitgæst* (l. 2670);   *nīðgæst* (l. 2699)[11]

The author establishes a conceptual affinity of the dragon to darkness (cf. l. 2833, *middelnihtum*), which counters the conceptualization of Beowulf as a hero connected to the light domain.[12] The two, hence, are constructed as naturally opposing narrative blueprints that, as co-existence becomes impossible, are bound to clash violently.

I now want to draw attention to an interesting notion of the character construction that relies on the conceptualization patterns as outlined so far, yet promotes a coming to terms with the overall *theme* by foregrounding not the contrast and opposedness of both Beowulf and the dragon, but rather their likeness. The term *āglǣc(e)a* was chosen several times in the dragon episode. It is used to refer to the dragon as a miscreant and induces further negative connotations such as fierceness (cf. e.g. ll. 2520, 2534). Modern translators might consider *monster* an adequate rendering of the concept. However, Beowulf himself is an *āglǣca*, too, on a par with the dragon when they meet each other to fight (cf. l. 2592).[13] By means of this lexical and hence concept choice, their antagonism is temporarily dissolved – which ultimately is in line with their dying together (cf. l. 2824). Beowulf and the dragon do match; they are even in their being depicted as superlative and extraordinary. Both are terrified of each other (cf. l. 2565) and thus share the same emotional setup. We may state at this point of narration that the dragon and Beowulf define and complete one another: DRAGON is BEOWULF and vice-versa.[14] This conceptual parallelism highlights the bestial in Beowulf as it stresses the human in the dragon.

In addition, the dragon features specific human traits and abilities, which may have made the original recipients – and we may assume so from a modern perspective – reconsider the nature of the dragon as a brutish beast all the more. The metaphorical conceptualization DRAGON is RULER (IN HALL) (cf. ll. 2211, 2320) likens the dragon, yet again, to king Beowulf. Further, the dragon can feel, think and plan like humans generally do. It acts consequentially in accordance with its own moral standards – it can tell wrong (e.g. the theft of a cup) from right (e.g. avenging the theft), can be enraged (cf. l. 2220), be joyful, and can bear hope and hate:

DRAGON'S EMOTION is HUMAN EMOTION   – cf. *Hāt* (l. 2296); *wēn* (l. 2323); *Hete* (l. 2554)

TREASURE is DRAGON'S DELIGHT   – cf. *Hordwynne* (l. 2270)

The dragon performs acts on its own account based on free will (cf. *wolde* in ll. 2294, 2315). The author, however, strives to ensure that the dragon, in all its relating to humanness, is conceptualized as a moral antithesis to man via strongly evaluative vocabulary. Further, it is positioned against the background of (humanoid) Grendel and his mother who were introduced as

Beowulf's opponents earlier in the text. The dragon is not only harmful, but ill-willed (cf. l. 2273) and false (cf. l. 2514). After its death, the author seeks to highlight the dissimilarities to the human sphere again: for instance, in contrast to Beowulf, the dragon is meant to be kept in mind as the hated one (cf. ll. 2909–2910), and its concealing of the hoard was unjust in the first place (cf. l. 3059).

Dragons, as sources suggest, were considered to be actually existing (physical) beings.[15] Their rarity, as it were, called for conceptualization. *Beowulf* is in this respect a continuation of an older textual tradition which survives in occasional instances of Old English gnomic poetry.[16] The author's specifications of the dragon in *Beowulf* are of particular interest as they go beyond its employment as a mere text-ornamental, generic adversary. In total, considerable text material is used to bring the dragon's characteristics and motives to the fore to make him a serious and concrete, albeit nameless, opponent. The dragon as a conceptual unit is developed in the text via extensive and creative patterning of metaphors in particular. The metaphorical (lexicogrammatical) expressions belong to Hasan's *verbalization* stratum (cf. ch. 2) and enable the individual recipient's contact with the text. These expressions are instantiations of conceptual metaphors that constitute a part of the *symbolic articulation* potential. The conceptual metaphors that have been emphasized here are exploited in particular for the construction of character such as the dragon's *vis-à-vis* Beowulf's. It is the dynamic conceptual approximation and deapproximation of both characters in particular that constitute artistic ruptures of the otherwise consistently patterned dragon-as-supreme-antagonist setup. In more general terms, deconstructing the pattern consistency is a window to the grammar of verbal art:

> [it] is the patterning of those patterns that foregrounds meanings in the text and creates a background against which the *break of a pattern* will be perceived as significant. (Pagano and Lukin 2015: 106, my emphasis)

In other words, we thus perceive a glimpse at the *theme*, i.e. at a deeper meaning which refers to matters that link up with the artist's text-creational intention on the one hand, and that affect the recipient's cultural environment, social organization, and the human condition in general on the other. The *theme* at hand in *Beowulf*, i.e. the text without its text particularities, encompasses moral integrity, the facing of social and existential challenges, the unavoidability of fate, emic versus etic viewpoints on culture and identity and, pointed out in particular here, the monstrous in man. The survival of the *Beowulf* text and its modern recognition as a work of art has, for instance, definitely contributed to the status of dragons as available and even essential narrative institutions (cf. Tolkien 1963: 68) that can, as cultural items, transport such *themes* that are also relevant for the here and now.

9.4. Example discussion: Metaphysical poetry

The history of English texts offers a plethora of opportunities that tie in with the *Beowulf*-related findings of conceptual metaphors as part of the fabric that constitutes verbal art. The literary text category of metaphysical poetry provides ample examples of dense patterning via metaphor. As in section 9.3, the following brief discussion is meant to bring expressly this tool to the fore in identifying conceptual metaphors that feed *symbolic articulation*.

The following poem by John Donne has become known as *Holy Sonnet XIV*. First published in 1633, it is a 14-line end-rhyme sonnet in predominantly iambic pentameter, arranged in three quatrains and a final couplet:[17]

> 1   *Batter my heart, three-person'd God; for you*
>   *As yet but knocke, breathe, shine, and seeke to mend;*
>   *That I may rise, and stand, o'erthrow mee, 'and bend*
>   *Your force, to breake, blowe, burn, and make me new.*
> 5   *I, like an usurpt towne, to'another due,*
>   *Labour to'admit you, but Oh, to no end,*
>   *Reason your viceroy in mee, mee should defend,*
>   *But is captiv'd, and proves weake or untrue,*
>   Yet dearly'I love you, and would be lov'd faine,
> 10   But am betroth'd unto your cnemie,
>   Divorce me, 'untie, or breake that knot againe,
>   Take mee to you, imprison me, for I
>   *Except you'enthrall me, never shall be free,*
>   *Nor ever chast, except you ravish mee.* (Donne 1961)

The quatrains each correspond to a set of metaphorical instantiations that can be traced to different, yet systematically and logically sequenced conceptualizations. The first quatrain (ll. 1–4) realizes and establishes a setting relying on the conceptual metaphor GOD is GLASSBLOWER.[18] Acts of forceful, yet metaphorical spiritual violence (cf. e.g. *Batter, knocke, bend, breake, burn*) are required against the speaker as a patient to recreate him (e.g. *breathe, shine, mend, blow*) according to divine will. In the second quatrain (ll. 5–8), the focus shifts from God as actor to the speaker whose inwardly torn condition is worded mainly in terms of the source domains WAR (cf. *defend, captiv'd*)[19] and POWER (cf. *usurpt, viceroy*). These semantically overlapping sets of *foregrounding* are intensified by the formal frame of the quatrains.[20]

In the third quatrain (ll. 9–12), the author takes up the previously fore-grounded conceptualizations of violence (cf. *breake, take*) and war/captivity (cf. *enemie, imprison*) and interweaves them with an exploitation of the meta-phorical domains (SPIRITUAL) LOVE (cf. *love, lov'd*) and MARRIAGE (cf. *betroth'd, divorce*). This is accompanied by a changing rhyme scheme (from enclosed to alternate rhyme), and followed by a couplet which repre-sents another disruption of the formal symmetry of ll. 1–8. The final couplet (ll. 13–14) provides a paradoxical, yet positive reinterpretation of the so far consistently employed negatively laden metaphorical expressions. With this peripetic move,[21] spiritual imprisonment means freedom (cf. *free*), and God's violence, which now includes sexual violence (cf. *ravish*), means chastity.

In the complexity of his *foregrounding* arrangements via metaphor, Donne keeps to a consistency which, finally, gives rise to unconventional and creative uses which go beyond common experience. This creative use in particular as part of verbal art grammar sheds light on 'the work's artistic intention' (Hasan 2007: 28) and, hence, the *theme*. The recipient, i.e. includ-ing the modern one, is enabled to reflect on the ambivalence of violence and freedom, as well as on questions of the relationship of the self and the divine, including hierarchies of power in general. In the event, these reflec-tions are propelled by the described *foregrounding* design.

The following discussion of Thomas Carew's 1640 poem *Red and White Roses* will complete the examples provided here in terms of the organiza-tion of conceptual metaphor patterns as a key element to render the deeper meaning accessible.

1   READE in these roses the sad story
Of my hard fate and your owne glory;
In the White you may discover
The palenesse of a fainting lover;
5   *In the Red the flames still feeding*
On my heart with fresh wounds bleeding.
The white will tell you how I languish,
And the Red expresse my anguish;
The White my innocence displaying,
10   *The Red my martyrdome betraying.*
The frownes that on your brow resided,
Have those roses thus divided.
Oh! let your smiles but cleare the weather,
And then they both shall grow together. (Carew 1870)

The particular linguistic deployment of metaphor in this poem of 14 end-rhyme lines follows its arrangement into a series of couplets.[22] The first couplet (ll. 1–2) sets the stage: The speaker's separation from a beloved one is exemplified via (concrete) roses that serve as metaphors to conceptualize his miserable inner state as the poem progresses. The (NEGATIVE) INNER STATE is PLANT conceptual metaphor governs the linguistic choice throughout. Building on this, the author maps attributes of a white (cf. ll. 3–4) and a red rose (cf. ll. 5–6) onto his lovesickness (cf. *palenesse, fainting, wounds*). The juxtaposition is intensified in ll. 7–10 where white and red are employed within the same couplets. Here, the metonymic colours are conceptualized as persons – as actors and at the same time as the speaker's instruments, they bring his emotional state (cf. the fourth couplet: *languish, anguish*) and his spiritual condition (cf. the fifth couplet: *innocence, martyrdom*) to the fore.

The speaker's addressee is identified in couplet six (ll. 11–12) as the causer of his disturbance (cf. the metonym *frownes*) by consistently taking up the plant metaphor (cf. *roses thus divided*). Yet, the focus shifts in the final couplet (ll. 13–14). In an emphatically introduced direct appeal (cf. *Oh!*), the addressee is positively reinterpreted as the solution to the speaker's problems. Via a newly introduced weather metaphor (PROBLEM is BAD WEATHER), the main conceptual metaphor is extended to include, with respect to the author's and the recipients' individual experiences, the impossible: the growing together of the different roses which reverses the conceptualization NEGATIVE INNER STATE is PLANT into positive.

In texts, *foregrounding* takes place in significant places (cf. Miller 2016: 65). Carew exploits a main metaphor to that end, namely artistically structuring the speaker's lament to highlight his health, emotion and spiritual state. Ultimately, it is a twist of the consistent patterning that pushes the coming to terms with the *theme* even further forward. The *theme* of wider sociocultural concern includes matters of difference and separation versus unity, and inner conflict due to religious moral understanding. Further, it cannot be excluded that the author refers to the historical War of the Roses to warn of domestic political tensions in the pre-Cromwellian era (i.e. at the time when the poem was composed).

As in *Beowulf* and in Donne's poem, the conceptual metaphor repertoire and its wording form part of the respective author's 'orchestration' (cf. similarly Hasan 2007: 23) and thus act out of *theme*-related responsibilities (cf. Lukin and Webster 2005: 422). On this basis, it is justified to state that the theoretical frameworks of Hasan's verbal art model with its rooting in systemic-functional linguistics and of conceptual metaphor as a cognitive approach are not only reconcilable, but complement each other for the benefit of substantial insights.

9.5. Consistency and distance

Text authors exploit metaphors as a common ground that is shared with text recipients from the same or a related sociocultural background, and as a creative means of meaning negotiation to stage the intricate and elusive. An artistic realization is consistent when it is manifested through patterned metaphorical linguistic expression. However, a link to the *theme* can only be suitably established beyond the linguistic analysis of the text proper, for instance by including the context of text creation. This context is often not fully retrievable, a condition that holds for historical texts in particular. Further, the deeper meaning value attached to a text must remain vague if the (future) recipients of a text and their sociocultural frameworks are not well enough defined. This criticism notwithstanding, by identifying verbal art as recontextualizing means we may discover socioculturally problem areas as well as conceptualizations and stylistic demands that were relevant for the authors of historical texts and that still are relevant for modern readers. Several conceptual metaphors stand as a cultural constant and as a traditional resource for *foregrounding* purposes.[23] Thus, a multiply distant[24] text such as *Beowulf* can still speak to us, as it were, as a piece of art with significance.

Clearly, recipients bring diverse and individual experiences to a text, including the processing of other (artistic) narratives (cf. Gerrig 2011a, b). So do subsequent generations of authors with their discourse that relies on established conceptualizations and genre expectations as well as on creativity and experimentation. Meaning negotiation and understanding is thus seen as a diachronic process in which linguistic, conceptual, and situational knowledge all take part (cf. Feldman 2008: 284).[25] The wider the spatiotemporal, and this means sociosemiotic, distance between author and recipient, the more meaning recognition potential is lost and art may not be recognizable as such. Still, it remains remarkable that 'the symbolically articulated theme [can] be capable of striking a chord in the reader across substantial distances in time and space' (Hasan 2007: 25).

Recipients recreate a work of art (cf. Foley 1987: 196) by performing Hasan's second-level semiosis (cf. Figure 9.1) in the author's inverse order. Usually, authors start out from the *theme* which creates the *symbolic articulation* potential, which itself gives rise to *symbolic articulation* choices, and to accompanying *verbalization* potential and choices. The recipients start with the actual language that gives these choices analysable form. Metaphorical linguistic expressions, for instance, serve as access gates that lead, via consistent patterns of underlying conceptual metaphor, to the *theme* and to its reflection (cf. Figure 9.2). For Hasan, meaning lies in the 'combined calibration' (1988: 53) of logical, experiential, interpersonal, and textual structure.

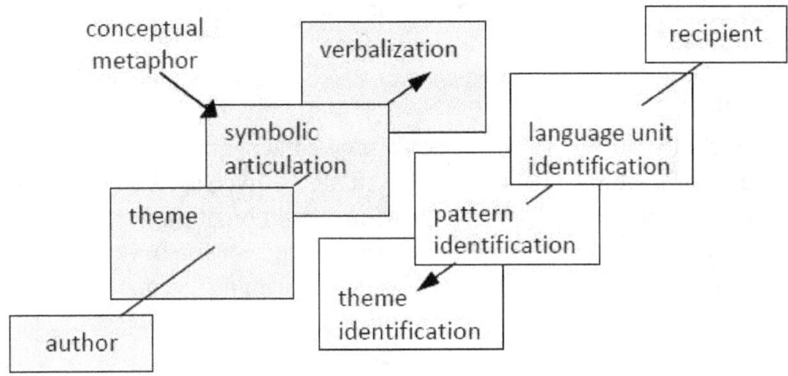

Figure 9.2: Author and recipient second-level semiosis including conceptual metaphor

Theme identification is the result of a process of convergence of meanings that surround these levels and that are created via language and, in terms of verbal art, an artistic toolset. Conceptual metaphors and their consistent instantiation (including breaks that rely on this consistency) have been identified here as belonging to this toolset. Yet again, the more sociosemiotically distant the author and the recipient of the same text are, the higher the likeliness of (a) an incomplete grasp of the conceptual metaphors involved; and (b) an incomplete congruence of the author's and the recipient's *theme*. If (a) and/or (b) applies, a full appreciation of verbal art is impeded.

Metaphor is not a predictor of art-ness, but an available resource to contribute to its establishment within a text. Only a small part of the artistic in *Beowulf* and Donne's and Carew's poems could be revealed here. Possible *foregrounding* patternings are manifold – they may dynamically overlap and act jointly as artistic 'moves'.[26] It will be rewarding to work out the co-functionality of metaphor and other *foregrounding* tools in more detail. It is fair to assume that future studies on the matter will not only contribute to our understanding of verbal art, but also provide insights into the complementarity of functional and cognitive theoretical approaches.

9.6. Conclusion

Hasan calls us to base our analysis of a potentially artistic text on strata beyond the Hallidayian semiotic framework. The claims about verbal art made here have been based on *foregrounding* via metaphor as a tool that contributes to transporting and identifying the *theme* and its contextualized significance. More particularly, conceptual metaphors as part of the *symbolic articulation* potential and their consistently patterned instantiations in text via lexicogrammatical choices help shape the grammar of verbal art – as do deliberate modifications, re-workings and breaks of these patterns. Yet, the degree and semiotic means of *foregrounding* establishment remain text-individual.

The text examples that have been discussed here are not intended to be seen as representing English literature in all its diversity. Still, these diachronic examples point on the one hand to a tradition of English verbal art, and to the construction (in terms of coherence and consistency) and deconstruction (in terms of contrast and asymmetry within a normative pattern) of *foregrounding* via metaphor on the other. *Foregrounding* appears to have been an instrument throughout the centuries which, in the case of the selected examples, allows modern recipients to still access and make assumptions about the original *theme* in spite of considerable spatiotemporal distance and related linguistic changes. Thus, the metaphorical conceptualization of the *Beowulf* dragon with its 'cognitive, emotive, and volitional capacities' (Evans 1985: 100–101), for instance, did not only contribute to developing the dragon-as-antagonist trope intra- and transtextually (cf. e.g. Rauer 2000), but to push the deeper meaning into the twenty-first century, as do the conceptual arrangements on the basis of metaphor in Donne and Carew. *Theme* construal, however, involves the recipient's willingness and socio-semiotic capabilities (cf. Hasan 2007: 26) – so it may either be more or less accessible to the individual recipient.

From a cognitive perspective, Hasan's model can be approached and enriched by justifiably assuming that literary reading involves the same mental processes and representations that are involved in comprehension generally (cf. Semino in Freeman 2006: 406). In this vein, the literary artistic text goes beyond the 'regular' language use. It is Hasan's concern that the artistic in terms of verbal art should not remain a mystery which everybody knows exists but is elusive to such a degree that it is not worth being examined and defined any further. Hasan's model of *double articulation* is, above all, an enabling one (cf. Hasan 2007: 34). It is open and cross-disciplinary enough to include cognitive theoretical assessments of conceptualization via language, i.e. the semiotic, and culture in general. Language remains the golden path to the identification of verbal art as a cultural activity. Hence, verbal art is a social process of meaning (re)negotiation[27] or, in other words, a traditional cultural opportunity that has extended our awareness and conceptualization of reality and realities. After all, referring to metaphor once again, it is the text itself that functions as a metaphor for the *theme* (cf. Butt 2016: 27). In this regard, choice-based patterned organization, some elements of which have been pointed out here, is employed to explain the elusive deeper meaning. For the author, the *theme* represents the beginning of the artistic effort, while its identification by the recipient accomplishes the meaning-making process.

Notes

1. Throughout this article, *theme* refers only to Hasan's use of the term as a stratal component of her semiotic system of verbal art; cf. section 9.2.
2. Cf. Miller (2010, 38) for a critical view on Hasan in this respect. Indeed, as social conventions are liable to change, a dynamic, fine-grained diachronic perspective is additionally required in order to assess potential spatiotemporal and sociocultural gaps between author and recipients that may read a verbally artistic text centuries after its composition. With respect to translations, cf. section 9.5.
3. On Mukařovský, related theoretical antecedents and Halliday as a particular influence on Hasan, cf. Mukařovský (1977); Hasan (1987); Lukin and Webster (2005: 413–418). For an inclusion of Jakobsen's insights into Hasan's framework, cf. Miller (2016).
4. For consistency in terms of semantic direction or 'drift', cf. Butt (1983).
5. Cf. Lothmann and Serbina (2017) on the lexicogrammatical realization of conceptual metaphors; cf. also Holme (2003).
6. Parts of the metaphor analysis relating to the Beowulf dragon have also been used in Lothmann (2016). On metaphors as a constitutive value in the mental construction of character identity in general, cf. Vaeßen and Lothmann (2014).
7. All Beowulf text quotations and line specifications in this chapter refer to Beowulf (1998). All Old English instances have been checked against Bosworth (1996) and OED (2016) in order to avoid entire text translations into modern English prose or poetry, and thus possible lexicosemantic distortions of the oldest source.
8. Here, 'being surrounded by fire' does not harm the dragon. His opponents, however, are in agony when the encasement metaphor is applied to them (cf. l. 2595), which underscores that *dragon*, and *fire* with its consumptive power, are intended to represent a conceptual unity.
9. This is in contrast to Beowulf who operates on land and in water; cf. the encounters with Grendel and his mother, for instance. Beowulf and the dragon contact at a border of each other's domains, i.e. the entrance of the barrow (cf. ll. 2551–2555). In this respect, the label *wyrm* stresses semantic connotations with crawling and earth, while the synonymously used *draca* comprises rather the flying and watching potential.
10. Interestingly, the term þēodsceaða ('people-harmer') is also used in the *Beowulf* text before the dragon attacks the Geatish dwellings that belong to Beowulf's dominion; cf. l. 2278 and Sorrell (1994: 59). Hence, the Beowulf author intends to channel the conceptualization of the dragon by the recipients. Recipients are guided to view the dragon as a malevolent creature in the first place. This is supported and filtered by the Beowulf character who himself, as an inside narrator, conceptualizes the dragon in a similar vein prior to meeting it (cf. ll. 2518–2523).

11.   On a possible mixed conceptualization of *gæst* ('guest') and *gǣst* ('spirit'), cf. Lionarons (1998: 37). The domain EVIL is not identified in my analysis due to its strong link to Christian readings (cf. e.g. Goldsmith 2013), which I consider unjustified for a text-based *dragon* conceptualization.

12.   Cf. e.g. Beowulf's radiant sword (cf. l. 2583: *hildelēoman*) and, earlier in the text, the light that surrounds him after the slaying of Grendel's mother (cf. ll. 1770–1772).

13.   The *Beowulf* author does not, and we may assume deliberately so, choose a more and unambiguously positively connoted lexeme instead. For instance, *ellenlǣca* ('champion', featuring the same compound head as *āglǣca*) would have been an available option. This decision clearly increases the complexity of the conceptualization of the Beowulf character, and his relation to the dragon as an opponent to overcome.

14.   In regard of the conceptual identity of both, cf. also Clark (1990: 126); Evans (2005: 250).

15.   Cf. e.g. the Anglo-Saxon Chronicle (cf. Shilton 1997: 70–71) and zoological studies (cf. Schneidewind 2008: 83).

16.   Cf. e.g. Maxims II (2011). Still, in this respect, fictional characters and events, however 'unrealistic' they may seem in view of life experiences of the recipients, possess 'the same potential for symbolic articulation of the theme as do the real ones' (Hasan 1975: 58).

17.   The poem combines formal elements of Petrarchan and Shakespearean sonnet arrangements.

18.   A different assumption in this respect is made for instance in Goatly (2010: 216). Cf. also there for metaphor-related analyses of further examples of Donne's poetic oeuvre.

19.   Reason acts as a personified soldier of the devout individual here. With respect to the war metaphor and its development in the history of English poetry, cf. Lothmann (2015).

20.   It can be argued in this respect that the form serves as a metaphor for the content. On the stanza representing a semantic area, cf. Elleström (2015: 211).

21   The move is supported by the double use of *except* and the chiasmus structure in the final couplet.

22.   The meter shifts non-systematically between iambic and trochaic tetrameter. It contributes, however, to a rounded-off form as the final couplet repeats the meter of the first.

23.   The notion of universality, either of values, topoi, or metaphor-based conceptualizations, is not discussed here.

24.   The distances include matters of language change, as well as varying aesthetic responses and evaluations of the *theme* across time. Cf. also Butt (2016: 49). On social distance and translations, cf. Hasan (1996: 48; 2007: 35). For more on the displacement between author and reader from a cognitive poetics perspective, cf. e.g. Stockwell (2016).

25.   In this regard, Hasan (1989: 102) states that '[it] is not an accident that the theme, the symbolic articulation, and the patterns of language display a great deal of similarity within any one period of verbal art.'

26.   Examples of semiotic devices that can be observed to contribute to *foreground-*

ing consistency are: the use of tense and sequentiality, finite vs. non-finite, pronouns and deictic markers, mood and modality, clause complexity, type-token frequency and further means of lexical and grammatical cohesion. On collocation as a control mechanism for verbal art, cf. Louw (2007). Next to intratextual patterning, intertextual strategies may be employed; cf. Butt (1988) on 'latent patterning'. In this regard, Butt uses the term *preoccupation* to assess inter-textual coherence beyond individual themes (cf. Butt in Lukin and Webster 2005: 425). For narratives, shifts between narrator perspectives are also among the *foregrounding* strategies. With respect to poetry in particular, mnemonic resources based on sound patterning are of additional relevance.

27. Cf. Butt (2016: 51): 'verbal art renews our potential to mean'.

References

[Beowulf] Anon. (1998). *Beowulf: An Edition with Relevant Shorter Texts* (Eds) B. Mitchell and F. C. Robinson. Oxford and Malden: Blackwell.

Bosworth, J. (1996). *An Anglo-Saxon Dictionary* (Ed.) T. N. Toller. Repr. Oxford: Oxford University Press.

Butt, D. G. (1983). 'Semantic "Drift" in Verbal Art.' *Australian Review of Applied Linguistics* 6 (1): 38–48. https://doi.org/10.1075/aral.6.1.04but

Butt, D. G. (1988). 'Randomness, order and the latent patterning of text." In D. Birch and M. O'Toole (Eds) *Functions of Style*, 74–97. London: Pinter.

Butt, D. G. (2016). 'Construe my meaning': Performance, poetry and semiotic distance. In W. L. Bowcher and J.Y. Liang (Eds) *Society in Language, Language in Society: Essays in Honour of Ruqaiya Hasan*, 24–55. Basingstoke: Palgrave Macmillan. https://doi.org/10.1057/9781137402868_2

Carew, T. (1640/1870). 'Red and White Roses.' In W. C. Hazlitt (Ed.) *The Poems of Thomas Carew*, 60. Arundel: Roxburghe Library.

Clark, G. (1990). *Beowulf.* Boston, MA: Twayne Publ.

Donne, J. (1633/1961). 'Holy Sonnet [XIV].' In H. Gardner (Ed.) *The Metaphysical Poets*, 83–84. Repr. Harmondsworth: Penguin Books.

Elleström, L. (2015). Visual, auditory, and cognitive iconicity in written literature: The example of Emily Dickinson's 'Because I Could not Stop for Death'. In M. K. Hiraga, W. J. Herlofsky, K. Shinohara and K. Akita (Ed.), *Iconicity: East Meets West*, 207–218. Amsterdam and Philadelphia, PA: Benjamins. https://doi.org/10.1075/ill.14.11ell

Evans, J. D. (1985). 'Semiotics and traditional lore: The medieval dragon tradition. *Journal of Folklore Research* 22: 85–112.

Evans, J. (2005). 'As Rare as They Are Dire': Old Norse dragons, Beowulf, and the Deutsche Mythologie. In T. Shippey (Ed.) *The*

Shadow-walkers: Grimm's Mythology of the Monstrous, 207–269. Tempe, AZ: Arizona Center for Medieval and Renaissance Studies.

Feldman, J. A. (2008). *From Molecule to Metaphor: A Neural Theory of Language*. Repr., Cambridge, MA and London: The MIT Press.

Foley, J. M. (1987). 'Reading the oral traditional text: Aesthetics of creation and response. In J. M. Foley (Ed.) *Comparative Research on Oral Traditions: A Memorial for Milman Parry*, 185–212. Columbia: Slavica.

Freeman, M. H. (2006). The fall of the wall between literary studies and linguistics: Cognitive poetics. In G. Kristiansen, M. Achard, R. Dirven, and F. J. Ruiz de Mendoza Ibáñez (Eds) *Cognitive Linguistics: Current Applications and Future Perspectives*, 403–428. Berlin: Mouton de Gruyter.

Gerrig, R. J. (2011a). Conscious and unconscious processes in readers' narrative experiences. In G. Olson (Ed.) *Current Trends in Narratology*, 37-60. Berlin and New York: De Gruyter.

Gerrig, R. J. (2011b). Individual Differences in Reader4's narrative experiences. *Scientific Study of Literature* 1: 88–94. https://doi.org/10.1075/ssol.1.1.09ger

Goatly, A. (2010). *Explorations in Stylistics*. London and Oakville: Equinox.

Goldsmith, M. E. (2013). *The Mode and Meaning in 'Beowulf'*. Repr., London: Bloomsbury.

Halliday, M. A. K. (1985). *An Introduction to Functional Grammar*. London: Arnold.

Halliday, M. A. K. (2014). *An Introduction to Functional Grammar* (rev. C. M. I. M. Matthiessen) 4th ed. London and New York: Routledge.

Hasan, R. (1967). Linguistics and the study of literary texts. *Études de Linguistique Appliquée* 5 : 106–121.

Hasan, R. (1975). The place of stylistics in the study of verbal art. In H. Ringbom (Ed.) *Style and Text: Studies Presented to Nils Erik Enkvist*, 49–62. Amsterdam: Skriptor.

Hasan, R. (1987). Directions from Structuralism. In D. Attridge, N. Fabb, A. Durant, and C. McCabb *The Linguistics of Writing: Arguments between Language and Literature*, 103–22. Manchester: Manchester University Press.

Hasan, R. (1988). The analysis of one poem: Theoretical issues in practice. In D. Birch and M. O'Toole (Eds) *Functions of Style*. London: Pinter.

Hasan, R. (1985/1989). *Linguistics, Language, and Verbal Art* (2nd ed.). Oxford: Oxford University Press.

Hasan, R. (2007). Private pleasure, public discourse: Reflections on engaging with literature. In D. R. Miller and M. Turci (Eds) *Language and Verbal Art Revisited: Linguistic Approaches to the study of literature*, 13–40. London: Equinox.

Hasan, R. (2011). A timeless journey: On the past and future of present knowledge. In *Selected Papers of Ruqaiya Hasan on Applied Linguistics*, xiv–xliii. Beijing: Foreign Language Teaching and Research Press.

Hasan, R. (2013). Choice, system, realization: Describing language as meaning potential. In L. Fontaine, T. Bartlett, and G. O'Grady (Eds) *Systemic Functional Linguistics: Exploring Choice*, 269–299. Cambridge: Cambridge University Press.

Holme, R. (2003). Grammatical metaphor as a cognitive construct. In A.-M. Simon-Vandenbergen, M. Taverniers, and L. J. Ravelli (Eds), *Grammatical Metaphor: Views from Systemic Functional Linguistics*, 391–415. Amsterdam and Philadelphia, PA: Benjamins. https://doi.org/10.1075/cilt.236.21hol

Lakoff, G., and M. Johnson. 2011. *Metaphors We Live by*. Repr., Chicago and London: University of Chicago Press.

Lakoff, G. and Turner M. (2009). *More than Cool Reason: A Field Guide to Poetic Metaphor*. Repr., Chicago, IL: University of Chicago Press.

Lionarons, J. T. (1998). Cultural syncretism and the construction of gender in Cynewulf's Elene. *Exemplaria* 10 (1998): 51–68. https://doi.org/10.1179/exm.1998.10.1.51

Lothmann, T. (2015). 'Oft in My Face He Doth His Banner Rest': War as a pervasive metaphor in early English literature. *Yearbook of the German Cognitive Linguistics Association* 3: 51–70. https://doi.org/10.1515/gcla-2015-0004

Lothmann, T. (2016). The ravaging and hoard-guarding antagonist: A cognitive approach to 'Dragon' conceptualisations in 'Beowulf' and selected writings of Tolkien. *Fastitocalon* 6: 169–184.

Lothmann, T. and T. Serbina. (2017). On the overlap of grammatical metaphor and conceptual metaphor in political discourse: A reconciliatory approach. In S. Neumann, R. Wegener, J. Fest, P. Niemietz, and N. Hützen (Eds) *Challenging Boundaries in Linguistics: Systemic Functional Perspectives*, 223–238. Frankfurt am Main: Lang.

Louw, B. (2007). Collocation as the determinant of verbal art. In D. R. Miller and M. Turci (Eds) *Language and Verbal Art Revisited: Linguistic Approaches to the Study of Literature*, 149–180. London and Oakville: Equinox.

Lukin, A. and J. J. Webster. (2005). SFL and the study of literature. In R.

Hasan, C. M. I. M. Matthiessen, and J. J. Webster (Eds) *Continuing Discourse in Language: A Functional Perspective. Vol. 1*, 413–456. London and Oakville: Equinox.

[Maxims II] Anon. (2011). InAnon. (Ed.) *The Complete Corpus of Anglo-Saxon Poetry: Maxims II*. http://www.sacred-texts.com/neu/ascp/a15. htm (accessed 16 May 2016).

Miller, D. R. (2010). The Hasanian framework for the study of 'verbal art' revisited … and reproposed. *Textus* 23: 29–51.

Miller, D. R. (2016). Jakobson's place in Hasan's social semiotic stylistics: 'Pervasive Parallelism' as symbolic articulation of theme. In W. L. Bowcher and J. Y. Liang (Eds) *Society in Language, Language in Society: Essays in Honour of Ruqaiya Hasan*, 59–80. Basingstoke: Palgrave Macmillan. https://doi.org/10.1057/9781137402868_3

Mukařovský, J. (1977). *The Word and Verbal Art*. New Haven, CT: Yale University Press.

[OED] *Oxford English Dictionary*. (2016). Oxford: Oxford University Press. www.oed.com (accessed 16 May 2016).

Pagano, A., and Lukin, A. (2015). Exploring language in verbal art: A Case Study in K. Mansfield's 'Bliss'. In S. Starc, C. Jones, and A. Maiorani (Eds) *Meaning Making in Text: Multimodal and Multilingual Functional Perspectives*, 92–108. Basingstoke and New York: Palgrave Macmillan. https://doi.org/10.1057/9781137477309.0012

Rauer, C. (2000). *Beowulf and the Dragon: Parallels and Analogues*. Cambridge: Brewer.

Schneidewind, F. (2008). Farmer Giles of Ham: The prototype of a humorous dragon-story. In M. Hiley and F. Weinreich (Eds) *Tolkien's Shorter Works: Proceedings of the 4th Seminar of the Deutsche Tolkien-Gesellschaft*, 77-100. Zürich: Walking Tree Publications.

Seneca, L. A. (2009). *De brevitate vitae ad Paulinum*. In D. Camden (Ed.) *Corpus Scriptorum Latinorum: A Digital Library of Latin Literature*. Repr. http://www.forumromanum.org/literature/seneca_younger/brev. html (accessed 18 May 2016).

Shilton, H. (1997). The nature of Beowulf's Dragon. *Bulletin of the John Rylands Library* 79 (3): 67–77.

Sorrell, P. (1994). The approach to the Dragon-fight in Beowulf, Aldhelm, and the 'traditions folkloriques' of Jacques Le Goff. *Parergon* 12: 57–87. https://doi.org/10.1353/pgn.1994.0002

Stockwell, P. (2016). 'The texture of authorial intention. In J. Gavins and E. Lahey (Eds) *World Building: Discourse in the Mind*, 147–163. London: Bloomsbury.

Tolkien, J. R. R. (1963). Beowulf: The monsters and the critics. In L. E.

Nicholson (Ed.) *An Anthology of Beowulf Criticism*, 51–103. Notre Dame, IN: University of Notre Dame Press.

Vaeßen, J., and Lothmann, T. (2014). 'Do you read me? Metaphor as a pathway to the conceptualisation of literary identity.' *International Journal of Literary Linguistics* 3: 1–18. http://www.ijll.uni-mainz.de/index.php/ijll/issue/viewIssue/6/4 (accessed 18 May 2016).

10 Openings in fiction: An approach to verbal art based on Hallidayian, cognitive and Hasanian Principles

Peter Wenzel[*]

10.1. Openings as a relevant research subject

Comparatively little systematic research work has been done so far on the openings of narrative texts. The multiplicity of possible types and their rhetorical strategies were last discussed from the viewpoint of a literary scholar in an article by Peter Erlebach (2011). A useful older approach to the subject was made by Helmut Bonheim (1982) in a study on narrative modes in the short story. Moreover, there are a few comments on text openings in classical handbooks on text linguistics (cf. Plett 1975; Werlich 1976: 150–157), and in postclassical narratology, there is one important collection of essays edited by Brian Richardson (2008). This is practically all worthwhile scholarly work available.[1]

This scarcity of research is astonishing, since many phenomena point to the particular relevancy of text openings. As Torgovnick (1981: 3–4) has put it, 'it is difficult to recall all of a work after a complete reading, but climactic moments, dramatic scenes, and beginnings and endings remain in the memory.' This particular memorability that beginnings share with endings could be due to the fact that these sections are often foregrounded against the rest of the text, being structured particularly densely with the help of repetition and symmetry, or some other eye-catching devices such as negations, questions, proverbs or intertextual references.[2]

---

* Peter Wenzel (*1953) is Full Professor of English Literature at RWTH Aachen University and has published on Shakespeare, literary genres and various fields of literary theory. His recent research interests focus on text openings and endings.

What makes text openings most important, last but not least, is their privileged cognitive function: At the beginning of a text, the reader will usually get some decisive clues for its intended reception, thus with regard to comprehension and interpretation, the text opening exerts what is called 'a primacy effect' (cf. Sternberg 1976). The situation, the persons and occurrences in a narrative text, the question of whether it is to be read as fictional or as non-fictional, the relationship of its story-world to that of the reader, the relevant cultural schemata and argumentative patterns against the background of which it is intended to be seen, all these essential sense-producing devices are usually either explicitly or implicitly contained in the text opening (cf. Herman 2009) so that there is strong need for studying openings in more detail.

As the present essay will show, some of Michael Halliday's essential notions about language can be of great use for that purpose, particularly the idea that for the author, openings involve the necessity of making systemic choices from a network of interrelated alternative strategies. Moreover, text openings are incontrovertibly functional, serving the social function of establishing a communicative bond between narrator and reader, the informational function of conveying knowledge about the story-world, and the interpretive function of already pointing the reader towards a thematic frame in which the presented story is intended to be processed and understood.

As will be shown in this essay, it is not difficult to support the notion of the relevancy of these functions with recent evidence from the investigation of cognitive mechanisms involved in text creation and text comprehension in general. Thus what is here presented as 'informational function' of a text opening can easily be related to what in cognitive stylistics has been called 'the scenario-mapping theory', while the 'interpretive function' has strong affinities with 'the rhetorical focusing principle' which has been used to explain how an author directs the reader's attention to those elements of the text that he intends to ground his message upon (cf. Sanford and Emmott 2012).

10.2. Openings and introductory information – systematic choices concerning the exposition

When an author is going to design a text opening, he is confronted with a system of alternative options: The expository information can either be given in a concentrated manner right at the beginning of the text, or it can be delayed and distributed in small quantities as the plot develops (cf. Pfister 1988: 87–88, and Neumann and Nünning 2008: 50). Another relevant decision is whether all introductory information is intended to be 'emic', i.e. entirely referenced within the exposition itself, or whether it is to be 'etic' in that it refers to persons or things outside the boundaries of the text (as when referentless pronouns occur). Yet another choice to be made is that between a narration which tells its story *ab ovo* and one which starts *in medias res*.

Of course, such choices are by no means arbitrary and made independently of another. Rather, they form part of the system of narrative discourse commonly used in a historical period. Still, there is such a thing as an unmarked case, the most far-spread type of exposition, namely the preliminary and concentrated one (cf. Neumann and Nünning 2008: 50). In combination with emic referencing and often an *ab ovo*-presentation of the story, it was the standard exposition, in the eighteenth- and nineteenth-century realist novel in particular. Delayed and distributed expositions, in contrast to that, often in combination with referentless pronouns and a beginning *in medias res*, are typical of modernist and postmodernist fiction in our time (cf. Neumann and Nünning 2008: 50). Lending themselves to the production of intended 'expositional gaps' (ibid. 50–51), these expository techniques can serve one of the main purposes of fiction in modern times, a strong involvement and activation of readers.

The gradual turn away from the traditional concentrated and fully referenced type of exposition to more open and flexible forms must certainly mainly be seen against the background of changes in world views and literary periods, but it can also be accounted for in terms of even more general phenomena, such as the firm establishment and conventionalization of such patterns. For it is only too plausible that the more deeply these patterns have become entrenched, the more easily they can be modified or even altered. Thus, it does not come as a surprise as we shall see in what follows that the primordial frames governing the construction of text openings are often only partly visible at the surface of a text and must largely be reconstructed from underlying cognitive expectations.[3]

10.3. Openings and their narrative functions: Narration-frame, story-frame, thematic frame

In the framework of a systemic and functional approach, text openings can be defined as fulfilling social, informational and interpretative functions. In cognitive terms, the fulfilment of these functions can be described as the fulfilment of various schemata or frames.

10.3.1. The narration-frame

Of all the frames of expectation to be filled in a text opening, the narration-frame, establishing an interpersonal and thus social relationship between author and audience, is the most elementary one. Who speaks (i.e. who is the narrator)? Who is the intended addressee? In what way will the narration be told and what will be its effect? To what degree is the narrative information reliable? Questions like these are of course often answered by default, because due to contextual information and readerly experience, they need not be problematized. But when no relevant information about these questions can be inferred from the medium, the text genre or some paratexts, information concerning the narration-frame will be conveyed right at the beginning of a text. This is the case for instance with the following broadside ballad in which not only the envisaged audience, but also the communicative occasion, the speaker and the intended rhetorical effect are all mentioned in the very first lines:

> Come all you gallant seamen that unite a meeting,
> Attend to these lines I am going to relate,
> And when you've heard them 'twill move you with pity,
> To hear how Lord Nelson he met with his fate;
> (Anon., "A new song composed on the death of Lord Nelson" [1805])

While in most narrations, readers are expected to fill the slots of the narration-frame by default, an explicit and often even somewhat awkward elaboration of the narration-frame becomes likely when the narrator is fallible, unreliable or even mad. Such narrators tend to address their readers in an explicit or implicit manner in order to defend the abnormality and excessiveness of their narration. A classic example of this type of opening is provided by one of the most famous unreliable narrations of Edgar Allan Poe ([1843] 1967: 320):

> For the most wild, yet most homely narrative which I am about to pen, I neither expect nor solicit belief. Mad indeed would I be to expect it [...] Yet, mad am I not – and very surely do I not dream. But tomorrow I die, and to-day I would unburthen my soul. My immediate purpose is to place before the world, plainly, succinctly and without comment, a series of mere household events.

An explicit discussion of elements of the narration-frame can further be found in some modern and postmodern narratives whose purpose it is to foreground and question the artificiality of their narrative conventions, sometimes even those that concern the function of the text opening itself. Graham Greene at the beginning of one of his novels, for instance, anticipating a notion that can also be found in the work of many later modernist writers,[4] voices the idea that the beginnings and endings of narrations are not given by nature, but arbitrary demarcation points helping one to structure his experience in a meaningless flow of time:

> A story has no beginning or end: arbitrarily one chooses that moment
> of experience from which to look back or from which to look ahead.
> (Greene [1951] 1962: F 1)

In an even more unconventional and self-referential manner, reference is made to the narration-frame in John Barth's 'Life Story', a typical postmodernist meta-story (cf. Wolf 1997):

> Without discarding what he'd already written he began his story afresh in a somewhat different manner. Whereas his earlier version had opened in a straight-forward documentary fashion and then degenerated or at least modulated intentionally into irrealism and dissonance he decided this time to tell his tale from start to finish in a conservative, 'realistic', unself-conscious way. He being by vocation an author of novels and stories it was perhaps inevitable that one afternoon the possibility would occur to the writer of these lines that his own life might be a fiction, in which he was the leading or an accessory character. (Barth [1963] 1969: 113)

From Barth's anti-conventional meta-reflections, many insights into the traditional structure of a text opening can be gained. To do justice to the conventional standards of an exposition, the story must be told 'from start to finish', i.e. *ab ovo* in a chronological fashion. Moreover, it is unlikely in a work of realist fiction that elements of the narration-frame will be discussed, because the readers of such a narrative will expect that the story is told in an 'unself-conscious way' (as Barth puts it, nicely punning on the seeming objectivity of such a narration). Finally, in a conventional work of fiction, the borderline between the narration-frame as an external and the characters as part of an internal system of communication must be strictly observed and never be crossed in the way Barth is playing with the two levels. It is this internal frame of a text opening that will be considered next.

10.3.2. The story-frame

In one of the few early analytical descriptions of the functions of text openings, Werlich (1976: 152–153) already distinguished an internal frame from the narration-frame as the other, outer structure. Referring to the news story as its prototype, he defined the function of this internal frame as 'anticipating answers to the so-called five Wh - interrogatives: the *who? what? when? where?* and *why?* of events' (ibid, 152: § 267). In the framework of empirical findings about the psychological mechanisms underlying narrative understanding (cf. Zwaan, Langston, and Graesser 1995), the outstanding relevancy of this story-frame with its W-questions can easily be accounted for: According to what became known in cognitive research as 'Situation models in language comprehension' (cf. Zwaan and Radvansky 1998) and has more recently been termed 'Fundamental scenario mapping' (cf. Sanford and Emmott 2012), the most 'basic processes by which interpretations can be made at all' require the construal of a particular 'scenario' (ibid.: 5). This is a situation model that contains 'information about five conceptual dimensions: properties of the protagonist, time, space, causality and intentionality ([giving evidence of] the goals of the characters)' (ibid., 37). Thus when readers encounter a text, they will immediately attempt to match textual information to a particular scenario, and early answers to the *who*? (protagonist or protagonists), *when*? (time), *where*? (space), *what*? (consequences caused) and *why*? (intentionality) are thus of utmost importance.

It speaks for the cognitive relevancy of this pattern, which differs from classical frame and schema theories by its more dynamic and constructive orientation (cf. Zwaan and Radvansky 1998: 162), that it was known in Medieval rhetoric already (cf. Erlebach 2011: 111),[5] and that in older narrations, most of the questions mentioned by Werlich are answered right from the start in a very systematic fashion. Nice examples of this are provided by the openings of Miguel de Cervantes' *Don Quixote* and Daniel Defoe's *Robinson Crusoe*, two novels which are time and again quoted as prototypical early works of their genre:

> In a village of La Mancha, the name of which I have no desire to call to mind [= where?], there lived not long since [= when?] one of those gentlemen [= who?] that keep a lance in the lance-rack, an old buckler, a lean hack, and a greyhound for coursing. (Cervantes [1605] 2014: n.p.)

> I was born [= who?] in the year 1632 [= when?], in the city of York [= where?], of a good family, tho' not of that country, my father being a foreigner of Bremen, who settled first at Hull. He got a good estate by merchandise [= what?] (Defoe [1719] 1987: 27)

It is very instructive that the concentrated transmission of information in the openings of these traditional novels has strong affinities with the transmission of information in the openings of prototypical nursery tales as they were studied in a well-known article by no less an expert in verbal art than Ruquaiya Hasan (1996). According to Hasan, a nursery tale is likely to open with an 'initial placement' which precedes the story's initiating event, passing on to the reader 'some nuclear semantic properties' that can again easily be ascribed to the famous set of W-questions, namely:

- person particularization ('a, some, one, two, …') [= who?]
- temporal distance (locative adjunct, temporal or spatial) [= when? where?]
- attribution (e.g. by an epithet) and habitude (e.g. 'used to, would, often') [= what?] (as elaborative properties).

It is true of course that even in nursery tales, an initial placement completely answering the W-questions is only optional, and that apart from being missing entirely it can be non-discrete, i.e. interspersed or included with the realization of the initiating event (cf. Hasan 1996: 65–69). But such flexibility is quite typical of frame structures in general: Their slots can always also be filled by default, and a filling can be delayed, which happens even more frequently in complex narratives such as the twentieth-century novel and short story, whose tendency towards 'informational gaps' was already discussed in an earlier section of this essay.

To what a degree a filling of the slots of the story-frame is still commonly expected in spite of all narrative flexibility, can be inferred best from some of its parodic treatments. Samuel Beckett (1953: 293), for instance, opens one of his experimental narrations, *The Unnamable*, with the formula 'Where now? Who now? When now?', thus directly drawing the reader's attention to the questions that ought to be but cannot be answered in the beginning of Beckett's text. The readers' conventional expectations of getting some background information on the main character's *where? when?* and *what?* are still more explicitly mocked in the opening paragraph of J. D. Salinger's famous critical youth novel *The Catcher in the Rye* ([1951] 1969: 5):

> If you really want to hear about it, the first thing you'll probably want
> to know is where I was born, and what my lousy childhood was like,
> and how my parents were occupied and all before they had me, and all
> that David Copperfield kind of crap, but I don't feel like going into it.

Of course, the traditional expository story-frame which is so scathingly ridiculed by Salinger here has always been further spread in the novel than in other, shorter narrative fiction. And yet, even in the short story, the story-frame is often filled right from the start – if not by biographical background information, at least by a detailed description of a character's situation. An example of this is provided by the opening of 'Chaff in the Wind', a typical mildly modernist narrative by the short story specialist H. E. Bates ([1953] 1992: 13):

> She was burning chaff in three big yellow separate heaps as he came
> across the field. A flame was darting up and along the blue-back edge
> of each heap like lamp-wick, leaving smoking ash behind.

She stood leaning on the long white handle of a hay-fork, arms firm and crooked, hands just below her chin, eyes rather low on the three smoking heaps, as if she was not really watching him at all. The wind was cold for October.

On the one hand, the informational input provided by this opening does not answer all of the W-questions a reader brings to the beginning of a text – the year of the action remains unspecified, the place is not named, and as often in modernist texts, the characters are referenced only by cataphoric pronouns so that the opening tends to be etic rather than emic – and yet, a model of the underlying scenario can still easily be construed. Burning some heaps of chaff in a field is a situation easy to process for the reader, and the subsequent time-reference 'The wind was cold for October' increases the familiarity of the scenario. Bates's text opening, in spite of its modernist elements, therefore still allows the smooth filling of a story-frame,[6] while cases of beginnings in which the reader 'is being thrown into a context to which he lacks the key, at least at the outset' (cf. Bonheim 1982: 115) and must therefore put 'unresolved input on a "wait and see" list' (cf. Sanford and Emmott 2012: 38) remain comparatively rare, even in radically modernist and postmodernist fiction.[7]

The filling of the necessary story-frame by mapping a familiar scenario is, however, only one of the purposes of Bates's opening. For in addition to this informational function the opening also has an interpretive function, because subliminally, it already gives the reader some hints about the plight and longings of the female protagonist: When the unknown man coming across the field gets into her vision, a symbolic flame standing for her unfulfilled interest in the opposite sex is darting up, but her eyes remain fixed on the 'smoking heaps, as if she was not really watching him at all'. The reader is thus subtly prepared for the theme of the story, the repressed erotic needs of the Cinderella-like protagonist. This is a finding which shows how necessary it is to analyse, in addition to the narration-frame and the story-frame, a third frame of expectation that determines the processing of a narrative in the reader's mind: the thematic frame.

10.3.3. The thematic frame

The following definition of the core of verbal art, given by Ruquaiya Hasan (2007: 23–24) in one of her excursions into the realm of literary studies, is an excellent starting point for a discussion of the central mechanism in the mental processing of a literary text opening:

> [...] we postulate that verbal art has a level of meaning organisation
> called *theme*. Theme is the deepest level of meaning in verbal art:
> meanings which concern the human condition [...]. But this deepest
> meaning is not declared to the reader directly by the author. Rather,
> it is inferred on the basis of the foregrounded patterns of relations
> [...]. I have referred to this level of foregrounding as symbolic artic-
> ulation. [...] The foregrounding is where the most crucial work of
> verbal art is done, and here language plays an important role.

Hasan's notion that meaning organization in a narrative text ultimately
depends on a writer's strategic use of linguistic foregrounding nicely ties
up with the attention recently paid in cognitive psychology to 'the rhetorical
focusing principle', i.e. the writer's task to 'cause a reader to pay attention to
X, and not to Y [...] because X constitutes something important, while Y is
simply the background against which X happens' (Sanford and Emmott 2012:
72). Such rhetorical focusing is only the psychological version of the principle
of foregrounding, which can be defined as 'the use of either unusual linguistic
forms or an unusually high or low density of particular linguistic forms, these
being sufficiently prominent to contribute to the overall interpretation of a
text, including controlling the attention paid to the different parts of it' (ibid.:
73). Going back as far as Shklovsky's and Mukarovsky's ground-breaking
insights into the significance of defamiliarization and deautomatization as the
basic principles that inspire artistic perception, foregrounding also guarantees
a deeper cognitive processing (cf. Sanford and Emmott 2012: 103–131). In
many concrete manifestations, it can be traced both at the level of the content
of stories and at the level of their form.

Foregrounding at the content-level takes place whenever a text starts
with some factual *non-sequitur*. Frequently, this is the case in the openings
of 'unnatural narratives'.[8] A good case in point is George Orwell's *1984*,
the first sentence of which has been cited time and again as one of the most
remarkable openings in world literature:[9] 'It was a bright cold day in April,
and the clocks were striking thirteen' (Orwell [1949] 1972: 5). Likewise,
the situation described in the first sentence may clash with accepted moral
standards and in this way attract the reader's attention right from the start.[10]

Formal foregrounding can be employed in openings at a multiplicity of
linguistic levels – in addition to typographical, phonological, lexical and
syntactic devices, discourse features disrupting the normal cohesion and
coherence of a work can contribute to its effects (cf. Sanford and Emmott
2012: 74ff.). The overlong, talkative and meandering first sentence of Lau-
rence Sterne's *Tristram Shandy* – again one of the best-known openings in
world literature – lends itself to illustrating how foregrounded discourse
strategies can prepare the reader for the theme(s) of a novel:

> I wish either my father or my mother, or indeed both of them, as they were in duty both equally bound to it, had minded what they were about when they begot me; had they duly consider'd how much depended upon what they were then doing; – that not only the production of a rational Being was concern'd in it, but that possibly the happy formation and temperature of his body, perhaps his genius and the very cast of his mind; – and, for aught they knew to the contrary, even the fortunes of his whole house might take their turn from the humours and dispositions which were then uppermost: – Had they duly weighed and considered all this, and proceeded accordingly, – I am verily persuaded I should have made a quite different figure in the world, from that, in which the reader is likely to see me. (Sterne [1760] 1965: 3)

The lack of syntactical coherence and the long-windedness of this passage, its numerous insertions, marked out by the repeated use of dashes – all these foregrounded discourse features make it clear right from the start that a narrator is speaking here who will never be able to confine himself to rational thought and purposeful direction of his deliberations.

Rhetorical focusing in an opening passage can, however, not only be achieved by deviating discourse features that are grounded on linguistic irregularities, but also by some obtrusive repetition (cf. Sanford and Emmott 2012: 75). A famous text opening in which this strategy of thematic foregrounding is lavishly employed is that of Vladimir Nabokov's *Lolita*:

> Lolita, light of my life, fire of my loins. My sin, my soul. Lo-lee-ta: the tip of the tongue taking a trip of three steps down the palate to tap, at three, on the teeth. Lo. Lee. Ta.
>
> She was Lo, plain Lo, in the morning, standing four feet ten in one sock. She was Lola in slacks. She was Dolly at school. She was Dolores on the dotted line. But in my arms she was always Lolita. (*Lolita* [1955] 1989: 9)

This enthusiastic invocation provides an outstanding example of what can be called, in Hasan's terms, 'symbolic articulation'. It is above all the excessive use of alliteration that characterizes the narrator as a person who is madly obsessed with pedophelism. As the repetition of the numerous *l*- and *t*- sounds in the passage strikes the impression of being forced and unnatural, one might even argue that Nabokov is already intimating the unnaturalness of the speaker's love-relationship to Lolita here. Further instances of strategic repetition endorse this impression: 'Lolita, light of my life, fire of my loins. My sin, my soul' – the very association of positive and negative terms in parallel constructions is a subtle hint that the narrator's fascination for this child is not an expression of pure and innocent feelings, but rather a case of taboo-breaking and destructive obsession.

It is clear that text openings will become most memorable when the use of obtrusive repetition is combined with other types of foregrounding, such as techniques of information-focusing and contrast-building. A superb example of this is provided by the opening of Charles Dickens's *A Tale of Two Cities* ([1859] 1962: 1):

> It was the best of times, it was the worst of times, it was the age of wisdom, it was the age of foolishness, it was the epoch of belief, it was the epoch of incredulity, it was the season of Light, it was the season of Darkness, it was the spring of hope, it was the winter of despair, we had everything before us, we had nothing before us, we were all going direct to Heaven, we were all going direct the other way – in short, the period was so far like the present period, that some of its noisiest authorities insisted on its being received, for good or for evil, in the superlative degree of comparison only.

An extreme density of foregrounding gives this famous passage its exceptional rhetorical force: The ample use of anaphora in the form of a repetition of the same phrases at the beginning of several consecutive clauses, in three different patterns ('it was the' – 'we had' – 'we were all going direct'), in the last but one instance amplified by epiphora ('before us'), is combined with the technique of constructing conspicuous opposing pairs ('best of times' and 'worst of times' – 'age of wisdom' and 'age of foolishness' – 'epoch of belief' and 'epoch of incredulity' – 'season of Light' and 'season of Darkness' – 'spring of hope' and 'winter of despair' – 'everything' and 'nothing' – 'to Heaven' and 'the other way' [= to Hell]), whose paradoxical quality is highlighted further by the numerous binary repetitions ('of times' – 'age of' – 'epoch of' – 'season of' – 'of' only in the case of the last items) contained in them. Along with its steady rhythm, syntactic foregrounding increases the passage's particular conspicuousness, not only because the long list of antitheses is presented in a single sentence, but also because the 'it was' - anaphora produces a powerful effect of grammatical focusing.[11] As many critics have confirmed, there is once again a close relation between the initial rhetorical focusing and the theme of Dickens's novel. To quote from the Routledge Sourcebook on *A Tale of Two Cities*:

> The moment of the opening long sentence through a series of balanced contrasting statements serves as an introduction to the central method of the novel, contained also in the title, *A Tale of Two Cities*. Contrasts, parallels, and doublings of character, incident, place,

time and theme enact the dualisms established in these statements. (Glancy 2006: 116)

Spelling out the interconnections referred to in this quotation, one can mention many central topics of the novel mirrored in its opening: The time of the French Revolution in which the novel is set is 'the best of times' for the oppressed civilians of Paris, but also 'the worst of times' for the adherents of the old regime. For the ones, it means 'the spring of hope', for the others 'the winter of despair'. The opening antitheses also suggest that as is typical of many of Dickens's works, the characters of this novel can be classed along the lines of wisdom and foolishness, light and darkness, Heaven and Hell, and that the novel's structure is grounded on the principle of presenting doubles, the most prominent of which is its two locations, Paris and London. Last but not least, by referring to the contrast between 'belief' and 'incredulity', the opening also already prepares the reader for the novel's concern with the English attraction to spiritualism and superstition and the atheism of the French Revolution. In summary, then, the opening of *A Tale of Two Cities* is a masterpiece of verbal art and symbolic articulation, densely foreshadowing the numerous structural tensions, contradictions and controversies of the ensuing novel.

While in *A Tale of Two Cities*, rhetorical focusing is patterned contrastively and remains centred on a general characterization of the novel's theme, time and setting, it is used more flexibly and for further purposes in other Dickensian openings. Particularly worth mentioning here is the famous first chapter of *Hard Times*, in which Dickens employs rhetorical focusing not only for striking a keynote of the theme of his novel, but at the same time and in combination with it for a deeply ironical description of one of his main characters. Moreover, he achieves the foregrounding that is necessary for these purposes not only through skilful verbal repetition, but also through a comical use of metaphor:

'Now, what I want is, Facts. Teach these boys and girls nothing but Facts. Facts alone are wanted in life. Plant nothing else, and root out everything else. You can only form the minds of reasoning animals upon Facts: nothing else will ever be of any service to them. This is the principle on which I bring up my own children, and this is the principle on which I bring up these children. Stick to Facts, sir!'

The scene was a plain, bare, monotonous vault of a schoolroom, and the speaker's square forefinger emphasized his observations by underscoring every sentence with a line on the schoolmaster's sleeve. The emphasis was helped by the speaker's square wall of a forehead, which had his eyebrows for its base, while his eyes found commodious cellarage in two dark caves, overshadowed by the wall. The emphasis was helped by the speaker's mouth, which was wide, thin, and hard set. The emphasis was helped by the speaker's voice, which was inflexible, dry, and dictatorial. The emphasis was helped by the speaker's hair, which bristled on the skirts of his bald head, a plantation of firs to keep the wind from its shining surface, all covered with knobs, like the crust of a plum pie, as if the head had scarcely warehouse-room for the hard facts stored inside. The speaker's obstinate carriage, square coat, square legs, square shoulders, – nay, his very neckcloth, trained to take him by the throat with an unaccommodating grasp, like a stubborn fact, as it was, – all helped the emphasis. (Dickens [1854] 1994: 1)

Repetition is again the most important focusing strategy in the first part of this opening – five times, the word 'Facts', additionally foregrounded by capitalization, appears in the first paragraph of this opening, three times the word 'nothing', twice the sentence 'This is the principle on which I bring up […] children'. While the reference to facts prepares the reader for what will become the central thematic opposition in the novel, the contrast between 'fact' and 'fancy', i.e. between Utilitarian Rationalism and Dickens's Christmas Philosophy (cf. Wenzel 1998: 317–318 and 323–324), the repetition of 'nothing' and 'this is the principle on which' is obviously intended already to produce some reservations against the rigidity of Utilitarian education (as it had been established in a new educational system by Sir James Kay-Shuttleworth in 1846 [cf. Simpson 1997: 25] and is sharply criticized by Dickens in the ensuing chapters). The most frequently repeated lexical items in the second paragraph of the opening are the words 'square' and 'to emphasize/emphasis', skilfully used to endorse the already suggested antipathy against rigid didacticism and rationalist education. Moreover, the combination of the notion of squareness with various of Mr Gradgrind's body-parts ridicules this schoolmaster right from the start – an effect which is further increased by the strange comparisons of the skirt of his hair with a 'plantation of firs' and his scalp with 'the crust of a plum pie'. In addition to these odd images, another striking metaphorical connection is established between the 'plain, bare, monotonous vault of a schoolroom' with which the second paragraph opens and the shape of Mr Gradgrind's head – including 'a square wall of a forehead', 'commodious cellarage' for his eyes, and 'warehouse-room' for his fact-loaded knowledge. The ridiculous, forbidding narrow-mindedness of the schoolmaster is in this way also mapped onto his school and its Utilitarian educational principles.

It is an open question, of course, to what degree an individual reader will be able to understand all the subtle symbolic articulation contained in Dickens's text openings. It can certainly be argued that the rhetorical focusing aimed at criticizing Utilitarianism, for instance, can only be grasped in a second reading of *Hard Times* – or perhaps by a reader who is very well acquainted with Dickens's political views from studying several of his other novels. Still, there are also important focusing effects – such as the ruthless mocking at Mr Gradgrind and his school – that are easy to comprehend for everybody, even without any further background information. Ultimately, then, only empirical reader research could give some evidence of the degree to which a theme becomes concrete in a specific reader's mind, but this is equally true of the two other frames discussed in this article and therefore hardly a valid argument against the relevancy of thematic frames.

4. Conclusion

In an insightful comment on the general development of theories of language and grammars in the second half of the twentieth century, Michael Halliday (1994: xxviii) stated that the most fundamental opposition was 'not that between "structuralist" and "generative"' approaches but that

> between those that are primarily syntagmatic in orientation (by and large the formal grammars, with their roots in logic and philosophy) and those that are primarily paradigmatic (by and large the functional ones, with their roots in rhetoric and ethnography). The former interprets a language as a list of structures […], tend to emphasize universal features of language [and] to take grammar (which they call 'syntax') as the foundation of language […]. The latter interpret a language as a network of relations, with structures coming in as the realization of these relationships; they tend […] to take semantics as the foundations […] and so to be organized around the text, or discourse.

It is clear that within this general framework, classical structuralism and even text linguistics pursued the former 'list of syntagmatic structures' approach, while only the later cognitive perspective on literature opened up the more fruitful 'network-and function-oriented' approach. As long as the former approach held the scene, research in the openings of narrative texts produced little results, since texts can be opened in a great variety of ways, using – a few fixed formulae in nursery tales notwithstanding[12] – a great variety of possible structures, both with regard to content and formal principles (such as narrative modes or rhetorical devices).[13] When text openings are, however, explored from a cognitive and functional viewpoint, focusing on the psychological mechanisms underlying their understanding, it becomes possible to identify some frames of readerly expectation that play an essential role in the reception of any narrative beginning and must therefore – sooner of later – be filled with the expected information. In this article, these frames of expectation were termed the narration-frame, the story-frame, and the thematic frame.

Of these frames, the narration-frame, establishing the bond between author and reader, is the most elementary one. It provides the necessary information on the communicative situation, unless it can be inferred as a default value from the medium, the text genre or paratextual indicators. Specified information concerning the narration-frame can refer to the nature of the narrator – in particular the degree of his reliability – and/or the intended addressees of the narration, possibly also to the nature of the narration itself – whether it is fictional or nonfictional, natural or unnatural, conventional or experimental with regard to its narrative technique. The second relevant frame is the story-frame which, serving a fundamental scenario mapping, answers the famous 'five W-questions': *who? what? when? where?* and *why?* thus providing the reader with the necessary information on the properties of the protagonist, his or her intentions, the time and the space as well as the causality of the action. Last but not least, any narrative text opening must provide some clues to the main themes and problems that the reader is intended to focus upon when pursuing the story. This is usually done with the help of various techniques of foregrounding, of which strategic repetition is the most frequent and conspicuous one. Using strategic repetition for thematic and symbolic purposes, authors subtly prearrange the reception of their works and foreshadow the network of themes, experiences and perspectives that will burgeon in the narrative after its opening.

Notes

1.   With the exception of the discussions in a few literary handbooks, such as Krings (2004: 164–171), and Neumann and Nünning (2008: 49–51).
2.   Cf. for an analysis of these features with regard to endings Wenzel (2014).
3.   This idea is in my opinion not yet sufficiently emphasized in the otherwise useful approaches to the subject in Richardson (2008), some of whose categories overlap with the distinctions made in this article.
4.   Cf. on this Vaeßen and Strasen (2015: esp. 89–90) with regard to Frank Kermode and Julian Barnes; and Hart (2015: 104) with regard to Iris Murdoch.
5.   The relevant questions listed by Erlebach with reference to Lausberg are: 'quis, quid, ubi, quibus auxiliis, cur, quomodo, quando', which shows how deeply conscious of scenario mapping early rhetoricians already were.
6.   Cf. for a similar classification of the informational specificity of the opening of this story Puschmann-Nalenz (1999: 193): 'Das "wer?", "wo?", "wann?", das der Leser fragen würde, ignoriert der Erzähler. Dennoch fühlt sich der Rezipient nicht desorientiert, denn es folgen präzise Informationen mit scharf beobachteten Details und im Verlauf der nächsten Abschnitte auch Orts- und

Zeitangaben: Oktober auf abgeernteten Feldern im ländlichen England' ('The "who?", "where?", "when?" that the reader is normally interested in is ignored by the narrator. And yet, the recipient is not left without orientation, since in what follows he gets precise pieces of information in closely observed detail and in the course of the next paragraph also references to place and time: harvested fields in rural England in October').

7.   As Bonheim (1982: 114–116) discovered already, non-referential text openings, 'although they do crop up in narrative, especially as a subcategory of speech and in first-person narration' (cf. ibid, 114) usually remain indeterminate for only a very short time – perhaps in a first sentence introduced by cataphoric *yes* or *and* – only then to fall back into a mode that allows a mapping of the input on a scenario.

8.   'Unnatural' narratives are 'texts that represent physically, logically, or humanly impossible scenarios or events' (Alber 2013: 135).

9.   Cf. the numerous collections of 'best first sentences' on the internet.

10.   A recent dystopian novel by Lydia Millet provides a good example: 'There was a time, not long ago, when it was illegal to kill people' (Millet 2014: 9).

11.   On grammatical focusing as a special type of foregrounding, cf. Sanford and Emmott (2012: 86–89), who use the term 'information structuring' for it.

12.   Cf. the summary of Hasan's article (1996) on the nursery tale in section 3.2 above: Even though she is able to make out some fixed patterns in the openings of this genre, she still feels it necessary to finally confirm their great flexibility.

13.   Cf. the article by Erlebach (2011) on first sentences in literature, which is marked by an amazing multiplicity of sentence forms, modes of narration and matter narrated at the beginnings of literary texts.

References

Alber, J. (2013). Reading unnatural narratives. *Anglistik: International Journal of English Studies* 24 (2): 135–150.

Barth, J. ([1963] (1969). Life Story. In *Lost in the Funhouse*. New York: Doubleday.

Bates, H. E. ([1953] 1992). 'Chaff in the Wind'. In *The Daffodil Sky*. London: Michael Joseph.

Beckett, S. (1953). *The Unnamable*. London: Faber & Faber.

Bonheim, H. (1982). *The Narrative Modes: Techniques of the Short Story*. Cambridge: Brewer.

Dickens, C. ([1854] 1994). *Hard Times*. Harmondsworth: Panguin.

Dickens, C. ([1859] 1962). *A Tale of Two Cities*. Harmondsworth: Penguin.

Erlebach, P. (2011). Literary assessment of the first sentence. *Anglistik: International Journal of English Studies* 22 (2): 107–118.

Glancy, R. (Ed.). (2006). *Charles Dickens's A Tale of Two Cities: A Sourcebook*. Milton Park, Abingdon: Routledge.

Greene, G. ([1951] 1962). *The End of the Affair*. London: Heinemann.

Halliday, M. (1994). *Introduction to Functional Grammar* (2nd ed.). London: Arnold.

Hart, T. (2015). Unexpected endings: Eucatastrophic consolations in literature and theology. In G.Hopps, S. Neumann, S. Strasen, and P. Wenzel (Eds) *Last Things: Essays on Ends and Endings,* 101–17. Frankfurt am Main: Lang.

Hasan, R. (1996). The nursery tale as a genre. In Carmel Cloran, David Butt, and Geoffrey Williams (Eds) *Ways of Saying, Ways of Meaning: Selected Papers of Ruquaiya Hasan*, 51–72. London: Cassell.

Hasan, R. (2007). Private pleasure, public discourse: Reflections on engaging with literature. In D. R. Miller and M. Turci (Eds) *Language and Verbal Art Revisited: Linguistic Approaches to the Study of Literature*, 13–40. London and Oakville: Equinox.

Herman, D. (2009). Narrative ways of worldmaking. In S. Heinen and R. Sommer (Eds) *Narratology in the Age of Crossdisciplinary Narrative Research*, 71–86, Berlin and New York: de Gruyter.

Hopps, G., Neumann,S., Strasen, S., and Wenzel, P. (Eds). (2015). *Last Things: Essays on Ends and Endings*. Frankfurt am Main: Lang. https://doi.org/10.3726/978-3-653-04320-4

Krings, C. (2004). Zur Analyse des Erzählanfangs und des Erzählschlusses. In P. Wenzel (Ed.) *Einführung in die Erzähltextanalyse: Kategorien, Modelle, Probleme*, 163–197. Trier: Wissenschaftlicher Verlag.

Millet, L. (2014). *Pills and Starships*. New York: Black Sheep/Akashic Books.

Nabokov, V. ([1955] 1989). *Lolita.*Harmondsworth: Penguin.

Neumann, B. and Nünning, Ansgar (2008). *An Introduction to the Study of Narrative Fiction*. Stuttgart: Klett.

Orwell, G. ([1947] (1972). *1984.* London: Martin Secker & Warburg.

Pfister, M. (1988). *The Theory and Analysis of Drama* (Trans. John Halliday). Cambridge: Cambridge University Press. https://doi.org/10.1017/CBO9780511553998

Plett, H. F. (1975). *Textwissenschaft und Textanalyse: Semiotik, Linguistik, Rhetorik.* Heidelberg: Quelle & Meyer.

Puschmann-Nalenz, B. (1999). H. E. Bates: Chaff in the wind. In R. Borgmeier (Ed.) *Englische Short Stories von Thomas Hardy bis Graham Swift*, 192–201. Stuttgart: Reclam.

Richardson, B. (Ed.) (2008). *Narrative Beginnings: Theories and Practices*. Lincoln and London: University of Nebraska Press.

Salinger, J. D. ([1951] 1969). *The Catcher in the Rye.* Boston, MA: Little, Brown & Co.

Sanford, A. J. and Emmott, C. (2012). *Mind, Brain and Narrative.*

Cambridge: Cambridge University Press. https://doi.org/10.1017/CBO9781139084321

Simpson, M. (1997). *The Companion to Hard Times*. The Banks, Mountfield, near Robertsbridge, East Sussex: Helm Information.

Sterne, L. ([1760] 1965). *The Life & Opinions of Tristram Shandy*. Harmondsworth: Penguin.

Sternberg, M. (1976). Temporal ordering, modes of expositional distribution, and three models of rhetorical control in the narrative text. *Journal for Descriptive Poetics and Theory of Literature* 1: 295–316.

Torgovnick, M. (1981). *Closure in the Novel*. Princeton, NJ: Princeton University Press.

Vaeßen, J. and Strasen, S. (2015). A history of Anthony in $3^1/_2$ endings: History, memory, and fabulation in Julian Barnes's *The Sense of an Ending*. In G. Hopps, S. Neumann, S. Strasen, and P. Wenzel (Eds) (2015). *Last Things: Essays on Ends and Endings,* 81–99. Frankfurt am Main: Lang.

Wenzel, Peter. 1998. Structural oppositions and contradictions in Dickens's *Hard Times* and Mrs. Tonna's *Helen Fleetwood*: A critical comparison of structuralist and poststructuralist methods of interpretation. *Zeitschrift für Angistik und Amerikanistik* 46: 316-24.

Wenzel, P. (2014). Hunting for signals of closure: Research on endings in literature. *Anglistik: International Journal of English Studies* 25 (2): 137–149.

Werlich, E. (1976). *A Text Grammar of English*. Heidelberg: Quelle & Meyer.

Wolf, W. (1997). Metafiction. Formen und Funktionen eines Merkmals postmodernistischen Erzählens. Eine Einführung und ein Beispiel: John Barth, 'Life-Story'. *Literatur in Wissenschaft und Unterricht* 30: 31–50.

Zwaan, R. A., Langston, M. C., and Graesser, A. C. (1995). The construction of situation models in narrative comprehension: An event-indexing model. *Psychological Science* 6 (5): 292–297. https://doi.org/10.1111/j.1467-9280.1995.tb00513.x

Zwaan, R. A., and Radvansky, G. A. (1998). Situation models in language comprehension and memory. *Psychological Bulletin* 123 (2): 162–185. https://doi.org/10.1037/0033-2909.123.2.162

11 'That's not normal rabbit behaviour': On the track of the grammar of fictional worlds

Rebekah Wegener[*] and Timo Lothmann[†]

> Drum hab' ich mich der Magie ergeben
> (Goethe 2013: 16)

11.1. Introduction

In this pilot study we investigate the conceptualization of fictional story worlds with a focus on fantastic worlds. An eye-tracking experiment was devised to test the reading of texts involving different types of transition into *secondary fantasy worlds*. Additional interview data revealed that the participants' constructions of *secondary worlds* are largely a response to the lexico-grammatical patterning of the textual stimuli. In the process of

[*] Rebekah Wegener is a researcher and lecturer in linguistics and semiotics at RWTH Aachen University. She has a background in linguistics, semiotics, psychology and cognitive science. Her research interests include theoretical and applied linguistics using corpus and experimental methods and modelling multimodal interaction in context and in real-time for smart computational applications. Rebekah was introduced to Hasan's work on verbal art by David Butt, whose own work on verbal art is the inspiration behind her current projects on verbal art and stylistics.

[†] Timo Lothmann is a researcher and lecturer of English linguistics at RWTH Aachen University where he completed his PhD on the Tok Pisin Bible translation in 2006. He has also taught at the universities of Münster and Paderborn. His research interests include reading and translation processing, pidgins and creoles, postcolonialism, and imaginary worlds. He lays particular stress on interdisciplinary perspectives. Recent publications comprise a metaphor approach to literary identity. Currently, he focuses on fields of application of conceptual metaphor and blending theory.

describing the fantastic, the *secondary world* is widely constructed as a conceptualization of a non-normal version of the *primary world*, or as a world from which *primary-world* elements are absent. Readers tend to take up the author's offer of 'otherness' to amplify and generalize this otherness.

This study is an investigation of particularities in the make-up and the understanding of fictional worlds. By putting the focus on story worlds of the fantastic, we intend to shed light on authors' and readers' constructions of *secondary-world* settings and in particular, the nature of the reader's transition into the *secondary world*. In this regard, special emphasis will be put on tools of foregrounding the elements that deploy, from a *primary-world* perspective, 'non-normality' or 'magic' in the textual stimuli.

A pilot eye-tracking experiment was devised to capture the reading of examples of different categories of authentic fictional texts that contain fantastic elements. The data yield significant differences in the tracking recordings of so-called normal fictional text passages compared to passages that display actual fantastic features. Further, the analysis of text-related interview responses by the participants strongly suggests that the individual constructions of *secondary worlds* are not merely a superficial reaction to changing frequencies of the author's lexical choices of description. Rather, following Halliday (1964) and Butt (1983; 1988), we claim that the reader responds to a complex ensemble of lexico-grammatical features.

The research makes a connection between cognitive approaches to literature (e.g. Gavins and Steen 2003; Stockwell 2002, 2005) and systemic-functionally inspired language analyses of artistic texts (e.g. Hasan 1989, 2007). In addressing readers' experiences and their response to texts in particular, this study represents a contribution to empirical studies of literary reading (e.g. Miall 2006; Jacobs 2015a, b; Mangen and van der Weel 2016).

11.2. Background, motivation and text basis

Reading or listening to a story entails the construction of mental representations of the content, including the narration of characters and the settings they live and operate in, as van Dijk and Kintsch (1992) outline in their model of discourse processing. Some of the processes involved in this discourse processing are biological processes, some linguistic and some contextual. This makes it necessary to clarify the exact relationship between these different aspects. Here, we consider it fruitful to draw on Hasan's notion that:

> in story-telling, two distinct orders of context operate: a primary context, that of telling the story [...] and a secondary context which

> is construed by the language of the 'storying' text […]. […To] a
> certain extent, the double context feature may be said to apply to all
> 'displaced' texts […]. (Hasan 2011: xxii)

Thus the readers' engagement with the text is one context, and the world within the text is another context.

Following Steiner (1991) and Wegener (2011), we extend this notion to see the different activities that are involved in writing, reading and indeed the experimental domain. Following Wegener (2011), we also consider the relationship(s) between the texts that are produced in these different activities and the extent to which they can be said to relate to each other and thus the ways in which they can be used as research data.

In our research, we see the writing process as one primary context, the reading as a second primary context and the interviews as a third primary context. These all have their own contextual configurations, so that, for example, the experiment has asymmetrical tenor relations because we had our students as participants, the field is shared because we discuss the text, but the language produced is distinct from that of the storytelling, such that while an author is unlikely to explicitly draw attention to strangeness, a reader describing this world might very well draw attention to this strangeness. Furthermore, we change the mode of discourse from writing to speaking.

For Hasan the story also has its own context that is a secondary context. The secondary context is the representation of the writer's *secondary world*, and for fantasy is likely to include multiple secondary contexts, for instance pre- and post-transition contexts. We also have multiple secondary contexts, because we get the readers to produce a reaction-based description.

In elucidating this other world in a story context, the recipient is a builder of mental realities[1] along the lines of, but not limited to, the narrative framework that the story text provides. The created *secondary-world* realities based on such a story text may diverge considerably from those induced by our everyday, *primary-world* settings – which renders them no less real or meaningful in our individual minds.

We use the term *primary world* to denote the world (i.e. the realities) that might be said to exist in the mind of the text author(s) and recipient(s) (readers and listeners, hereafter referred to as readers since this study focuses on written text reception). This world includes common uses of language, other cultural experiences, and physical laws. Because they exist as abstract constructs in the minds of individuals, neither *primary* nor *secondary worlds* are accessible to us, however, we can access approximations through analysis of discourse that describes the *secondary worlds* or through contextual parameters that might impact on the *primary worlds*.

In the diversified fantastic literature genre in particular, non-*primary-world* entities help constitute the fictional *secondary world*. These entities, which may simplistically be labelled 'magic' or 'Faërie' (Tolkien 2014),[2] represent a vast input potential for the creation of coherent fictional worlds (Lothmann and Scholz 2016).

Hsu *et al.* (2015) also operationalize the 'magic' or 'Faërie' for their research as '[s]upra-natural events, or magical events in discourse [that] involve world-knowledge anomalies' (Hsu *et al.* 201: 2) that should require greater processing from the reader. We pick up on this operationalization for our own study. However, we use the term *magical elements* because we include both events and entities that are 'supra-natural' in the sense of being distant from the readers' *primary-world* settings. Of course, not all *magical elements* are impossible in the non-fictional world. Clear-cut definitions are of course difficult. When one enters the realm of, say, quantum mechanics at one extreme or superstition on the other, otherwise magical or unnatural elements become possible and the notion of a shared lived reality becomes much fuzzier.

Indeed, as can been seen in Figure 11.1, we assume non-congruence between the *primary worlds* of the reader and writer and the *secondary worlds* of the reader and writer. The *primary world* of an author writing in 1865 or even 1937 or 1997 is likely to be quite different from that of our relatively young readers reading in 2016. They are also reading English language authors writing about English culture. Neither are they likely to share conceptualizations of the *secondary world*. Our only point of access for these worlds is through the shared discourse of the writer (in our case text excerpts) and that of the reader (in our case interview transcripts).

In the vein of Fauconnier and Turner's theory of conceptual integration (1998, 2003), *secondary worlds* of the fantastic may be seen as blends of (several) Faërie and *primary-world input spaces*. These abstract blends thus constitute substantial world-building tools. They are necessary for readers to follow, let alone immerse in, story events. This ability and readiness to make use of blends during the processes of writing and reading underlie the fantastic, and hence fiction, in general. In turn, emergent meaning may accrue from the blends, which has potential (and actual) rebound effects on the readers' everyday life spheres.

During the blending operations, Coleridge's widely known postulate of the 'willing suspension of disbelief' (see his *Biographia Literaria* (2013) [1817]: chapters XIII–XIV) is realized. The readers' willing suspension of their disbelief co-creates the story on the basis of what has been termed *secondary belief* (e.g. Tolkien 2014). Whenever we are willing to dismiss the exclusivity of *primary-world* realities in this manner, we open our minds to story worlds

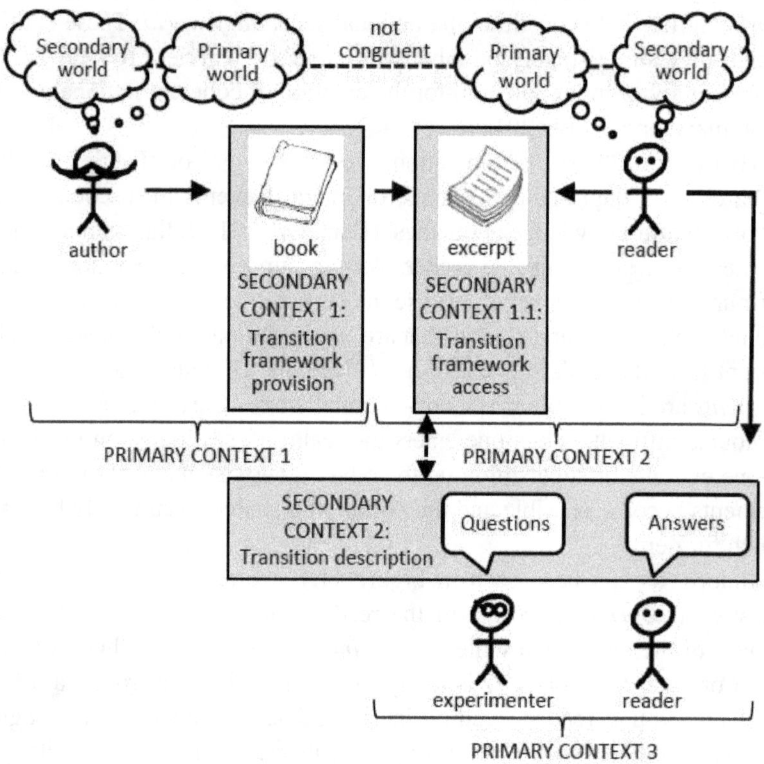

Figure 11.1: Complexity of worlds and contexts.

in general, and to those that are commonly labelled fantastic in particular. The present study focuses on such fantastic texts. We intend to bring an additional metaphor perspective to the table by arguing that metaphors can be used to explain and qualify non-*primary-world* entities and processes.

Manifested through linguistic expression, metaphors may help define our realities (Lakoff and Johnson 2011), including the realities of story worlds. It is our aim to corroborate here that metaphors are apt storytelling instruments that can be used to conceptualize and foreground *secondary-world* particularities and can, thus, contribute to consistent world-building.[3] On the basis of the assumed overarching conceptualizations that the fantastic *secondary world* is either a non-normal version of the *primary world*, or a world from which *primary-world* elements are absent, we seek to investigate the extent to which the author uses foregrounding, including metaphor, to introduce the *secondary world* to the reader. There may be variation depending on the type of fictional text. Further, we expect differences in foregrounding usage between the author's introduction of the *secondary world* setting and the reader's retelling it to a person who is purportedly not acquainted with the respective text.

As our textual stimuli, we selected the initial passages of the following texts: *Harry Potter and the Philosopher's Stone* (Rowling 2014 [1997]), *Alice's Adventures in Wonderland* (Carroll 1982 [1865]), and *The Hobbit* (Tolkien 2007 [1937]). We consider these texts to be not only influential and widely known classics that are likely to be accessible to our students as non-native readers of English, but, more importantly, representative of different types of fantastic literature with different types of transition to a fantasy world. In this respect, we follow the typology of Mendlesohn (2008) who identified three main categories of fantastic texts, namely intrusive fantasy (such as *Harry Potter*), portal-quest fantasy (such as *Alice*), and immersive fantasy (such as *The Hobbit*).[4]

11.3.   Types of transition into a fantasy world

We set out in this study to examine the reader experience for different types of transition into fantasy fictional worlds. For the purposes of this study, our classification of transition styles is based on those of Mendlesohn (2008), who provides a number of different transition styles including *Intrusion, Portal-Quest,* and *Immersion* and provides both instantiations of these categories and language features that can be used to identify category membership.

Intrusion is a transition style that, according to Mendlesohn (2008: xxii), 'takes us out of safety without taking us from our place'. The foundation of this category is that there is a normal world and this is disrupted or intruded upon by the fantastic. Thus, as Mendlesohn (2008: xxii) suggests, 'it has as its base the assumption that normality is organized' and that 'fantasy and "reality" are often kept strictly demarcated'. Mendlesohn proposes that fantasies in this category rely heavily on explanatory language and have the 'normal world' as a base. We have selected *Harry Potter and the Philosopher's Stone* (Rowling 2014 [1997]) as our example for the category of *Intrusion* fantasy. From a reader's perspective, the story features a subsequent disruption of a presumptively normal story world (that resembles the reader's *primary world*) by elements from a different, more fantastic origin.

The *Portal-Quest* fantasy is 'a fantastical world entered through a portal' and one where 'individuals may cross both ways, [but] the magic does not' (Mendlesohn, 2008: xix). Mendlesohn refers to this as a situation where the magic does not 'leak'. Mendlesohn (2008: xix) suggests that 'the language of the Portal-Quest fantasy is often elaborate, […] intensely descriptive and exploratory rather than assumptive'. As our example of the *Portal-Quest* fantasy transition, we selected *Alice's Adventures in Wonderland* (Carroll 1982 [1865]), taking this as a prototypical example of the *Portal-Quest* transition and one of the novels that Mendlesohn also suggests as representative of this category.

Immersion fantasy 'invites us to share not merely a world, but a set of assumptions. At its best, it presents the fantastic without comment as the norm both for the protagonist and for the reader' (Mendlesohn, 2008: xx). Our text selection for this category is *The Hobbit* (Tolkien 2007 [1937]) because it displays linguistic features that set it apart from the other texts and it meets many of the criteria for this category. In the immersive fantasy, the characters must 'take for granted the fantastic elements with which they are surrounded; they must exist as integrated with the magical' (Mendlesohn 2008: xxi) and this is certainly the case for *The Hobbit*.

While they are not the focus of our research, these categories are very useful for examining the reader's reaction to transition from the 'normal' fictional to the fantasy fictional world and our research goes some way to testing these three categories for their linguistic differences, and their relation to the reader in terms of differences in eye-tracking results and in terms of reader response during interview.

11.4. The experiment

11.4.1. The design

Our experiment was designed to test how readers react to different types of transition into a fantasy fictional world. To do this, we had 14 readers from our English Linguistics and Literature student population at RWTH Aachen University read the three texts, with questions asked after each text and further questions at the end of the readings. Appendix 1 shows the profile of our readers. Notice that all of our readers are non-native speakers of English and all texts included are English original texts shown in English. We intend to extend the experiment to matched samples of native speakers of English to compare the differences.

11.4.1.1. Ethics statement

All participants were recruited from our classes and participation was entirely voluntary and unpaid (except for chocolate and drinks). All participants were extensively informed about the study both verbally and in writing and all participants signed written consent and data release forms. The forms were stored separately to maintain participant privacy. After the experiment the participants were given the opportunity to withdraw their data. None of them chose to withdraw their data and all feedback was positive.

11.4.1.2.   Participants

All participants had normal or corrected to normal vision. All participants had at least C2 English language competence and are all enrolled in English language and literature studies. Their ages ranged from 20–29, three self-identified as male and 11 as female. All had German as a first language and most spoke more than two languages.

11.4.1.3.   Materials

All testing took place in our eye-tracking lab on campus at RWTH Aachen University using a Tobii TX300 eye-tracker. As well as the eye-tracking, which also collects video data of the reader, we used audio recording with *Audacity* (Mazzoni 2016) and an unobtrusive desk-top microphone. The audio recording was used during the entire experiment and captured both acoustic signals during reading (breathing, laughter, gasps, etc.) and the spoken interview records. The spoken interviews were later transcribed and analysed.

11.4.1.4.   Method

After an introduction that included a calibration phase, participants were then shown the first text and instructed to read the text silently to themselves at their own pace and to notify us when they had finished. This allowed us to synchronize the video, eye-tracking and sound later on. Once they had finished reading the first text, participants were asked a number of semi-structured interview questions which can be seen in Appendix 2. The same protocol was followed for text two and text three.

Once this was complete, participants were asked several demographic questions. The experiment was then concluded. After that we provided participants with an opportunity to see their eye-tracking graphs and to find out more about the experiment. The whole process took no more than 1 hour in total.

11.4.2. The stimuli text excerpts

We selected three text excerpts that are representative of the category for which they were chosen. The details of these texts are outlined in Table 11.1. Our texts range across a fairly large time span, from 1865 to 1997, but are similar in readability and they are quite similar in length, each excerpt covering the first pages of the novel and being about 2,100 words in length. The lengths do not match exactly, but have been cropped to finish at a relatively natural end point (e.g. at the end of a paragraph). These 'natural' segments cover the start of the respective novel and the first introduction of the fantastic.

Text	Author	Date of publication	Word count	Transition style
Harry Potter	J.K. Rowling	1997	2,059	Intrusion
Alice	L. Carroll	1865	2,147	Portal-Quest
The Hobbit	J.R.R. Tolkien	1937	2,100	Immersion

Text	Flesch-Kincaid Grade Level	Readability Score (Flesch-Kincaid)[5]	Avg. predicted reading time
Harry Potter	4.4	81.4	8 mins
Alice	8.9	74.6	12 mins
The Hobbit	6.6	76.6	10 mins

Table 11.1: Overview of the texts selected for the experiment

Further, the excerpts needed to cover not only the moment of transition to the fantastic, but also enough of the fantasy world to enable a measurement of *magical elements* to compare with the non-magical fictional world. This meant that we selected reasonably large portions for the experiment (i.e. four pages of on-screen text). Because the stimuli texts cover four screens each, readers moved forward in the text by hitting the right arrow key. This was practised during the calibration phase and is recorded as a keyboard item in the data.

The combined reading time of the texts is exactly 45 minutes for the slowest reader in our sample. All our texts were shown in Arial font, size 12 point, margins of 1.5 cm with expanded spacing and were typically classified as fantasy novel excerpts. Our text layout can generally be considered to follow best practice for texts used in eye-tracking experiments that Beymer, Russell and Orton (2008) suggest for on-screen readability, including suggestions for font size, font type and general accessibility. We also take into account Rello and Marcos' (2012) suggestions for spacing, colour, contrast, and other guidelines for readability. We have not matched or optimized our texts for line length (Dyson and Haselgrove 2001), however we have tried to match our texts on aspects such as readability and we limited the test time to 45 minutes to avoid screen reading fatigue effects.

In this pilot study of ours, the selected texts represent a natural variation of several different language features, such as modal adjuncts,
narration style (incl. dialogue) and the realization of *magical elements*,
to provide indications for future research.[6] The challenges for testing
these findings further will be discussed in detail in the discussion
section.

Usefully for our purposes, Mendlesohn's categories are each instantiated and
linguistic features specific to each category are well set out. Because of these
linguistic differences, we keep the categories separate when testing for differences in reader reaction both through eye-tracking and reader response
interviews.

The categories, Mendlesohn (2008: xvi) suggests, are 'the result of an
extended thought experiment' and are 'intended solely in terms of "this is
what I observe over a wide range of texts". But it is not the categories themselves which are necessarily of interest. Mendlesohn (2008: xviii) states
that it is the reader's relationship to the framework that is of interest.

11.4.3. The analysis

The audio recordings were transcribed and measured for lexical density,
metaphor usage, negation usage and description. These were then compared
with the same measures in the texts. Within the texts we also annotated
magical (i.e. unambiguously non-*primary world*) elements, dialogue and
narration. Measuring the location of the *magical elements* within the text
allowed us to identify the boundaries of the transition to the fantasy world.
This enabled us to identify areas of interest to compare fixation duration
between the 'normal' fictional world and the fantasy fictional world.

The identification of the transition to the fantasy fictional world also meant
that we were able to compare the building of the fantasy world by the author
with the representation of this fantasy world by the reader in their interview.
Our rationale for this procedure was that if the author had favoured a particular type of construction technique for the fantasy world, then the reader's
reaction to this stimuli text (secondary context 1.1) captured during the interview (secondary context 2) should show some relationship to the patterning evident in the stimuli text. The nature of this relationship is not exactly
straightforward and unproblematic because of the contextual complexities
outlined in Figure 11.1 earlier, however, it does provide a small window onto
the otherwise inaccessible construction of the *secondary world* by the reader.

We use the results of this analysis to guide a targeted grammatical analysis of the texts and the interview data. In particular, due to limitations

in space, we focus on the distribution of metaphors, negation and representation of normality and expectation through modal adjuncts. In choosing modal adjuncts, we follow Halliday's (1982) discussion on the use of modals in Priestley's *An Inspector Calls*. Here Halliday suggests that lexicogrammatical selections encoded in categories such as the probability type of modality (see also Halliday and Matthiessen (2014: 156) on its interpersonal and textual metafunctions) realize the speaker's subjective judgement on likelihood and validity of information (Halliday 1982: 147), which is of particular interest in the context of judgements of 'normal' versus 'magical' or fantastic.

11.5. Results

The first of our results comes from the identification of the transition point in each of the excerpts. This was done by annotating the incidence of magical (i.e. Faërie) elements in the texts. Following Alber *et al.* (2010), and Hsu *et al.* (2015), *magical elements* were identified as the introduction of elements (temporal or physical situations, actions and entities) that would be considered impossible in the *primary world* and thus are likely to represent world-knowledge anomalies for the reader. This was aligned with the readers' identification of *magical elements* to ensure that the transition point for each reader was clearly identified. For clarity and to reflect how these areas were established, we will refer to these two areas of interest as *low-density magical element* and *high-density magical element*.

For the identification of transition points, this approach works very clearly with *Portal-Quest* fantasies such as *Alice's Adventures in Wonderland* (Carroll 1982 [1865]) because the reading of the text begins with an area featuring no *magical elements*, then there is a magical portal of some kind, then there is a fantasy world with a high density of *magical elements*. This means that when we examine the text we get a clear section with no *magical elements* and a clear section with a high density of *magical elements*, and it is possible to make these parts balanced areas of interest for eye-tracking measurements. What we see in these cases is expressions of surprise coinciding with an increase in the density of *magical elements* (see also Appendix 11.4).

By comparison, *Intrusion* fantasies present more of a challenge. Here, the *magical elements* are distributed throughout the text with higher or lower density of *magical elements* occurring in a wave-like pattern. This distribution can be seen in Figure 11.2, which shows the annotations as they occur in the text and the different features with which these co-occur. Here, the large box encloses the area with higher density of *magical elements* and the smaller (horizontal) boxes highlight the features that are most frequent in the text. In the *Intrusion* fantasy, we do see the intrusion of *magical elements* into the 'normal' fictional world context, but what we also see in *Harry Potter and the Philosopher's Stone* (Rowling 2014 [1997]) is the foregrounding of the normality of the 'normal' fictional world so that the *magical elements* appear more strange by comparison.

In *Immersion* fantasy the reader is directly immersed into this fantasy world as though it were the 'normal' world, so what we see is a process of habituation rather than transition. But what we find in these instances is that the reader often has a 'friend' in the narrator to guide them and orient them to the world. When we examined *The Hobbit* (Tolkien 2007 [1937]), what we found was that the highest density of *magical elements* occurred almost exclusively within the narration sections. It may be a potential characteristic of the entire category of *Immersion* that *magical elements* occur primarily in the narration in contrast to *Portal-Quest* texts such as *Alice*, for instance, where the dialogue also contains these elements. Within the *Hobbit*, even the few *magical elements* that can be seen after the dialogue begins are located in the narration segments between the dialogue parts, with only two *magical elements* located within the dialogue.

| Text | Dialogue | Magical elements | Metaphor | Modal adjuncts | | | | | |
				Probability	Typicality	Obviousness	Usuality	Evaluation	Prediction
Harry Potter	22	27	27	3	1	2	23	4	3
Alice	33	35	7	7	6	3	15	2	6
The Hobbit	25	37	18	3	1	2	3	2	4

Table 11.2: Distribution of features across all three texts

For this pilot study, we limited the textual analysis to showing the distribution of the modal adjuncts of probability, usuality, typicality and obviousness (Halliday and Matthiessen 2014: 109). Because of their frequency in *Alice*, we also annotate the modal adjuncts of evaluation and prediction (ibid.). This forms the initial part of a larger study of the grammar of fantastic story worlds.

In *The Hobbit*, we see the modal adjuncts cluster around the narration, and they are fairly evenly distributed across the different categories. In *Alice*, the focus is on usuality and probability and is fairly evenly spread

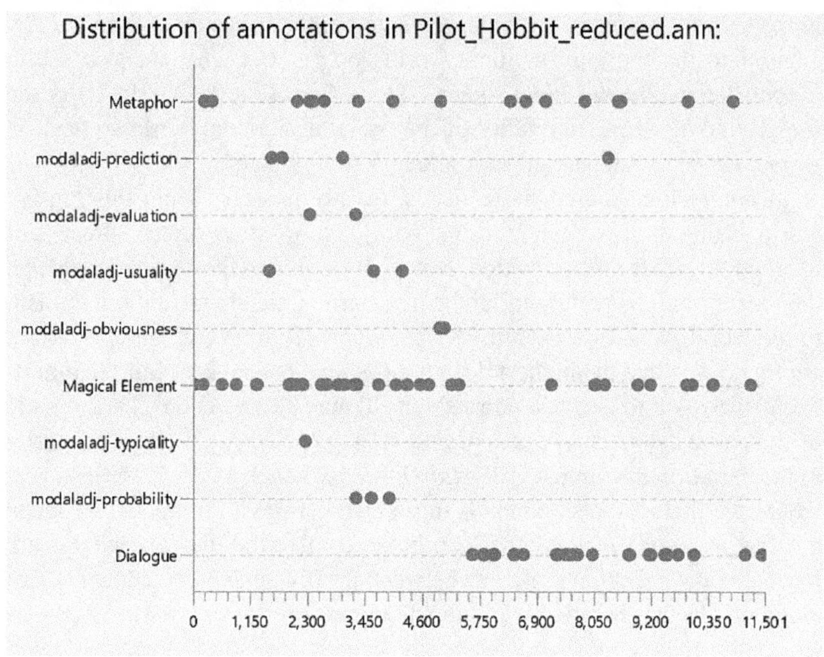
Distribution of annotations in Pilot_Hobbit_reduced.ann:
Metaphor
modaladj-prediction
modaladj-evaluation
modaladj-usuality
modaladj-obviousness
Magical Element
modaladj-typicality
modaladj-probability
Dialogue
0   1,150   2,300   3,450   4,600   5,750   6,900   8,050   9,200   10,350   11,501

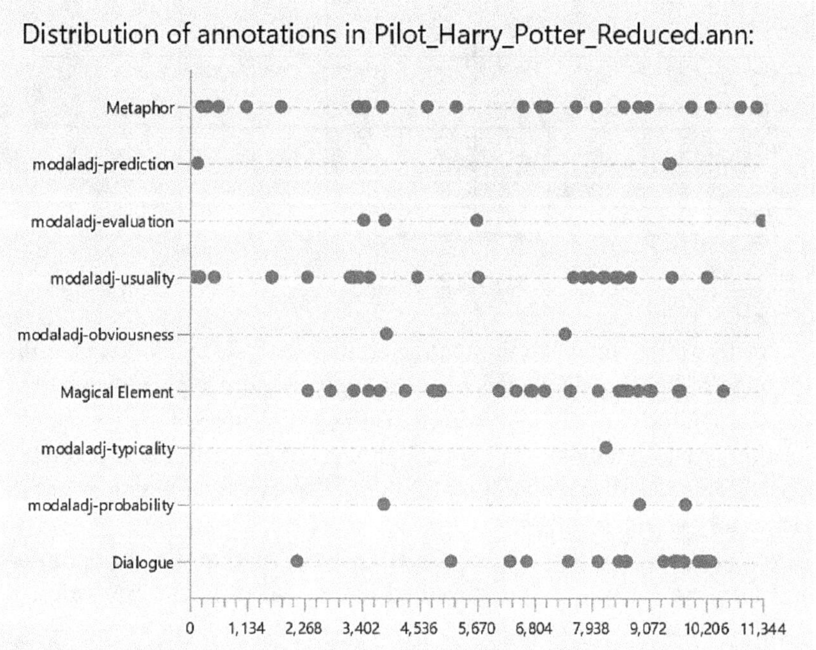
Distribution of annotations in Pilot_Harry_Potter_Reduced.ann:
Metaphor
modaladj-prediction
modaladj-evaluation
modaladj-usuality
modaladj-obviousness
Magical Element
modaladj-typicality
modaladj-probability
Dialogue
0   1,134   2,268   3,402   4,536   5,670   6,804   7,938   9,072   10,206   11,344

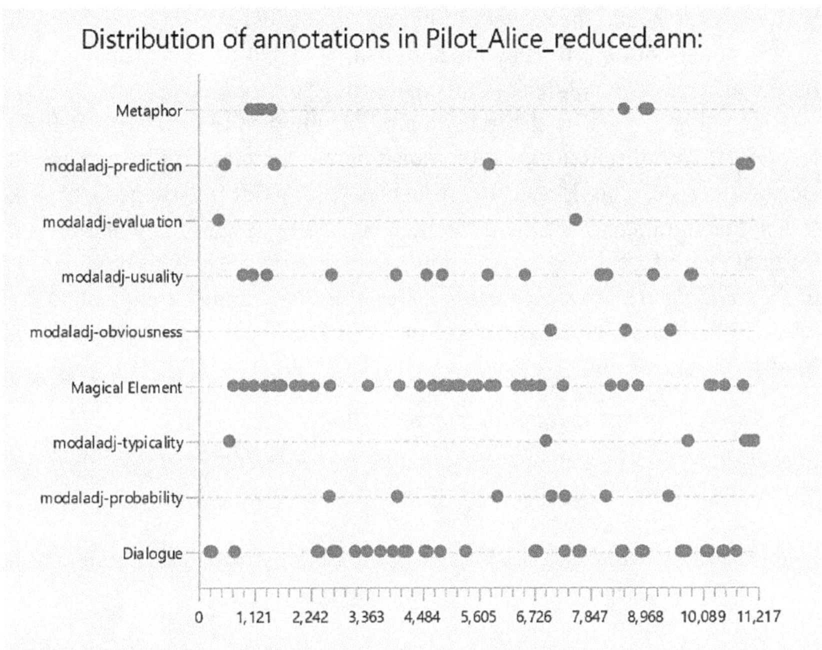

Figure 11.2: Annotation of language features in the texts shown as they occur in the text
x-axis: progression through the text at the level of cell
y-axis: different annotation categories

through the excerpt. It should be noted that the dialogue in *Alice* is almost exclusively mental projection at this stage and this is reflected in the verb *think* being ranked among the highest in the lexical density. Like *Alice*, *Harry Potter* shows a propensity for modal adjuncts of usuality, however here they are almost exclusively focused on normality. There are two very distinct clusters that align quite closely with clusters of *magical elements* and in these cases the tendency is towards negated normality – that is, the modal adjuncts of usuality have been negated.

Metaphor usage in *The Hobbit* and *Harry Potter* is quite evenly distributed and fairly similar in quantity. There is very little clustering and the metaphors are what might be called metaphors of everyday language use. In fact, *Harry Potter* has the highest metaphor usage of the three. *Alice* has markedly fewer metaphors than the other two excerpts, but it is unclear whether this is a pattern that continues and it is unlikely to be a feature of the transition category, but rather an idiosyncrasy of the text.

Crucially for our present question, the readers do not pick up any of the metaphors in describing the worlds, nor do they use metaphors for describing the characters. Metaphor usage in the conventional sense was low for both the authors and the readers. What we do see instead is a foregrounding of strangeness or otherness by the authors that is picked up and accentuated by the readers. We will discuss this patterning further below.

Being able to identify the transition points allowed us to test the readers' reaction to the different types of transition to the fantasy fictional world. Because this is a classic repeated measures study with fully dependent data, to test the significance of the difference between the total fixation duration[7] for areas with low density of *magical elements* and areas with high density of *magical elements*, we ran paired T-Tests[8] for each transition type and this revealed the following results (see Appendix 11.3 for the raw scores of total fixation duration):

> *Harry Potter and the Philosopher's Stone*:
> The value of t is 2.201321. The value of p is 0.046385; significant at $p \leq 0.05$.
> *Alice's Adventures in Wonderland*:
> The value of t is 7.548220. The value of p is < 0.00001; significant at $p \leq 0.01$.
> *The Hobbit*:
> The value of t is 6.573693. The value of p is 1.8E-05; significant at $p \leq 0.01$.

In all cases, the area with high-density *magical elements* has a significantly longer total fixation duration than the area with low-density *magical elements*, implying, if we follow Henderson *et al.* (2015), that there is greater attentional and language-processing engagement for areas with a high density of *magical elements* compared to areas with a low density of *magical elements*.

While *The Hobbit* and *Alice* are significant at the more stringent 0.01, *Harry Potter* is significant only at 0.05. Furthermore, both *The Hobbit* and *Alice* show a difference in total fixation duration that is consistent across all participants, while *Harry Potter* varies across participants. We can see this difference in Figure 11.3, which shows the raw eye-tracking fixation duration for all participants across all texts and compares the fixation duration for areas with high-density *magical elements*.

Having established that there is a significant difference in fixation duration between 'normal' fictional and fantasy fictional world for all categories, we were interested to see what exactly it was that readers were giving attention to and we turned to the interviews that the readers gave after each text.

In analysing the readers' interview texts, we compared the authors' representation of the respective fantasy world with the readers' representation of that fantasy world after reading. In follow-up research, the analysis of the

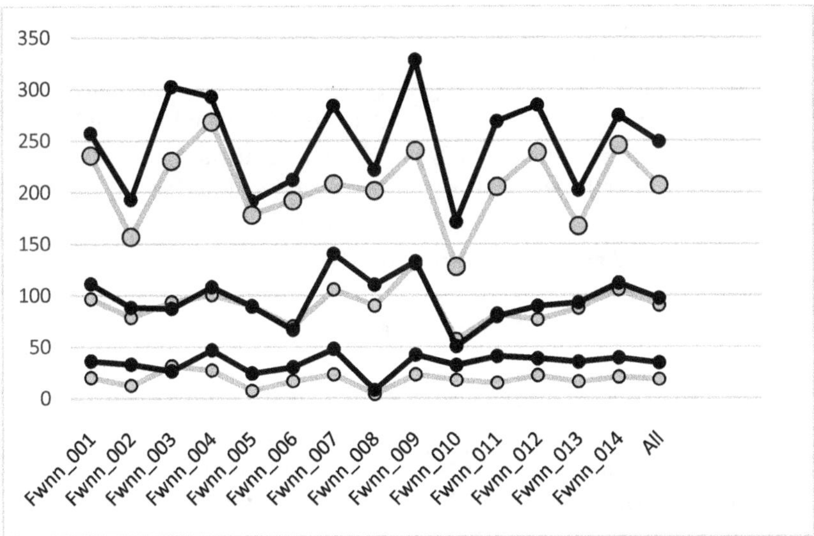

Figure 11.3: Fixation duration for all participants and all texts. In each case, the darker line represents the area of the text with the higher density of magical elements and the lighter line indicates the area with lower density of magical elements. The topmost pairing is The Hobbit, the middle is Harry Potter and the lower is Alice in Wonderland (see end notes for raw scores).

identification of the distribution and alignment of different types of modal adjuncts and metaphors will be extended to further categories.

As we discussed briefly above and see in Figure 11.2, the texts show evidence of clustering in modal adjuncts of usuality and probability (Halliday and Matthiessen 2014: 109) for both *Alice* and *Harry Potter*. In *Alice*, we also see high use of prediction. What these modal adjuncts are foregrounding is a pattern of normality and non-normality or strangeness, expected and unexpected, probable and improbable, common and uncommon. This patterning is picked up by our readers and is extended or amplified, so that we see readers extrapolating single instances in the *secondary world* to generalizations of strangeness of otherness.

The high density of words to assess the Faërie elements of the story, that is the strange or even impossible in *primary-world* terms, is further illustrated here by quotes from the participants' interviews, one for each type of fantasy text (emphasis ours):

Intrusion (Harry Potter)
[…] **this prototypical life of normal people and on the other hand you have this magical world** besides which the protagonists at least in this context – the Dursleys – seem to know something about but to avoid it at any cost and this is I guess the first instance where **these two worlds clash.** (FWnn_001)

Portal-Quest (*Alice*)
Alice sees this rabbit, and the rabbit is talking, and it also has a watch, and it says 'I'm going to be late' and **that's not normal rabbit behaviour** and also the fact that she's in this rabbit hole and keeps falling and falling, **that's not a normal normal rabbit hole either,** and also the room in which she is with and the cake she eats that makes her smaller or makes her grow and yeah, **it's many elements that are not from this world**. (FWnn_012)
Immersion (*The Hobbit*)
In the beginning **it didn't seem to be too different**, I mean they start off very early saying **hobbit and you don't really know what that means so you already get the sense that this is different** and then it's about this hole in the ground and how it looks like which is also different, but other than that for a very long time it seems at least **somewhat ordinary with ordinary things**. (FWnn_001)

We observe that an additional focus is on negation when the readers conceptualize the otherness of the *secondary world*. What we see is that readers take up the author's offer of strangeness (in terms of conceptualization and lexical choice) and amplify and generalize this strangeness. In so doing, negation in particular appears to be used as a lexico-grammatical tool for the purpose of this conceptualization. For example, below are some of the (negative polar) conceptualizations of the worlds that we see from the readers which include the realization of morphologically marked negative polarity via prefixation (emphasis ours).

[...] it's where everything **im**possible is possible [...]	(FWnn_005)
[...] the laws of physics **don't** apply in this world [...]	(FWnn_006)
[...] but they're **not** like humans [...]	(FWnn_012)
[...] they have some relatives who're **not** quite that normal [...]	(FWnn_007)
[...] **not** the world we are living [...]	(FWnn_014)

Such evaluation against *primary-world* knowledge[9] rebounds into the *primary world* itself in the context of the participants' description of the story as a result of their individual blending efforts. The description makes the story a story that is shared between social subjects beyond the author, and thus beyond the private experience of engaging with the *secondary world* (see also Hasan 2007). The participant, again, will construct the *secondary world* setting on the basis of the double-context input[10] and previous knowledge of *primary* and *secondary worlds*. Our data of author and reader representations of *magical elements* support the view that in the process of retelling, the conceptualization of the *secondary world* as a strange or absent *primary world* applies. We conclude that this overarching metaphor, in which the *primary world* domain acts as a source of mappings onto the *secondary world* target, is at the heart of coming to terms with the fantastic in fictional worlds.

11.5. Outlook

While our pilot study was designed to guide our future investigations, the findings reveal many new areas of investigation (see below) and raise the real possibility that it may be possible to identify clear and measurable indices for Mendlesohn's (2008) categories on the basis of how readers engage with the text.

With respect to our sample population, our sample size was deliberately small and limited to non-native speakers of English. We are already making plans to extend this to far larger sample sizes that include different populations of native speakers of English. The current restriction for building much larger samples sizes is the difficulty in getting large sample sizes for natural reading-based eye-tracking experiments. Lab-based collection is not only costly in terms of finances; it is very costly in terms of time. Further challenges include accessing and investigating large samples of native-speaker populations. These challenges are behind Wegener *et al.*'s (2016) work towards the development of mobile eye-tracking and annotation technology that will eventually allow us to easily reach and test much larger samples in more natural settings.

In addition to these extensions, we plan to re-run the experiment with different texts that fit into the categories used here to test whether the patterns that we see in our pilot study hold true for a larger sample. It appears from our current study that there is a significant difference between the different categories, but it is unclear from our small sample whether or not this will hold over a wider range of texts. Furthermore, it is impossible to test without seeing how other texts behave with respect to both language patterns and fixation duration.

One of the first aspects that we are following up is the duration of the transition effect in fixation duration. We have examined aspects that are boundary effects. We do not as yet know for how long these effects will be maintained. We hypothesize that, since the function of a transition point such as those we examine is to habituate the reader to a fantasy world, we should see a gradual drop in fixation duration. However, this gradual drop should reflect the different transition styles. To measure this, we are currently running tests of sequential, matched areas of interest within the areas with high-density *magical elements*.

The differences in fixation duration offer us an opportunity to explore further the findings of Henderson *et al.* (2015), who combined fMRI with eye-tracking to 'demonstrate that fixation duration is correlated with activity in cortical structures associated with attention, oculomotor control, and language processing' (Henderson *et al.* 2015: 396). In so doing, they showed that 'fixation duration in reading reflects ongoing cognitive processes associated with text understanding, and with the interface of language processing, attentional systems, and eye movement control' (Henderson *et al.* 2015: 396). This opens up the potential to investigate what cognitive action is taking place when readers transition into the fantasy world much as Hsu *et al.* (2015) have done with their work on fMRI and reading.

The differences in fixation duration also suggest the need for a more comprehensive lexico-grammatical analysis of the different sections of text to identify the concrete linguistic features that characterize the areas with high-density *magical elements* and those with lower density. We have also begun to analyse the corresponding sections in the readers' interview data so that we can compare the linguistic features that readers use to characterize their conceptualization of the fantasy world.

Finally, we have only just begun to touch on the role of the reader (and the author) as social subjects (see Hasan 1989). The contextual features that pertain to both the reader and the text offer fruitful areas for future investigation. We have not yet examined the demographic and personal reading behaviour data that we collected on our participants. Beyond the experimental opportunities, the research has presented many opportunities to connect with cognitive linguistic and experientialist frameworks such as text world theory (e.g. Gavins 2007).[11] An integrating approach including Wolf's (2012) work towards a theory of imaginary worlds as well as the constitutiveness of metaphor and blending in world-building will bring us closer to understanding fictional worlds, and hence literature, in general.

If literature is the fusion of discourse and art (Hasan 2007: 16), the elusive notion of art is shaped by the particularity of language and its functioning in text (Hasan 1989: 91). In this respect, this study is a contribution to tracing the artistic in the combined effort by authors and readers to construct fantastic worlds. As Hasan writes:

> It is by using language that the artist is able to explore some set of fundamental cultural elements that have become – or are on the way to becoming – part of our consciousness/ our mental habits, and these foreground for us the deepest concerns of humanity [...]. (Hasan 2011: xvi–xvii)

Notes

1. For an in-depth discussion of (cultural) models involved in the construction process, see e.g. Strauss and Quinn (1997); Schneider (2001); Strasen (2008).
2. Faërie represents the perilous realm of enchanting beauty (see Tolkien 2014: 27) where beasts dwell and actions are possible that cannot be traced in the *primary world*. By addressing Faërie, Tolkien intended to challenge the customary apprehension of reality of the recipients of fictional story worlds.
3. See Lothmann (this volume). See also Vaeßen and Lothmann (2014) for a metaphor approach to literary character construction. On foregrounding and systematic patterning that fosters textual coherence, see e.g. Hasan (1989).
4. We would like to thank all our very keen students who participated in the study. Additional special thanks go to our assistants Sven Hintzen, Marvin Nowak, and Charlotte Rosenow.
5. We use the Flesch-Kincaid measures for reasons of comparability with existing studies. Furthermore, because we did not carry out comprehension tests and have non-native readers of English, the readability scores were used as a proxy for reader comprehension. This was combined with a reader supplied evaluation of the difficulty of the text.
6. Please note that this is a pilot study that is intended to guide future research on a much larger scale and thus, while we have provided statistical measures of our findings, these are indicative rather than conclusive findings.
7. This metric measures the sum of the duration for all fixations within an area of interest. We use this measure because it has been shown by Henderson *et al.* (2015) to correlate to brain activity during natural reading tasks, specifically, that it reflects attentional engagement and language processing.
8. This is a classic repeated measures design which compares the difference between the total fixation duration for the same participant reading the same text in two sequentially adjacent areas of text. The design is comparable to that of Hsu *et al.* (2015) although their method of investigation includes fMRI.
9. In this respect, see the experimental data on counterfactual world contexts in Ferguson and Sanford (2007).
10. On the double-context input consisting of primary and secondary contexts, see Hasan (2011) and section 11.2 of this paper.
11. In the context of text world theory and negation, see Hidalgo Downing (2000) in particular.

References

Alber, J., Iversen, S., Skov Nielsen, H., and Richardson, B. (2010). Unnatural narratives, unnatural narratology: Beyond mimetic models. *Narrative* 18 (2): 113-136.

Beymer, D., Russell, D., and Orton, P. (2008). An eye tracking study of how font size and type influence online reading. In O. Abuelmaatti and D. England (Eds) *People and Computers XXII: Culture, Creativity, Interaction. Proceedings of HCI 2008, Vol. 2*, 15–18. Liverpool: BCS.

Butt, D. (1983). Semantic 'Drift' in verbal art. *Australian Review of Applied Linguistics* 6: 38–48. https://doi.org/10.1075/aral.6.1.04but

Butt, D. (1988). Randomness, order and the latent patterning of text. In D. Birch and M. O'Toole (Eds) *Function of Style*, 74–97. London. Pinter Publishers.

Carroll, L. (1865/1982). *Alice's Adventures in Wonderland and Through the Looking-Glass*. Oxford: Oxford University Press.

Coleridge, S. T. (1817/2013). *Biographia Literaria*, (Eds T. Riikonen and D. Widger). *Project Gutenberg: E-book 6081*, <http://www.gutenberg.org/files/6081/6081-h/6081-h.htm#link2HCH0014> (accessed 20 December 2016).

Dyson, M. C., and Haselgrove, M. (2001). The influence of reading speed and line length on the effectiveness of reading from screen. *International Journal of Human-Computer Studies* 54: 585–612. https://doi.org/10.1006/ijhc.2001.0458

Fauconnier, G. and Turner, M. (1998). Conceptual integration networks. *Cognitive Science* 22: 133–187. https://doi.org/10.1207/s15516709cog2202_1

Fauconnier, G., and Turner, M. (2003). *The Way We Think: Conceptual Blending and the Mind's Hidden Complexities*. New York: Basic Books.

Ferguson, H. J. and Sanford, A. J. (2007). Anomalies in real and counterfactual worlds: An eye-movement investigation. *Journal of Memory and Language* 58: 609–626. https://doi.org/10.1016/j.jml.2007.06.007

Gavins, J. (2007). *Text World Theory: An Introduction*. Edinburgh: Edinburgh University Press. https://doi.org/10.3366/edinburgh/9780748622993.001.0001

Gavins, J. and Steen, G. (Eds). (2003). *Cognitive Poetics in Practice*. London: Routledge. https://doi.org/10.4324/9780203417737

Goethe, J. W. (1808/2013). *Faust: Eine Tragödie*. North Charleston, SC: CreateSpace.

Halliday, M. A. K. (1964). The Linguistic Study of Literary Texts. In H. Lunt (Ed.) *Proceedings of the Ninth International Congress of Linguistics*, 302–307. The Hague: Mouton.

Halliday, M. A. K. (1982). The de-automatization of grammar: From Priestley's 'An Inspector Calls'. In J. Anderson (Ed.) *Language Form and Linguistic Variation: Papers Dedicated to Angus McIntosh*, 129–159. Amsterdam: Benjamins. https://doi.org/10.1075/cilt.15.09hal

Halliday, M. A. K. and Matthiessen, C. M. I. M. (2014). *Halliday's Introduction to Functional Grammar*, 4th ed. London: Routledge.

Hasan, R. (1989). *Linguistics, Language, and Verbal Art* (2nd ed.). Oxford: Oxford University Press.

Hasan, R. (2007). Private pleasure, public discourse: Reflections on engaging with literature. In D. R. Miller and M. Turci (Eds) *Language and Verbal Art Revisited: Linguistic Approaches to the Study of Literature*, 13–40. London: Equinox.

Hasan, R. (2011). A timeless journey: On the past and future of present knowledge. In *Selected Papers of Ruqaiya Hasan on Applied Linguistics*, xiv–xliii. Beijing: Foreign Language Teaching and Research Press.

Henderson, J. M., Choi, W., Luke, S. G., and Desai, R. H. (2015). Neural correlates of fixation duration in natural reading: Evidence from fixation-related fMRI. *NeuroImage* 119: 390–397. https://doi.org/10.1016/j.neuroimage.2015.06.072

Hidalgo Downing, L. (2000). *Negation, Text Worlds, and Discourse: The Pragmatics of Fiction*. Stamford, CT: Ablex Publications.

Hsu, C.-T., Jacobs, A. M., Altmann, U., and Conrad, M. (2015). The magical activation of left amygdala when reading Harry Potter: An fMRI study on how descriptions of supra-natural events entertain and enchant. *PloS ONE* 10 (2): e0118179, 1–15. https://doi.org/10.1371/journal.pone.0118179

Jacobs, A. M. (2015a). The scientific study of literary experience: Sampling the state of the art. *Scientific Study of Literature* 5: 139–170. https://doi.org/10.1075/ssol.5.2.01jac

Jacobs, A. M. (2015b). Neurocognitive poetics: Methods and models for investigating the neuronal and cognitive–affective bases of literature reception. *Frontiers of Human Neuroscience* 9 (186). https://doi.org/10.3389/fnhum.2015.00186

Lakoff, G. and Johnson, M. (2011). *Metaphors We Live by*. Repr., Chicago, IL: Chicago University Press.

Lothmann, T. (this volume). Striking a chord in the reader: On metaphor as a constituent of the grammar of verbal art.

Lothmann, T. and Scholz, J. (2016). Derived from and flowing into reality: Faërie as a conceptual framework for the blending of story rooms. *Hither Shore* 12 (2015): 8–20.

Mangen, A. and van der Weel, A. (2016). The evolution of reading in the age of digitisation: An integrative framework for reading research. *Literacy* 50: 116–124. https://doi.org/10.1111/lit.12086

Mazzoni, D. (2016). *Audacity 2.1.2*. Audio recording software. <http://www.audacityteam.org> (accessed 13 January 2017).

Mendlesohn, F. (2008). *Rhetorics of Fantasy*. Middletown, CT: Wesleyan University Press.

Miall, D. S. (2006). *Literary Reading: Empirical and Theoretical Studies*. New York: Lang.

Rello, L. and Marcos, M.-C. (2012). An eye tracking study on text customization for user performance and preference. In *2012 Eighth Latin American Web Congress: Proceedings*, 64–70. Piscataway, NJ: IEEE. https://doi.org/10.1109/LA-WEB.2012.13

Rowling, J. K. (1997/2014). *Harry Potter and the Philosopher's Stone*. London: Bloomsbury.

Schneider, R. (2001). Toward a cognitive theory of literary character: The dynamics of mental-model construction. *Style* 35: 607–640.

Steiner, E. (1991). *A Functional Perspective on Language, Action, and Interpretation: An initial approach with a View to Computational Modelling*. Berlin: Mouton de Gruyter.

Stockwell, P. (2002). *Cognitive Poetics: An Introduction*. London: Routledge.

Stockwell, P. (2005). *Texture: A Cognitive Aesthetics of Reading*. Edinburgh: Edinburgh University Press. https://doi.org/10.3366/edinburgh/9780748625819.001.0001

Strasen, S. (2008). *Rezeptionstheorien: Literatur-, sprach- und kulturwissenschaftliche Ansätze und kulturelle Modelle*. Trier: WVT.

Strauss, C. and Quinn, N. (1997). *A Cognitive Theory of Cultural Meaning*. Cambridge: Cambridge University Press.

Tolkien, J. R. R. (1937/2007). *The Hobbit or There and Back Again*. London: HarperCollins.

Tolkien, J. R. R. (2014). *Tolkien on Fairy-stories* (Eds V. Flieger and D. A. Anderson). London: HarperCollins.

Vaeßen, J. and Lothmann T. (2014). Do you read me? Metaphor as a pathway to the conceptualisation of literary identity. *International Journal of Literary Linguistics* 3: 1–18. <http://www.ijll.uni-mainz.de/ index. php/ijll/issue/viewIssue/6/4> (accessed 10 January 2017).

Van Dijk, T. A. and Kintsch, W. (1992). *Strategies of Discourse Comprehension* (3rd pr.). San Diego, CA: Academic Press.

Wegener, R. (2011). *Parameters of Context: From Theory to Model and Application*. PhD thesis, Macquarie University, Sydney.

Wegener, R., Kohlschein, C., Jeschke, S., and Schuller, B. (2016). Automatic detection of textual triggers for reader emotion in short stories. In J. F. Sánchez-Rada and B. Schuller (Eds) *Proceedings of the LREC*

2016 Workshop "Emotion and Sentiment Analysis, Portorož, Slovenia, 80–84. <http://www.lrec-conf.org/proceedings/lrec2016/workshops/ LREC2016Workshop-ESA_Proceedings.pdf> (accessed 13 January 2017).

Wolf, M. J. P. (2012). *Building Imaginary Worlds: The Theory and History of Subcreation*. New York: Routledge.

Appendices

Appendix 11.1: Participant demographics

ID	Age	Gender	Languages spoken at home	Other languages	Highest level of education
Fwnn_001	27	Male	German	English, French (basic), Latin (basic)	MA equivalency
Fwnn_002	25	Female	German	English, French, Dutch, Norwegian	BA
Fwnn_003	23	Female	German and French	English, Italian, Spanish, French	Abitur
Fwnn_004	27	Female	German and Bosnian	English, French, Spanish, Bosnian	Abitur
Fwnn_005	23	Female	German	English, French (basic), Spanish (basic), Chinese (basic)	Abitur
Fwnn_006	23	Female	German	English, French, Italian, Japanese, Latin, Korean (basic), Swedish (basic)	Abitur
Fwnn_007	21	Female	German	English, French, Italian	Abitur
Fwnn_008	22	Female	German and Croatian	English, Croatian, French, Spanish	Abitur
Fwnn_009	29	Male	German	English	MA
Fwnn_010	22	Female	German	English, Spanish, French (basic)	BA
Fwnn_011	23	Female	German	English, Dutch, French (basic)	BA
Fwnn_012	20	Female	German	English, French (basic), Spanish (basic)	Abitur
Fwnn_013	21	Female	German and Greek	English, French, Greek	Abitur
Fwnn_014	26	Male	German and Persian (Farsi)	English, Urdu, French (basic), Italian (basic), Persian (Farsi)	Abitur

Appendix 11.2: Interview questions

(a) 'Imagine talking to someone who hasn't read this story. Please briefly describe the setting of the story for me.'

(b) 'Did you notice a second setting in the story? Can you briefly describe this for me?'

(c) 'Did you notice any magical elements in the story? What was the first magical element that you noticed?'

Appendix 11.3: Raw scores for fixation duration by participant and transition type

RAW	Intrusion		Portal-Quest		Immersion	
	Harry Potter		*Alice*		*The Hobbit*	
ID	Low Magical Element Density	High Magical Element Density	Low Magical Element Density	High Magical Element Density	Low Magical Element Density	High Magical Element Density
Fwnn_001	96.66	111.07	20.50	36.51	235.83	257.14
Fwnn_002	78.46	88.20	12.66	33.22	157.01	193.10
Fwnn_003	93.55	87.12	31.55	26.64	230.33	302.46
Fwnn_004	100.27	107.84	27.48	46.93	268.18	292.95
Fwnn_005	89.63	89.18	7.49	24.40	178.22	191.35
Fwnn_006	69.96	66.57	16.81	30.36	192.06	212.18
Fwnn_007	105.55	140.24	23.39	48.07	208.29	283.95
Fwnn_008	89.88	110.08	4.02	8.22	201.53	221.60
Fwnn_009	130.67	132.60	23.30	42.34	240.36	328.40
Fwnn_010	57.36	50.59	17.78	32.22	127.75	171.20
Fwnn_011	81.77	79.52	15.01	40.89	205.45	268.42
Fwnn_012	76.31	89.37	22.23	38.60	238.71	284.54
Fwnn_013	87.41	92.69	15.99	35.28	167.24	201.95
Fwnn_014	105.31	111.56	20.66	39.30	245.45	274.08
All	90.20	96.90	18.49	34.50	206.89	248.81

Appendix 11.4: Overview of the three stimuli texts under both conditions

Eye-tracking metric by area of interest	*Harry Potter*	*Alice*	*The Hobbit*
Total Fixation Duration: low magical element density	90.2	18.49	206.89
Total Fixation Duration: high magical element density	96.9	34.5	248.81
Fixation Count: low magical element density	385.14	82.86	937.21
Fixation Count: high magical element density	422.93	147.57	1051.64
Total Visit Duration: low magical element density	105.35	22.66	252.77
Total Visit Duration: high magical element density	112.89	40.72	292.5
Visit Count: low magical element density	9.86	6.36	21.64
Visit Count: high magical element density	12.5	6.5	37.43
AOI word count: low magical element density	400	100	1118
AOI word count: high magical element density	473	153	1011

12 Future directions in the study of verbal art

Wendy L. Bowcher[*]

12.1. Introduction

Professor: Well, what do you think?

Maggie: Good.

Professor: Unacceptable answer. What's the poem about?

Maggie: I don't know.

Professor: Yes you do. What's it about?

Maggie: Losing?

Professor: What.

Maggie: Love?

Professor: Ah. And how about that. Is the love lost already? Is Bishop writing about it as a possibility? A probability? What?

[*] Wendy L. Bowcher is a Professor in the School of Foreign Languages at Sun Yat-sen University, China. Her main research interests include the study of context in the theory of Systemic Functional Linguistics, multimodal discourse analysis, and English intonation. She is the editor of *Multimodal Texts from Around the World: Cultural and Linguistics Insights* (2012), co-editor (with Jennifer Y. Liang) of *Society in Language, Language in Society: Essays in Honour of Ruqaiya Hasan* (2016), co-editor (with T. D. Royce) of *New Directions in the Analysis of Multimodal Discourse* (2007, 2014), and co-editor (with B. A. Smith) of *Systemic Phonology: Recent Studies in English* (2014). Wendy was instrumental in the formation of the Japan Association of Systemic Functional Linguistics (JASFL) in 1993 and served for several years as the Vice President of the association. From 2011 to 2014 she was Vice-Chair of the International Systemic Functional Linguistics Association (ISFLA).

Maggie: Um. In the beginning she's talking about losing real things, like keys. And then she … she gets like … she lost a continent.

Professor: Getting grandiose.

Maggie: Yeah. And the way she says it, it's like it doesn't matter.

Professor: Ah. Her tone? Would you call it detached?

Maggie: I think she wants to sound detached. She wants to sound like it doesn't matter, because she knows deep down how bad it's going to feel to lose.

Professor: Lose what? Or whom? Is it a lover?

Maggie: No. It's a friend.

Professor: A plus. Smart girl.

(transcript of scene from *In Her Shoes* 2005 Twentieth Century Fox Film Corporation/2009 Twentieth Century Fox Home Entertainment)

Maggie is a dyslexic, and having failed at school, and in most of her life so far, is now working temporarily in an aged care home where her grandmother lives. The professor is blind, and is one of the residents in the home. He senses there is something more about Maggie than she projects, and guesses she is dyslexic when she first resists reading to him. Nonetheless he persuades her to read 'One Art' (although somewhat abbreviated from the original) by Elizabeth Bishop. In the conversation that follows we see that the Professor is not satisfied with Maggie's evaluation of the poem as being 'good', and so through a series of questions, together Maggie and the Professor arrive at the 'theme' of the poem, its deep meaning: loss, and coping with loss in a stoic way. Although they have, essentially, bypassed the crucial 'symbolic articulation' utilized by Bishop, we get a hint of it when they work through the building up of the significance and size of things lost: trivial items such as keys to big items like continents. This little movie scene illustrates the difference between evaluation and interpretation of a literary work – a key theme in Hasan's research on verbal art.

Evaluation is akin to appreciation. We can 'like' something. We can feel it is powerful, or beautiful, and like Maggie, we can say it is 'good'. But on what basis are we making such a judgement? In the conversation between Maggie and the Professor, a type of analysis ensues after the Professor asks, 'What's it about?' However, the discussion surrounding the professor's question about Bishop's 'tone', and Maggie's opinion that Bishop wants 'to sound detached' is not supported in the same way as the conversation concerning the 'what' of the poem. Rather, it derives simply from what they both 'sense' from the poem. Hasan contends that 'analytical frameworks are needed when the basis of appreciation has to be made explicit; and at that point focus on language becomes necessary' (Hasan 1985: 28). She also points out that paraphrase is not enough to describe the nature of verbal art (Hasan 1985: 98), and that the analytical framework needs to include 'two levels of semiosis': a first order semiosis, which represents the language choices, and a second order semiosis, which is 'the product of the artistic system through foregrounding and repatternings of the first order meanings' (Hasan 1985: 98). It is on this basis that Hasan explains her framework for understanding how verbal art makes its meaning, and hence how it is recognized as 'art', and the chapters in this volume have presented some ways of applying and extending her ideas.

But where to from here? In order to consider the possible future directions of linguistic analyses of literature, utilizing Hasan's framework, it is worth pausing for a moment to consider what has been gained from analyses that have already been conducted? After all, like Maggie and the Professor, we could simply be content with discussing literature and arriving at its deep meaning(s) without doing the kind of meticulous analysis that Hasan has demonstrated, and that her framework demands. And in doing so, if we are in an educational context, we might still receive an 'A +' as Maggie does from the Professor by working through to an understanding of a work of literature by a less than rigorous linguistic analysis. So the question arises: what has been the point of those analyses and have they delivered anything of interest that is worth pursuing? In order to answer this question, this chapter briefly presents some key highlights of Hasan's ideas on verbal art and the application of these by various scholars. The chapter does not propose to conduct an in-depth description and evaluation of these applications. Rather, the brief overview provides a background against which future research might make sense. The overview is organized in terms of the following general domains.

(a)   The place of verbal art in society;
(b)   Theory, models, corpora and tools;
(c)   Verbal art and pedagogy;
(d)   Hasan's verbal art framework and other theories and approaches; and
(e)   Verbal art and translation.

12.2. The place of verbal art in society

12.2.1 Language, society and verbal art

In literate societies it is the written word which is particularly valued in that the functions of writing 'tend to be the prestigious functions, those associated with learning, religion, government, and trade' (Halliday 1985: vii). Within this set of prestigious functions we find literature. However, unlike other types of written texts, literature is characterized by a quality that transcends the everyday, and is typically associated with a society in which time can be devoted to more than the means of survival, a society in which a greater focus can be placed on liberty, art, beauty and culture rather than anything explicitly practical. In this regard, consider, for instance, the place of poetry in the following quotation from John Adams, president of the United States of America between 1797 and 1801:

> I must study politics and war, that our sons may have liberty to study mathematics and philosophy. Our sons ought to study mathematics and philosophy, geography, natural history and naval architecture, navigation, commerce and agriculture in order to give their children a right to study painting, *poetry*, music, architecture, statuary, tapestry and porcelain.

> (from a letter to Abigail Adams, 12 May 1780, see federalistpapers. org emphasis added)

There is no disputing that literature (verbal art) is ranked as a highly valued creative art within society, but far from being 'impractical', most descriptions of literature point to what it 'does'. For instance, in her explanation of the function of literature in society, Kusch (2016) says:

> Literature *conveys* sacred knowledge, *teaches* moral and social lessons, *announces* new ideas, *records* revolutions, *tests* the limits of cultural values, and *shows* us our best and worst selves. As the set of stories we tell of ourselves through narrative, performance, lyrical reflection, and many other forms, literature *encapsulates* human experience and *records* the messy, painful, triumphant, and sublime realities of the passage of humans through our world. ... Literature *offers* us the human life in total – not reduced – with its inconsistent logic, morality, and identity on full display. (Kusch 2016: 1 italics added)

The italicized words in this quotation highlight what literature is said to DO within a society. But even when scholars describe what literature IS, the focus still tends to be on what literature DOES. For example: 'literature is a way to experience a way of life, a time period, a culture, an emotion, a deed, an event that you are not otherwise able, willing (as, say, in the case of murder), or capable of encountering in any other manner' (McGee 2001: 2).

Researchers working in the systemic functional theoretical framework, emphasize that literature is language, and that what it *does* is intimately tied to what it *is*. This is not to say that other scholars do not recognize that literature is language (cf. Kusch 2016), but the SFL model of language provides a rather different perspective on the 'language' that literature is. The oft cited quotation of Hasan that for verbal art 'language is not as clothing to the body; it *is* the body' (Hasan 1985: 91), resonates with the SFL perspective on language. Of language, Butt says:

> Languages are not platonic forms waiting to be called into actualization. Rather, they are fine calibrations of behavior, learnt in response to the specific socio-cultural conditions within which the network of speakers is operating. As emphasized by Wittgenstein, one's language is rooted in 'forms of life'. 'Sharing a language' is not agreement in opinions but in 'forms of life'. (2009: 374)

If language is rooted in the living of life and is an essentially social activity, then verbal art must also be so, and if sharing a language is sharing 'forms of life' then it stands to reason that verbal art is a means through which these forms of life might be shared. Thus, to understand the place of verbal art in society, we must see verbal art as a 'necessary' part of human social existence. Why? Because it has evolved to be so. That is, if language is as it is because of how it has been [and continues to be] put into service in the living of life (cf. Halliday 2003: 29) and if literature is language (it cannot be anything else), then it, too, is a part of this ongoing change; it, too, is as it is because of what it has evolved to do, and what it does, apparently, is convey, teach, announce, record, etc. (cf. Kusch 2016). These are what we understand as the social functions literature over time has come to serve.

However, we know that there are other language-based activities which also 'have' these functions (cf. Hasan 1985: 100; Kusch 2016: 1). So why have different language activities evolved to serve what appear to be the same functions within society? What is different about verbal art from these other language-based activities? Can those functions really be the same if the linguistic choices differ? If language changes over time because of the functions it is pressed to serve, then a possible direction for research could be a more penetrating focus on the part that verbal art plays in the evolving nature of a language, and in its own evolution *vis-à-vis* society, and on how and why it has evolved as a means of fulfilling certain functions and of 'sharing' specific 'forms of life' in the way that it does.

12.2.2 Verbal art and community

The concept of sharing mentioned in the previous section suggests community. Indeed, verbal art through the ages has provided an opportunity for sharing and creating community. Akerejola (2012) for instance explains that the oral telling of folktales in Òkó society is a part of a community activity 'aimed at negotiating communal meaning' (2012a: 35). Consider also the Euskaran tradition of 'bertsolaritza', or oral improvisatory poetry telling, which it is believed has played a role in cementing a sense of community in the Basque population and of keeping the Euskaran language alive (BBC2 *Before Babel* 1992). Hasan's framework offers a way into investigating how verbal art re-contextualizes 'the kind of knowledge that is based on the experience of everyday life as it is lived unselfconsciously by the members of some community' (Hasan 2007: 25). In this sense, verbal art mirrors community, at least in the sense that that community is refracted through the eye (or pen, or voice) of the verbal artist. Hasan says 'one of the reasons that verbal art can never be dissociated from the community in which it was created is precisely because the stratum of theme is closest to a community's ideology' (Hasan 1985: 99). She further explains:

> the challenge of the creator of verbal art is that the symbolically articulated theme has to be capable of striking a chord in the reader across substantial distances in time and space, even though the roots of theme lie in the artist's own ideological stance. (Hasan 2007: 25)

This 'striking a chord in the reader' may not be done directly in verbal art. The controversies of life when embedded in verbal art 'are inferred and generally not debated explicitly' (Hasan 1985: 100). This is perhaps why Maggie and the Professor sensed Bishop's detachment, but were not able to support their sense linguistically. However, Butt demonstrates how the artist's striking a chord may be through a form of 'latent patterning' (Butt 1988) manifest in such features as clause complexing and textual arrangement, which 'constitute a profound, even visceral, dimension of the embodiment of language' connecting meaning to the bodily experience of language, and becoming a resource in verbal art which is latent, but powerful in the expression of the aesthetic meaning being conveyed (Butt 2016). This is akin to Halliday's remark that the theme of 'time' in Priestley's work is 'a motif that permeates the interaction of the participants, and is more or less covertly woven in to the dialogue' (Halliday [1982] 2002: 129). In connection with this is Halliday's reference to Eco (1976) who 'compares a work of art to a language, saying that "there must be an underlying system of mutual correlations, and thus a semiotic design which cunningly gives the impression of non-semiosis"' (Halliday [1982] 2002: 130).

Although the theme of verbal art may be subtly threaded through or infused in the text (to various degrees of subtlety), its reception may nonetheless rally together or polarize groups of people and thus solidify people's sense of belonging to a community. Consider the effect Salman Rushdie's

The Satanic Verses, D. H. Lawrence's *Lady Chatterley's Lover*, Oscar Wilde's *Salome* or Harriett Beecher Stowe's *Uncle Tom's Cabin* have had on certain segments of society, or the many cases of book burning that have taken place over the course of history reflecting one community pitched against another. There is also the role of verbal art in engendering a sense of national pride and/or identity – the lyrics of national anthems, the ancient *manyou shu* in Japan, *Waltzing Matilda* and *The Man from Snowy River* in Australia. Verbal art can certainly rally people around a way of thinking, or a shared emotion, such as is done through poetry at funerals, hymns, chants at football matches, teasing rhymes, or nursery rhymes that bring a closeness and intimacy between carer and child.

This communalizing function of verbal art suggests many directions for future research. For example, in what moments in history is verbal art used (whether consciously or not) to rally others to a cause? How is this done? How does it do it differently from literary works such as Marx and Engels' *Communist Manifesto* or Thomas Paine's *Common Sense*? How might verbal art be used as, say, a 'bonding icon' (cf. Stenglin 2012)? Research into community-forming and community inspiring verbal art could provide fascinating insights into what brings one community together in contrast to another, and could highlight what underlies the historical and cultural reach of such works.

It should be remembered, however, that communities are complex entities and their parameters are difficult to define (cf. research into the concept of 'speech community'). Hasan's identification of the context of creation and the context of reception are important in this regard, as is the theoretical position taken up in SFL that 'text is text because of its relevance to a context, and contexts are themselves constructed by text' (Butt 1988: 78). With such a theoretical model of language, we can begin to see how verbal art constructs context(s) and at the same time may be comprehended within different contexts of reception. Butt comments that 'poetry cannot come from anything except a poet's engagement with cultural particularities' (Butt 2009: 369), and he demonstrates how writers of varying cultural backgrounds within an English-speaking speech community can contribute to a deeper and richer picture of the potentials of the English language, and in doing so of the potential in descriptions of the community of English speakers. His analyses of Ee Tiang Hong's poetry show a rich tapestry of life that the resources of the English language can construct, and he argues that:

> In confronting the poems of Ee Tiang Hong, we have a chance to understand more deeply that variation is the dominant of experience, the deepest principle of consistency in our evolving, systemic potential, the source of our ability to confront change with creative,

> polyphonous personae. Rather than an aberration from, or a threat to, the notions of structure and coherence, our variations are the surest sign of our place in an open, dynamic, system. (Butt 2009: 391)

Hasan's methodology provides a means of evaluating 'the techniques with which [verbal art] organizes linguistic and cultural values to an aesthetic purpose' (Butt 2009: 369). That is, analysis can reveal how verbal art strikes the community chord through symbolic articulation, which is essentially 'experiments in textual organization or semantic design' (Butt 1996: 86) thus making it possible for linguistic choices to transcend their everyday uses to become a work of art with a recognizable message (or theme). Future work on analysing verbal art from a range of authors drawing on the resources of a specific language can open up new vistas in the potential ways of meaning of that language and at the same time widen our understanding of the relationship between verbal art, language and the complex composition of a speech community.

12.2.3 Verbal art and its themes

It is generally asserted that through studying literature we learn more about who we are as human beings: what preoccupies us, how beauty, for instance, is linguistically construed and understood. It gives us access to the parameters of the world as different cultures construct them because language itself is a mirror on society – its varieties are symbolic expressions of social variation, 'created by society, and help[ing] to create society' (Halliday [1978] 2007: 255). Verbal art is both the most abstract and perhaps the most intimate of all the arts – abstract because the experience of our world is resemioticized into language to be experienced again through language, and most intimate because language is a part of who we are as humans. As the author Toni Morrison (1993) says: 'We die. That may be the meaning of life. But we do language. That may be the measure of our lives'. We are born to communicate, to socialize, to discourse, to imagine and to share those imaginations. Verbal art is the medium through which we can share in a way that our sharing touches the hearts of those with whom the sharing is done. Although John Adams suggests that poetry is a part of the liberalized life, and the prerogative of those no longer needing to fight for life's necessities, there is plenty of evidence that such fights themselves motivate the sharing of experience through verbal art. Thus, verbal art is a necessary part of the human existence, as is evident across the spectrum of human existence, beliefs, and walks of life. Take for example King David's *Psalms*, the tragedies of Aeschylus, Chaucer's tales, Shakespeare's comedies, Wilfred Owens' war poetry, Hitler's youth poems, Mao Zedong's poetry, or Agota Kristof's provocative trilogy.

Hasan has demonstrated that literature 'does' something different with language than with other language activities which may appear to function in the ways that we have mentioned. She has demonstrated that 'language IN literature' is doubly articulated such that it configures to reveal a 'theme' – 'the deepest level of meaning' and 'what a text is about when dissociated from the particularities of that text' (Hasan 1985: 97). It is the theme that points directly to the role of verbal art in society: 'the theme of verbal art is very close to a generalization, which can be viewed as a hypothesis about some aspect of the life of social man' (Hasan 1985: 97). Butt enhances this definition by saying that 'verbal art is the central problem-solving activity in [a] culture, [and] that its function is to address the culture's deep difficulties' (Butt 1996: 86).

While both Maggie and the Professor identified Bishop's theme in 'One Art' as concerned with coping with loss, a general human experience, writers themselves are aware of the function of tackling 'difficulties' through their art. Take for instance, Günter Grass's comment during his Nobel Prize lecture:

> books can cause offence, stir up fury, even hatred ... writers should consider the condition of permanent controversiality to be invigorating, part of the risk involved in choosing the profession ... nothing is sacred to them, not even capitalism, and that makes them offensive, even criminal. But worst of all they refuse to make common cause with the victors of history: they take pleasure milling about the fringes of the historical process with the losers, who have plenty to say but no platform to say it on. By giving them a voice, they call the victory into question, by associating with them, they join ranks with them. (Grass 1999)

There is much scope for comparing and contrasting the ways in which humans convey, teach, announce, test and challenge cultural significances and trivialities. That is, given that verbal art is one of the ways that humans do this, how does it compare and/or contrast with other ways in both the themes it takes up and the means with which it does so? Research into verbal art within the SFL framework has really only scraped the surface of our understanding of which 'difficulties' verbal art tackles, why and how it tackles those and not others, and what this tells us about the role of verbal art in society.

12.3. Theory, models, corpora and tools

12.3.1 Verbal art and language variation

Hasan maintains that variation 'is a central concept in linguistics ... [b]ecause it is one point in the study of language where you can see how certain aspects of culture actively enter into the process of language, perchance making their way to the system' (Butt and Liang 2016: 389). Butt remarks that 'variation is the dominant experience, the deepest principle of consistency in our evolving, systemic potential' (Butt 2009: 391), and with specific reference to verbal art he says 'stylistics has always focused on variation – the problem of how the morphologically similar can have a contrastive "valeur" (de Saussure 1974 [1915]) in its means, and how the apparently contrastive can take on a similar valeur' (Butt 2009: 390).

Varieties of language are called registers in SFL, and verbal art as a whole can be considered a register. However, Hasan has demonstrated that there is something different about verbal art and its subregisters from other registers in that while verbal art utilizes the same resource, language, it does so in a different way. Nevertheless, in order to understand the specific nature of verbal art, analysis begins at the same place as with all other language varieties: the study of the language of the text using a set of descriptive categories such as clause complexing, Transitivity choices, cohesive ties and lexical choice, and as in any kind of discourse analysis, one looks for patterns of features. But the patterns that are found 'are not the prerogative of literature' (Hasan 1985: 92). This is evident in work utilizing Hasan's methodology as in this present volume, and is shared by other scholars working within literary criticism outside the framework of SFL (e.g. Kusch 2016). That is, the linguistic method of analysing literature, is a means of relying not on 'an individual's sensibility, but of a maximally explicit and therefore replicable, methodology', one which relies on conventional discourse analytical tools and methodologies (Lukin and Webster 2005: 419; cf. Kusch 2016: 6).

Once the initial analysis has been conducted, however, Hasan's framework and her methodology diverges from all other approaches to the analysis of literature. Hasan argues that limiting the study of literary style to counting the frequency of certain features or accounting for variation in literary form with variation in context are unhelpful in highlighting the nature of verbal art because verbal art is characterized by two planes of operation or 'orders of meaning'. That is, the study of the linguistic features of a literary text, its 'verbalization', must be complemented by an investigation of two other levels of meaning: 'theme' and 'symbolic articulation'. Symbolic articulation is an interface in that it is the means whereby the 'ordinary' (for want of a better term) meanings of language are re-semioticized to shape an 'artistic' message. It is interesting to note that Hasan claims that 'the need for this stratum is recognized in most schools of literary criticism' (Hasan 1985: 98), and yet it is her work that has advanced a replicable way of modelling this level of meaning and relating it to the artistry of verbal art.

Symbolic articulation involves a certain backgrounded patterning of the language of the text and a foregrounding – a means of making salient through contrast what is backgrounded (cf. Halliday [1971] 2002, [1982] 2002, [1987] 2002). She argues that:

> the stratum of symbolic articulation is where the meanings of language are turned into signs having a deeper meaning. Foregrounding and patterning of patterns play an important role in ascribing the second order meanings to the patterns of the first order meanings; and in doing this, they provide a principle for discriminating between the crucial and the incidental. (Hasan 1985: 98)

The development and explication of the concept of foregrounding is a key outcome of the application of Hasan's framework. This is evident in her own work and that of others, including many of the chapters in this volume (e.g. Tilney and Tuckwell this volume). Foregrounding, as we have seen applies to elements that are highlighted, and highlighting is done through contrast (see e.g. Hasan 1985: 33). I do not need to go into detail about this here, as the chapters within this volume do that adequately, and a reading of Hasan's own explanations and demonstrations of this are clear and readily accessible (e.g. 1985). But developments in Hasan's ideas of foregrounding suggest interesting avenues for further research. For instance, with regard to variation in language and in verbal art, Butt's proposal of 'latent patterning' is an argument for and a means towards 'understanding the latent patterns of our habitual behaviours' (Butt 2009: 391). Further investigations into foregrounding and latent patterning and variations in their manifestation and meaning are important for understanding the way in which language is put to use in different forms of verbal art.

Relevant to this discussion is that a key feature of an SFL approach to studying language is that the investigative findings should also play a role in 'developing and/or contributing to [the] theory of language' (Mahboob and Knight 2010: 3). Thus, given that the insights gained through analyses of verbal art demonstrate the way in which language 'becomes' art, what and how does this contribute to our theory of language? Miller observes that 'symbolic articulation makes the theme accessible to us – *just as*, in the semiotic system of language, the lexicogrammar makes the semantics, i.e. the stratum "above" it, accessible to us' (Miller 2016a: 65). So how can we further our understandings and explanations of the place of the 'art' of verbal art in relation to other theoretical concepts and features? That is, how does 'theme', 'symbolic articulation', 'semantic drift' (e.g. Butt 1983, Caffarel-Cayron this volume), and 'latent patterning' (e.g. Butt 1988: 2016) relate to context of situation, realization, register, text structure, and/or texture? What more do we learn about the potentialities of configurations of linguistic choices in relation to context? In this regard, take for example, Butt's (2009) finding that changes in clause complexing play a role in the generic phases of Ee Tiang Hong's poetry, or Caffarel-Cayron's (this volume) analysis of how changes in de Beauvoir's Transitivity choices over time reflect changes in her (de Beauvoir's) own relationship with literature, or Li's (this volume) description of Austen's strategic use of clause complexing in *Northanger Abbey* to differentiate narrative voice from character voices in dialogue and what this means within the greater context in which Austen was writing. There appears to be much scope for the development of the theoretical description and model of language through a consideration of these questions.

12.3.2.   Corpora and verbal art

One of the most significant advances in understanding discourse in recent years has been the development of a means of storing and retrieving large corpora of language. This is because corpora provide a means of standing at a far enough distance to see patterns that were not visible from close quarters. In Roald Dahl's story 'The Great Automatic Grammatizator' Adolf Knipe is 'struck by a powerful but simple little truth'. He notices, after studying a corpus of magazines, the rule-governed nature of English grammar and the consistency in types of stories correlating with types of magazines. Knipe's observation reminds us that an examination of a corpus of literature can highlight 'orderliness' of language in use in literature (cf. Hasan [1992] 2009: 309). However, 'a large corpus of discourses occurring in different types of social contexts' can also reveal the variability of language and how variation responds to 'meeting speakers' communicative needs' (Hasan 2009: 17). How might a corpus linguistic approach be of use within the study of verbal art?

Butt's (2016) study of *Troilus and Cressida* uses concordance tools to investigate certain key words in the play and to compare these key words with other works by Shakespeare in order to build a picture of the logogenesis of the play – and not simply build a picture, but to show how lexical strings and their interactions 'multiply at a rate not easily tracked by a listener or reader' (p. 34). He demonstrates how these interactions play a role in Shakespeare's verbal artistry, his specific symbolic articulation of patterns of language to realize a theme.

Miller (2016b), too, applies a corpus linguistics approach. This time to the study of Shakespeare's *Coriolanus*, and specifically to an appraisal analysis of occurrences of the word 'noble' in the play. However, while she finds the corpus concordance of 'noble' useful in that it 'flags candidates for manual probing', it 'does not provide sufficient co-text' including those participants being appraised as noble or as appraising others. Further, because automated corpus analysis does not deal with full clauses or semantic analyses, it is useful only for 'word patterns and low-ranking lexicogrammatical patterns' (Miller 2016b: 212). These latter features are useful at a preliminary level of analysis in verbal art, but cannot provide usable details on 'the mechanisms symbolically articulating the theme' of a text (Miller 2016b: 225).

In both of these studies, corpus tools are used to assist an analysis of the text, particularly in the initial stages of the analytical process, but they cannot, as Adolf Knipe's computer does in Dahl's story, do a complete analysis such that one could feed grammatical information, plot, and other details into a computer and the computer would then produce stories *en masse*. Aside from this being somewhat of a science fiction at this point in time, it needs to be remembered that the difficulty also lies in the fact that 'the patterns of a verbal artefact … create a "chemistry", the nature of which cannot be stated within the limits of any one set of choices' (Hasan 1985: 47). In both Miller's and Butt's analyses, a manual analysis of grammatical choices was needed to investigate the aesthetic or higher stratum of meaning of each work.

Nevertheless, there seems ample scope for putting corpus tools to much greater use in the study of verbal art. For instance, the UAM corpus annotation tool (see www.corpustool.com) offers a number of possibilities for opening up the study of larger corpora of verbal art as it can annotate texts in terms of noun phrases, clauses and sentences, and can search for specific instances of grammatical or lexical features, thus providing an opportunity for comparison across different texts. These would go a long way in assisting in the identification of patterns and patternings of patterns. With advances in technology, corpus studies in verbal art could shed much light on things such as the 'preoccupation' or 'the "thesis" which integrates the majority of the themes of individual artifacts in the body of an author's work' (Butt 1984: 49). Tuckwell (this volume), in her analysis of Auden's sonnet 'Who's who', suggests a future corpus study when she states that her analysis 'may serve as the beginning of a series of analyses or sonnets' with a view to uncovering what, other than the '14 line' typicality, may characterize the nature of sonnets. This points to the value of a corpus approach in categorizing different subregisters of verbal art thus increasing our description and understanding of the potential for human artistic expression. A corpus approach could also provide an insight into the specific techniques deployed across an artist's ouvre in the service of making the realizational link between theme and verbalization.

Other questions which could be investigated through corpus approaches might include: If variation is found across an author's oeuvre, where and to what end is that variation put? Is it idiosyncratic or significant, and how do we know? In what ways do the themes and linguistic strategies deployed by authors within a specific cultural domain compare or contrast, and how do those comparisons lead to a deeper understanding of each artist's 'take' on the society in which they each operate? The groundwork for investigating such questions has already been laid, but the territory offered in terms of mass data is still waiting to be explored. Ultimately, a large corpus of different instances of verbal art from different cultural and linguistic contexts, could provide a means of better understanding how language is deployed across the social contexts of verbal art.

12.3.4.   Visualization

Related to the need for further advances in technology associated with analysing large corpora is the possibility of visualizing the linguistic characteristics of verbal art. Zappavigna explains that techniques of text visualization allow viewers to be presented with a synoptic view of a text but at the same time 'preserve a dynamic view of logogenesis' (2011: 216). However, text visualization is characterized by techniques which focus on lexical features rather than clause-based or semantic features, indicating a direct link between the model of language informing the development of the technology and the kind of information that the techniques are able to convey. Zappavigna notes that 'to date, visualization techniques have not been used to explore meaning beyond the clause in all its prosodic complexity' (2011: 216) as a robust SFL analysis would do. It is such complexity that is at the heart of verbal art; the 'chemistry' of verbal art goes beyond words and combinations of words (Hasan 1985: 47).

Nevertheless, there seems to be considerable scope for utilizing and developing the current visualization techniques. For instance, Zappavigna demonstrates how 'streamgraphs' can be used to visualize the tracking of multiple features of a text and can represent the 'weighting' of certain features across an unfolding text. She notes that streamgraphs have been used to visualize the 'salience of particular characters' in Mark Twain's *Tom Sawyer* (Zappavigna 2011: 222). Another form of visualization is a 'text arc'. These are useful in visualizing repetitions across unfolding texts. Certainly, for simple rhyming texts, these kinds of visualizations would be readily applicable. 'Animated networks' present three dimensional interconnected systems. One such visualization system is called 'Valence'. This system uses frequency of lexical adjacency and 'affords a way for the user to move around inside the text and explore relationships between words' (Zappavigna 2011: 226). Such systems are useful for visualizing more complex texts wherein changes and variations within a text 'have repercussions throughout the system' (Zappavigna 2011: 223). Zappavigna suggests that 'a logical extension' could be developing a system that handles annotated data which specifies 'different kinds of relationships between annotation series' (2011: 224). Zappavigna is positive in her evaluation of the future of visualization and suggests that a future direction could be to develop visualization techniques in conjunction with annotation tools such as the UAM CorpusTool (e.g. O'Donnell 2008) and SysAM (Matthiessen and Wu 2001).

Visualization systems would seem to be particularly useful for verbal art to highlight foregrounding and latent patterning. Since 'foregrounding is a device by which the attention of the reader is directed to the organisation of the various strands of meaning in the text' (Hasan 1985: 95), visualization could be a means of representing this, and of comparing and contrasting foregrounding across the whole text and across different parts of a text. As for latent patterning, it seems possible that visualization could one day provide a means of representing this, however, in both cases, developing the appropriate input features would need to go hand in hand with the type of visualization technique utilized, and that would mean an SFL-informed development of such technology.

12.3.5.   Tools for a reasoned debate of appreciation

On realizing that many discussions of artworks such as painting and sculpture revolve around information and details from outside the work itself, O'Toole (2011) argued for and proposed a shared language for talking about visual art. The study of verbal art too needs 'collective rules and assumptions and a shared vocabulary to describe literary effects' (Kusch 2016: 6). The development of a way of talking about verbal art is one of the areas in which Hasan's framework has made great strides. This is due to Hasan's insistence on not relying on 'isolated patterns of language' to describe literature, but on explaining 'why we pull out the patterning of patterns as significant in literature, while ignoring its occurrences elsewhere' (Hasan 1985: 94). The overall approach has been to investigate 'language **in** literature' rather than the language **of** literature, the former of which Hasan explains is looking at how language 'functions' in literature (Hasan 1985: 94). That is, grammatical features such as tense and Transitivity choices, lexical cohesion, sound play such as alliteration, and other features such as grammatical parallelism do not have artistic value in and of themselves; it is how they function in verbal art (cf. Hasan 1985: 94). Butt confirms this view when he says

> in verbal art we are dealing with 'language all the way' – it is not realistic to abstract, as some critics have, an artistic or aesthetic system

as 'parasitic' on language. Verbal art is a form of language that needs explanation in terms of system and function just as any other use of text requires a representation in the interpretation of culture. (Butt 2007: 26)

This approach has led to 'a strong distinction between "explication de texte" and stylistic analysis' placing the focus on the linguistic evidence for claims about the nature and function of verbal art (Butt 2016: 30).

While there have been advances in demonstrating the importance of a rigorous linguistic analysis of literature and proposing a vocabulary and techniques for investigating this language, there is still a long way to go in developing a shared vocabulary to describe literary 'effects'. At present, the kinds of categories of literary effects that we have are very general in nature. We can make an analogy here between other categories and concepts in SFL theory. For instance, we know that all contexts of situation have a Field, a Tenor, and a Mode. But simply saying a context has a Field, Tenor and Mode, does not give any useful details about the context itself and how it might compare or contrast with other contexts. Likewise, claiming that each instance of verbal art has a theme is hardly saying anything at all. It is far too general. Further, identifying the theme of a specific piece of verbal art while interesting in and of itself, is too locally-focused. Future studies in verbal art could explore the various categories of theme, and the basis for developing those categories. For instance, are there specific linguistic strategies (symbolic articulations) typically associated with certain types of theme in certain social contexts? The same could be said for such strategies as 'latent patterning' or 'semantic drift'. Can we categorize 'types' of latent patterning, or 'types' of semantic drift? To do so, could go a long way in developing a description of the different ways in which language functions in verbal art, and would provide a fuller description of the strategies deployed in the creation of language as art. It would also provide the basis for 'contribut[ing] to a reasoned debate – something that has often been difficult to achieve with traditional literary criticism because of its many hidden assumptions' (Hasan 1985: 91).

12.4. Verbal art and pedagogy

12.4.1. The potential to be a verbal artist

In her Nobel Prize lecture, author Doris Lessing (2007) said: 'The story-teller is deep inside every one of us. The story-maker is always with us … it is our imaginations which shape us, keep us, create us – for good and for ill'. If it is true that there is a 'storyteller deep inside every one of us' why is it that relatively few people 'become' storytellers, novelists, poets, raconteurs? Does one's environment effect one's chances of becoming a great novelist? For example, does a great (i.e. a culturally valued) writer only emerge from a background such as that of Grazia Deledda: a 'family [which] nurtured a love of nature as well as a love of literature and storytelling' (*Grazia Deledda: Voice of Sardinia*)? Does a writer require a significant other to influence and bring out the storyteller – perhaps like Toni Morrison whose father's stories 'became an element in her own writing' (*Toni Morrison – Facts*)?

Hasan has commented that 'the potential for creativity and imagination is a part of the child's nature' (Hasan 1985: 2). In the child's development of language, Halliday has hypothesized that the imaginative function (perhaps the function most associated with verbal art) is the last function that a child develops. Verbal art comes in many forms and is found across divergent social and cultural contexts. When it comes to storytelling, there are, as Hasan (1985: 91) observes, some who 'kill' a story and others who can tell it effectively, in an entertaining manner, and in a way that inspires or conjures a vivid imagery and a sense of delight in the wording. As she explains, the difference is in 'the way that the story is "discoursed"' (Hasan 1985: 91). Much has been made of the relationship between spoken storytelling and written stories and the importance of interactive/joint reading in the home to future reading and learning abilities (e.g. Durkin 1966; Rose 2011: 205). Williams (1999) points out, though, that differences deriving from social background in how this activity is conducted can have pedagogical consequences once a child enters school, and in any case, not all families have storytelling and joint reading activities in the home. So the question arises, do certain social contexts inhibit the development of future verbal artists, or, perhaps, do specific verbal artists emerge from certain social situations and not others?

Bernstein's (1971) sociological research found that the written and spoken language of children from working class families differs from that of children from middle class families in terms of the degree of explicit verbalization. Since it is the manipulation of language itself that is a key to verbal art, do the processes of 'verbal elaboration' linked with social background play a role in the development of specific kinds of verbal artists? That is, if some children are encouraged or surrounded by those whose typical discourse patterns involve 'verbal elaboration of subjective intent [and a] sensitivity to the implications of separateness and difference' (Bernstein 1971: 61), do such children feel more at ease in expressing their observations of life through socially valued forms of poetry and literature? This raises the question: does the creation of verbal art manifest differently and is it differentially distributed across social groups?

Across society verbal art takes various forms and each is valued differently. That is, descriptions of verbal art range from that which is considered low-brow, high-brow or no-brow (cf. Swirski 2005; Swirski and Vanhanen 2017) – such descriptions themselves being social evaluations. Across the spectrum verbal art includes limericks, bawdy jokes and storytelling, puns, poetry, short stories and novels (of various kinds). Nevertheless, each of these involves 'verbal risk taking' and specific forms of 'verbalization'. Thus, if verbal art is a necessary social activity within a society, as we have already established, a possible research direction could be the investigation of which types of verbal art arise predominantly in one social group and not another, and which types are found across different social groups, and why this may be so. Such investigations could provide insights into the relationship between verbal art, social codes and socialization, and these insights could be valuable for a variety of pedagogical purposes and contexts.

12.4.2.   Learning verbal artistry

How much time is spent in verbal art pursuits in comparison with other artistic pursuits in a child's early years both before and after they enter formal educational institutions? In elementary schooling much time is spent finger painting, model making, playing physical games, and singing. Do language-based games figure as prominently? A hallmark of verbal art is the focus on the language itself, and a child's involvement in word play and nursery rhymes 'exposes the child to the pleasures of patterning in language' and works to prime a child for verbal art (Hasan 1985: 2). Hasan claims that a child who expresses delight on hearing a rhyme such as 'To market, to market, to buy a fat pig, Home again, home again, jiggety jig' 'is probably receiving an early lesson in the appreciation of verbal art' (Hasan 1985: 2). While appreciation of verbal art does not necessarily metamorphose into an ability to create verbal art, there remains the question of which children may enter school more likely 'primed' for engaging in and creating socially valued types of verbal art, particularly the written forms.

Part of the problem with teaching verbal art lies in the understanding of what verbal art is. Hasan's analytical framework has demonstrated where the 'artistry', or 'creativity' of verbal art lies, but there are still those who credit the artistry of verbal art as something outside the language of the text itself. This attitude often flows through to classrooms wherein children are asked to 'write creatively', but given little instruction in terms of the nature of what it is they are asked to write. Gilbert notes the following:

> Many students never progress beyond a basic competence with subject-verb agreement and spelling and punctuation conventions; they

> never progress to an understanding of the conventions of literary narratives. And some of this failure to master the conventions of literary 'authorship' must lie in the mistaken belief that writing is not craft but imagination; not construction but creation. (Gilbert 1990: 76)

With regard to teaching written forms of language, including creative narratives, which would fall within the realm of verbal art, of note within SFL research is genre pedagogy (e.g. Christie 2012; Martin 1986, 1993). Genre pedagogy has primarily aimed at developing a form of interventionist pedagogy in order to demystify writing for children at school and to provide all children with the tools to succeed in the kinds of writing tasks they are likely to encounter throughout their education. In the early stages of research into the genre approach to writing, researchers found that teachers often asked children to 'write a story' no matter what the actual genre required, and a common form of writing that was encouraged was narrative, or storytelling (Martin 1984). However, as children progressed through the school system, other kinds of writing, such as reports and expositions were in higher demand and valued more in the subject fields. The genre approach emphasizes the overall structure of a piece of writing (a genre), knowledge surrounding the type of genre itself, and typical grammar forms associated with different stages of the genre. However, while genre pedagogy has gone a long way in developing an understanding of the differences between, say, a 'report' and a 'narrative', it does not adequately deal with the nature of verbal 'artistry'.

Hasan demonstrates through her analytical framework that language patterning and symbolic articulation underlie the artistry of verbal art, but it is in her work on *literacy* pedagogies that the key to teaching the artistry of verbal art may lie. That is, simply teaching the recognition of certain forms of verbal art and teaching generic features such as the 14 lines of a sonnet, or the staging of a narrative in the hope of creating future verbal artists would miss the point of what verbal art is. Such approaches are examples of 'recognition literacy' and 'action literacy' respectively (see Hasan [1996] 2011 and Lukin this volume). Both forms of literacy are naturally of great importance to children's educational success, but perhaps, in teaching verbal art, a kind of 'reflection literacy' is needed. Reflection literacy, according to Hasan is a type of pedagogy through which students produce, not simply *re*produce, knowledge. It is a means through which pupils learn to not simply accept the knowledge passed down to them, but to question it and to produce new knowledge (Hasan [1996] 2011: 193). Günter Grass's claim that 'writers should consider the condition of permanent controversiality to be invigorating, part of the risk involved in choosing the profession', points to the verbal artist's role in the production of such 'new' knowledge.

While the focus in verbal art is on the language, the language itself is symbolically articulating a deeper issue, or social theme. The question is, if analysing, unpacking and explaining the theme of a verbal artefact is possible, is it also possible to teach how to artistically create a theme? Perhaps we need a reflection verbal art pedagogy (RVAP) which would involve teaching children to produce novel 'experiments in textual organization or semantic design' (Butt 1996: 86), and new ways of artistically addressing a society's 'deep difficulties' (Butt 1996: 86; cf. Hasan [1996] 2011: 198). Important to RVAP would be children's exposure to and engagement in different forms of verbal art suited to different levels of educational advancement. Along with this would be an appropriately pitched means of leading children through to an understanding of the place of verbal art in society, the employment of an empowering model of language, and of instruction in the ways in which 'society's difficulties', including their own, can be artistically-linguistically articulated (cf. Hasan 1986: 26). In addition to these general pedagogical aims, a RVAP would also include a sensitivity to the kinds of socialization processes pupils have experienced (as mentioned in the previous section) since certain socialization processes predispose children to taking individualized verbal 'risks'. As with reflection literacy, so with RVAP: 'what is specifically relevant to reflection literacy is semantic orientation … since it is speakers' orientation to meaning, their ideological stance that underlies their disposition to make enquiries, analyses and challenges of one kind or another' (Hasan [1996] 2011: 198). There are rich opportunities for investigating any number of questions that arise from a consideration of these issues relevant to teaching and learning verbal art.

12.4.3 Pedagogy and writing about literature: Literary criticism and verbal art

McGee (2001) says:

> Often, students are intimidated when it comes to writing about literature because they feel that they do not know enough about literature to write about it or that the author is surely hiding some meaning in the text that they just can't find. It is important, though, to keep in mind that readers are integral to making meaning with literary texts. Readers complete the writer's work, bringing their own life experiences and ideas to it to make meaning. (p. 3)

McGee offers several suggestions for 'reading' and 'responding' to (writing critically about) a piece of literature, including a set of terms like plot, character, personification, setting and symbolism, and a set of sample questions such as 'Why does the narrator and not one of the characters tell the story?',

'In what way does the title give clues to the meaning of the story?', 'How does your culture feel about …?' (2001: 10). While such questions assist students in understanding the meaning of a piece of literature, can they lead to an objective evaluation of a piece of literature and an understanding of its artistry? Butt references Hasan as saying: 'If we are to claim a teacher's role with respect to literature and verbal art, we need to be able to address the central claim of the activity: namely, "wherein lies the artistry"?' (Butt 2016: 50). The gateway to the artistry, as has already been established, is the language. But it is a particular view of language that is needed to guide students to a deep appreciation of verbal art. Hasan says:

> the specialist domain that enables us to acquire knowledge about language is linguistics; without linguistics, the study of literature must remain a series of personal preferences, no matter how much the posture of objectivity is adopted: being objective implies knowing the nature of that which one is being objective about. An understanding of the nature of language, of how the system works, is essential and it is not a natural by-product of knowing how to use language. … Understanding about language has consequences for understanding the meanings of the work of literature. (Hasan 1985: 104)

This implies that any pedagogical approach to literary criticism must incorporate a study of linguistics, and specifically a theory of language that is adequate for analysing verbal art.

Butt (this volume) sets out an agenda for being 'better informed' about verbal art and its place within society from a linguistic point of view. Being better informed means that both teachers and students better appreciate the 'artistry of verbal art'. Objective, replicable analyses of verbal art require an approach which is scientific in its methodology: a method based on observation of the language itself, and an approach which 'respects the decisions the artist has made' without evaluating those decisions on the basis of any cultural or social bias (cf. Butt this volume). In her early years teaching English language and literature in Pakistan, Hasan wanted to enable her students 'to produce their own reasoned analysis of a literary work; [in order to] to free themselves from simply following renowned critics, whose unquestioned reputation for taste rendered their literary taste unquestionable' (Hasan 2011: xv). Butt relates how Hasan encouraged her students and colleagues to dispense with teaching literature 'through the hegemonies of taste', and 'to be methodical about semiotic and semantic differences: examine the cultural parameters and grammatical systems through which a work is interpreted, as well as those in which it may have been constructed' (Butt 2016: 50). In order to fulfil this kind of pedagogy, there is a need for a SF approach to make greater inroads into the broader field of literature education and of literary criticism in general. It is important for scholars to highlight the value of the SF model of language and demonstrate the utility of SF tools for conducting objective, replicable linguistic analyses of verbal art of all kinds. It is important for a wider audience of literary critics and educators to see how SF tools can be used to reveal that the artistry of verbal art is linguistically-based, not something that derives from outside the text itself. And it is important to show the kind of linguistic analyses that can access this artistry. Furthermore, such analyses can highlight the difference between verbal art and the study and evaluation of literary texts (Hasan 1985: 101) – literary texts being those in which the patterning of patterns are not 'utilized for a second order semiosis, resulting in metaphorisation' (Hasan 1985: 101). Ultimately, SFL theory can provide a basis for developing a common language for appreciating verbal art not tied to cultural biases and tastes. Hasan has pointed this out on a number of occasions (e.g. Hasan 2007), but there remains much scope for developing a pedagogy which places this issue at its core.

12.5.   Hasan's verbal art framework and other theories and approaches

There have been various attempts to incorporate into Hasan's work other approaches and ideas. Miller (e.g. 2007, 2016a) for example argues for accepting Jakobson's idea of grammatical parallelism, and specifically his 'pervasive parallelism' into Hasan's framework, because Jakobson is not simply identifying grammatical patterns per se, but those patterns which are exploited to bring about a certain 'meaning'. She demonstrates that Jakobson's grammatical parallelism can be 'likened to … Hasan's patterning of patterns … the motivated consistency of semantic direction for the symbolic articulation of verbal art' (Miller 2016a: 67).

One of the more recent analytical approaches to take hold in SFL research is the application of Martin and White's (2005) appraisal framework. Miller (2016b) incorporates this framework into her corpus study of the use of 'noble' in *Coriolanus*. Although Miller's study focuses more on the usefulness of corpus linguistic methodology rather than the relationship between the appraisal system and Hasan's verbal art framework, her study does bring the possibility of a useful engagement of these two frameworks to light. Perhaps future investigations could cover questions such as: how is evaluation manifest in verbal art? What is the focus of the evaluation? Does evaluation play a role in foregrounding, and how and why might it do so? What is the relationship between the deployment of appraisal resources and the symbolic articulation of theme in an instance of verbal art? That is, how do appraisal resources contribute to the second order linguistic patterns which transform 'the first order meaning into the inferred theme, by the working of patterns of foregrounding' (Hasan 2007: 33). Further engagement with the appraisal framework could yield interesting insights into the role of evaluation in foregrounding, in the construal of theme, and of the role of evaluative resources deployed in different forms of verbal art.

While symbolic articulation itself is a means of 'metaphorization' (Hasan 1985: 101), Lothmann (this volume) considers the place of conceptual metaphors in Hasan's verbal art framework. He demonstrates that metaphor is a contributor to the artistry of a text and suggests that future research could highlight the complementariness of Hasan's framework and cognitive approaches to discourse. Future work could indeed clarify and test such claims.

While Wegener and Lothmann (this volume) also raise the possibility of including an account of conceptual metaphors in foregrounding, their study attempts to make several interesting connections – both theoretical and methodological – between other ideas and Hasan's model of verbal art. For instance, using Mendlesohn's (2008) categories of the way language transitions into a fantasy world in fantasy-based literature they consider the possible impact these transitions have in the context of reception of a fantasy novel through utilizing the technology of eye tracking. They add support to their eye tracking findings through interviews with their subject-readers finding that there is 'a significant difference in fixation duration between "normal" fictional and fantasy fictional world' in a novel. Technology associated with corpus annotation and visualization in the context of verbal art studies has already been mentioned (cf. Section 12.6.2 this chapter), but advances in eye tracking technology would seem to hold interesting opportunities for considering the context of reception of verbal art, some of which Wegener and Lothmann mention in their chapter.

In the previous section Bernstein's social codes were mentioned in relation to verbal art and pedagogy, but there have been some interesting applications of Bernstein's ideas in relation to the analysis and interpretation of verbal art. For instance, Li (this volume) frames her discussion and interpretation of narrative voice and character voice by appealing to which of these manifest the properties of a restricted or an elaborated code. In a similar vein, Lukin and Pagano (2016) use the concept of Bernstein's coding orientation to discuss the ways in which Katherine Mansfield distinguishes between different characters in the story 'Bliss', such that 'the wording of the characters establishes their social positioning and preoccupations' (Lukin and Pagano 2016: 98). This is manifest in a kind of 'semantic drift'

– 'the ensemble effect of patterns of choices from a number of systems' (Butt and Lukin 2009: 198), and used in an implicit way to move the story along. Lukin and Pagano show how Mansfield deftly uses the features of essentially an elaborated code to mark off characters as belonging to the middle classes, making 'the style of middle class talk an object of scrutiny, and a thing of curiosity' (Lukin and Pagano 2016: 107) for the reader. Given the plethora of work in SFL utilizing the concept of coding orientation, or semantic orientation, the interpretation of different types of verbal art and different 'voices' expressed in verbal art suggests a very exciting and rich direction of future research. Future research could focus on interpreting characterization in terms of social positioning and semantic orientation and the role of these in foregrounding and in the kind of human experience and social difficulties that writers convey through verbal art.

Another area of engagement is in the comparison of verbal art with the language and thinking of science (e.g. Halliday [1987] 2002; [1990] 2002; Butt 2007; Halliday and Butt forthcoming). Halliday reveals 'science in poetry' in his study of Tennyson's 'In Memoriam' and 'poetry in science' in his study of Darwin's *The Origin of Species* (Lukin and Webster 2005; cf. Halliday [1987] 2002 and [1990] 2002). Butt argues that science and verbal art should be seen as complementary; both science and verbal art metaphorize and symbolically interpret and represent the world and 'draw upon – albeit in different ways – a pre-existing metaphoric architecture' established within their creative fields (Halliday and Butt forthcoming). They do this by 'com[ing] to terms with the complexity of language … a complexity in which things do not exist of themselves, but only as a function of the role played within the totality of other terms' (Butt 2007: 91). In both verbal art and 'verbal science' 'the habitual patterns of the conventional linguistic system are reworked to serve purposes at the limits (and beyond) of current collective understandings' (Halliday and Butt forthcoming). Both, according to Butt (2007), involve 'thought experiments'. Making the analogy between verbal art and science is both innovative and inspiring; innovative in that science and verbal art are rarely seen to be complementary and yet they each present their own metaphorization of human experience; and inspiring because this analogizing opens up possible future investigations into comparing verbal art with the way in which different disciplinary languages create their own 'take' on how to question, construct and interpret life and society.

12.6. Verbal art and translation

Like the study of verbal art, translation has often been approached with the idea that something outside language can inform the evaluation of a translated text. However, an intuitive approach to the study of translation results primarily in 'a subjective and arbitrary evaluation' (El-dali 2010, 34). Jakobson (1959/2004) and Catford (1965) are often cited as early advocates for linguistic theory to inform translation theory, and Catford is of particular importance for SFL scholars as his seminal work on the relationship between translation theory and linguistic theory was informed by Halliday and Firth (1965: 1). Taking the view that language can be described across several levels (although not quite the same as those expounded by Halliday), and that meaning is not found within a single level or is a feature separate from language, Catford expounded the concepts of translation shifts 'departures from formal correspondence in the process of going from the SL [source language] to the TL [target language]' (1965: 73) and translation equivalence proposing that '[a] central task of translation theory is that of defining the nature and conditions of translation equivalence' (1965: 21). With the benefit of the development of SFL theory, recent descriptions of the concepts of equivalence and shifts have been refined (e.g. Halliday 2010; Matthiessen 2001), and over the years, translation scholars have demonstrated the usefulness of SFL (or aspects of SFL) as an informing theory for the study of translation (e.g. Baker 2011; Hatim and Mason 1990; House 1997; Steiner 2004; Steiner and Yallop 2001). The focus of this section is on those studies which have specifically incorporated Hasan's ideas on verbal art to analysing translations of verbal art and the possible future directions that these studies suggest.

12.6.1.   Good translations?

Of importance in evaluating translations is defining what makes a 'good' translation, and the answer often revolves around the notion of 'equivalence'. But depending on one's theoretical approach, equivalence is defined very differently (cf. Halliday 2001; House 1997, 2001). Catford (1965), Halliday (1966, [2009] 2013) and Matthiessen (2001) (to name just a few), deal with this question using the SF model of language. For instance, Halliday explains that the theoretical dimensions of 'stratification', 'instantiation', 'rank', 'metafunction', 'delicacy', and 'axis' 'are critical to any comparison of two or more different languages; and hence to the process of translation, because they are the parameters that define equivalence (and therefore also non-equivalence, or shift)' (Halliday [2009] 2013: 109). Halliday (2001: 15) also observes that

> equivalence at different strata carries differential values; that in most cases the value that is placed on it goes up the higher the stratum –

semantic equivalence is valued more highly than lexicogrammatical, and contextual equivalence perhaps most highly of all; but that these relative values can always be varied, and in any given instance of translation one can reassess them in the light of the task.

Considering Hasan's model of verbal art, how might the concept of equivalence apply to translations of verbal art? In comparing an English translation of Dario's poem 'Caracol' with its original in Spanish, Lukin (2010) demonstrates that although the basic experience in Dario's poem is translated without issue, the deeper meaning of the poem, achieved through consistency of foregrounding of tense and voice in the original, is not achieved in the translated version. Lukin and Pagano (2012) are also concerned with what makes a good translation, but consider this at the level of context of situation. Their focus is on a sequence of talk by different characters at a dinner party in Mansfield's 'Bliss'. The talk is a display of different instances of middle-class 'elaborated code' (cf. Bernstein, 1971) wherein each move in the talk 'is about the presentation of the individual's individual preoccupations and sensibilities' (Lukin and Pagano 2012: 126). While the sort of dinner party Mansfield constructs is itself a cultural phenomenon, Lukin and Pagano explain that 'the complexity of the social situation becomes apparent' when the dinner party is backgrounded by an account of the context of situation and the context of culture (2012: 126). The language, in this case, is on display as representing social positioning, and 'social positioning is central to the theme of Mansfield's story' (126). They close their discussion with the question of how to translate this kind of 'semantic drift' from one language to another. That is, it is not about translating a dialect, or dialectically-marked passages from one source text to a target text, but translating a social code, a social positioning (in Bernstein's sense) that is symbolically articulated; 'code is not visible in the same way that dialect is since its variation is at the semantic stratum of language' (127). Given that verbal art is located within the SF multidimensional model of language, how are the symbolically articulated patternings of patterns translated? That is, how does one translate the organization of 'linguistic and cultural values' which have been put 'to an aesthetic purpose' (Butt 2009: 369)? These studies lay the groundwork for such ventures into translation and of determining what makes a good translation.

12.6.2.   Translation and the context of creation and context of reception

It is perhaps in the act of translation that the mutual indebtedness of culture and language come to the fore. The translation of verbal art from one language to another involves 'a complex process of *refraction* in a *mediated* interlingual, intercultural communicative transposition' (Aljahdali 2016: 82). Aljahdali's analysis of the Turkish, Arabic and English versions of *O Alquimista (The Alchemist)*, makes use of Hasan's concepts of the context of creation and context of reception, showing patterns of language that bridge the cultural and social divide between the original version of the book and the modern cultural contexts of the proposed readers, including the attempts by translators to incorporate into the internal narrative of the story features that best reflect the international bestseller context in which this novel is placed.

Butt (this volume) suggests that an analysis of linguistic patterning across different translations of a source text into one specific language can highlight the 'semantic consequences' of different linguistic choices. Future research could ask: How can analyses of translations contribute to a cross-cultural description of contexts of reception? How can they provide diachronic or synchronic descriptions of shifts or variations in world view within a specific society? For instance, consider the different English translations of the Bible, and specifically, the artistry of books (or passages) such as the Song of Songs, the Psalms, or Ecclesiastes. How do modern translations differ from earlier translations? What is there in the context of reception that certain translations are appealing or responding to (cf. Gregory 2001)? Are there shifts in the way the themes are symbolically articulated? How and for what purposes? Other related questions could include what insights into societal 'difficulties' and 'preoccupations' do we gain from the context of reception of translations across time periods or multiple translations within a short span of time? And how might these different translations provide insights into the translators' interpretations of the context of creation of the source text?

Although I have located the concepts of context of creation and context of reception in this section on translation, these two concepts are relevant across the study of verbal art. Wegener and Lothmann (this volume) for instance, consider the use of eye tracking technology and interviews as a way into understanding features of the context of reception of fantasy texts. Other technologies and technological considerations might also be of value in future studies of verbal art, such as the effect of digitizing texts, how internet platforms change the face of the context of creation and affect the resultant forms of verbal art, as well as the way in which the world-wide web opens up opportunities for access to all kinds of verbal art, thus changing and 'complexifying' the context of reception. There is also the issue of readily available translation software, such as Google Translate. How does such software manage the translation of verbal art, what effects do such translations have on the contexts of reception, and how can this kind of software be improved to take into account the second-order semiotic of symbolic articulation?

12.6.3.   Translation and the place of verbal art in society

I began my descriptive background for raising ideas or suggestions about the possible future directions of research into verbal art by focusing on the place of verbal art in society. It is fitting, then, to end with this topic in this section on translation as translation is the means whereby we can gain access to the ways in which verbal art is placed in different societies. Through the act of translation, we can discover what kind of knowledge and cultural values are conveyed, and how human experience is encapsulated and recorded in vastly different societies and languages. Translation can lead us to a better understanding of which themes one society picks up as significant, which social difficulties are worked out in different forms of verbal art, and how these themes and difficulties are symbolically articulated. The higher levels of the language system, the semantic level and the level of context, are where the greatest potential for equivalence lies (Matthiessen 2001: 75) – the metafunctions being universal, and language events typically construing a Tenor, a Mode, and a Field. This does not mean that there will always be equivalence, there will no doubt be translation shifts, either subtle or more pronounced depending on the languages qua cultures involved; shifts in terms of 'depth of detail' and in 'matching the degree of specificity' of contexts, for instance (Halliday [2009] 2013: 106). Halliday ([2009] 2013) has demonstrated interpersonal shifts in an English version of a Forward to a Chinese-English dictionary; Aljahdali's (2016) study shows that translations of *O Alquimista* differ in order to suit the contexts of reception of the novel; and Lukin's (2010) study of the translation of 'Caracol' exposes a shift in lexicogrammatical choices which has consequences for the construal of the theme of the poem. Locating equivalence and shifts across the various dimensions of language organization can highlight similarities and differences within instances of verbal art, and reveal more deeply how verbal art plays a role in the expression of these similarities and differences.

The translating of verbal art is perhaps the most fertile site for examining how and where (linguistically) the flux of human existence and human experience may converge. Hasan's model of verbal art with its level of symbolic articulation interfacing the levels of theme and verbalization, requires that any translation of verbal art must 'translate' the symbolic articulation in order for the artistry itself to be translated. After all, it is the symbolic articulation which is at the heart of the artistry of verbal art and through which verbal art is able to strike a chord with its readers. If the theme is constructed through a symbolic articulation of patterns of patternings, which patterns of patternings in the target text are most suited to constructing such a theme and to conveying and evoking the theme of the text to the target readers? Consider Halliday's comments regarding the translation of Japanese haiku and tanka into English ([2009] 2013: 118). We've possibly all experienced reading poetry from a different culture from our own and have either been left flat by it or have been drawn into a way of feeling that we perhaps had never experienced before. Hasan's approach can help get to the core of where and why a translation may fall flat, or at best may not quite hit the mark that the original version did (cf. Lukin 2010).

A consideration of future directions in the translation of verbal art should be extended to the teaching of translation techniques. When a translator understands the nature of the artistry in verbal art, their understanding of what is involved in translating this artistry can be refined, as can their understanding of where equivalence is best located for the translation of a specific piece of verbal art. The study of verbal art using the techniques proposed by Hasan can enrich the field of translation studies, and using translations as sites for investigating the linguistically construed aesthetic purposes can enrich our understanding of verbal art in general.

Final word

I hope that this chapter has demonstrated that much has been gained from previous work in verbal art utilizing the ideas proposed by Hasan, and that this work has set a fertile ground for future research into the nature of verbal art, its place in society, how it may be analysed, represented, critiqued, taught, learned, and translated. While there are no doubt many other issues and ideas that could have been included, I hope that the few ideas included in this chapter act as a springboard for identifying many other areas in which research into verbal art could move forward. Above all, it seems important to me that we must see verbal art as a necessary language activity in society, as part of the 'mix' of language variation and as an important contributor to the potentiality of the language system, and not as an optional extra open to study or creation by only a few. By engaging in a broader and more earnest way with verbal art we can be assured of gaining a rich and meaningful insight into this feature of culture and of who we are as human beings.

Note

*   I use the terms 'literature' and 'verbal art' interchangeably in this chapter.

Acknowledgements

- This chapter was supported by the Project of Humanities and Social Sciences, Ministry of Education, People's Republic of China (Grant no. 13YJAZH001).
- I wish to thank Dr Annabelle Lukin and Dr David Butt for comments on an early draft of this chapter. I alone am responsible for any short-comings in the chapter.

References

Akerejola, E. (2012). Multimodality in Òkó folktale discourse and its sociosemiotic purposes. In W. Bowcher (Ed.) *Multimodal Texts from Around the World: Cultural and Linguistic Insights*, 11–38. Basing-stoke: Palgrave Macmillan. https://doi.org/10.1057/9780230355347_2

Aljahdali, S. A. (2016). Narrative structure, context and translation in Paulo Coelho's O Alquimista in English, Arabic and Turkish. *Journal of World Languages* 3 (1): 79–97. https://doi.org/10.1080/21698252.2016.1224138

Baker, M. (1992). *In Other Words. A Coursebook on Translation*. London and New York: Routledge. https://doi.org/10.4324/9780203327579

BBC2 (1992). Before Babel. *BBCTWO Horizon Television Documentary*, Episode 12, UK.

Bernstein, B. (Ed.) (1971). *Class, Codes and Control: Theoretical Studies Towards a Sociology of Language*. Vol. 1. London: Routledge & Kegan Paul. https://doi.org/10.4324/9780203014035

Butt, D. G. (1983). Semantic 'Drift' in verbal art. *Australian Review of Applied Linguistics* 6 (1): 38–48. https://doi.org/10.1075/aral.6.1.04but

Butt, D. G. (1984). *To be without a description of to be: The relationship between theme and lexico-grammar in the poetry of Wallace Stevens*. Unpublished PhD thesis. Macquarie University, Australia.

Butt, D. G. (1988). Randomness, order and the latent patterning of text. In D. Birch and M. O'Toole (Eds) *Functions of Style*, 74–97. London: Pinter.

Butt, D. G. (1996). Literature, culture and the classroom: The aesthetic function in our information era. In J. James (Ed.) *The Language-Culture Connection*, 86–106. Singapore: SEAMEO.

Butt, D. G. (2007). Thought experiments in verbal art: Examples from Modernism. In D. R. Miller and M. Turci (Eds), *Language and Verbal*

Art Revisited: Linguistic Approaches to the Study of Literature, 68-96. London: Equinox.

Butt, D. G. (2009). Technique and empire in the poetry of Ee Tiang Hong. *World Englishes* 28 (3): 365–393. https://doi.org/10.1111/j.1467-971X.2009.01598.x

Butt, D. G. (2016). 'Construe my meaning': Performance, poetry and semiotic distance. In W. L. Bowcher and J. Y. Liang (Eds), *Society in Language, Language in Society: Essays in Honour of Ruqaiya Hasan*, 24–55. Basingstoke: Palgrave Macmillan. https://doi.org/10.1057/9781137402868_2

Butt, D. G., and Lukin A. (2009). Stylistic analysis: Construing aesthetic organization. In M. A. K. Halliday and J. J. Webster (Eds) *Continuum Companion to Systemic Functional Linguistics*, 190–215. London: Continuum.

Butt, D. G., and Liang, J. Y. (2016). In her own words. In W. L. Bowcher and J. Y. Liang (Eds) *Society in Language, Language in Society: Essays in Honour of Ruqaiya Hasan*, 381–411. Basingstoke: Palgrave Macmillan. https://doi.org/10.1057/9781137402868_16

Catford, J. C. (1965). *A Linguistic Theory of Translation. An Essay in Applied Linguistics*. Oxford: Oxford University Press.

Christie, F. (2012). *Language Education Throughout the School Years: A Functional Perspective*. Chichester: John Wiley & Sons.

de Saussure, F. (1915/1974). *Course in General Linguistics* (Trans. W. Baskin). London: Fontana Collins.

Durkin, D. (1966). *Children Who Read Early: Two Longitudinal Studies*. New York: Teachers College Press.

Eco, U. (1976). *A Theory of Semiotics*. Bloomington, IN: Indiana University Press. https://doi.org/10.1007/978-1-349-15849-2

El-dali, H. M. (2010). Towards an understanding of the distinctive nature of translation studies. *Journal of King Saud University – Languages and Translation* 23: 29–45.

Gilbert, P. (1990). Authorizing disadvantage: Authorship and creativity in the language classroom. In F. Christie (Ed.) *Literacy for a Changing World*, 54–78. Hawthorn, Vic.: ACER Press.

Grass, G. (1999). *To be Continued …* Nobel Lecture. http://www.nobelprize.org/nobel_prizes/literature/laureates/1999/lecture-e.html. Accessed 2 February 2017.

Grazia Deledda, Voice of Sardinia. Nobelprize.org. Nobel Media AB 2014. Accessed 15 Mar 2017. http://www.nobelprize.org/nobel_prizes/literature/laureates/1926/deledda-article.html

Gregory, M. (2001). What can linguistics learn from translation? In E.

Steiner and C. Yallop (Eds) *Exploring Translation and Multilingual Text Production: Beyond Content*, 19–40. Berlin: Mouton de Gruyter. https://doi.org/10.1515/9783110866193.19

Halliday, M. A. K. (1966). The comparison of languages. In A. McIntosh and M. A. K. Halliday (Eds) *Patterns of Language: Papers in General, Descriptive, and Applied Linguistics.* London: Longmans.

Halliday, M. A. K. (1971/2003). Linguistic function and literary style: An enquiry into the language of William Golding's `The Inheritors'. In S. Chatman (Ed.) *Literary Style: A Symposium.* London: Oxford University Press. Reprinted in J. J. Webster (Ed.) *Linguistic Studies of Text and Discourse. The Collected Works of M. A. K. Halliday, Vol. 2,* 88–125. London and New York: Continuum.

Halliday, M.A.K. (1978/2007). An interpretation of the functional relationship between language and social structure. In J. J. Webster (Ed.) *Language and Society. The Collected Works of M. A. K. Halliday, Vol. 10,* 251–263. London: Continuum.

Halliday, M. A. K. ([1982]2002). The de-automatization of grammar: From Priestley's 'An Inspector Calls'. In J. J. Webster (ed.) *Linguistic Studies of Text and Discourse; Volume 2 in the Collected Works of M.A.K. Halliday,* 126-148. London: Continuum.

Halliday, M. A. K. (1985). *Spoken and Written Language.* Geelong: Deakin University Press.

Halliday, M. A. K. (1987/2002). Poetry as scientific discourse: The nuclear sections of Tennyson's 'In Memoriam'. In J. J. Webster (Ed.) *Linguistic Studies of Text and Discourse. The Collected Works of M. A. K. Halliday, Vol. 2,* 149–168. London and New York: Continuum.

Halliday, M. A. K. (1993). The construction of knowledge and value in the grammar of scientific discourse: Charles Darwin's *The Origin of the Species.*" In M. A. K. Halliday and J. R. Martin (Eds) *Writing Science: Literacy and Discoursive Power,* 86–105. London: The Falmer Press. Reprinted in J. J. Webster (Ed.) *Linguistic Studies of Text and Discourse. The Collected Works of M. A. K. Halliday, Vol. 2,* 168–192. London and New York: Continuum.

Halliday, M. A. K. (1993). Towards a language-based theory of learning. *Linguistics and Education* 5 (2): 93–116. https://doi.org/10.1016/0898-5898(93)90026-7

Halliday, M. A. K. (2003). Introduction: On the 'architecture' of human language. In J. J. Webster (Ed.) *On Language and Linguistics. The Collected Works of M. A. K. Halliday, Vol. 3,* 1–29. London: Continuum.

Halliday, M. A. K. (2009/2013). The Gloosy Ganoderm: Systemic functional linguistics and translation. In J. J. Webster (Ed.) *Halliday in* the 21st Century. *The Collected Works of M. A. K. Halliday, Vol. 11,* 105–125. London: Bloomsbury Academic.

Halliday, M. A. K. (2010). Pinpointing the choice: Meaning and the search for equivalents in a translated text. In A. Mahboob and N. K. Knight (Eds) *Appliable Linguistics,* 13–24. London: Continuum.

Halliday, M. A. K. and Butt, D. G. (forthcoming). Language and science; language in science; and linguistics as science. In G. Thompson, W. L. Bowcher, L. Fontaine, D. Schöntal, and J.Y. Liang (Eds). *The Cambridge Handbook of Systemic Functional Linguistics,* Cambridge: Cambridge University Press.

Hasan, R. (1971). Rime and reason in literature. In S. Chatman (Ed.) *Literary Style: A Symposium,* 299–326. New York: Oxford University Press.

Hasan, R. (1984). The structure of the nursery tale. In L. Coveri (Ed.) *Linguistica Testuale: Proceedings of the 15th International Congress of the Italian Linguistic Society,* 95–114. Rome: Bulzoni.

Hasan, R. (1985). *Linguistics, Language and Verbal Art.* Geelong: Deakin University Press.

Hasan, R. (2007). Private pleasure, public discourse: reflections on engaging with literature. In D. R. Miller and M. Turci (Eds) *Language and Verbal Art Revisited: Linguistic Approaches to the Study of Literature,* 13–40. London: Equinox.

Hasan, R. (1992/2009). Rationality in everyday talk: From process to system. In J. J. Webster (Ed.) *Semantic Variation: Meaning in Society and in Sociolinguistics. The Collected Works of Ruqaiya Hasan, Vol. 2,* 309–352. London: Equinox. https://doi.org/10.1515/9783110867275.257

Hasan, R. (2009). Wanted: A theory for integrated sociolinguistics. In J. J. Webster (Ed.) *Semantic Variation: Meaning in Society and in Sociolinguistics. The Collected Works of Ruqaiya Hasan, Vol. 2,* 5–40. London: Equinox.

Hasan, R. (1996/2011). Literacy, everyday talk and society. In R. Hasan and G. Williams (Eds) *Literacy in Society.* London: Longman. Reprinted in J. J. Webster (Ed.) *Language and Education: Learning and Teaching in Society. The Collected Works of Ruqaiya Hasan, Vol. 3,* 169–206. London: Equinox.

Hatim, B. and Mason, I. (1990). *Discourse and the Translator.* London and New York: Longman.

House, J. (1997). *Translation Quality Assessment. A Model Revisited.* Tübingen: Gunter Narr Verlag.

House, J. (2001). How do we know when a translation is good? In Steiner,

E. and C. Yallop (Eds) *Exploring Translation and Multilingual Text Production: Beyond Content*, 127–160. Berlin: Mouton de Gruyter. https://doi.org/10.1515/9783110866193.127

Jakobson, R. (1959/2004). On linguistic aspects of translation. In L. Venuti (Ed.) *The Translation Studies Reader*, 138–143. London: Routledge. https://doi.org/10.4159/harvard.9780674731615.c18

Kusch, C. (2016). *Literary Analysis: The Basics*. Abingdon: Routledge.

Lessing, D. (2007). *On not winning the Nobel Prize*. Nobel Lecture. http://www.nobelprize.org/nobel_prizes/literature/laureates/2007/lessing-lecture_en.html.

Lukin, A. (2010). Translating modernist preoccupations. In C. Wu, M. Herke and C. M. I. M. Matthiessen (Eds) *Voices around the World: Proceedings of the 35th International Systemic Functional Linguistics Congress (Volume 2)*, 86–91. Sydney: Macquarie University.

Lukin, A. and Pagano, A. (2012). Context and double articulation in the translation of verbal art. In J. Knox (Ed.) *To Boldly Proceed: Papers from the 39th International Systemic Functional Congress*, 123–128. Sydney: The Organising Committee of the 39th International Systemic Functional Congress.

Lukin, A. and Pagano, A. (2016). Inner and outer worlds: Speech and thought presentation in Mansfield's *Bliss*. *Journal of Literary Semantics* 45 (2): 97–116. https://doi.org/10.1515/jls-2016-0007

Lukin, A. and Webster, J. J. (2005). SFL and the study of literature. In R. Hasan, C. M. I. M. Matthiessen, and J. J. Webster (Eds), *Continuing Discourse in Language: A Functional Perspective. Vol. 1*, 413–456. London and Oakville: Equinox.

Mahboob, A. and Knight, N. K. (2010). Appliable Linguistics: An introduction. In A. Mahboob and N. K. Knight (Eds) *Appliable Linguistics,* 1–12. London: Continuum.

Martin, J. R. (1985). Systemic functional linguistics and an understanding of written text. In B. Bartlett and J. Carr (Eds) *Proceedings of the 1984 Working Conference on Language in Education*, 22-40. Brisbane: Brisbane College of Advanced Education.

Martin, J. R. (1986). Intervening in the process of writing development. In C. Painter and J. R. Martin (Eds) *Writing to Mean: Teaching Genres across the Curriculum*, 11–43. Occasional Papers 9. Applied Linguistics Association of Australia.

Martin, J. R. (1993). Genre and literacy – Modelling context in educational linguistics. *Annual Review of Applied Linguistics* 13: 141–172. https://doi.org/10.1017/S0267190500002440

Martin, J. R. and White, P. R. R. (2005). *The Language of Evaluation.*

Appraisal in English. Basingstoke: Palgrave Macmillan. https://doi. org/10.1057/9780230511910

Matthiessen, C. M. I. M. (2001). The environments of translation. In E. Steiner and C. Yallop (Eds) *Exploring Translation and Multilingual Text Production: Beyond Content*, 41–124. Berlin and New York: Mouton de Gruyter. https://doi.org/10.1515/9783110866193.41

McGee, S. J. (2001). *Analyzing Literature: A Guide for Students.* London: Longman.

Mendlesohn, F. (2008). *Rhetorics of Fantasy*. Middletown, CT: Wesleyan University Press.

Miller, D. R. (2007). Construing the 'primitive' primitively: Grammatical parallelism as patterning and positioning strategy in D. H. Lawrence. In D. R. Miller and M. Turci (Eds) *Language and Verbal Art Revisited: Linguistic Approaches to the Study of Literature*, 41–67. London: Equinox.

Miller, D. R. (2013). Another look at social semiotic stylistics: Coupling Hasan's 'Verbal Art' framework with 'the Mukarovsky-Jakobson Theory'. In C. A. M. Gouveia and M. F. Alexandre (Eds) *Languages, Metalanguages, Modalities, Cultures: Functional and Socio-Discursive Perspectives*, 121–140. Lisbon: BonD.

Miller, D. R. (2016a). Jakobson's place in Hasan's social semiotic stylistics: 'Pervasive Parallelism' as symbolic articulation of theme. In W. L. Bowcher and J. Y. Liang (Eds) *Society in Language, Language in Society: Essays in Honour of Ruqaiya Hasan*, 59–80. Basingstoke: Palgrave Macmillan.

Miller, D. R. (2016b). On negotiating the hurdles of corpus-assisted appraisal analysis in verbal art. In S. Gardner and S. Alsop (Eds) *Systemic Functional Linguistics in the Digital Age*, 211–228. London: Equinox.

Miller, D. R. and Turci, M. (2007). Introduction. In D. R. Miller and M. Turci (Eds) *Language and Verbal Art Revisited: Linguistic Approaches to the Study of Literature*, 1–12. London: Equinox.

Morrison, T. (1993). Toni Morrison – Nobel Lecture. <http://www.nobelprize.org/nobel_prizes/literature/laureates/1993/morrison-lecture. html> (Accessed 2 February 2017.)

O'Donnell, M. (2008). Demonstration of the UAM CorpusTool for text and image annotation. In *Proceedings of the ACL-08: HLT Demo Session (Companion Volume)*, 13–16. Columbus, Ohio: Association of Computational Linguistics. http://www.aclweb.org/anthology-new/P/ P08/P08-4004.pdf. https://doi.org/10.3115/1564144.1564148

O'Toole, M. (2011). *The Language of Displayed Art*. London: Routledge.

Rose, D. (2011). Meaning beyond the margins: Learning to interact with books. In S. Dreyfus, S. Hood, and M. Stenglin (Eds) *Semiotic Margins: Meaning in Multimodalities*, 177–208. London: Continuum.

Steiner, E. (2004). *Translated Texts: Properties, Variants, Evaluations.* Frankfurt a.M.: Peter Lang Verlag.

Steiner, E., and Yallop, C. (Eds). (2001). *Exploring Translation and Multilingual Text Production: Beyond Content.* Berlin: Mouton de Gruyter. https://doi.org/10.1515/9783110866193

Stenglin, M. (2012). Glocalisation: Exploring the dialectic between the local and the Global. In W. L. Bowcher (Ed.) *Multimodal Texts from Around the World: Cultural and Linguistic Insights,* 123–145. Basingstoke: Palgrave Macmillan. https://doi.org/10.1057/9780230355347_6

Swirski, P. (2005). *From Lowbrow to Nobrow.* Montreal: McGill University Press.

Swirski, P. and Vanhanen, T. E. (Eds). (2017). *When Highbrow Meets Lowbrow: Popular Culture and the Rise of Nobrow.* Basingstoke: Palgrave Macmillan. https://doi.org/10.1057/978-1-349-95168-0

Toni Morrison – Facts. Nobelprize.org. Nobel Media AB 2014. Accessed 4 February 2017. <http://www.nobelprize.org/nobel_prizes/literature/laureates/1993/morrison-facts.html>.

Williams, G. (1999). The pedagogic device and the production of pedagogic discourse: A case example in early literacy education. In F. Christie (Ed.) *Pedagogy and the Shaping of Consciousness*, 88–122. London: Cassell.

Zappavigna, M. (2011). Visualizing Logogenesis: Preserving the dynamics of meaning. In S. Dreyfus, S. Hood, and M. Stenglin (Eds) *Semiotic Margins: Meaning in Multimodalities,* 211–228. London: Continuum.

Author Index

Auden, Wystan Hugh 3, 45–49, 80,
83–85, 102–105, 107, 290
Austen, Jane 3, 6, 166–185 (Chapter 7),
289
Northanger Abbey 172–177, 182,
289

Balzac, Honoré de 6
Barrell, John 168–9
Beauvoir, Simone de 3, 132–164
(Chapter 6), 289
Mémoires d'une jeune fille rangée
132–135, 137, 139–141
Beowulf 4, 211, 214–226
Brontë, Charlotte 167, 183

Carew, Thomas 220–224
Carey, Peter 3, 109–112, 115, 121, 125,
128
Carroll, Lewis 258
Alices' Adventures in Wonderland
255–256, 258, 260–261, 263–
266, 276–277
Cervantes, Miguel de
Don Quixote
Chaucer 43, 285
Coetzee, J.M. 2, 53–54, 72–74
Foe 2, 53–54, 57–58, 60, 62–63, 66,
68–69, 72–73
Committed literature 137
Corpus-assisted Systemic Socio-
Semantic Stylistics (SSS) 53–59

Defoe, Daniel 54, 57–58, 72, 237
Robinson Crusoe (RC) 54, 237
Dickens, Charles 166, 242–245
Hard Times 243, 245
A Tale of Two Cities 242–243
Donne, John 219–226

Gaskell, Elizabeth 166, 183
Gibbon, Edward 3, 166–167, 178, 183,
185

Golding, William 8
Free Fall 8

Hasan, Ruqaiya 1–22 (Introduction &
Chapter 1), 26–27, 29, 35–36, 39–40,
49, 53–57, 60, 72–73, 80–81, 84, 94,
107, 110, 114–115, 119, 132–134,
137, 139–140, 162–163, 166–167,
170–171, 174, 185, 211–214, 218,
222–226, 232, 237, 239–241, 247,
250–252, 269, 278–288, 292, 294–
296, 298–306, (Chapter 12)
PhD thesis 8–9, 11–12, 14
stratal model 10, 211, 225
tristratal framework 213
Hazlitt, William 167–170, 173, 180–181,
185

Johnson, Samuel 3, 166–167, 172–179,
181, 183, 185
Rasselas 172–178

Kristof, Agota 285

Murray, Les 11, 19–20, 80, 94, 107
Widower in the Country 11, 80, 107

Owen, Wilfred 285

Priestley 283
An Inspector Calls 260

Rowling, J.K. 258
*Harry Potter and the Philosopher's
Stone* 255, 258, 261, 263–266,
276–277

Sexton, Anne 11
Old 11
Shakespeare, William 7, 11, 27, 43, 83,
226, 232, 285, 289
As You Like It 11
Coriolanus 289

Hamlet 27
King Lear 27
Troilus and Cressida 289
Spenser 43

Tolkien, J.R.R. chapters 9, 11
The Hobbit chapters 9, 11

Vázquez Montalbán, Manuel 4, 188–192, 194, 198–199, 205, 208
Los mares del Sur 188–190, 193

Wilson, Angus 8, 11, 15
Anglo-Saxon Attitudes 8
Woolf, Virginia 166–170, 179, 181–183, 185
A Room of One's Own 166–167
Wyatt 43

Yeats, W. B. 11, 19, 32,
Old Men Admiring Themselves in the Water 11

Zedong, Mao 285

Subject Index

affect 68
affiliation 17, 189–193, 207
agency 3, 46, 93–97, 140–142, 146, 150, 155, 161–163
agent / agentive relation 18, 35, 46, 48, 73, 93–102, 142–163
allegory 110–112, 120, 127, 197
alliteration 169, 214, 241, 292
anaphora 242
Anglo-Saxon poetry 38
appraisal 2, 4, 21, 59–60, 63, 66–67, 74, 180, 188–189, 191, 195–196, 199, 202, 205–206, 289, 299–300
    appraisal resources 205, 299–300
    appraisal systems 53–54, 63–65, 68, 299
appreciation 63–65, 74, 192, 198, 201–206, 279–280, 292, 295, 298
article (definite) 119
articulation
    double-articulation 18, 55, 213, 224
    symbolic articulation 2, 4, 9, 13–14, 16, 22, 29, 39, 55–56, 139–140, 211–214, 218–219, 222–223, 226, 240–241, 243–244, 279, 285, 287–289, 293, 296, 299–300, 305–306,
assonance 214
attitude 59, 71, 195–199, 202, 206–207

beginning 4, 224, 232–339, 242, 245, 247, 290
blending 4, 211, 250, 253, 266, 268

cataphoric 239, 247
causation 93, 99
choice(s) 15, 32, 84, 102–104, 118–119, 121, 123–125, 127, 139, 193, 202, 206, 212, 217, 222, 224, 233–234, 280, 287, 289–290, 292, 301
    grammatical 82, 174, 290
    lexicogrammatical 189, 214, 216, 224, 305

lexical 174–175, 197, 203, 251, 266, 287
linguistic 13, 120, 133, 137, 163, 213, 215, 221, 282, 285, 289, 304
of Subject 89–90, 98, 102–104
textual 88, 124, 207
Circumstance 20, 89, 93, 95–96, 98–99, 101, 104, 120
cline of dynamism 19–21, 94, 96
code (restricted / elaborated) 166–172, 183, 295, 300–301, 303
cognitive
    approaches / processes 28, 109, 214, 221, 223–224, 232–234, 268
    linguistics 4, 211, 237, 268, 300
    psychology 240
    science 28, 250
    stylistics / literary studies 115, 128, 226, 245, 251
coherence / coherent 1, 18, 23, 193, 198, 208, 214, 224, 227, 240–241, 253, 269, 285
cohesion / cohesive 119, 240, 287
    grammatical 227
    lexical 292
collocation 59, 61–62, 66, 70, 204–205, 227
communitative
    act 104, 189, 195, 304
    function / purpose 39, 103, 114, 233
    needs 289
    situation / process 61, 102–103, 235, 246
community habits 2, 27
complexity 1, 14, 18, 26, 32, 37–38, 65, 170, 180, 189, 220, 226–227, 254, 291, 301, 303
concordance 54, 59, 63, 65–68, 289
connotation 74, 217, 225
context
    author-reader context 10, 68, 250–254
    inner – outer 17–18, 35, 250–254

cultural distance 8, 17–18, 214,
250–254
field, tenor, mode 16–18, 125, 170,
250–252, 293, 305
text-in-context 9, 16, 250
intra-text context 4, 250–254
corpus 3, 8, 53–54, 57–58, 72, 125, 134,
163, 174–175, 289–291, 299–300
corpus-assisted 57, 59 *see also
Corpus-assisted Systemic Socio-
Semantic Stylistics (SSS)*
corpus-based 57
corpus linguistics 3–4, 28, 53, 250,
289–290, 299 *see also UAM
Corpus Tool*
crime novel / crime fiction / detective
fiction 188–191, 194, 201
criticism 74, 181, 222
literary criticism 8–9, 12, 22, 42,
107, 287, 293, 297–299
social criticism 189
translation criticism 193
cross-linguistic perspective 3
culture 1–4, 14, 17–23, 26, 29–32, 39–
40, 42, 49, 53, 83, 111, 112, 128, 166,
188–196, 200,   207, 218, 224, 253,
281–287, 293–298, 303–306
cultural 7–8, 17–18, 23–36, 43–60,
190–199, 206–207, 213–225,
233, 252, 268–286, 291–299,
303–305
socio-cultural 1, 7, 17, 60, 172, 177,
221–222, 282
culture-specific 4, 207

defamiliarization 3, 28, 109–110, 113–
115, 119–120, 123–124, 127, 240
deictic / deixis 119, 125, 128, 207, 227
density 240, 242, 259–265, 268, 276–
277
lexical density 259, 263
deviation 82
dialogue 69–70, 166, 171–179, 181,
183–185, 188–189, 191, 199, 259,
261, 263, 283, 289
discourse 7–8, 21, 31, 59, 124, 179, 183,
188–190, 205, 212, 222, 234, 245,
251, 253, 268, 278, 285, 289, 294, 300
discourse analysis 109, 132, 190,
252, 278, 287
discourse features 240–241
discourse strategies 240
free indirect discourse 126, 166,
203
spoken discourse 205, 252
written discourse 252
double articulation *see articulation*
dynamic 2, 19–21, 94, 114, 136, 170,
211, 218, 223, 225, 237, 285, 291

effective voice 93
elaboration 91, 116
ellipsis 85, 102
emotion 1, 4, 23, 28, 98–99, 101,
105–106, 121, 124, 142, 144, 156,
158, 162, 180, 188–189, 191–192,
195–196, 204–205, 217, 221, 281, 284
embedding / embedded clauses 41, 46,
85–95, 97, 99, 102–103, 106, 137,
168–169, 171, 173, 179, 189, 283
endophoric 119, 128
engagement 61, 70–71, 199, 252, 264,
269, 284, 297
enhancement 116, 121
ethnicity 190–191, 198–199, 206
evaluation / evaluative 3, 11, 22, 32,
53–54, 59, 65–66, 68, 71–73, 136,
180, 188, 191–192, 199–200, 205–
207, 217 226, 261, 266, 269, 279–280,
292, 295, 298–302
existence 1, 20, 23, 56, 133, 137–138,
141, 150, 154, 156–159, 161–163,
202, 213, 217, 282, 285, 305
existential 162, 218
existential process 141, 152–154,
161–162
existentialism 138
exophic 119
expansion 92, 116
experimental
evidence / data 28, 269
methods 4, 250, 252, 268
narrations 238, 246
experimentalism 190
exposition 233–234, 236, 296
extension 91–93, 115–116, 179, 292
eye-tracking 4, 250–251, 256–260, 264,
267–268, 277, 300, 304

fiction 18, 29, 31–32, 54, 72–73,

109–111, 120, 127, 134, 146, 166, 172, 181–183, 188–192, 206, 226, 232–234, 236, 238–239, 246, 250–251, 253–254, 300 *see also fictional words, crime fiction, science fiction*
fictional world(s) 1, 4, 115, 121, 124, 128, 250–251, 253, 255–256, 258–259, 261, 264, 267–269, 300
fictionality 183
figurative 31
finite(ness) / non-finite(ness) 15, 19, 41, 44, 86–89, 174–175, 177–178, 227
foregrounding 2–4, 11, 13–15, 23, 28, 38, 48, 55–57, 72, 81–84, 87, 90, 94, 98, 102–105, 109–110, 113–115, 118–121, 123, 125, 127–128, 133, 140–142, 144, 146, 150, 153, 161, 183, 198, 203, 206, 213–214, 217–224, 226–227, 232, 235, 240–244, 246–247, 251, 254–255, 261, 264–265, 269, 280, 288, 292, 299–301, 303
Formalism 113–114, 245
    Russian Formalism 27, 29, 39, 49, 82, 110, 113
frame 17, 103, 190, 219, 233–234, 236–238, 245–246
    of expectation 234, 239, 245–246
    narration-frame 234–236, 239, 246
    story-frame 234, 236–239, 246
    thematic frame 234, 239, 245–246
functional approaches 26, 29, 128, 214, 223, 234, 245 *see also Systemic Functional Linguistics*

gender 3, 83, 106–107, 169, 172, 191, 274
    gendered sentence 168, 172
Generativism 245
genericity 109, 167, 218, 289, 296
    generic "you" 98, 102, 104
genre(s) 8, 11, 22, 27, 29, 31, 103, 133–134, 182, 184, 189, 201, 205, 211, 213, 222, 232, 235, 237, 246–247, 253, 296
grammar 7, 22, 41–42, 46, 53, 56, 85–86, 107, 132, 141, 167, 211, 214, 218, 220, 224, 245, 250, 261, 289, 296 *see also Systemic Functional Grammar, Structuralism, Generativism, lexicogrammar*

grammatical 8, 15–16, 19, 22, 38–39, 41–42, 44, 48, 55, 61, 82–89, 96, 102, 119, 140, 167, 174–175, 227, 242, 247, 259, 290, 292, 298–299 *for grammatical metaphor, see metaphor*

identity 21, 141, 188–192, 196, 199, 205, 207, 211, 218, 225–226, 250, 281, 284
    master identities 188–191, 206
ideology 6, 11, 13, 17, 115, 119, 121, 189, 207, 283, 297
imagery 31, 214, 294
immersion / immersive 253, 255–256, 258, 261, 266, 276
immortality 112, 153–154, 163
individualism / individuality 2, 22, 138, 170, 183
informational function 233, 239
interpersonal 11, 28, 59, 86–88, 90, 93, 98, 102, 176, 183, 222, 234, 260, 305
intertextuality / intertextual 134, 191, 198, 200, 227, 232
intrusion / intrusive 255, 258, 260–261, 266, 276

judgement (appraisal) 64–65, 68, 71, 188, 195–200, 204–206, 279

keyness 175, 177

language processing 264, 268–269
lexical 3, 8, 37–38, 42, 54, 58, 61, 71, 95–96, 101, 171, 174–176, 189, 196–197, 203, 205, 207–208, 217, 227, 240, 244, 251, 266, 287, 289–291 *for lexical density, see density*
lexical cohesion 292
lexicogrammar / lexicogrammatical 37, 57, 139–140, 174–175, 177, 189, 205, 211–212, 214, 216, 218, 224–225, 260, 288, 290, 303, 305
lexis 7, 36–37
literacy
    action literacy 12, 296
    female literacy 167
    literacy education 12
    literacy pedagogies 12, 296
    recognition literacy 12, 296
    reflection literacy 12, 296–297
    universal literacy 3, 183

literal 195–197, 203–204, 208
literary language 3, 134
logical 15, 90–92, 98, 102, 222, 292

magical element(s) / event 253, 256,
    258–264, 267–268, 275–277
magical world 4, 258, 266
metafunction(al) 3, 81, 85, 260, 302,
    305 *see also Systemic Functional
    Linguistics*
metaphor / metaphoric(al) 1, 4, 14, 23,
    29, 31, 71, 171, 204, 211–212, 214–
    215, 218–226, 243–244, 250, 254,
    259–261, 263, 265, 267–269, 300–301
        conceptual metaphor 4, 211, 214–
            215, 217–226, 250, 300
        grammatical metaphor 169, 173,
            179–181
        metaphorization 299–301
metaphysical poetry 211, 214, 219
middle voice *see voice*
modal adjunct 87, 98, 105, 259–261,
    263, 265
modality 15, 88, 121–123, 174–175, 178,
    227, 260
monologue 125, 191
mood 82, 86, 88, 174–175, 178, 227
        declarative mood 82
        imperative mood 44
        interrogative mood 67, 70
        mood adjuncts 123
        moodless 41
morpheme 3, 203, 266
multicultural(ism) 192
multimodality 31, 80, 250, 278

narrative 4, 69, 120–121, 125–126, 166,
    171–179, 181, 183–184, 188–190,
    195, 215, 217, 219, 222, 227, 232–
    236, 238–240, 245–247, 252, 281,
    289, 296, 300, 304
narratology 232
new novel (nouveau roman) 137
nominalisation 166, 171, 173, 181, 183
normality (appraisal) 65, 198, 205
normality (as opposed to fictionality)
    / non-normality 251, 255, 260–261,
    263, 265

Old English 215, 218, 225

opening (in literature) 69, 84, 116, 142,
    232–247 (Chapter 10)
orality 170, 188, 197, 206, 283

paradigmatic 208, 245
parallelism 80, 181, 217
        grammatical parallelism 292, 299
        pervasive parallelism 55, 58, 299
paratext(ual) / paratextuality 195, 197,
    200, 235, 246
passive (vs. active) 142, 175
passive (vs. dynamic) 19–20, 94, 101
pattern(ing)
        of communication 103–104
        of counterexpectancy 103–104
        cultural patterns 27
        exchange / interaction patterns 54
        foregrounded patterns 15, 48, 72,
            83, 87, 94, 98, 103–104, 127,
            133, 140, 142, 146, 223, 240, 300
        grammatical patterns 15–16, 22,
            83–84, 89, 140, 299
        language patterns / linguistic
            patterns 12–15, 22, 28, 39–40, 55,
            82, 107, 110, 113, 115, 127–128,
            133, 214, 226, 267, 287–289,
            292, 295–296, 300–301, 304
latent patterning 283, 288, 292–293
lexical patterns 8
lexicogrammatical patterning 140, 214,
    250, 290
of meaning /semantic patterning 55, 59,
    85, 87, 104, 107, 140, 144, 280, 288
of metaphors 211, 214–224, 263
        of normality 264–265, 267
        patterning of patterns 55, 57–58, 72,
            80, 102, 107, 140, 213, 218, 288,
            290, 292, 299, 303, 306
        sound patterns 7, 227
        of speaking 27
        of structure / organisation 4
        clause / text patterns / organisational
            patterns 29, 33, 38, 40, 48, 82–83,
            90–91, 99, 180, 214, 218, 227,
            233–234, 237, 242–243, 247,
            259–260, 269, 294
        of thematic progression 89
        of transitivity 3, 18, 94, 99, 101,
            132, 142, 162–163, 204

phonological / phonology 197, 205, 240, 278
phraseology 184
planes of narration 16, chapter 1
poetics
    Classical poetics 113
    Cognitive Poetics 226
    Prague School Poetics 114
polarity 65–66, 121, 174–175, 178, 183, 266
portal quest 255–256, 258, 260–261, 266, 276
postmodern(ism) 74, 111, 234–236, 239
pragmatics 7, 28
Prague School (Linguistics) 11, 29, 82, 110, 114
prefixation 266
primary world 251–255, 259–260, 265–267, 269
process(es) 20, 41, 46, 61, 74, 93–104, 115, 120, 124–125, 140–143, 146, 149–150, 152–160, 162, 169, 176, 180–181
projection 15–16, 91–93, 102–103, 106, 116, 124–125, 184, 263
propensity 18, 175, 263

qualitative analysis 57, 59, 177, 189
quantitative analysis 3, 57, 59, 173–174, 177

reader(s) 4, 12–13, 16–22, 35, 38, 40, 42–43, 46, 49, 54, 68 73, 98, 104–105, 109, 116, 119–124, 127–128, 132– 139, 141, 155, 163, 172, 182–185, 188–193, 195, 197–208, 211, 222, 226, 233–247 (Chapter 10), 251–269 (Chapter 11), 283, 289, 292, 297, 300–301, 304–306
    reader response criticism 42
realis vs. irrealis 65
realism / irrealism 28, 110–111, 185, 190, 234, 236
register 12, 14, 18, 20, 31, 39, 41, 53–54, 83, 87, 183–184, 188, 206, 214, 287–288, 290
Renaissance 41, 43
repetition 189, 202–203, 208, 232, 241– 244, 246, 291

rhetoric(al) 67, 106, 116, 235, 242, 245–246
    arts 32
    devices 245
    Medieval rhetoric 237
    rhetorical focusing principle 233, 240–245
    strategy 232
rhythm 133, 169, 205, 242

scenario / scenario-mapping 233, 237, 239, 246–247
science fiction 290
secondary world 4, 250–255, 259, 265–267
self-engendered process 93–94, 142
semantic 7, 15–16, 19, 22, 27–29, 33, 37–38, 42–46, 59–60, 66, 68, 72, 74, 82, 87, 119, 144, 191, 197, 199, 204, 206, 213, 215–216, 219, 225–226, 237, 285, 290–291, 297–299, 303–305
    logico-semantic relations 115–117
    semantic consequences 304
    semantic drift 115, 140, 163, 288, 293, 300, 303
    semantic orientation 169–170, 297, 301
semantics 56, 132, 139, 245, 288 *see also Corpus-assisted Systemic Socio-Semantic Stylistics (SSS)*
semiosis 13–14, 212, 283
    first order semiosis 55, 212, 280
    second order semiosis 4, 13, 55–56, 134, 140, 213, 222–223, 280, 299, 305
    secondary semiosis 2
semiotics 1–2, 14, 17–18, 23, 36, 41, 55–56, 80, 167, 171, 184, 211–213, 223–226, 250, 283, 285, 287–288
    semiotic difference 35, 298
    semiotic distance 35
    semiotic stylistics 53 *see also Corpus-assisted Systemic Socio-Semantic Stylistics (SSS)*
    socio-semiotic 9, 14, 17, 213, 222–224
simile 214
social – particularly chapter 1, but see throughout for different aspects

social stereotypes 4, 188, 198–199,
205–206
sociology (sociologically) 2, 6–7, 294
source text 45, 188, 190, 193, 197, 203,
205–206, 208, 303–304
speech 28, 70, 125–126, 166–167, 170,
178, 181–182, 184, 194, 198, 208, 247
direct speech, free direct speech
(FDS) 125–127, 179, 183, 190,
203
indirect speech, free indirect speech
(FIS) 125
reported speech 183
speech act (theory) 7, 28, 125, 204
speech community 27, 170, 284–
285
speech presentation 127
spoken 74, 125, 137, 178, 183, 202–203,
205, 214, 257, 274, 294
story world 4, 119–120, 124, 127, 233,
250–255, 261, 269
Structuralism 4, 110, 114, 245 *see also
Prague School*
style 8–9, 12, 28, 133–136, 181, 183,
194, 198, 208, 301
critique of 12
epistolary novel style 69
literary style 1, 116, 287
narrative style 259
of criticism 12
semantic style 60, 72
transition style 255, 258, 268
writing style 3, 11
stylistics 8–13, 19, 22, 28, 42, 82, 109,
113–114, 126, 132, 188, 212, 250, 287
cognitive stylistics 115, 128, 233
literary stylistics 3, 29, 80, 109
socio-semantic stylistics 3, 14,
53, 73 *see also Corpus-assisted
Systemic Socio-Semantic
Stylistics (SSS)*
symbolic articulation 2, 4, 9, 13–14, 16,
22, 29, 39, 55–56, 139–140, 211–214,
218–219, 222–223, 226, 240–241,
243–244, 279, 285, 287–289, 293,
296, 299–300, 305–306
symbolisation 13
syntactical coherence 241
syntagmatic 208, 245
syntax 11, 189, 197, 203, 245

Systemic Functional Linguistics (SFL),
Systemic Functional Grammar 3–4,
11, 17–18, 29, 42, 53, 59, 73, 80–82,
85, 96, 109–110, 115, 118, 123, 132,
134, 167–169, 174, 185, 189–190,
211, 221, 251, 278, 281–282, 284,
286–288, 291–293, 296, 299, 301–302
Systemic Functional Stylistics 82, 109

target text 193, 303, 306
taxis 34, 46–47, 115
hypotaxis 37–38, 42, 115, 118, 169,
179, 181
parataxis 38, 115, 169, 173
tense 15, 43, 69, 86–88, 102–104, 121,
127, 174–178, 197, 203, 227, 292, 303
textlinguistics 80
textual 9, 18, 35, 45–46, 54, 57, 74, 98,
128, 169, 184, 189, 218, 237, 283
analysis 171, 206, 261
choices 88, 124, 207
coherence 269
importance / significance 15, 72,
140
location 15, 72, 214
meaning 88–89, 91, 98
metafunction 260
organisation 29, 169, 285, 297
orientation 170
stimuli 250–251, 255
structure 115, 222
theme 89–90
texture 27, 288
theme
theme (as a stratal component in
Hasan's work) 2, 3, 11, 13–16,
18, 22, 55–56, 58, 72–73, 84,
102, 115, 128, 139–141, 155,
162–163, 180, 188, 197, 211–227
(Chapter 9), 239–240, 242–243,
245–246, 279, 283, 285–291,
293, 297, 300, 303–306
Theme (as a label within the textual
metafunction) 35, 88–91, 97–99,
102, 107, 116, 120, 128, 133,
176–177
transcendence 3, 138–139, 141, 153,
155, 162–163
transcendent(al) 138, 141, 162
transition style 255, 258, 268

transitivity 3, 18–20, 93, 132, 134, 137, 141–142, 144, 162–163, 204, 287, 289, 292

translation 3–4, 11, 42–43, 49, 128, 138, 140, 142, 147, 153, 155, 159, 161, 164, 188–191, 193–194, 197–200, 203–208, 211, 225–226, 250, 280, 301–306
    Spanish-English translation 3, 188–190, 197–199, 203–207, 303
    Spanish-German translation 3, 188–190, 194, 199–200, 206

transtextual(ity) 224

trope(s) and / or figure(s) 31, 224

UAM corpus tool 174–175, 290, 292

veracity 58, 64–66, 68, 71–72

verbal art 1–8, 11–18, 21–23, 26–32, 36, 39, 42, 49, 53–57, 73, 80–81, 107, 113–114, 133–134, 137, 139–140, 163, 166, 171, 185, 211–214, 218–227, 232, 237, 239, 240, 243, 250,, 278–306 (Chapter 12)
    and pedagogy 12, 21, 280, 293, 296–300

verbalization 13, 39, 55, 139, 212–213, 218, 222, 287, 290, 294–295, 305

voice 16, 31, 60, 70, 95, 100, 126, 133, 137, 174–175, 178–179, 185, 190, 195, 244, 283, 286, 189, 300–301, 303
    see also middle voice
        effective voice 93
        middle voice 46, 93–94, 96–97
        narrative voice 69, 177, 289, 300

W-questions 237–239, 246

written 2, 40, 58, 69, 137, 170, 189, 194, 203, 206, 214, 252, 280–281, 294–296

9 781781 794470